The Isle of Sheppey

The Isle of Sheppey

by

Sheila M. Judge

Carved oak chest at Harty Church, Sheppey. About 13th century.

ROADMASTER PUBLISHING

in association with

BAGGINS BOOK BAZAAR

First Published by
Rochester Press 1983
This Revised Edition 1997

© Sheila Judge 1983 and 1997

ISBN 1 871814 61 8

ERRATUM TO FIRST EDITION

Original Page 1, Paragraph 14:

Further research informs us that a 'celt' was in
fact a flask holder and not a flask itself

Page 81, Paragraph 3:

Parker sailed into Sheerness on the Sandwich
and not the Monmouth as stated

Published by Roadmaster Publishing, PO Box 176, Chatham, Kent ME5 9AQ
in association with Baggins Book Bazaar, 19 High Street, Rochester, Kent ME1 1QB
Printed by Bookcraft (Bath) Ltd, Somerset

Contents

Bibliography

Castles in Kent. David Waldron Smithers. Rochester Press.

Elizabeth the Ist. Neville Williams.

Windmills and Watermills. William Coles Finch.

Bibliotheca Cantiana, Volume I. Rochester Press.

Guide to the Kent County Archives. Dr. Felix Hull, B.A. Ph.D.

Volumes of Bygone Kent, published by Meresborough Books.

Catalogue of English Charters and Documents, 12–19th Century, from the collection formed by Sir Thomas Phillips, Bart., Sothebys.

The Benedictines in Britain. The British Library.

Journals of Kent Local History, published by the Kent Voluntary Service Council.

Guide to Kent Archives Office, first supplement, 1957–68.

Catalogue of Estate Maps, 1590–1840. First supplement, 1957–68.

A History of the Abbey Church of Minster. The Reverend W. Bramston, M.A.

Introduction to Archives. F. G. Emmison.

Kings and Queens of England and Great Britain. Eric R. Delderfield.

Rambles in the Island of Sheppey. Henry T. A. Turmine.

Social Institutions in Kent 1400–1660. W. K. Jordan. (K.A.S.)

Sheppey Church Magazines, 1884, et sequentes.

Perambulation of Kent. William Lambarde, 1576.

History of Kent. Dr. John Harris, 1719.

Archaeologica Cantiana, volumes I–XCVI.

Kentish Yesterdays. South Eastern Magazines.

Shurland. H. Davies.

The Victoria History of Kent.

The Dutch in the Medway. P. G. Rogers.

Kent. Edward Hasted, 1778–99.

Faversham's Court of Orphans. Canon W. Telfer.

From Coast and Country; From Crown Quay Reach. Richard-Hugh Perks.

The Prison Hulks of Woolwich. James Porter.

They all want Putting Down, Rural Unrest in the 1830's. Margaret Askew.

The Parish Chest. W. E. Tate.

Kentish Sources, Some Roads and Bridges.

Kentish Sources, Kent and the Civil War.

Kentish Sources, Aspects of Agriculture and Industry.

The Place Names of Kent. Judith Glover.

The Local Historian's Encyclopaedia. John Richardson.

Congregational Churches, Sheerness, Queenborough, Minster and Grain. 1725–1898, compiled by John Gordon, Senior Deacon.

Agricultural Records, A.D. 220–1977. J. M. Stratton.

The Life and Times of Henry VIIIth. Robert Lacey.

Henry VIIIth and his Court. Neville Williams.

Kentish Sources, IV, Crime and Punishment. Edited by Elizabeth Melling, B.A.

Kent Records. (K.A.S.) Medieval Kentish Society.

Kentish Sources, V, Some Kentish Houses. Edited by Elizabeth Melling, B.A.

Anglo-Norman Armory. Cecil R. Humphery-Smith.

A Complete Guide to Heraldry. A. C. Fox-Davies.

Boutall's Heraldry. J. P. Brooke-Little.

Public Records Office. Ancient Deeds, Feet of Fines, Kent. Survey of Sheppey, 1572.

Sir Roger Twysden, M.S.S.

The Community of Kent and the Great Rebellion. Everitt.

George Ist. John Clarke.

Hammer of the North. Magnus Magnusson.

Samuel Pepys' Diary.

The English Village. Richard Muir.

Anglo-Saxon England. Lloyd and Jennifer Laing.

The Celts. Graham Herne.

A Distant Mirror. Barbara W. Tuchman.

The Devil's Crown. Richard Barber.

Here comes an Old Sailor. A. T. Sheppard.

English Social History. G. M. Trevelyan.

Kentish Sources. The Poor. Edited by Elizabeth Melling, B.A.

The England of Elizabeth Ist. A. L. Rowse.

The Elizabethan House of Commons. J. E. Neale.

Domesday Book, a guide. R. Welldon Finn.

Life in Kent at the Turn of the Century. Michael Winstanley.

Seventeenth Century Kent. W. Chalklin.

Roman Britain. Anthony Birley.

A Chronicle of Kent, 1250–1760. R. M. Filmer.

The Thames Estuary. William Addison.

The Formation of England, 550–1042. H. P. R. Finberg.

Plant Hunters. Tyler Whittle.

History of the Sheerness Economical Society Ltd, 1816–1916. W. Henry Brown.

Queenborough as a Naval Port. T. J. Woodthorpe, F.R.S.M.

Postal History. Jeremy Greenwood.

Edward Ist. E. L. G. Stones.

The Shellness News. By courtesy of G. V. Bull, esq.

The History of Faversham. Edward Jacob, 1774.

Dormant and Extinct Peerage. Banks.

Arden of Faversham, a play.

Textus Roffensus. Hearne.

Archbishop Robert Winchelsey's Register.

The Reign of Queen Elizabeth Ist. Black.

Grose's Antiquities.

Stothard's Monumental Effigies.

Calendarium Geneologia.

Close Rolls. Fine Rolls. Patent Rolls. Pipe Rolls.

State Papers Domestic.

History of Kent. H. F. Abell.

Local History Jottings. J. Fitzgerald Hogg. (Archives.)

Churches of Kent. Sir Stephen Glynne.

North East and East Kent. John Newman.

Kent Views.

Weever.

A Saunter through Kent with Pen and Pencil. Charles Iggulsden.

Numismatic Chronicle, 1971.

Camden (died 1623) Clarenceaux King at Arms.

Kent Keepers of the Peace (K.A.S.)

Kingsborough Law Day Records (Archives.)

A Survey of Monastery Lands, Henry VIIIth. P.R.O.

Britain Before the Norman Conquest.

South East Survey. Richard Wyndham.

Kent. Arthur Mee.

Companion into Kent. Dorothy Gardiner.

Kent. Winbolt and Ward.

Ingoldsby Legends. Barham.

The Vikings and their Origins. David Wilson.

The Ingoldsby Country. C. G. Harper.

Sir Francis Drake. George Malcolm Thomson.

The Anglo-Saxon Chronicle.

Bede's Ecclesiastic History.

Nicholson's Progresses (of Queen Elizabeth Ist.)

CHAPTER I

In the beginning

People generally have never heard of the Isle of Sheppey, and then the reaction is 'where is it, somewhere in Scotland?' or they know it, and either like or dislike the place heartily. There seems no middle way, but there are reasons for these attitudes.

The island is a bare 50 miles from London, in north-east Kent. It lies at the mouth of the Thames, at the junction where it is joined by the Medway, although it is the River Swale, a tributary of the Medway, that separates the island from the mainland. The north shore faces the North Sea and the north east winds that go with it. In length it is about nine miles, in width approximately four to five miles, and it was certainly larger in bygone days, as will be seen.

Although it seems a small and unimportant place, Sheppey has a colourful and exciting past, which is fast becoming forgotten and lost under the present spread of building development and caravan and chalet sites. To prevent this history being altogether lost, this story is being written.

It is not possible to put an exact date on the origin of the island. We are told that millions of years ago England and the continent were one great land mass. Over a long, long period of time the world went through a series of ice ages, which altered lands and oceans. The great reptiles lived, and as conditions altered, died, and other living things changed their form and life style by evolution. In this way the world as it is today was formed, and the Isle of Sheppey was part of it.

Fifty million years ago Sheppey was in a tropical zone. It is thought that the basin of the North Sea was fed by the rivers of Europe, and the eastward flowing rivers of England. In time this flow of water receded, and the climate altered once again. Evidence of this period can be found in the mud of Sheppey cliffs, and fossils discovered there can be seen in the British Museum.

Mr. Edward Jacobs of Faversham, in A.D. 1757 was one of the first geologists to seriously attempt to identify and catalogue his findings. Mr. Shrubsole of Sheerness, a hundred years later, was another.

Mr. Jacobs is recorded as having found the skull and tusks of a long extinct type of elephant. Other fossils listed are those of crocodiles, molluscs, a mammalian skull, and the bones of a primitive animal with hooves. Six different species of extinct birds have been identified; birds of prey, gannets, an ancestral type of tropical bird, and an unknown bird the size of an ostrich. Skeletons of snakes have been found, tortoises with soft shells, and various large extinct varieties of turtle. Bones of fish are plentiful, among them the earliest evidence of the sturgeon family, and a rather horrifying extinct variety of hard scale fishes with crushing teeth, one of which is regarded as peculiar to Sheppey, the Pynodus Bower bankii. No-one so far has unearthed a dinosaur, or similarly exciting large reptile, so whether they roamed the island is doubtful.

Following the glacial upheavals and the floodings, the island emerged shaped much as it is now. Certainly the tropical climate did not survive! In 1977-8 Nipa Palmpods, small fruits and seeds, and fossilised tropical vegetation were collected, together with the vertebrae and teeth of different kinds of sharks, as further evidence of the warmer past. To generations of islanders who have faced the easterly winds it sounds like a fairy story, but it was fact, millions of years ago.

The island, as first recorded, rises from marshland on south, east and west to a ridge of hills along what was once roughly the island's centre. The north side consists of cliffs of London clay, where the hills end rather abruptly. The islands of Harty and Elmley are now part of Sheppey, but in Anglo-Saxon times they were separated from the larger island by fleets, or small rivers, which needed a ford, or a ferry to cross them. These have long since gone, and access is now by road.

The island in its beginnings would have appeared as a large green area of marshland, which was subject to repeated flooding, with a large range of hills, rather like a backbone, which stretched from what is now Scrapsgate Road, through Minster and Eastchurch, to Warden Point. Coming on to the island via Kings Ferry, the view would have been of a vast expanse of flat marshes, with a line of hills rising three miles ahead. There were more trees in Sheppey then, and the hills were quite heavily wooded.

The Swale encircled the island, and the North Sea washed the base of the cliffs on the north. Approaching the island via the Swale, the usual way in days gone by, sailors would find a small creek entering the river between Harty and Minster. This was Windmill Creek, a small tidal river that ran through the fields at the back of the farms on the Lower Road, and served Minster and Eastchurch as an island water-way.

The island was known to the Greeks, who were among the earliest explorers. Ptolemy, the geographer of the second century A.D. mentions two islands in the mouth of the Thames, Tolicepus and Counsus. Although he gave latitude and longitude, his measurements did not correspond with those that the British understood, and learned men have argued ever since about these names. The weight of opinion appears to favour Counsus as Sheppey.

What the ancient Britons, or Celts, to give them their proper name, called the island isn't certain. That the island was inhabited in the centuries B.C. is certain. In 1873 the stock of a Bronze Age founder was discovered in Harty, and this appears to be the first known settlement on the island, as no others have been found.

There were moulds for celts (a celt being a kind of flask) the celts themselves, gouge moulds, gouges, hammers, knives and other things. This hoard gave valuable information on the method of bronze casting in the first century B.C.

In 1935 a bronze axe of palstave form was found on the beach at Warden Bay. This was apparently remarkable largely for the poor workmanship — it was judged to be the early effort of a workman learning his trade! Various coins have been found, often in the cliffs. Not for the reason that the men lost them as they were climbing the cliffs, as the local children thought, but because there has been so much cliff erosion that land now on the cliff edge was once many acres inland, where the action was. Coins of Dubnovellaunus, usually uninscribed, are not uncommon. One of these was found in 1932 and is now in the British Museum. The museum says that it is a gold quarter-stater of the King Dubnovellaunus, 15-1 B.C. With this were found two bronze dress ornaments, a pin and a broach, of Celtic origin. King Dubnovellaunus was king of one of the minor British tribes, allied to the Trinovantes, who were one of the chief tribes in the south-east at that time.

It is hard to believe that the only Britons in Sheppey were in Harty. Harty was the obvious place for an encampment (which was, incidentally, above marsh, and high tide level) because settlers there were in a position to defend the approaches from the Swale, and the island's inland water way, but there must have been other settlements. There have been fisherman, and oyster and mussel gatherers with settlements at Queenborough and Minster since time immemorial. There have also been sheep and ponies.

Where the humans and animals originated is debatable. Did they arrive before the separation of England from the Continent, or did they come by sea later? Probably both. There was certainly a sea trade with Britain in pre-Roman days, which points to a resident population in the British Isles. Britain was famous for her hunting dogs, corn, cattle, hides, iron, tin from Cornwall and slaves. Whether the slaves went willingly is another matter.

Julius Ceasar arrived in Kent in 54 or 55 B.C. He found the Britons intractable and warlike, a tall, fair haired, blue eyed people. They washed their hair in lime, which bleached it nearly white, and caused it to stick up in stiff spikes. Their usual dress was trousers and tunic, but when they fought they stripped naked and painted themselves all over with bright blue patterns, using woad for the purpose. Hence Caesar's repeated references to 'Sky Blue Britons'. They were expert with ponies and chariots, and caused him not a little bother. He knew Sheppey, if not intimately, and remarked on the number of sheep grazing there. It is to be hoped that the Sky Blue Britons gave him a warm welcome. Their wild shrieks as they drove into battle unnerved many a Roman, until the soldiers became used to the method. Caesar did not stay long, but after his visit to Britan the island was known as Insula Ovinium, the Island of Sheep.

It was almost another hundred years before Claudius arrived, in which time Britan had presumably forgotten it was supposed to be a Roman province, and Sheppey went along with that.

Claudius's invasion was definite. He took over Britain, although not without early troubles in the creeks and small rivers round the Medway. However he had come to stay, and Romans were stationed in Sheppey. Whether the Britons 'took to the hills', or stayed and became Romanised, no one has any real idea. Some probably stayed and continued to fish, collect oysters, live in their round timber homesteads, and work for Roman masters.

There is no evidence of Roman villas on Sheppey, apart from some foundations that were found when the prison was being built, but then nothing conclusive was proved. The artefacts found so far consist of roofing tiles, and samian ware in Harty, together with coins of Constantine. A quern was also found in this area. At Shellness, a kiln for burning shells was identified. Coins have been found in many places on the island. Copper coins of Hadrian, A.D. 117–138 and of Maximinus A.D. 286–310 were found at Minster, and both emperors are said to have visited Sheppey, to inspect defences. In recent years a bronze Roman ring was picked up in the beach at Sheerness, and was considered an important find, and in 1969 a collection of five hundred coins was dug up on the mud flats at Warden Bay. These coins included examples from the reigns of Trajan, Hadrian, Maximinus and others, the latest date being A.D. 260.

The Romans interest in Sheppey was purely military. The island was an important defence position and indeed has continued to be so up to the present day. To understand its importance, both to the Romans and the peoples that followed them, it is necessary to understand the route that ships took round Britain. Ships were small, powered by sails or oars. They would choose the shortest passage across the North Sea, which would bring them to the Kent coast in the vicinity of Thanet.

Thanet, until, roughly, Tudor times, was separated from the mainland by a navigable stretch of water called the Wantsum. Ships would sail up there, away from the sea and storms, and then push on for London or Rochester, keeping well into the coast. They avoided the open sea at the mouth of the River Thames by creeping up the River Swale, and sailing

past Sheppey to enter the Medway, or the Thames, when they had rounded the point by Queenborough. Therefore it was necessary to have garrisons in Sheppey, where all incoming shipping could be observed, and repelled if necessary. It is believed that the Romans had fortifications at Shurland and Minster, the two highest points of the island, which gave a commanding view of the Swale and the marshes to the south and east, and the North Sea to the west and north. It is also likely that there were smaller outposts at Shellness, Leysdown and Harty. There have been many Roman coins collected around Leysdown, and Shellness is the furthest point of the island facing Whitstable. Harty is the first place an invader coming up the Swale would reach on the island, and the approaches to the island waterway could be observed from here.

No records have been found of the Roman soldier's reactions to Sheppey. Dressed in tunics and sandals, they must have found it a cold inhospitable place, and doubtless thought the same unrepeatable things about it as troops in years to come thought about Sheerness.

There was no difference in the climate of Sheppey then from that of Sheppey today, and no difference in the marshes and mud. The cliffs and hills were as they are now, stiff London clay, dark and thick, with overlying beds of buff or yellow coloured clay, Bagshot Beds, on the highest points. The marshes were as wet, rich grazing in summer and frequently flooded in autumn, winter and spring. The winds were as biting and sentry duty cannot have been a comfortable outing.

Queenborough also had an army outpost, and a small fishing settlement on the edge of sea and marsh. At Shurland and Minster Abbey Roman titles and bricks have been identified and have been repeatedly re-used in subsequent buildings.

There is a story that the Romans had a temple to Diana on the site where the abbey now stands, but there is no proof of this, and in fact it is unlikely. From the tiles, hypocausts, and other stones and bricks found it is obvious that there were Roman buildings on the site, but it was most likely a small barracks or guard house.

The Romans were tolerant about religion. With soldiers from many different countries in their legions, they did not attempt to enforce the Roman Pantheon in the army, but allowed the men to worship their own gods. There was no church parade, or set religious observance as people now understand it. Gods were worshipped privately, often by a man alone. Although the Roman soldiers acknowledged Juno and Mars, different branches of the army often had a special god they sacrificed to, so uniformity would have been difficult to enforce.

A temple, then, would have been a small building. There could easily have been several small temples situated near a barracks, depending on the number of different religions or gods worshipped, by the serving troops. A usual plan for a Romano-Celtic temple was a square 'cella', the inner shrine, surrounded by a square outer wall which enclosed the te menos, the sacred precinct. The large, opulent temples associated with Roman cities would not have been considered for an outpost like Sheppey, the Insula Ovinium.

The Britons had dark gods of their own. There is an old story that Druids held meetings on the Isle of Elmley, but there is no proof of this. Elmley has always been marshy, and Druids needed oak trees. Caesar, whose invasion is remembered in Sheppey purely by a number of silver coins dug up when trenching, accused the Britons of burning human beings in large wicker baskets made in the shape of a man. The Romans also distrusted the Druids, the British priests.

There is no way of knowing how all these elements combined in Sheppey. No old tales exist of ghostly

2

centurions doing their rounds, or ill treated Britons. Emperors visited, presumably to make sure that the garrisons were in order, and for the four centuries the Romans were on the island one can only imagine that they kept the guard as ordered and the Britons who remained tended their sheep and fished.

No Roman roads were made on the island, and how they managed King's Ferry, whether by bridge or boat, is not recorded. They left no Roman names for places, or if they did then they were quickly forgotten. Unless some new discovery is made, it seems very little is left of four centuries of Roman occupation on the island.

CHAPTER II

The founding of the Menstre

The Romans finally left Britain in the fifth century, but before they finally abandoned Britain troubles with the Saxon 'pirates' had started, and by A.D. 407 there were not enough troops left to defend the northern borders or the southern shore line. There was a line of forts along the south-east coast, known as the Saxon Shore Forts, with a special command in charge of them, 'the Court of the Saxon Shore'.

Despite this, the Angles, Saxons and Jutes raided Britain, and caused damage and havoc. After the departure of the Romans, a local leader called Vortigern, invited the Saxons to settle in parts of the coast, to help repel sea-faring Picts from the north. This was the beginning of the end. By A.D. 442 the Saxons had rebelled against Vortigern, and fetched more of their race to help them. War, turmoil and chaos followed. The Britons made a final despairing appeal to Rome for help, the famous 'groans of the Britons' mentioned by the writer Gildas. No help was forthcoming, Britain was on her own. The invaders completely ignored the previous civilisation and towns became ruined and decayed, trade declined, slaves escaped and Britain returned to the dark ages.

During the fifth century Ambrosius and the legendary Arthur kept the Saxons out of the south-west, but in Kent they were well established. Sheppey was an obvious place for settlement, due to its unique position and military importance. Remains of a moated earthwork is easily traced at Sayes Court, Harty. Once again a defence position in the Swale, where the river could be constantly under surveillance, was chosen. There were earthworks at Queenborough, placed in a commanding position, and a fishing settlement known as Bynnae. Roman fortifications at Shurland and Minster were taken over and adapted by the invaders. Minster was then known as Cyningburg, the King's borough, and the name is still extant in Kingsborough Farm.

The monk Bede, who in later times wrote an ecclesiastical history of the English people, said that the invaders were Angles, Saxons and Jutes, the Jutes mainly settling in Kent, but that rather over-simplifies matters. Frankish and Frisian tribes have also been identified, and by the end of the seventh century they regarded themselves as the 'English Nation' although they were divided into several kingdoms.

They were pagans, worshipping the Scandinavian gods, Odin, or Woden, Thor and Freya. Any Christians there may have been in Britain (for Christianity had spread gradually, and many Romans were converted to it), had fled. The Britons also fled, to Wales, and to the west of England. Any that did not escape the invaders were captured and became slaves, if they lived.

By the late fifth century the south and east of Britain was divided into kingdoms, all fighting among themselves for supremacy. The king who was most powerful was considered overlord of them all. The third overlord in the succession was Aethelbert of Kent, who had vanquished the powerful Ceawlin of Wessex. It was to King Aethelbert of Kent, in A.D. 597 that St. Augustine came, to convert the heathen English. Augustine's task was probably made easier by the knowledge that Aethelbert's wife, Queen Bertha, was already Christian. Her father, King Chanbert of Paris, had only consented to her marriage on the condition that she would be allowed to practise her own religion. In view of this perhaps it wasn't surprising that King Aethelbert agreed to conversion, and forsook the pagan gods. Once the king was a Christian, his nobles and lesser subjects had not much choice, they had to follow him. In fact, King Aethelbert was the head of a royal family that for several generations were to be renowned for their religious zeal, and the number of monasteries they founded in Kent.

There was no dramatic attempt to convert the English overnight. Instead, temples were reconsecrated as churches and the idols destroyed. Ancient festivals became religious feasts e.g. the mid winter Yule Tide holiday became Christmas.

In spite of all endeavours, for a time Augustine's influence did not extend beyond Kent and Essex, and periodically there was backsliding into old beliefs. The British bishops in Wales, who practised the Celtic Christian teachings, would not acknowledge Augustine, and the Church was not united under the Pope in Rome until A.D. 690. Augustine baptised several hundred people in the Swale, and it is more than possible that some of the settlers from Sheppey were among them.

Aethelbert was one of the first kings to make new laws for England. The system behind the laws was old, for a framework of law had grown up through the years, based on the unity and kinship which the Anglo-Saxons used as the basis of their society. The laws were comprehensive and just, and they were the first in England to be influenced by Christianity. They were written in English, not Latin, and are the earliest written record of English social structures.

King Aethelbert's Son, Eadbald married Emma who like Queen Bertha was Frankish, and Christian. They had a daughter and son; the daughter Eynswith (or Eadswyde) was the first abbess of the nunnery at Folkestone; the son, Ercombert, became King of Kent, and married Sexburh. Sexburh, or Sexburga as she is usually called, was the daughter of Anna (or Annas, Ennis) who was king of the East Anglians, a Christian and described by the Monk Bede as 'a very good man.' Sexburh had three sisters, described by Bede with admiration. He seemed devoted to them in a religious sense, extolling their virtues as a pious, holy family. All the sisters became nuns.

After her husband Ercombert died in A.D. 664, Sexburh

asked her son Egbert for land on which to build a monastery. Egbert was King of Kent until he died in A.D. 673 when his brother Hlothere, or Lothaire, became King. It is generally supposed that the monastery was founded between A.D. 664 and A.D. 673 but it must be understood that all the accounts of this period were written at least one hundred years later, often more, and until that time history was passed on by word of mouth. This leads to some doubt about exact dates. The land given her was in Insulae Ovinium, or as the Saxons now called it, 'Schepeye' which literally means Sheep Island, and that is the name it has been known by ever since the Saxon invasion, albeit with a variety of spellings at different periods.

An extract from '*A Fragmentary Life of St. Mildred and other Kentish Royal Saints*' describes the building of the Monastery.

Now Erminhilda lies at Ely with her mother (Sexburh) and Aunt Audrey and their powers are often demonstrated there. And St. Sexburh and St. Erminhild received the Holy Veil in the Minster which is called Milton in Kent.

And the Island of Sheppey belongs to Milton; it is three miles broad and seven miles long.

Then for delight, and for honour, it pleased the Holy Woman Sexburh to found and build a minister for herself there, so that men of old said that the sound of creaking cart and complaining harrow never stopped for thirty years.

Then, when the minister was built, an angel of God came to her in a vision at night and announced to her that before many years a heathern people should conquer the nation. She had then held the kingdom on behalf of her son Hlothere for thirty years. And she then bought his share of the territory from him, and enfranchised it to the minister for as long as Christianity should be maintained in England. And she obtained a blessing from Rome for these who, in God's service, — the estate . . .

There it ends. It was taken from the writings of Florence of Worcester, Simeon of Durham, and others, England's early historians. Thirty years is, of course, an exaggeration. It was a way of saying 'a long time'.

Hlothere was Sexburh's second son. She had done her duty as seen at the time, made sure of the succession, and then made sure of the future of her minister. One of her sisters, St. Etheldreda, or Audrey, married twice, but remained a virgin, which seems rather tough on both husbands, but the lady was esteemed for it.

Sexburh founded her monastery, or nunnery, for royal or noble widows and spinsters, a place where devout ladies could have refuge and glorify God. There are two lives written about her, and preserved in the British Museum, in which one writer says 'her grace of form was as conspicuous as that of her mind' and much more in that vein.

The site she chose to build on, on top of the hill at Minster, was one of the fortified look-out posts for the island. It commanded every approach by land, sea and creek, with a view stretching for miles around. The minister admitted ladies of noble birth, who wished to renounce the world, take the vows of a nun, and devote themselves to prayer and good works.

It may seem incongruous for widows to become nuns, but if they did not wish to remarry, and many didn't, having lived through one arranged marriage, a nunnery was the only alternative. Some unmarried women really wished to become nuns, others were perhaps not good marriage prospects for one reason or another, or perhaps were rebellious and would not accept the husband chosen for them. No family wanted unmarried daughters at home to keep, so if no suitable match could be made a convent was the answer; it carried a certain

prestige and could perhaps be relied upon for intercession with those above — such was the outlook of the times.

Sexburh built a monastery for seventy-seven nuns, with herself as first abbess. There was a chapel, a refectory, cloisters, kitchens, dormitory, hospital, a separate house for the chaplains, and possibly a rest house for pilgrims and wayfarers. In addition there was the farm, for this was a minster that had to be self supporting, so there were farm buildings, land, stock, and probably fishing rights. All the buildings, apart from the chapel, would have been built of timber and wattle, for there was little stone for construction work in Sheppey and timber and wattle, or daub and wattle, were the usual materials used. The chapel was made of Kentish rag stone and flint, and part of the original nuns' chapel can be seen in the present church at Minster.

Anglo-Saxon churches were small, consisting of a narrow nave and small chancel, with little windows set high up in the walls. The walls were very thick, two feet thick, or more. All this is apparent in the north aisle of Minster Abbey, where the first nuns' chapel was built. It incorporated stone, flint, and Roman tiles, much of the material from older buildings, some of Roman origin, which were already on the site.

There was probably some fortification on the site and the farm workers and the villagers would build their crude huts and live round the outskirts of the monastery. There must have been a chaplain to take services and hear confession, and apart from the nuns' servants there would possibly have been men capable of bearing arms and fighting should it be necessary. From the position of the monastery on the top of the hill, and the manner in which the village and roads encircled it, it appears very likely that the nunnery was built on a fortified hill, with the cliffs and sea to the north and a steep drop to the marshes below on the southern side.

The nuns were of the Benedictine order, which was a strict order. The day was divided into period for prayers, devotions and church services, duty and work. The nuns were duty bound to aid the sick, help the destitute, offer hospitality to travellers, and pray for the souls of the sick, the dying, and the dead. At the same time they were not supposed to leave the nunnery, mix with strangers, or become too worldly, and the lay sisters and servants must have been responsible for the duties in kitchen and rest house.

There was a seal for the priory, a lozenge shaped lead seal with a likeness of Sexburh in the centre. She is represented as standing, holding what appears to be an olive branch in one hand and weights in the other. Round the edge is inscribed in Latin, 'This is the seal of Sexburh'. She is wearing a nun's habit and coif.

There is a remarkable story about this seal. In the year 1868, during restorations at Canterbury Cathedral, a floor and ceiling were removed from St. Andrew's Chapel, which had been divided into an upper and lower chamber. In the flooring were found several charters and other documents, which had slipped through. The seal of one was the seal of the charter of the Prioress of Minster, Sheppey. The charter in question was of an exchange of some houses in Canterbury for marshland in Sheppey, between Canterbury and the Abbey of Minster.

Sexburh was joined by her daughter Erminhild in A.D. 675, when Erminhild's husband Walfere, king of Mercia, died. Sexburh left Sheppey in A.D. 670 (again, it is claimed, as the result of a dream) and joined her sister Ethdreda at Ely, where she later succeeded as abbess, A.D. 679.

Erminhild became the second Abbess of Sheppey. In A.D. 699 King Wihtred was King of Kent, and by a charter made in that year granted the monasteries and churches of Kent freedom from all demand of public taxation and 'charge or vexation'. He declared he would stand by this, and so must posterity. 'Things he has allowed must not be brought to nought by any chicanery'. This the King signed, as did

Beorhtwald the archbishop, other bishops, presbyters and abbots in the presence of the renowned abbesses, Hirminhilda, Irminburga, Aeba and Nerenda, on the 6th day of the Ides of April, 8th year of reign, at Ceiling. Hirminhilda, presumably, was Irminhild, Abbess of Menstre, Schepeye, later to succeed her mother at Ely.

The Abbey became known as Sexburh menstre, and was the centre of the island. It was the largest settlement, the Menstre owned all the land from Sheerness to Eastchurch, and at that time the island was Minster, that was the place of importance. Sexburh died at Ely in A.D. 699, and was buried there near her sister. There is an odd statement extant that 'she laid down her life at Milton church door' but there is no verification for this. She was later canonised, and the Minster was dedicated to her. Her feast day is July 6th. King Egbert her husband, and her two sons, were buried in St. Augustine's Abbey at Canterbury.

It appears to have been a strict and well run monastery, managing its lands, receiving the tithes, and celebrating holy days with church services, rejoicing and merriment, as was the custom. Income from the farm was supplemented by offerings, tithes and Church Scot, a form of tax. Soul Scot was an offering to the priest for prayers for the dead man's soul. One tenth on income was set aside for maintenance of the clergy, and for relief of pilgrims and the poor.

While the monastery was there, farm workers and villagers were sure of protection and help. The various trades knew their duties, their dues, and their privileges. Only the slaves had little or no privileges, but even they were allowed to join in the feasting at Christmas and other holy days. Ploughing, harvest and other rural occasions were all an excuse for a revel.

Sheep were the important animals, the backbone of the economy, and as well as providing wool and meat, they were milked, and cheese and butter made.

Sexburh Minster is claimed by some to be the oldest abbey in Kent, but this is a debatable point, and Minster in Thanet makes the same claim. There were several Kentish foundations endowed by King Aethelbert's family in the seventh century.

This was a time of intense religious zeal and work in the monasteries, and it is reasonable to suppose that the small chapel was richly decorated, lighted with many small lamps and hung with valuable tapestries and linens considered worthy of an abbey. There would be books, missals and holy books beautifully handwritten and decorated in the style of the time.

All this was done to the glory of God, and for the good of man and his immortal soul, and the abbey continued to grow and prosper for the space of two hundred years, despite the warfare between the kingdoms, until Sexburh's prophetic dream came true, and disaster struck the Sheppey Minster.

CHAPTER III

Then the Pagan came

There is no record extant of the prioresses who followed Sexburh and her daughter Irminhild, but there is no reason to suppose that the nunnery did not flourish and run smoothly. The abbess, or prioress, had complete jurisdiction over her nunnery, her nuns and also over the farm, land, lay sisters and various grades of farm workers. These included slaves, for the Anglo-Saxons had no qualms about using slaves, and becoming Christian seemed to make no difference. The prioress also had the right to nominate a priest to serve the chapel and the nuns, although later this ceased.

Over the centuries, the kings of the different kingdoms fought for supremacy, but all seemed to have respected the convent, and allowed the nuns to live in peace. King Offa of Mercia was overlord in A.D. 774. He made laws and charters which were favourable to the monasteries, and added to their privileges. He is believed to have died whilst visiting Sheppey in A.D. 796 and one of the old stone coffin lids in Minster Abbey was alleged to be that of King Offa. In fact, he was buried at Bedford.

Apart from the priory, the island was regarded as 'Kings Land' and there were different posts at strategic places, with soldiers on guard. This did not seem to be of much help when Queen Sexburh's prophetic dream came true, and the Vikings came in their long boats. The *Anglo-Saxon Chronicle* states laconically A.D. 832(835): 'In this year the Pagan devastated Sheppey'. The date, due to time and other factors, is approximate, and the chronicle did not waste words. The heathen were getting in just about everywhere, so what was one small priory among so many others.

The following year 'they didde come in greater force, and in this year didde come Athelstan of Kent and fought with five and thirty pirate shippes'. It seems that by A.D. 855 the Danes, or Vikings as they are popularly known, had established Sheppey as a convenient headquarters for themselves, and remained in control of this corner of the coast until the final exodus of the Danes when William the Conqueror appeared.

In A.D. 893 'three hundred an fifty sayle of shippes under Hoestan arryved in Sceapige and spoiled it, the lyke did they four years later'. Off the coast of Sheppey Hoestan defeated King Alfred's navy, and then strengthened the three fortresses on the island before moving inland to build a stronghold at Milton. Two of the strongholds in question were known to be the abbey and what was later Shurland Hall. The chronicles tell us that 'the Danes had wrought great destruction to the Abbey, and expelled the Prioress and nuns, many of whom were put to the sword. If these nunnes of Sceapige had better privileges than the Religeuse of other parts of this realm, they were exceedingly ille handeled with Danish pirates'. Eventually, Hoestan was beaten by Alfred, and then converted, but by then the damage was done. Alfred managed to defeat the Vikings, up to a point. By allowing them to settle in the north-east of England, a territory known as the Danelaw, he kept the south and south-west free of them, but the coastal areas were always at risk.

After King Alfred's death fighting broke out again, as successive kings, good and bad, struggled for mastery of the British kingdoms, and attempted to keep the Vikings in check. By the end of the ninth century many monasteries had been despoiled, and despite King Alfred's attempts to promote schooling and education, monastic life and learning were at a low ebb. A Kentish will of A.D. 835, which left certain rents to St. Augustine's of Canterbury, made provision for the case that in some years payment might be impossible 'through heathen folk'.

During the tenth century an attempt was made to tighten up the discipline in the churches and monasteries. Churches tried to get their lands back, bishops and abbotts were given more authority, and married priests were turned out of office, and replaced by monks. It is possible that the priory of Sheppey enjoyed a little breathing space at this time, but by the end of the century this temporary respite was lost again in more raids, rapings, burnings and murders. By the end of the tenth century the British were paying Danegeld to keep the Vikings away, but as one party of raiders quickly replaced another it had little effect, apart from impoverishing Britain.

In 1002 the infamous Massacre of St. Brice, in which the skins of the Danes were hung on church doors, led to worse things. Throughout the eleventh century fighting continued, until eventually the Danes ruled England, first Swein, and then his son Cnut, or Canute. Cnut's reign was not without troubles, and he visited Sheppey frequently — it appears to have been a useful naval base. Cnut also managed to get some order out of the chaos of a country that was part British, part Danish, and when Edward the Confessor became king in A.D. 1042 he inherited a relatively well managed country, with land workers supporting the land owners, and manning the army when called upon to do so. The great abbeys provided art, scholarship and religion. However the coastal areas did not recover so easily, and it is generally thought that from the time the raiders first wintered in Sheppey no civilised community could have existed in the lower valley of the estuary.

In 1002 King Ethelred (the Unready) convened a Witan at Canterbury which all the bishops attended. This was apparently to discuss the current situation, for in 1001 the chronicle reported constant fighting in England because of the pirate army. They harried and burned almost everywhere. The second payment of Danegeld was £24,000, and appeared to be doing little useful, or stopping the raids. West Kent was ravaged in 999 and the Danes rode about the countryside on horses they had stolen.

During this period of roughly one hundred and fifty years there were no organised Danish (or Norse) communities in Kent. In the north and east of England the Vikings settled, and left traces of farming and merchant life, place names, legends and customs. In Sheppey they left nothing, which seems remarkable. Apart from the two 'Nesses', Sheerness and Shellness, whose names are attributed to the raiders — Ness being their word for nose, or in this case, headland — there are almost no stories, no history of battles, nothing. Neither have any artefacts been discovered, or if they have, they have remained unrecognised — unreported.

There are two local stories current about the raiders. For many years Sheppey men have been convinced that the islanders are descended from Vikings. This is more than possible providing the families have been on the island long enough, but no-one worries too much about proving the point. The other story, in which children at least believed implicitly, was that the mounds, or cottrels, along the Old Ferry Road were the burial places of Viking chiefs, following some of the battles for the abbey and the island. They contained untold treasure, of course! but no-one would dare to dig it up, for fear of the ill luck that would surely follow. Even now there is a reluctance to discredit the story entirely, although the cottrels in question are more likely to be safety mounds for the cattle and sheep to take refuge on in times of flood.

The only other legend is a Danish one. When the Vikings raided the abbey, one of the raiders made to attack a nun, but before he could strike her he found himself frozen to the ground, transfixed by the look she gave him. He could not

understand it, his limbs felt weak and he was unable to move. The nun continued to gaze at him, half pleading and half defiantly. The warrior put his sword away and beckoned the nun to follow him, which she did, quite calmly and confidently. He led her away from the scene of carnage, down to where the boats were moored. Quite uncharacteristically, he helped her quietly into a small boat, and rowed away. Safely back in his native land, the ill-assorted pair lived in a deep cave cut in a cliff, close to the seashore. The Viking respected the nun's vows and never attempted to molest her in any way, but looked after her and served her faithfully. The nun continued with her dedicated life of prayer and service to others, and there were many tales told of her kindness, and her help when people were in trouble, or ill. Her powers of healing were renowned for many miles, and so the nun from Sexburh Minster in Sheppey became a folk heroine and a legend in a far-off land. If there were any similar tales locally there is no trace of them now.

It seems incredible that a monastery should have been almost completely obliterated, but it happened. Even allowing that the chronicle was possibly written at a later date, and by monks who could find nothing bad enough to say about the detested heathens, it is doubtful if the facts were over-exaggerated. The raiding bands of Vikings were pagans, and found the monasteries and abbeys a storehouse of treasure, which they had no scruples about taking. Women meant little to them, nuns or otherwise, and those that weren't raped or killed would in all probability be taken as prisoners, if only to provide amusement for their captors.

The abbey at Minster stood on the highest point of the island, easily seen. There were various approaches, although Vikings were known to prefer creeks, as they could sail up a creek easily, and then moor or beach the long ships. Raiders could put in at Queenborough, then Bynnee, and take on the small fort there coming across the marshes to Minster. Anywhere along the marshy coast between Queenborough and the present White House would have been an easy landing place: Scrapsgate has long been a convenient beach for small boats. The most likely way, though, would have been to leave the Swale by Harty and sail up Windmill Creek. From the head of the creek it was only a short distance across marsh and field to the abbey and long-boats could easily be moored there. A stolen pony or two would shorten the journey, and probably make the ensuing battle easier for the invaders. For battles there were, although according to the records the defenders were usually overcome.

The look-outs at the abbey would have ample warning of raiders, as there was an uninterrupted view for miles around. What their thoughts were when they saw the high-prowed long-boats snaking up the creek no-one has recorded. The boats with their fiercely carved figure-heads, the wild yellow-haired men with their long beards and moustaches, great swords and axes and gleaming metal caps must have struck fear into many hearts. They were a bigger race of man than the British, and if they did wear horned head-dresses (which modern historians assure us is not so) they must have appeared like devils indeed. The fighting men would take up defensive positions and the farm workers belonging to the abbey, and the villagers, would be expected to grab some sort of weapon and fight too. No-one mentions the nuns. Presumably they took refuge in the little church, together with the women and children from the village, and prayed for deliverance.

If the defending garrison ever won a battle it is not recorded. In successive raids the nunnery and the village round it were burnt down, and any attempt at rebuilding suffered by fire again, later. It was not so difficult to burn a priory and village. All the buildings were made of wattle and daub, and wood, and would burn away merrily once they got going. Only the church remained, or part of it and this we know is true because many stones and tiles in the nuns' chapel show signs of having been in a fire. Anything of value would have been stolen before the place was fired. Doubtless many of the nuns and their people were killed. Those who survived and tried to rebuild would have similar ordeals again. The Vikings wintered in Sheppey, living off the land and using the island as a base. They probably found the sheep very useful, both for food and clothing. It is not too much to imagine that any islanders left alive would try to live as inconspicuously as possible, to avoid more reprisals. Invaders being what they are, local girls may well have been pressed into service, and not argued about it if there lives were at stake. This would give rise to the tale of the islanders' Viking ancestry.

It seems impossible that no signs of any battles should have been found, and it is likely that artefacts have been found over the centuries, and simply not recorded. There are examples of this. In the late 1920's workmen were digging a trench down the length of Imperial Avenue, Minster, a road running at right angles from Queens Road to the cliff edge. During the trench digging they unearthed skeletons, not just one or two, but several dozen at least. They were all lying longitudinally, as though they had been buried in a trench, somewhat hurriedly. When the bones were lifted from the trench, they quickly dissolved to powder. The only things that remained intact were the jawbones, and teeth, beautiful big, strong white teeth that many present-day men would envy. One or two local people who were interested in island history wanted the skeletons reported, but apparently nothing was done. The contractor did not want work stopped. The only thing they could do was to examine the skeletons in the hope of learning something of their origin. Their conclusions were that the bones belonged to tall men, as the long bones were of great length. The size of the jaws and teeth also suggested men of large build.

Several years later, when another trench was being dug down the side of an adjacent road, and parallel with the earlier trench, more skeletons were found, but these were relatively small, and the diggers presumed they were the remains of women, and promptly decided that the bones were those of murdered nuns. Once again, the finds were not investigated further. Of course there is absolutely no proof, but could these burials have followed one of the battles for the abbey, when the resident men-at-arms fought so hard to defend the nuns and their church? It is possible, at least, for there are no other reports of burials on the cliffs, almost under the abbey walls, and indeed no local history of battles since the Viking raids.

When Edward the Confessor became king in 1042 there was very little of the priory left; in all probability little more than a rough settlement around the remains of the church. Any hope of peace for Sheppey under Edward was short-lived, as the king quarrelled with his powerful barons, and in 1052 Godwin, Earl of Kent, ravaged the island and left it desolate once again. Local stories maintain that because of his wickedness his land was swallowed up by the sea and covered with sand and became the Goodwin Sands. Also, that he choked to death at a feast given by the king, which, apparently, was no more than his just dues and served him right.

Be that as it may, the Goodwin Sands are certainly there, and once were land that was lost late in the eleventh century. This was a time of great storms, Flanders and the low countries suffered in Europe, Sheppey marshes were badly flooded and much land was lost from the cliffs. The names Goodwin, Godwin and Godden are still common names in Sheppey, and go a long, long way back. King Harold, who reigned for such a short time, was the son of Earl Godwin. There were various stories, not all polite, about the Earl's parentage, and he was in part, at least, of Danish stock. When William the Conqueror arrived in Britain the monastery of Sexburh Minster was in ruins, and the fortified hill settlement almost deserted.

CHAPTER IV

William the First of Sheppey

William the Conqueror, rightly or wrongly, but it would seem inevitably, made himself King of England in A.D. 1066, at Battle in Sussex. He then had to bring some law and order into the rest of England.

Kent always maintained that the county was not conquered. Kentish men and men of Kent treated with King William on Penenden Heath, and as a result were allowed to retain the old laws and customs of their county. This was accepted as a literal fact in years to come and was referred to and given credence in court actions. However, this did not prevent the Norman nobles, and the knights whom the king wished to reward, taking over, or being allocated land in Kent as freely as in other counties. They used the Anglo-Saxon framework of laws, which was a sound one, but appointed officers of their own, and introduced the feudal system.

The Normans had originally been Vikings, who had settled in France, and been given land there; they adopted the language and outlook of the French but insisted on their individuality as Normans. England, used to Anglo-Saxon and Scandinavian tongues, now had a ruling class who spoke only French. It says a great deal for the English that over the years the court language, French, gradually died out, and the nation spoke English, albeit with differences of dialect.

Sheppey was soon compensated for the loss of population due to raids and pillaging. Foreign lords, and their retainers, took up residence as Norman nobles were granted land on the island. De Shurland, De Northwode, Peyforer, De Montfort and many other strange names appeared. Some lived on the island, they were sent there to garrison and defend it, but not all. Many simply had grants of land there, as can be seen from the charter rolls, fines and inquisitions and similar documents that formed part of the king's legal system.

The Church was one of the biggest land owners. One of King William's first charters referring to the Isle of Sheppey was headed 'King William the First de Scapeia', Scapeia being the Norman version of Sheppey, and in it he promised that the abbey and daughter churches should retain all the privileges they had been used to in former days.

King William made his half brother Odo, the Bishop of Bayeaux, the new Earl of Kent, and put him in charge of all ecclesiastical matters. He also left him to act as regent for a year after the Conquest. When William returned to England he had problems in the north to attend to. During this time Odo was becoming too powerful, and more interested in worldly matters than spiritual ones. So William asked Abbot Lanfranc to come to Canterbury and take charge.

Abbot Lanfranc wasn't too keen, but nevertheless he came, and the Anglo-Saxon Register 1070–82 reports that William I sent to brother Odo, Bishop of Bayeaux and Earl of Kent, and to Hamo the dapifer (Sheriff) this command: that he grant to Abbot Lanfranc all the customs which his predecessors enjoyed in the Church of Newington, St. Martin of Dover and the Menstre in Scapeia. These customs were recorded in the Domesday Monarchum and the white Book of St. Augustine.

This is, in fact, a list of churches and the dues they paid to the Mother Church at Canterbury during the year, and is in the Chapter Library at Canterbury. A second list showed certain churches that had others grouped under them. The third list has fewer names, and the dues paid 'before the coming of the Lord Lanfranc the Archbishop'. The churches subordinate to Milton and Newington are stated to have been given to the Abbey of St. Augustine by William the Conqueror, so it is presumed that the lists back to A.D. 1070–89 and were probably drawn up the first year Lanfranc was archbishop. Some churches had Saxon names, which the Normans disliked, and so altered.

Dues were paid in 7^d, or a multiple of the same. There are the dues from St. Augustine to Christchurch in Canterbury, and a reference to the last Saxon Bishop, who fled in 1070. The churches in Sheppey are listed.

Heortege. 7^d. That is Harty in Sheppey. Largely owned by the Church.

Churches subordinate to Milton Regis.

Northcip, which is thought to be Warden (North Sheppey). St. Augustine was a landowner.

Legesdune (Leysdown) and Eastcyrce (Eastchurch).

Subordinate to Newington were Hartlip, Rainham, Upchurch, Lower Halstow and Sexburga Minster.

This list was of Saxon origin, as the name was unchanged. All these churches were given to St. Augustine's Abbey.

The third list recites the dues from Middletune (Milton) which were two sesters of honey, two sheep and eight lambs, and sixty loaves and twelve pence and at Pentecost six hundred pence. Sheppey's contribution was amongst this levy.

A later list says that Middletune with all its chapels by grant of the kings namely William, Henry and Steven these are the chapels of the same church where they receive the Chrism (Holy Oil) and there pay their pence. Two churches in Scapeia, Leysdown and Warden. Elmlie is a very small island and pays threepence halfpenny. Again, there are Chapels of Newentone receiving the oil there, to wit at Middletune, and paying pence.

Two Churches in Sheppey, Minster and Eastchurch.

By this it appears that all the island churches belonged to St. Augustine, or other monasteries. All obtained the Chrism from Milton, but Minster Abbey was the mother church on the island, and the only church licensed to perform the rites of baptism, marriage and burial. It is also noticeable that in the later lists the name Sexburg was omitted, Saxon saints were not liked or recognised, and the priory became the Minster of Scapeia.

King William found the Minster in ruins, and almost deserted. How many nuns were there and whether they were lay sisters or professed nuns, has never been ascertained. He ordered some rebuilding, and towards the end of the eleventh century heard that the Prioress of Newington had been strangled in her bed, by the cook. No reason is given for this anarchy in the priory, but King William dealt with it

firmly and swiftly. He took the manor of Newington and added it to his own possessions, and transferred the remaining nuns to the ruinous Minster in Sheppey. How they managed is not clear. A new prioress must have been elected, and a certain amount of rebuilding completed. At the very least the little ragstone chapel would have been made fit for the nuns to worship in.

It was a trying time for all religious foundations, as Odo had appropriated to himself much of the Kentish Church property, and Archbishop Lanfranc was fighting to regain it for the Church.

The old lists of dues were not re-issued by coincidence at that time, the archbishop needed all the money he could raise, church dues and all, to help him in the struggle. In A.D. 1083 the king committed Odo to prison on a charge of robbing the Church of land and revenues, and Odo was tried, and found guilty, at Penenden Heath.

During this period of clerical upheaval the nuns of Sheppey can have received scant attention or help.

It is doubtful if the rules of the Benedictine Order were as strictly kept as they had been in the original foundation. The nuns were still drawn from the ranks of the nobly born and wealthy and would not have been admitted to the priory without a sizeable dowry. One cynic remarked that 'nunneries were in reality a home for wealthy unwanted spinsters and widows'. Unmarried female relatives were not popular in the great halls of nobles. Little is heard of Minster until Archbishop Corbeuil became Archbishop of Canterbury in 1126 and rescued it from ruin.

Apparently the nuns had been struggling desperately to keep the priory alive. The monastery that had started so gladly and courageously in A.D. 664 or thereabouts somehow continued until the general dissolution in A.D. 1546, but at no time does life appear to have gone as smoothly or uneventfully as one would imagine the life of cloistered nuns should.

The archbishop rebuilt the church, adding a second nave and chancel as a parish church, so that the abbey became in fact two churches, one for the nuns and one for the parish. The nomination of a priest was granted to the abbot and convent of St. Augustines, who allocated two monks to act, one as chaplain and confessor, one as vicar for the parish. They lived in the east gable of the gate house. Later a parsonage was built, commenced, it is thought in the thirteenth century.

The monastery was rebuilt; the gate house, which is all that remains of it, standing next to the abbey as it does now. The domestic buildings were on the north side of the church, where in the last century it was said the cloister garth was still smooth. There was a refectory, a dormitory, a chapter house, cloisters, cellarage, kitchens and other household accommodation. Quite where they were all situated can only be conjectured, as the site has never been officially surveyed or excavated, one of the few in England that hasn't. The position of the gate house is the only clue — behind here, with a vigilant porter in charge to prevent unwanted visitors, lay the convent buildings.

There were also farm buildings, and outside the priory wall houses for farm and domestic workers.

The Minster owned most of the land from Sheerness to the manor boundary of Shurland in Eastchurch, and the prioress held the rights of Lord of the manor.

The abbey was rededicated to St. Mary and St. Sexburga, at long last Queen Sexburga was recognised and allowed her rightful title as the founder of the abbey and the Isle of Sheppey's patron saint.

Although the church was rebuilt as two churches, as it is seen now, it is unlikely that the interior resembled that of the abbey as it is today.

Medieval churches were the centre of village life.

However their religion is regarded now, it meant a great deal to the people of the Middle Ages. England's economy was based on agriculture, and the majority of the village people were bound by work to the land, and the lord of the manor. Their holidays were the holy days, when they had a day free from work, attended church, and then had some kind of merrymaking to follow. The church must have been a place of beauty and light after the darkness and drabness of their cottages.

Church walls were painted in bright colours with Biblical scenes, and religious stories, for how else could an illiterate countryman understand the teachings he only heard in Latin. There were two altars, the high altar, and one to our Lady. There was a great rood, or cross, with statues or pictures of Mary and John on either side, attached to the top of the rood screen. Later a loft was built above this, the rood loft, and stairs were provided for singers and musicians to get up there.

In Lent, a veil was hung across the chancel between the choir and the altar, from the first Sunday in Lent until the Wednesday of Holy Week. Seats were in rows facing north and south with a clear alley between. There were fixed seats in the chancel, on the south side of the altar, called sedilia. Usually near the east end of the south wall, they were for the use of those ministering at the altar. Near them was a piscina.

The sedilia and the piscina can be seen in the nuns' chapel in the abbey. There is another piscina to the south of the high altar, in the parish church of the abbey. The piscina in the nuns' chapel has been broken, Cromwell's men are blamed, rightly or wrongly, for this.

On the north side of the altar, under the easternmost window, was the recess for the holy sepulchre, and if there was no recess something wooden was made up before Easter.

In the nuns' chapel there is a tomb in a recess on the north side of the altar, filled by a nameless knight in armour, an unknown Yorkist. He could have been placed in the Easter sepulchre at a later time of upheaval, but no-one knows now.

There were side altars and images and candles, wax candles, giving light and colour. It is recorded that in the abbey there was the high altar, an altar to the Virgin Mary, and another to St. Katherine. There were images of St. Mary le Piety, of the Holy Cross, and of St. James, but it is not known where they stood. Only the outline of St. Nicholas is still discernible, in a niche to the right of the altar in the parish church. The corresponding niche on the left side is empty. In the churchyard stood a small chapel to St. John the Baptist about which very little is known.

When the abbey was restored in 1851 the workmen found Roman flue tiles, originally used in a Roman bath, in the north wall. They were built into the wall to form an opening going through it, the wider mouth opening inside. It is claimed there were builders' marks on these tiles. They are thought to have been put in the wall for acoustic purposes, as there is some evidence of a covered way once having been built against the outside of the north wall. Nuns coming into their chapel via the covered way could hear, or be heard, without being seen by the congregation. These interesting tiles, or jars as some call them, are now plastered over.

On either side of the church tower is a semi-octagonal turret or buttress; there were once two belfreys here, one for the parish bell ringer, the other for the nuns' servant, to chime the hours. There is a large, very old, door in the tower, facing west. It is seldom used now, and the tower is kept locked, and only used by the clergy and church wardens.

There seems to be no knowledge of how many nuns were in the priory at this time, and the record of prioresses is very incomplete. They all came from wealthy, noble families.

There were many gifts to the priory. In the register called 'Honour and knight's Fees', it states that in 1086 Geoffrey de Ros held lands in Kent of the Bishop of Bayeaux, and some in Middletune (Milton). In 1130 Geoffrey de Ros (the son) accounted in Kent thirty shillings for his father's land (i.e. a final instalment of a much larger fine). He gave to the priory with his daughter a rent in the Holme of Grain in Kent. Date of death is not given, but in 1166 his son William held much land. The son died before 1194, but a further entry says that William de Ros I gave to the Nuns of Sheppey the Church of Bobbing, Kent, forty-seven acres of wood, e.g. Woods Court, Badlesmere, and three and a half acres of Grave in Pinegrave. (The location of that is unclear.) He or his son also gave a marsh in Sheppey called slipe. It would seem that the priory was being helped to a fresh start, and plenty of support was forthcoming.

In 1186 Roger, Abbot of St. Augustines, gave Agnes the Prioress tithes in Bobbing for a rent of ten shillings yearly. In 1188 the tithes of 'Westlande' for fourteen shillings yearly were added. There must have been a fire, with damage to buildings, for in 1225 Henry III allowed the prioress three marks to aid the repair of houses burnt. Priory houses, or houses of villagers, it seems that one way or another the Minster was in trouble again. This is not really surprising, as in the stormy reign of King John, England was laid under an interdict from the Pope, and the king was excommunicated.

During these years the churches were closed. No masses were said, and the people were denied the full rites of the sacraments. Relics were put away in ashes, so it is told, the priests lost a great deal of revenue, and so did the religious houses.

There were no pilgrimages, bells did not peal, candles were not lighted, and many people were made very unhappy. It is probable that the Minster lost revenue at this time, as there would be no pilgrims visiting the Abbey, and no Church revenues from funerals, baptisms and weddings.

In April 1234 Henry III granted on the priory a charter confirming their possessions and liberties in detail, pursuant to a charter of Richard I.

During Richard the 1st's reign there is one of the first appearances of the Shurlands of Eastchurch. The first mention of the name Shurland, or de Scirland as it was then spelt, paid a yearly due to the Priory. In 1198 the first of the Roberts, Robertus de Scirland, rendered an account to the treasury. Cecilia de Scapeia, presumably his wife, is also mentioned as rendering an account.

In these 'Great Rolls of the Pipe' there are many references to the abbey, 'The moniales de Scapeia', and to the Lady Cecilia who was reputed to be a generous patron of the priory.

In 1190 Osbernus de Scapeia was the prior of the Monastery of St. Andrew of Rochester, and he councelled the Lady Cecilia to give a window to the altar of St. Peter in Rochester Cathedral, of which there is now no trace. Lady Cecilia was obviously of a pious nature.

Despite grants and gifts the Minster was still in a bad financial state, for it is recorded that in 1286 Roger de Northwode did much to relieve the poverty of the house, which had fallen into ruin 'owing to defect of right government'. 'He, with no sparing bounty, relieved it from the greatest penury, on account of the great affection Sir Roger bore to the monastery of Saint Sexburge.' 'Wherefore, among the servants of God there, he is to this day called the restorer of that House.'

When the inevitable happened, and death claimed them, Roger and his wife Bona were buried before the altar, neither the first nor the last of the Norwoods to be buried in the abbey. Two Norwood brasses only remain, and the identities and age of them are still debated to this day.

What happened that time to reduce the monastery to such poverty, one wonders. Perhaps they had not recovered completely from King John's calamitous reign. There had been several years of drought, shortage of fodder, and disease amongst the sheep, which would affect the priory farm adversely. It must be remembered, too, that although the prioresses were educated ladies from good families, they were not necessarily good organisers and administrators. There are many examples of this in their history.

It is interesting to find King Henry III so generously disposed towards the priory. He was a great patron of monastic foundations, and contributed much to the building of Westminster Abbey, and many of the other great cathedrals.

Dover Hospital was given the custody of the King's Warren (Rabbit Warren) in Sheppey, and in 1231 he granted to Maison Dieu land in Sheppey, and to Saint Mary in Dover the Church of Saint James in Warden. The King's gift was for the support of the brethren and the poor of the hospital. This shows that the Normans had built several small chapels on the island soon after their arrival, but Minster Abbey remained the Mother Church, and for many years was the only church in Sheppey with the authority to carry out the rites of baptism, marriage and burial.

Feast days were celebrated at the abbey, with processions around the church. All mediaeval churches had to be built with open space or a wide path going completely around the building to enable processions to pass.

In these days there were twelve consecration crosses outside the church, and twelve inside. There was a bracket for a light below the cross, in order that a light may be burnt on certain days e.g. the anniversary of consecration, or the patron saint's day.

The porch was used for the first part of baptism, marriages, and the churching of women. A decree in 1215 ordered that a child baptised by a lay person must be brought to the porch for the priest to complete the ceremony.

Many things took place at the church door. Bequests were paid, solemn contracts made, and sometime cases, both civil and criminal, were tried, until this was forbidden at the end of the twelfth century. Naturally there was a stoop for holy water. A recess for this can be seen inside the church door at the abbey. The font was near the entrance then, and in 1305 Archbishop Winchelsea ordered that fonts were to be kept covered, and a lock and key provided. They are still covered today.

The church was a busy place, and the villagers treated it as part of their lives, in what now would be considered a very familiar manner. Church ales were held in and around the church to aid church funds, people danced, sang and often drank too freely, and there are records of the complaints made by the parishioners whose duty it was to clear up.

Pilgrims thronged the church porch, many pilgrims visited Minster Abbey. The abbey has a large porch, and the interior door which leads into the church is very old, and has the appearance of once having been an outside door. It has been suggested that it was removed from the nuns' chapel when Archbishop Corbeuil rebuilt the abbey, as at the restoration in 1881 foundations of a great doorway were found at a place where the two churches are now joined.

On the stone surround of this great door scratch marks can be discerned, where crosses have been scratched or graven into the stone. These are probably the old pilgrims' marks, and similar crosses can be seen in the large upstairs rooms of the gate house, where pilgrims were lodged.

Monasteries and priories were obliged by rule to allow pilgrims and travellers a night's lodgings. After one night further hospitality could be refused, but no-one could be turned away if they asked for a night's shelter.

With their religious duties to attend to, domestic duties, the manor rights, a farm to oversee, and the duties due to the parish and villagers, which included help, medical attention, nursing, and relief in times of need and crisis, the nuns had a full programme. This without the visits, requests and hospitality due to the island's knights, barons and gentry; the de Shurlands, the de Northwoods, and their friends, families and relations.

It is not surprising that at times they could not cope, and their performance fell short of the high ideals expected of them.

CHAPTER V

The priory, five hundred eventful years

Life was not all gifts and reverence for the prioress and her nuns. Henry III, at Windsor, generously liberated to the prioress and nuns of Scapeya forty shillings of the King's gift, and at the same time ordered 'to cause thirty shillings to be received of them for the King's use, for his thirtyeth of their lands and possessions'.

Archbishop's visitations were not full of fun, either. In 1286, on May 11th, Archbishop Peckham wrote to the convent forbidding them to receive secular women, young or old, without his special licence, as the priory had been troubled by the long stay of these. It sounds as though the nuns had been somewhat too generous, either that or they had been allowing personal friends to stay for long visits, something that was forbidden but not unknown.

In April 1296 Archbishop Winchelsea's visitation was even worse. Following his visit he sent them a list of injunctions. Starting amiably enough, with salutations and blessings, he then orders that silence must be observed in the choir, cloister, refectory and dorter (dormitory) and that the nuns should not be garrulous or quarrelsome, hold secret conventicles, or acquire money without express licence from the prioress. He criticised their habits (clothes), forbade the wearing of ornaments, and accused them of lapsing in their prayers and divine offices. These faults were to be punished by solitary confinement, and if necessary by more severe measures.

On May 1st more injunctions followed: there was to be more silence and discipline, and more penances. In 1299 there was a mandate to the prioress and nuns of Sheppey to take steps forthwith to secure the due observance of Pope

10

Boniface the Third's decretal for the strict inclusion of nuns. The nuns were not to leave the monastery, it had been noted that the rule had become very lax on this point. It is only fair to add that when the archbishop died he left to the 'monialibus in Scapeya' *centure solidos* — a respectable sum of money at that time. His admonitions, after all, were for their own good!

In 1303 a licence was granted to the prioress and nuns to acquire land from Henry de Northwode to find a chaplain to celebrate divine service daily in their church for the souls of Roger and Bona his wife, for ever.

In 1322, in Archbishop Reynold's Register at Lambeth there is a curious entry relating to the priory, which states that both church and cemetery suffered pollution from bloodshed. The archbishop was requested to grant a faculty for holding a special service of reconciliation. This is tantalising. What happened at Minster to cause bloodshed and consecration, and cause the church to be defiled? So far, an answer has not been found, but there is a local legend that could have a bearing on the question. Directly in a line with the church, at the top of what is now Parsonage Chase, a vicarage was built in which visiting priests and monks were housed. It is believed that the original building was commenced in the thirteenth century. Monks would proceed to the abbey in single file, following a path from the parsonage that is still traceable, and in parts still unmade, the Old Parish Road. The monks would chant as they walked, and the only other sounds was of the swish of robes, the click of beads, and the soft 'plop-plop' of sandalled, or bare feet. One monk forgot his vows and fell in love with a nun from the priory. She did not return his feelings and rejected his advances. He would not accept her rejection, and increased his attentions to the point of becoming a nuisance, and offending other members of his brotherhood. He ignored remonstrances from the prioress, and from the priests, until eventually someone in the community, whether a monk or a layman is not clear, lost patience and in the manner of the age resorted to violence, and slew the amorous monk.

Since then the monks are said to have passed along the same road once a year in procession. Some of the older people in the village used to say they had seen, or heard, the monks coming up the stone stairway that leads from Back Lane to Minster Street, and then cross the road to the abbey. As there are two public houses adjacent to both the stairs and the abbey, their story was regarded with scepticism. However, there are people today who swear that they have heard the monks walking along the Old Parish Road, the chanting, the swish of gowns, the click of beads — it is, so far, an unproven story.

Archbishop Reynolds had further troubles with the priory in 1326, when he gave orders that disputes with the parishioners of Minster were to cease. This seems to have presaged a spate of troubles. Perhaps the prioress at that date was lacking in diplomacy.

Edward III became King in 1327. Throughout his reign he showed great regard for the priory, probably because he visited the island frequently, and King Edward and his sons were devoutly religious, as religion was understood at that time. In 1329 he confirmed Henry III's charter, which had gone missing when Leeds Castle was besieged by Edward II, and he also granted additional liberties. Among these was the right to hold a fair on Palm Monday, for the sale of toys or similar knick-knacks. The dues from this would go into the priory's coffers, but the fair continued long after the dissolution and was still held outside the church until the early nineteenth century. The Fair did not seem to do much towards propritiating the villagers. In 1332 the prioress complained that her pillory at Minster had been cut down. As she held the manorial rights she would be responsible for the pillory, the stocks, and any other form of village

correction that might be needed. Perhaps she was too free with the use of these correctives.

In 1339 came a cry for help. The prioress had been besieged for more than five days in the priory. It is hard to imagine just how the villagers managed to do this. The two gateways of the gatehouse must have been closed and barred firmly, in order to keep the local people out, but at the same time that meant that the prioress and nuns were forced to stay in. Whether they could leave the priory for their chapel is not revealed. At that time the nuns' chapel was separated from the parish church by a wall between the two, the present arches came at a later date, but even so going to the chapel could have been dangerous. How the difficulties were overcome is not known. In 1340 Archbishop John de Stratford confirmed appropriation to the priory of all churches belonging to it. The evidence was letters of Archbishop John de Peckham, saying he had inspected letters and muniments of William and Theobald, Archbishops, relating to the Church of Bobbing (William de Ros) which grant was confirmed by kings Richard I and John, and the Church of Gillingham and the Chapel of Grain which was the grant of Richard, Archbishop of Canterbury. Despite grants and confirmation of grants in 1343 the nuns complained they had been hindered from holding their yearly fair at Minster, and other liberties had been interfered with. Quite who or what was causing the interference is not clear, but presumably the feud with the villagers was still going vigorously.

Throughout the centuries all the kings seem to have confirmed and ratified the priory's rights and liberties: Richard II in 1381, Henry IV in 1400, Henry V in 1414, Henry VI in 1429 and Henry VII in 1504 — an imposing record.

The Kent Lay Subsidy Roll of 1334–5, which in effect records the taxes due from the members of the county who were considered to have enough wealth or property to pay, show that the Prioress of Sheppey was due to pay tax of £2, but that the priory was exempt from tax, so none was taken. The Charter of King Wihtred, made in the seventh century, was still honoured.

A fourteenth century Act Book of the Consistory Court of Canterbury records the following, which must have caused an uproar in the cloisters:

On July 2nd 1347, before John Leck and Laurence Falstolf, sitting in Saltwood Church.
Robert Perot alias Northo, who is accused of abducting Joan de Grofherst (Grovehurst) a nun of Sheppey, is to be examined as to whether
1) He was present when Joan first took the habit of the order
2) On what day he saw her wearing the said habit
3) On what day she disclosed to him her intention to abandon her vows and quit the monastery

There is a gap in the narrative here, as the case seems to have been continued in another folio, but then, on July 26th, 1347, it resumes as follows:

before Lech and Fastolph sitting in the Chapel of the Ville of Mortelak.
Case against Perot alias Northo for abducting Joan (a nun of Sheppey), daughter of Richard Grofherst.

To certain questions the accused replied that he did not know the day on which Joan took the habit, but that he had seen her wearing it, that he caused a secular dress to be brought to her by a certain boy on the day in which she left the monastery, and that he took her away on his horse without leave of the prioress or anyone else; also that for three years past or more, the said Joan had told him that she was desirous of leaving the monastery, and that certain other persons had heard her express this wish; that the said Joan did not ask leave of the prioress but of Olivia Pawythorn, a nun of the same monastery. And here the case was adjourned to Lambeth, leaving an unfinished story. What happened to the unfortunate pair? Did they get away with it, or was Joan returned to the monastery and suitably chastised? We don't know.

The affair raises many queries. One wonders just how strict the discipline was in the priory, as Joan and Robert had obviously been meeting frequently. The bold Robert seems to have had no difficulties about the elopement, finding 'a certain boy' who apparently had no trouble in smuggling in a dress for the journey, and then carrying Joan away on his horse, in the approved manner, without let or hindrance.

Thirteen forty-seven was the year the Black Death first appeared in England, and although there are no definite records of the plague in Sheppey, doubtless the priory was affected by the unrest it generated and worried by the possibility of its appearance. As the Black Death decimated the populace, there were fewer land workers available. The peasants soon found that this worked to their advantage, and demanded more freedom from 'boon work' (work done for the Lord of the Manor) and higher wages. The priory had a bad record of relations with the villagers, and all these things may have combined to weaken the discipline.

The Black Death was also followed by a certain amount of religious disaffection, encouraged by the Lollards, who were labelled as heretics by the establishment. The general tendency to riot and civil commotion ended in Watt Tyler's rebellion of 1381. Possibly Sheppey men took part, and although the mob was dispersed and there were heavy and cruel punishments, thankfully the peasants obtained some improvement in their rather dreary conditions in the following century. All this must have contributed to the gradual deterioration of many of the religious foundations. Certainly from this date it is harder to find facts and details of the priory.

The reign of Edward III brought different problems. The Hundred Years War with France meant that there were recurring scares of invasion. Threats like this were not unknown in former reigns, and in Edward II's reign men on the Kent coast had been alerted and beacons ordered, but in Edward III's reign French naval raids on the coast became a fact, and the manning of the beacons became part of the national defence. As a result of this, the Prioress of Sheppey found herself responsible for providing three men-at-arms, that is, men carrying arms, and three hobeliers, light horsemen who could gallop and relay messages, to watch and ward at Rodmer in Sheppey. The beacon there was just one of the Sheppey defences, which were very thorough. Three of the force are named, they were Willemus de Middletune (William of Milton) Bartholomus de Watton, and John Peyfore of Sheppey. It is not clear if these three were the men or the hobeliers, but their names and standing suggest that they were the horsemen.

Rodmer was a point somewhere along Minster Cliffs. No two old maps show it in the same place; it is variously shown as Merrimans Hill, the Royal Oak, and Hensbrook. The beacon was placed at this point, and the six men guarding it had the job of 'watching and warding' Minster Cliffs. This stretch was known locally as Wards, and doubtless this is where Wards Hill obtained the name it is still known by. In 1360 Edward III decided to build a castle at Bynne, which was called Newtown for a short while and finally officially named Queenborough. He showed great kindness to the priory, and in 1361 granted the nuns three stanks, or wells, 'In a Place called Bynne rainwater falls and is received by the Swale. Licence is granted for the Prioress to make four dykes, furrows or baulks with a plough, the width 3 feet 20 poles round the well for the water to run in. The water may be carried by ships' boats, carts, horses etc. and they may come

and go as they please by the causeway which goes to the castle.'

It has been suggested that the building of the castle interfered with the nuns' water supply, but buildings at Queenborough would not be likely to affect wells on Minster Hill. On the other hand, it may well have interfered with the water available for farm stock. The priory lands stretched almost as far as Queenborough, and what is now the town of Sheerness was at that time simply a vast area of marshland, called Minster Marshes. To be able to obtain extra water for stock summering there would have been a great advantage.

It is possible that the king visited the priory with Queen Phillipa, as they frequently stayed at Queenborough Castle, and the king's son, John o' Gaunt, was one of the first governors of the castle. The actual building of the castle must have created some excitement, as it would have been visible from the abbey, a new and imposing building seen across the intervening marshland. Inevitably, there would have been new faces on the island, and more visitors to the Minster.

The king built a chapel of ease for his new castle and town, it became a daughter church of the abbey, and paid dues to the priory, something which caused grumbling from Queenborough people in years to come. The new church had a priest, and celebrated the services, but was not licensed for baptisms, weddings or burials, and all ceremonies were performed at Minster Abbey.

This applied to Eastchurch and Leysdown churches also, and probably to Elmley, Harty and Warden. In 1355, when the prioress was reputedly Joan de Cobham, it is recorded that the Abbess of St. Sexburg complained to Archbishop Islip that William de Riphall, Vicar of Leysdown Parish Church, had buried certain bodies in his churchyard and received fees. The vicar was admonished, and fined, by the legal auditor. The fees were due to the Mother Church of Minster, and the bodies were ordered to be taken there. They are listed; John Sanders, threepence halfpenny, Joan Gamone, sevenpence halfpenny. Joan daughter of John Haucchyn, tuppence farthing. Juliana daughter of John Aleyn, threepence. Elias Spayland, threepence. John Keyn, fourpence. How the amounts of money per burial were arrived at one can only guess, and all had to be exhumed, moved to Minster and re-interred, a gruesome procedure. It seems a great to-do for the amount of money involved, but a penny was worth a great deal more than it is today, and Joan de Cobham has a history of demanding her rights.

Isabel de Hunyngton was elected as prioress in 1368, and there are no more complaints of quarrels with the villagers, so perhaps she understood the local people better than her predecessors had done. Records of the priory are scanty for this period. Presumably it was a busy time with the war with France, watch and ward duties, and a new castle and town developing on the island.

William Cheyney had succeeded Sir Robert de Shurland at Shurland Hall, and doubtless when Sir Robert, the Baron of Sheppey, died in 1327 (approximate date) there was a splendid funeral at the abbey, many prayers and masses, and the island mourned. Several of the Norwood family had died during the century, and they were also buried in the abbey. Marriages were celebrated, and the baptisms of infants from the local great houses must have been notable occasions.

In 1396 Archbishop William once again confirmed former charters, and added coolly that he had found from documents that by the foundation of the priory there should be a prioress and a certain number of canonesses professing the rule of St. Augustine, and received the profession of the order from them; Henry IV confirmed this in 1400.

This is confusing. The original monastery could not have belonged to the Augustinian Order, and the only explanation is that William de Corbeuil may have been responsible for a re-foundation, as he had been an Augustinian canon. At the same time, it seems strange to change the order that had continued for so long; and to complicate matters further, the priory was alluded to as a Benedictine foundation at the time of its dissolution.

There seem to be fewer available records for the fifteenth century. The war with France was over, for the time being. During the war it had been forbidden by law to ring more than one church bell if the church lay within seven leagues of the coast, as a peal of bells would signify invasion. Presumably the nuns were now permitted to have the abbey bells rung again. It is apparent in bequests in wills that the priory was hoping to build a tower on the abbey, which perhaps would also serve as a beacon in time of need, and be a guide for mariners. Despite the disaffection towards the clergy that was apparent in the second half of the fourteenth century there was still a preponderance of loyal churchmen.

Richard II was murdered in prison in 1400, and Jack Cade's rebellion and the Wars of the Roses were soon to follow. How much this affected the priory is hard to say, but certainly there is the effigy of an unknown Yorkist knight in the abbey. Once it was thought he was the notorious Duke of Clarence who was drowned in a tub of Malmesbury wine, according to legend, but this has been proved otherwise. The brass lettering that was once on his tomb has long since been ripped off, and the coats of arms are too worn to be identifiable. This poor Yorkist has a choice of characters. It could be Sir Hugh de Badlesmere, although why he should end in Minster Abbey is not clear. The only clue is that the Norwoods and the Badlesmeres were related by marriage. Another theory is that he was the husband of one of the Shurland ladies, Winifred de Shurland. It is not likely that he was a Cheyney, as they were staunch Lancastrians, although there is always the odd man out to reckon with. It is all very theoretical, and likely to remain so, unless some fresh evidence is discovered, which is always possible.

Sir William Cheyne of Shurland died early in the century, and in his will, proved in 1441, left directions that he was to be buried in the chapel of St. Katherine, within the Abbey of Sts. Mary and Sexburga, in the Isle of Sheppey. He also left a bequest of money for the abbey. That must have been another magnificent funeral, with a mighty feasting to follow, according to the custom then. He was the Lord of Shurland Hall, a descendant of Sir Robert de Shurland, through his daughter Margaret. His ancestors had also been buried in St. Katherine's Chapel, where the image of St. Katherine stood, surrounded by candles and beautifully decorated.

Now there is no indication of where the chapel stood, only suppositions. Neither is it known where William Cheyne lies. He could be the figure who was found six feet beneath the ground in the churchyard in 1833, either buried there at the dissolution, or hidden later from Cromwell's men, for between his hands, which lie together in the attitude of prayer on his breast, is a small image representing his soul. Such figures are rare in England, and would certainly have incurred the wrath of the Roundheads. The figure, carved in marble, is depicted clad in fifteenth century armour. One of his descendants, John Cheyne of Eastchurch, took part in Jack Cade's rebellion in 1450, taking with him men from Eastchurch and Minster, the Mayor of Queenborough, John Cokeran, and several Queenborough men described as mariners. The reason for the rebellion was the fear that Kent was about to be destroyed 'by Royal power, as a revenge for the death of the Earl of Suffolk'.

However, John Cheyne and his men were pardoned, and returned home to the island, and Miles and John Symond de Mynstre in Insula Scapaye, husbandmen, came back to their village. Later John Cheyne became a noted Lancastrian. Jack Cade did not give up easily, he continued his depredations and attacked Queenborough Castle, with no success. This must have created a disturbance on the island and caused some perturbation in the priory.

At some time in the first half of the fifteenth century Constance Septvans was the prioress. She is not included in the list of past abbesses or prioresses, so the actual date is uncertain but the family tree of Septvans (compiled by Sir Reginald Tower) states that John de Septvans the second had four children. His second child, and second son, died in 1453. His third child, a daughter, was Constance, and became Abbess of Sheppey. The priory has no history of disturbance when under her care.

William Rede of Minster, buried in 1472, left the abbey a very definite bequest in his will. 'My bay horse to be sold, and the money to buy an image of Saint George to be set in the Church.' The abbey must have been very well furnished with images by this time, and there were more to come. Bequests came from the mainland, generosity to the abbey was not confined to the island.

Robert Wybern of Sittingbourne whose name is still alive in Minster in Whyburn's or Whybourne's Farm, died in 1473. In his will, after a list of relatives and what they were to receive, he continues, 'Katherine, my daughter, a nun (muliere religiose) to have five rods of land in the field Beggars Thorn during her life, then to the Prioress and Nuns of Sheppey forever, to pray for my soul, parents, friends'.

William Randolfe of Sittingbourne, 1487, after bequests to his family, says, 'To the works (operibus) of Minster Church, the Tower, fifty three shillings and four pence'. That was indeed a handsome sum of money! He continues, 'to William and Thomas, sons of Stephen my son deceased, when they are twenty, all tenements lands within the Burgh (Borough) of Holte and Seden except lands in Eastchurch, and to their heirs, etc. ... Son Henry, all lands and tenements in Eastchurch, and my tenement called the Hall in the Borough of Ossynden (in Minster) after the death of my wife.' William Randolfe was obviously a land owner of some extent on the island, but where his ground was cannot be traced now.

There are many more wills leaving land, money, sheep, cattle and in one case honey, to the priory. Some of these bequests were to be used specifically for the tower, others were for candles and prayers, but it seems that the idea of a tower for the abbey church had fired the imaginations of the local people.

The islanders had another great devotion, which may come as a surprise to people today. This was to King Henry VI. Usually considered to be a weak king, subject to bouts of insanity, he was yet revered and acclaimed as holy by the ordinary people, and his burial places and relics were venerated. The Lancastrians disliked this and did their best to put a stop to it. The Archbishop of York issued a monition forbidding the veneration of images of King Henry VI in 1479. This did not deter the populace, many churches had an image of King Henry VI, and Minster Abbey was almost certainly among them.

A miracle is said to have taken place at Minster, which is recorded and verified. It concerned a child called Ann, the daughter of Thomas Plott, who lived in a cottage 'before the gates of the Convent'. This child was wandering along the 'public road' when she was run over and crushed by the wheel of a dung cart, which was being driven to the fields by a 'factor' (farm hand) who worked for the nuns. To put it briefly, the cart was loaded with dung, the wheels were strengthened with iron plates, and the child was pinned down by the shoulders 'so that it left her young body shattered on the ground, well nigh as flat as a pancake'. (This statement has an added interest. It is one of the first known written records of the expression Flat as a Pancake.) Naturally the neighbours ran to her aid, making a great deal of noise about it, and the mother, hearing the wailing came 'in great fear' and picked her little girl up and embraced her. She was certain the child was dead, so she put the body down and ran after the driver of the cart 'with her heart embittered, for indeed her anger was thoroughly aroused'.

Meanwhile another woman there, 'whose heart was firmly established in the Grace of Christ, with courageous faith snatched out her purse and bent a penny over the lifeless corpse, as if to implore the pity of our lord and the prayers of his most devout servant King Henry by this promise of an offering'. Everyone standing with her prayed, and requested a miracle, that they might have their wish by the intercession of so holy a man, And, it continues, a wonderful thing followed. Hardly was the prayer ended when the little girl came to life and cried for her mother — 'which was all the more marvellous, as she had never learned to speak before. The little one was but one year old.' After that she speedily recovered, and before dusk was playing and dancing in the street again.

The mother went to King Henry's tomb at Windsor on pilgrimage a week later, barefoot and in rough clothes. The other witnesses were named as John Besy and his wife Alice, and Agnes Andrew who symbolically bent the penny. It is all too far away in time now to know what really happened. To modern minds, one year old is rather young to be playing in the street, but the street in 1480 would only have been a dirt track between the little houses that huddled near the convent. One thing is sure, the villagers had a strong feeling of devotion to Henry VI, and doubtless his image was in the Abbey Church.

There are no more miracles recorded, or any other excitements. Archbishop Warham made a visitation in 1511, and the report gives a definite feeling of the priory slowly running down. Other priories shared the same fate at this time. The priory at Davington was deserted by the time of the Reformation, the last nun there having been found sitting nursing her baby, the local chaplain being the father in the case.

The prioress at this visitation was Agnes Revers, or Rivers. She said everything was in order, except that she doubted whether Advice Tunfield, chantress, behaved well to the nuns and provided properly for the observances in the choir. She had heard there had been seventeen nuns, and knew of fourteen, and wished to increase the number if she could find anyone wishing to enter religion (this is the first time a definite number has been mentioned since the seventy-seven nuns of A.D. 670).

Evidence was also given by Agnes Norton, sub prioress, Avice Tunfield, Elizabeth Chatok, Elizabeth Stradlyng, Mildred Wigmore, Dorothy Durell, Agnes Bolney, Anne Pettit, and Ursula Gosborn. These said that they had no maid called the convent servant to serve them with food and drink, and other necessaries, but the house was served by an outsider, a woman from the town. There was no infirmary, but those who were ill died in the dormitory; the gate of the cloister was closed too strictly, not only after supper, but at the time of vespers; and the prioress never gave any accounts. One said the manservants of the prioress spoke contemptuously and dishonestly of the convent. The prioress was ordered to render accounts and to make an inventory, to provide an honest woman servant, to make up the number to fourteen as soon as possible, and to build an infirmary at her earliest convenience. The chancel of Bobbing was to be repaired before midsummer.

It is a gloomy picture. There were probably not enough nuns for the work that they were supposed to do. It seems incredible that there should be no infirmary in use, unless it was used solely for nursing the sick and old of the village, which is a possibility. The nuns themselves do not seem to have been on the best of terms, and there was still a marked antagonism between the priory and the local people. However, although they could not know it, this situation was soon to end in a manner they had never foreseen.

CHAPTER VI

The first Normans in Sheppey

In Saxon times Sheppey was known for its Menstre, sheep, and very little else. Apart from fortifications at Harty and Shurland, and a small wooden fort at the fishing village of Bynne, there were few buildings beyond the huts of the local farming community, and not many inhabitants at that. Small areas around the forts would be cultivated, but the greater part of the island was empty of people, a big area of marshland, wooded on the hills, winding muddy tracks that served as roads, and the whole separated from the mainland by the Swale. Water transport was used freely, and the now defunct Windmill Creek was a recognised way of bringing goods to within a mile of the abbey. This emptiness did not suit King William I, and he distributed land generously amongst his knights, and the many religious foundations.

Domesday Book does not give much information about Sheppey, and leaves many blank spaces. Hugh de Port holds of the Bishop Stepedene (in Sheppey) Osward held it in T.R.E. that is, before 1066, then it was assessed at one sulung all but one yoke.

Land for two ploughs. On the demesne is — ? (and here are a pair of empty brackets) with one serf and four bordars, worth thirty shillings. This is not the place for long explanations, but a sulung was a Kentish measurement of land, roughly the amount of land that could be cultivated using an eight-ox plough team. It was divided into four yokes. Serfs and bordars were the lord of the manor's men, bound to their lord with the land. The slight difference in their rank was defined by the amount of land they worked for themselves and the amount of work they were obliged to do for their master.

Godfray de Melling holds half a sulung of land in Scapeya from the Archbishop, worth £4, nevertheless he pays one hundred shillings. Osward indeed held this same sulung from the Archbishop of Canterbury T.R.E. Osward had apparently been dispossessed, and under the new management all the rents had gone up. There are many records about disputes about the ownership of marshland, grazing rights, and similar questions, as leases and rents were argued over by the different religious houses.

Small chapels appeared on the island, all belonging to monasteries and religious orders. The Church of Harty was one of the earliest, belonging to the Priory of Davington. It is said to be one of the remotest churches in Kent, and one of the smallest. It is a beautiful little church, very simple, with many interesting features. It still relies on candles and oil lamps for light in the dark winter evenings, and is lovingly cared for. One of its greatest treasures is an old wooden chest, with a scene of knights engaged in a tilting match carved on the front. This is not, as has been sometimes claimed, a picture of the last 'Trial by Combat' which took place in the sixteenth century, and was caused by a dispute over land in Harty. This chest is far older, a probable estimation placing it in the fourteenth century or early fifteenth century and the carving appears to be of German, or low countries, origin. How it came to Harty is impossible to guess, but as almost all ships sailing from the Continent passed Harty, it could easily have been left by one of these voyagers. Eastchurch, Leysdown, Warden and Elmley all had small churches, but at that time none of them was licensed to perform the rites of burial, baptism or marriage.

In the Kent Feet of Fines, 1199–1200, many names are mentioned as owners of land in Sheppey, but not all of them lived on the island. A Feet of Fines consisted of copies of agreements made after disputes about land ownership. Some of these disputes were artificial, 'set up' in order to register ownership.

Aifrod de Broc and his wife Mabel argued about a place in Leysdown called Hokeling, to which one Margery de Sconington also laid claim.

Walter de Petrapoint granted to his mother Lucy a yoke of land in Stupendune in Sheppey. This appears again later, and the rent was paid by 'a pair of gilt spurs yearly'. In 1244 Benedict de Harty was accused of not paying the rent for a seam of salt in Harty. He admitted to owing the rent to the church. Arguments about seams of salt were not uncommon. Geoffrey de Sconington also owed 'salt rent' to John de Wadeton.

In Henry III's reign Robert de Greuling (probably Graveling) and his wife Dionisis were the plaintiffs against Roger de Thornfield and his wife Joan regarding a messuage, and sixteen acres and half a perch of land in Minster. It was agreed this was the right of Dionisis which she had as a gift, and was to 'hold to' Robert and Dionisis and their heirs. They were to pay John the Baptist one penny yearly and render all services due to the chief lord. Also the plaintiffs gave a sore sparrow hawk, presumably in gratitude.

There are many records of fines, and their main interest is the names of places, many now gone, the names of the people involved, and the settlements made. Many of these agreements stipulate that the land holders must do all services required by the chief lord. A rose yearly, on a specific day such as the Nativity of St. John the Baptist, was a common part of the settlement as was the sore sparrow hawk. This simply meant that it was a young hawk trained to hunt.

A fine of especial interest relates to the Peyforers. Osborne Peyforer was a domesday tenant, who was granted large areas of land in Kent. In Henry III's reign William Peyforer and his brother Richard claimed land from Fulke Peyforer and a fourth brother, as part of their inheritance from their father William Peyforer. William's land was divided between the four by the Kentish custom of gavelkind. Fulke's share included the manor of Borstal, in Minster. This was a small manor, subservient to the priory, but a manor of standing for all that, and the Peyforers were a notable family on the island until the fourteenth century when through marriage their manor passed to the Potyn family.

It is said that due to Kent retaining the old custom of gavelkind there were more small farmers who owned their land than in other parts of England. That might have been true up to a point, but the greater part of the working population came under the jurisdiction of the lord of the manor, for this was the Norman method of running the country. The nobles were answerable to the king, and their tenants and retainers were answerable to the lord in their turn.

Apart from the Church, the two biggest land holders of

importance in Sheppey after the conquest were the de Shurlands and the de Northwodes. Behind both families is the shadowy figure of Jordanus de Scapeia, said by some historians to have been the Lord of Sheppey, where he was given a large grant of land. He lived at Shurland Hall, and different branches of his descendants took the names of de Shurland and de Northwood. That is one story. The other is that he was the first of the Norwoods before they took that name. One fact is certain. The names of the Shurlands and the Norwoods before they came to the island is not known. Like many other Norman knights, they took their names from the land they conquered.

Shurland was the chief manor. Originally Shireland, sometimes spelt Scirland or Shoreland, the name means Kings Land, land given by the king. De Shurland's coat of arms, azure, six lioncels rampant argent and a canton ermine, shows a relationship with the ruling families of the time, as lions usually signified a connection with the royal families of the period, legitimate or illegitimate.

The Leybourne family also had six lioncels as their coat of arms, and the de Shurlands have been credited with an alliance there, but many of the leading military families showed lions on their arms, using variations to differentiate. Ermine was the coat of arms of John de Montfort, the Duke of Brittany and Earl of Richmond. All this points to a family of high rank in the world of William I. The first mention of the de Shurlands is in 1188, when one Adam occupied certain lands in Sheppey, upon which a tithe was payable to the prioress of Sheppey.

In the reign of Richard I, in 1198, the first of the Roberts appeared, rendering an account of twenty marks to the treasury. In the treasury was ten marks and ten pence, so he owed nine marks, twelve shillings and sixpence. Cecilia de Sheppey, apparently his wife, also had an account of forty marks to render. She only managed to pay ten, and so owed thirty marks. She was a devout lady, and generously inclined towards the Menstre.

Little is heard of the family in John's unsettled reign, but in 1225 King Henry III appointed Sir Geoffrey de Shurland Warden of the Cinque Ports and Constable of Dover Castle. This was an important post, more so because at this period the king was not on the best of terms with France, and the lord warden needed to be vigilant. The king taxed his people cruelly, and was more likely to appoint his wife's French relatives to posts of importance than resident Anglo-Normans. Sir Geoffrey must have been a man of ability.

In King Henry III's reign fighting broke out between the King and his brother-in-law Simon de Montfort. If Sir Geoffrey was related to the de Montforts, this could have had some bearing on his appointment as lord warden. Although Simon de Montfort was killed, the Westminster parliament he fought to establish continued, and two knights and two burgesses from certain towns were summoned to Westminster every year. Kings who came after Henry III continued this practice, and it was the start of the present House of Commons.

Henry III was a great founder and patron of religious institutions. He is said to have founded the Holy Cross of Sweinestre, a small hospital in the Sittingbourne area.

A charter of 1243 states that Simon de Wardune grants to God and the Holy Cross of Sweinestre and the proctor thereof and the ministers who serve God there and their successors two small casks of salt yearly. Witnesses:—Robert de Wardune, chaplain. Thomas chaplain of Hestchirce. Scapeia, Robert de Shurland, Jacob de Tugelstone, John de Hokelyng, Stephen de Ride, Giles my servant, Osbert chaplain to Middletune, Richard chaplain to Bobbing, Walter chaplain to Morristune.

This grant gives the names of many local people, and the

island's chaplains. Hokelyng has long since disappeared, but Stephen de Ride is still remembered by Great Rides, Old Rides and New Rides, farms between Eastchurch and Leysdown. Again, Sir Robert de Shurland is mentioned, and this leads many people to confuse him with the Sir Robert of the Sheppey Legend, whereas he appears to have been that famous Robert's grandfather.

In a fine, dated 1271, all the lands of John, son of William de Hokelynge in Leisdune, are disputed, and it seems likely that they were acquired by the de Shurland family. Between 1264 and 1286 there are frequent references to a Sir Roger de Shirlande, or Chirlande, presumably the son of Robert. The spellings are variable, as spelling was left to the scribe's own interpretation in the Middle Ages.

In the forty-eighth year of Henry III, 1264, the patent roll in Nottingham states laconically: Item. Touching the lands of Titemanston Co. Kent late of William de Titendene which are committed to Sir Roger de Chirlande value £10. The following July, the patent roll at St. Paul's: 'was granted safe conduct after the feast of the translation of St. Thomas the Martyr and the whole of that day, for Simon de Crie and his son Simon, John de Rokele, Ralph de Ginges and Roger de Shurlaunde, coming to the king at London'. It would be interesting to know why he had to travel to London to the king. Kent was not a safe county for travelling then, being plagued with outlaws and small bands of robbers, hence the safe conduct.

After the Baron's revolt in 1265 and the defeat of Simon de Montfort by the king's son Prince Edward, inquests were held a few months later to ascertain how many rebels were at large, and if there was much discontent in the counties. Such an inquest was held in the Hundred of Middletune, on the Sunday after St. Faith, October 1265. It was stated that there were no rebels in the Hundred. Sir Roger de Shirland immediately after the battle of Evesham took into his hands all the tenements of Robert de Raleghe worth twenty pounds, but he allowed Robert's men to do their work. There were Michaelmas rents of eight shillings which the Reeve received.

Sir Roger was an honest king's man, whoever his relations may have been. He went with Roger Leyburn to Gascony for service with Prince Edward in 1269, and the rolls relate that in August 1272 he was granted protection for three years whilst serving overseas. This protection was important, as no messages could be sent easily to men away from home, and it ensured that no action for debt could be taken against him during his absence. Five years later Sir Roger was in Wales, assisting King Edward I in overcoming Llewellyn, the last native Prince of Wales. Something for which many of the Welsh people have still not forgiven England!

In 1279 he was again granted protection until a month after the following Easter, while he went overseas on a pilgrimage. By May 1280 he had returned, but his recent pilgrimage did not seem to have altered his natural bent for fighting and hunting, for he was caught trespassing in Sherwood forest. The only reason for trespassing in forests was to hunt the deer, and that was a major crime in the eyes of the early Norman kings. Sir Roger was referred to as Knight of John de Vesey's household, and, as expected, he was pardoned.

In the reign of Edward I, in January 1282, there is one of the most interesting references to the de Shurlands. From a record of inquisitions in Chauncery come details recorded at the Inquisition at Middletune, the Thursday after St. Matthew.

Sir Roger de Shurlande and his ancestors used to have from time beyond memory in their Manors of Shurland and Uffeton in the Hundred of Milton, Wreck of the Sea, bloodwyte, childwyte, and amercements of bakers and brewers of their own tenants, and no bailiff of the king was

wont to distrain in the said manors without their (bedle) beadle or servant.

The said Roger renders yearly to the king thirty shillings of rent. The *Calendarium Geneologica* of the same year says 'Rogerus de Shirland, De libertatibus suis infra maneria de Shirland et Uffeton'. Sir Roger was granted the liberty of both manors, subject only to the king. There are only two more references to Sir Roger. In 1284 Philip de Especer of Gloucester admitted that he owed Sir Roger fifty pounds, which had to be levied on his goods and chattels in default of payment. Two years later Sir Roger went overseas yet again with John de Vesey on the king's business, and then no more is heard of him. Perhaps he died overseas. During his life he had accomplished a great deal, and for someone living off the beaten track in Sheppey he had travelled widely.

He had established Shurland Hall as a liberty, which meant that he literally ran and owned his own small village, holding a manor court in which he, or his son or representative, heard and judged local complaints and petty crimes, answerable to no-one but the king. What exactly are all the 'rights' given him, one might ask. The expression 'time beyond memory' meant that the manor had had these rights since before Richard I's time, but until the inquisition in question they had never been recorded. One of the reasons for holding such inquisitions was to ascertain who was, or was not, entitled to such rights, and record the findings.

Wreck of the Sea meant that the lord of the manor was allowed to claim for himself any wreck that he could reach with his lance at low tide. To do this effectively enough to make any real gain, he needed to be able to manage a swimming horse and to have a horse that would swim freely. This proved important to his son Robert.

Bloodwyte was the right to fine any of his retinue or servants for the shedding of blood and not keeping the peace in his domain.

Childwyte was a fine paid to the lord by the father of an illegitimate child. It was regarded as a compensation for cheapening the value of one of the lord's bondswomen. Amercement of brewers and bakers was simply the right to fine these tradesmen if they gave short measure or inferior produce, or to regulate their trade if necessary. Whatever he decided to do no-one could interfere.

All this suggests that he had a large establishment, with the staff dependent upon him for everything. This was true. Most of the people on a manor were dependent on their lord. There were graduations in the social scale, from the 'freeman' at the top of the list who rented ground and owed no service, to the lowest serf, who worked for his keep and little else. In between these came various grades who were allowed various amounts of land, and a number of beasts, in return for an allotted number of days' work on the manor land. This included repairs, road work, maintenance and the like. There were also bakers, brewers, butchers, blacksmiths, farriers, domestic servants, horse keepers and grooms, men at arms, squires, pages, reeves and a chief steward. All this without the women of the family, wife, mother possibly, children, and their personal and domestic staff. If the lord of the manor was just and kind, the people were lucky. They had food, shelter, clothing and protection in time of danger. If he was one of the wicked squires so popular in novels and political harangues, they had no chance.

It can be truthfully said that there have never been any stories of wicked squires in Sheppey, quite the reverse, and the islanders apparently had a real affection and respect for the de Shurlands, for it has lasted through the centuries up to the present day. It is the greatest pity that there are no manor records to refer to. It is said that there was an old book which contained accounts of the way in which the work of the manor was allocated at Shurland Hall, but earlier this century it was unfortunately lost in a fire. Perhaps, some day,

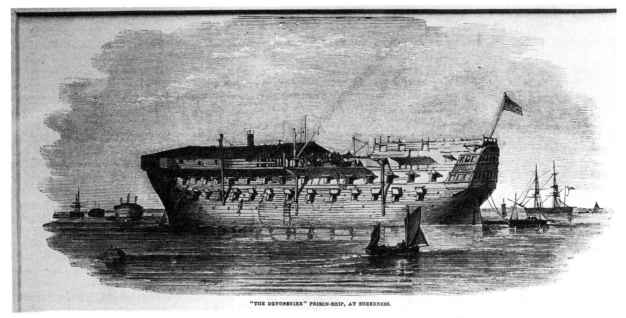

The *Devonshire*, a prison-ship moored at Sheerness; a floating hell of disease and overcrowding.

Russian prisoners aboard the *Devonshire*.

An old print showing a row of cottages built from the remains of Queenborough Castle.

One of the very few pictures of Queenborough Castle that have survived.

Queenborough High Street from an old print of 150 years ago.

A view of Queenborough High Street from the Western end with the artist Hogarth and his friends in the foreground, on their jaunt around Kent.

19

An early view of Sheerness dockyard with construction work going on in the foreground.

The waterside at Sheerness with dockyard buildings behind.

other records may be discovered amongst old manuscripts — these things do happen.

After Sir Roger came Sir Robert the Baron of Sheppey, about whom wonderful stories are told. Hasted says that in 1272 he was Warden of the Cinque Ports, but for various reasons this is very doubtful. It is much more likely that it was his grandfather Robert. The first definite record of Sir Robert is in 1290, and by then he had already been in Wales with Edward I, fighting in the wars there.

In the close rolls of the eighteenth year of Edward I, in June, it is recorded as follows:

Order to cause Robert de Shirlande to be acquitted of thirty marks of the fifty marks in which Robert de Shirlande his grandfather was indebted to Pulet a Jew lately deceased, which debt is in the King's hands by reason of the Jew's death, and to permit him to pay the remainder by five marks yearly and to cause this to be enrolled as the King has granted him these terms, by reason of his services in Wales.

This shows clemency on the part of Edward I, but references to Sir Robert in different rolls and charters indicate that the king had a very real regard for him. In one charter Edward referred to him as 'my good yeoman knight'. King Edward also had no liking for Jews, and during his reign he banished them from England.

Sir Robert won great renown in the Scottish wars, by reason of his bravery and daring. In 1291 he was granted protection until Christmas, as he was staying in Scotland on the king's service. He fought throughout the whole campaign, saw Wallace defeated at the Battle of Falkirk, and in 1300, at the siege of Caerlaverock, he was created a knight Banneret on the field of battle, in recognition of his boldness and strength in battle. This was a higher honour than knighthood, for that was no longer a proof of martial prowess, as Henry III had compelled all men with an income of over £20 to take up their title of knight as he needed the cash.

He was granted protection and respite of debts to the king again in 1304 as with John de Alta Repa and William de Roucester he was staying with the king on his service in Scotland until Michaelmas next. Then, as an afterthought, is added 'unless they return to England before that'. He returned to Shurland Hall for a while in 1305, but only for a short stay, because there was a grant in October for protection going overseas until Easter with Henry de Lacey, Earl of Lincoln, on the king's service.

Edward I died in 1307, and it is agreed by many historians who have studied the question that between 1305 and 1307 Sir Robert was involved in something out of the ordinary, some daring scheme or rash act, which gave rise to the famous legend that has continued all through the centuries. So just what was it? It has been referred to by all the historians who have written about Sheppey. Some are patronising, some commenting 'that it is a tale believed by the lower orders, and does not need any consideration'. Hogarth and his friends wrote about it in the eighteenth century. Barham satirised it in the *Ingoldsby Legends*, and many people imagine that his is the true version, but it is not. Grose, in his *Antiquities*, says that 'some pretend it was due to an excellancy he possessed in teaching horses to swim'. Others say he was so clever with horses that he must have used magic.

Whatever the reason, he is still to be seen lying at full length on his tomb in Minster Abbey, wearing his long surcoat, his head resting on his helmet, and his lance complete with pennants and streamers beside him. From his effigy it is apparent that he was a tall, well-built man. He has lost his right arm, but his sword hilt is visible on his left side, under his left hand. At his feet lies his page, which is unusual,

and by his side is his horse's head rising from the waves. It is all much defaced now, and covered with graffiti, some of which date back to the sixteenth century, but it is there and unexplainable. The more logically minded say the horse's head represents the wreck of the sea, but other manors had that right, and there is no other tomb like this one.

The legend that has followed him for so many years, and that for centuries the islander's believed implicitly, is this:

A sailor was found washed up on the shore drowned, and the local priest refused to bury him without payment. On hearing this Sir Robert went to deal with the matter himself. Finding the priest stubborn in his refusals, Sir Robert lost his temper and slew the cleric, saying that they could both be buried together, for he had no time for worthless priests.

Now Sir Robert had committed a major crime and sin, and the Church was furious, and demanded retribution. The Sheriff of Kent could not interfere with Sir Robert, or dispence justice or punishment, only the king could do that. Sir Robert was in bad trouble, and doubtless knew it. Even for him the King was not likely to condone the killing of a priest. So Sir Robert shut himself up in Shurland Hall, and refused admission to anyone, while he tried to think of a way out of this.

The king was on his way to France, and when Sir Robert heard this he saddled his best horse Grey Dolphin, and swam out to the king's ship as it was passing the Nore. Here he made full confession and asked for pardon. The king was so impressed by his daring and his boldness in swimming a horse such a long distance that he pardoned him and promised no punishment.

That settled, Sir Roger swam back to Sheppey where he is supposed to have reached the beach near Scrapsgate. Here the local wise woman, or witch was waiting. She laughed at him mockingly and said 'you think your good horse has saved your life, but within a year he will cause your death'.

Sir Robert was more than annoyed by this and probably replied with something like 'that's what you think!' or whatever the equivalent was then.

He promptly drew his sword and killed the horse, telling the witch she could do what she liked about it.

A year later he was walking on the beach, kicked something buried in the shingle, and it proved to be the skull of his horse.

There are two known endings to this tale. One says that the bone pierced his boot, cut his foot badly, and he returned to Shurland to die within forty-eight hours of blood poisoning. The second, which is more likely to be the original, states that he fell and hit his head on the horse's skull, and was rendered unconscious. He was taken home, where he recovered consciousness long enough to ask for his horse's head to be represented on his monument, as he had never forgiven himself for killing the animal. Then he died.

To this day no-one knows what really happened. He may well have committed a crime, and then swam out to the king's ship to ask pardon. The Nore was nearer to the island in the fourteenth century; much land has been taken by the sea since then. It is quite possible that the horse was exhausted after the return journey and collapsed on the beach, where it died or had to be killed because there was no alternative. Sir Robert probably did feel badly about it, he had a reputation as a wonderful horseman and he trained his horses well. He certainly had a name for training them to swim, presumably in order to claim as much wreckage as he could.

He could not have trained horses without having a certain amount of feeling for them, even in those barbarous times, and this horse was his favourite. He did not die a year later, but the seeds were sewn, and the legend grew and survived.

His life was far from uneventful, and he was frequently involved in hair-raising schemes.

In 1310 he was Overlord of Mere, in Kent, and in 1313 at the Great Assizes at Canterbury, he defended a case of forcible entry and won it. There is no clue as to what he had been up to that time! He then had to answer to the king, now Edward II, as to what warrant he had to claim the right of wreck, assize of bread and wine, and his other rights. Sir Robert pleaded his rights as his father had done, the Roll was inspected and the case dismissed — his rights were on record. However, it was made clear to him that his rights only applied to Shurland, and not to any other manors he might own. He saw more service in Scotland in 1314, and was at Bannockburn when the English were defeated there. After that he was sent on a commission of oyer and terminer (hear and determine) to settle feuds in Romney Marsh.

In 'Kent Keepers of the Peace' 1316–17, it states that he was appointed on many commissions, as he was known as a fair and just man. There are letters to the Prior of Christchurch, Canterbury, which prove this. At this time he was involved in a case of his own. Three of his men, sometarri (goods carriers) were set upon at Tremhythe (Kings Ferry). They were robbed, and one was badly mutilated. It is easy to imagine Sir Robert's anger at this. Five groups of jurors made presentments at different courts in July and August, but only four out of thirteen assailants were caught, and they were aquitted. He must have been furious! There were no laws regarding the ferry at that time, and it was becoming a problem.

After 1317 he was exempted from assizes, juries and like commissions for life, but in June of that year he was sent to Dover to escort two cardinals from Rome, Sir Luko de Flesco and Sir Gauselin, to London.

The next year he was employed in a parliamentary writ, and 'by oath of good men' into malpractices and oppressions by sheriffs and their deputies in the county. Many people were complaining in King Edward II's reign. Following that he was head of a commission enquiring into an accusation by Florentine traders that their ships loaded with wool, travelling from London to Sandwich, were robbed off Sheppey by men of Gravesend and Milton. How that concluded is uncertain, but in the same year 1319, the Sheriff of Kent was ordered to question the men of Clive in Kent about the goods of a ship driven into the shore near the town, to retain the ship for the king's use and no man to meddle. Regarding this, an inquisition made by Henry de Cobham and Robert de Shirland stated that the ship was going from Flanders to Scotland, and the value of the cargo of wheat and the ship was given, the said goods belonged to the king's enemies and all the men in the ship were killed by the men of Clive as evil-doers and rebels. No account of what happened to the goods is given, so perhaps Henry and Robert had a share in them.

It was recorded in 1320 that Roger de Northwode held twenty acres within the said manor of Northwode of Robert de Shirland by the service of eight shillings and four hens and one lamb and suit at court of 'Shirland'. This settles the argument about which was the chief manor. Sir Robert was overlord. In the same year he went overseas yet again with Edmund de Woodstock, the king's brother presumably on a mission for the king, and on his return went to Westminster as a knight of the shire, to represent Kent in parliament. The following year found him engaged in a commission on banks and dykes at Rainham, despite the former promise of exemption from such tasks.

Inevitably, he became involved in the barons' revolt led by Thomas of Lancaster, against the weak and unpopular king. For this rashness he was imprisoned in the Tower and must have been in fear of losing his head. However, the order for his release came in 1323, and ordered to come to the king on finding mainpernors (people to guarantee sureties) for coming according to king's orders. He was finally released and acquitted, having been 'imprisoned on suspicion'. There is a definite feeling that he did not enjoy the same friendship and rapport with Edward II as had been apparent in his relationship with King Edward I.

He was once again a knight of the Great Council of Westminster in 1324, and then little is heard of him until his death in 1327. By his own wish he was buried in St. Katherine's Chapel, in the Abbey of St. Sexburg and St. Mary in Sheppey, with his ancestors. His tomb, as stated, showed him lying on his side, complete with his page and his horse's head. His wife Catherine outlived him, and was still alive in 1329. Her life with him must have been hectic, as he was away from home for long periods of time, when she would have been responsible for the running of the manor, with all the problems of administration that entailed. Also, as the saying goes, she never could tell what devilment he was up to!

He comes through the ages as a bold, reckless man, given to deeds of daring, headstrong and sometimes thoughtless, but kind and just withal. Certainly he has always been regarded with esteem and affection by generations of islanders. He had no son, his only child, as far as is known, was his daughter Margaret, she was married to William Cheyney of Patrixbourne, whose father Sir Alexander Cheyne had been on campaign with Sir Robert in Scotland. All marriages were arranged in those days and this was obviously a marriage arranged by two old friends who had fought side by side. In this way Shurland Hall passed from the Shurlands to the Cheyneys, and Margaret started a new line of warriors.

In the list of Kent fines, of the 4th to 7th year of Edward III, which would be approximately 1330, it was recorded that on the Quinzain of St. Martin, William Cheyney and Margaret his wife claimed from Hugh de Dunham, Chaplain, and Thomas Pynke land round Doddington and Lynsted, which they were granted.

At Westminster they claimed the Manor of Shyrlande, with appurtenances, and one mill, four hundred and ten acres of land, ten acres of meadow, seven hundred acres of Marsh, ten pounds rent and rent of eight quarters of wheat, forty quarters of Barley, ten quarters of oats, one hundred and fifty cocks, two hundred hens and two thousand eggs, with appurtenances, in Eastchurch, Menstre, Leysdown and Warden in the Isle of Sheppey. All this was granted to William and Margaret, and to the heirs of William.

Among other claims Margaret also claimed that she held a moiety of the Manor of Uffeton, held in dower of the inheritance of Robert. In other words she held it for her son Robert, evidently named after his grandfather. When she dies, Robert said, it should go to Matilda, who was wife of Robert de Maryns, and to Roger and his heirs. If there be no heirs, it should return to Robert, 'by service of a rose at the nativity of Saint John the Baptist'.

So Baron de Shurland's estate was made over safely to his descendants, who continued to live there in much the same manner and were rebels and fighters in their turn, until the time of King Henry VIII.

The Lords of Sheppey

Next to the Manor of Shurland in Eastchurch stood the Manor of the de Northwoods. Northwood, or Norwood Manor was not such a large estate as Shurland, but the Norwood family owned other manors and land in Milton Regis and adjacent villages, the manor in Sheppey was only a part of their domain.

They do not seem to have been as headstrong or turbulent as the de Shurlands, and while they occupied a high position in the county, and performed their knight's service when asked, they seem to have avoided any trouble, which was not always easy to do in difficult times.

There are no legends or stories about the family. They were renowned for their devotion and generosity to the priory, and at the dissolution, long after the family had left the island, their coat of arms was still displayed prominently in the abbey. The other notable thing about them is their genealogical history which was recorded between 1385 and 1405, with further additions some years later. It is extremely rare to have such a record dating from such early times.

This roll was in the Surrenden collection, which was auctioned at Sotheby's in April 1981 when the collection of documents belonging to Sir Thomas Philips came on the market. The roll is considered to be the work of Thomas Brumpston, who was employed by the family. It is an interesting history, but far too long and involved to repeat in full.

The chronicle starts with Sir Stephen de Northwode, Knight, and omits the perplexing Jordanus de Sheppey entirely. In the reign of Henry III Sir Stephen was siezed of three hundred and ten acres of land, five hundred acres of marsh, in the Isle of Sheppey and other lands and manors in Kent. His son Roger inherited all this on the death of his father. Here the covenants relating to the holding of the land were altered, possibly at Sir Roger's request, for in 1256 (King Henry III) there are letters patent which record 'Grant to Roger de Northwode; that all the following lands in the hundred of Milton which hitherto has held in gavelkind shall in future be held by knight's service'.

Here the amount of land is stated, with a proviso about the rent. Rent forty shillings and half a farthing, and twenty eight and three quarters of a pound of cheese. Further parcels of land on the island are listed for which the rent is seven shillings, half a farthing and twelve and a half pounds of cheese, followed by the land at Milton and other villages. All the land in Sheppey amounted to roughly nine hundred and fourteen acres. Forty shillings was a knights fee, and certain services were due as well, among them military service when required. The demand for large quantities of cheese is not explained!

Sir Roger married Bona Fitzbernard, and was the Sir Roger who rescued the priory from penury, and when he died in 1286 he and Bona, who apparently died at much the same time, were buried before the altar in the parish church.

The two Norwood brasses that are lying on the floor of the south chancel were for many decades believed to be Sir Roger and Bona, but now they are generally attributed to Sir John and his wife Joan de Badlesmere. The lady Joan is a fine example of a lady of the early fourteenth century with her braided hair, elaborate headdress and flowing robes. She has a little dog at her feet, which is looking up at her in evident discomfort and annoyance at being used as a foot rest. Sir John is not so handsome, over the years he has been badly botched up. In 1511 the parishioners of Sheppey asked

permission to remove the knight and his lady from the chancel 'as they were sorely worn and broke'. Permission was refused, and they were advised to mend the brasses. This they did, and the portion of the knight from just above the knees is a palimpset, on the reverse side can be seen flowing draperies, which must have been part of a different brass altogether. For some reason the restorer chose to give the knight crossed legs, which give the brass a ludicrous effect, as they are not in proportion to the upper part of the figure. For a long time he had a gap between the top and bottom half, until in the late nineteenth century one of his descendants took pity on him and had a new 'middle' inserted.

The brasses show distinct signs of French influence, and even now questions abound regarding them. One theory is that they were never made to be a pair, but are two brasses from separate tombs. They are a fascinating example of fourteenth century dress and armour, and well worth studying.

Sir John succeeded his father, Sir Roger, and did homage to King Edward I for his lands.

In the calendar of Inquisitions 1285 (and here the dates are doubtful, but this occasionally happens) it records manors given in London, five in Kent, on the morrow of St. Andrew in the fourteenth year of Edward I, which brings the date to 1286 once again.

Northwood without Sheppey (Scapeyham) and Northwood within Sheppey. The extent of the lands and the rent is recorded, and John is named as next heir. The names of the manors are the main interest. The Northwoods had a manor at Milton called Norwood Chasteners. There is some doubt as to which Norwood was the first, one story being that the Manor in Sheppey was so called after the Manor at Milton.

Sir John married the Lady Joan de Badlesmere, who naturally brought manors and lands as dower, and they produced a family of at least seven children, all boys. The eldest, of course, was named John.

In 1291 he was Sheriff of Kent, and again two years later. In 1298 he was fighting in Scotland in company with other Sheppey knights. As it is quite likely that the Island contingent all left for the Scottish wars together, it being safer to travel in a large company, it must have been a glittering cavalcade of knights, squires, pages, men at arms, retainers and pack horses that rode across the marshes and crossed the ferry to the mainland.

Sir John cannot have seen out the whole of the Scottish campaign for he was Sheriff again in 1300. He was commanded to attend the coronation of King Edward II, and then in 1313 he was summoned to parliament as a baron. Later, he saw service in the north of England again.

His eldest son John married Agnes de Grandisson, and with his father's consent endowed his wife with the manor of Norwood Chasteners at Milton.

It was the custom of Kent that a wife when widowed had a right to half of her husband's possessions. The English common law stipulated a third, but Kent had its own laws. The dower made at marriage was a special provision, as it ensured that the widow had a place recognised as her own, to which she could retire, when she wished, with no arguments. Sir John junior also *produced* six sons, and then died before his father. His eldest son and heir was Sir Roger.

This led to problems, when, aged fifty nine, Sir John senior died in 1319, as the heir was a minor. The Lady Joan died in the same year and they were buried in Minster Abbey. Sir

Roger inherited the estate that was held by knight's service, other 'tenements' which were still held in Gavelkind had to be divided among the remaining sons, Roger's uncles and his brothers. There were so many co-heirs that it inevitably led to a certain amount of litigation.

As Roger was only twelve years old the king held the manor in capite, as was the custom. A year later he committed the custody of the lands, and the marriage of the heir, to Sir Bartholomew de Badlesmere. The marriage of an heir, **marita guin**, was an incident of knight service. During the 'nonage' of an heir this right belonged to the king over his tenants in capite. The king had the power to arrange a suitable match, and if the infant refused he had to pay the value of the marriage, and he forfeited it. If he married without the king's consent he paid a forfeit of double the value. These rights also belonged to the great feudal lords over tenants held to them by knights service, and all manor lords had similar rights over their tenants and workers. Wardships and marriages were valuable sources of revenues, the wards were saleable and treated as chattels.

Sir Roger's wardship was Sir Bartholomew's to hold until the legal age of the heir. He sold the marriage to the Lady Idonia de Leybourne, who had two daughters by a previous marriage. She married one of these, Juliana de Say, to young Sir Roger. At the time, in the year 1321–2 approximately, Roger was between fourteen and fifteen years of age and his eldest son, John was baptised before his father was fifteen years old. This rather incredible fact is well vouched for, and Roger himself made no secret of it.

As soon as he was considered old enough, which would be roughly in 1327, he obtained livery of his inheritance from the king. His wife Juliana died after a good nine years of marriage, leaving four children. Two years later Sir Roger married again, a widow named Elizabeth Ffoliat, née de Segrave. Four years later Elizabeth died, childless. She was buried in the abbey, 'nearly at the head' of Roger the restorer, with an engraved stone over her, of which all traces are now lost. The only remarkable thing on record about this stone is that the workmen at the time made a mistake of one hundred years in the date of her death when they inscribed the memorial.

Four years later Sir Roger married his third wife, Margaret or Margery, who had been married previously. One of her daughters from this marriage married Sir Roger's second son Roger from his marriage with Juliana, confusing the family even further.

Margery was not long married before she managed to get herself smothered whilst digging out a fox from an earth. The record says 'she was not killed on the spot' and after the accident she made her will, with Sir Roger's permission, and died on the last day of December 1340.

Two years later Sir Roger made yet another marriage, his fourth to Joan, widow of Thomas de Ffaversham. By this time his oldest son John needed his own establishment, and Roger junior was married, so he granted them both extra allowances from his other manors and lands. Sir Roger's mother, Lady Agnes, died in 1349 and left to him Norwood Chasteners where she had been living.

Then one of the things that occur at times in all families happened. In 1350 Sir John, the eldest son and the heir, married against his fathers will, one Joan Here of Faversham. Sir Roger was implacable, and considered disinheriting John because the marriage seemed to him 'manifestly in dispuragement of his blood'. At this point Sir Arnauld Savage intervened, and with much difficulty prevented this happening.

Sir Roger wanted nothing more to do with his son after this marriage, but 'to exonerate himself from supporting them, more for honour than love, he gave Sir John the manor of Norwood Chasteners'. To complicate life for Dame Joan,

Sir Roger reserved for himself £50 yearly for life if his son John died before him. Sir Roger's fourth wife Joan died in 1357, she had managed to live longer than the previous three. Nothing deterred, in little less than a year Sir Roger made yet a fifth marriage to Lady Agnes, widow of Sir John de Lobeham.

It is claimed that Sir Roger held Agnes in great affection and had rents and lands made over for her use. Agnes produced two daughters for Sir Roger, and the first one 'he caused to be called Juliana, in memory of Juliana his first wife'.

Sir Roger was summoned to Parliament as a knight of the Shire in 1360. In November 1361 he made his will and died.

Sir John was his heir, and by that time was more than forty years old. Dame Agnes sued for her dower, and it all seemed to have been arranged peaceably, with Sir John acting fairly and generously, for he agreed that even if Lady Agnes re-married, yet she could retain this income for life. Then Lady Agnes, with Fulco Peyforer and Richard Blore, the executors, put out a writ of debt against Sir John for arrears of rent of Norwood Chasteners.

Once again Sir Arnauld Savage helped to sort things out, Sir John paying £250, for which he said he had no thanks, and the rest remitted.

Lady Agnes re-married, keeping her dower as arranged, but Sir John was eager to avenge himself, and looked for ways to annoy her. This led to a great deal of litigation, with writs of debt and many compromises, and it is doubtful if Sir John had any satisfaction from it. He and his wife Joan had five children, the eldest, needless to say, called Sir Roger. Sir John died in February 1379. Sir Roger was heir to all manors and lands held by knight's service, and of the tenements held in gavelkind the co-heirs were his brothers William and James.

Here the record ends, apart from a later transcript which relates to the disputes which took place between members of the family about the estates.

A William de Northwood was knighted for gallantry at Agincourt in 1415. This may have been one of Sir Roger's sons, but by then there were many Norwoods in Kent. The last of the family in Sheppey was John de Northwode, who was Constable of Queenborough Castle in Edward IV's reign, in 1461. He was the last male of that line, and after he died the manor was sold to William Warner esq.

Norwood lost its importance as a manor from that time, and soon became just another farm on the island. The Norwoods were a noble family with a long history. One of the first Norwoods was a Crusader with Richard I, and over the years different members were Sheriffs of Kent, knights were sent to Westminster, and all of them undertook willingly the commissions that would be expected of a family of their standing. They were a large, prolific family, owning large estates in different parts of Kent, where they continued to live for many years after they left Sheppey. Different branches emigrated, and their descendants return from America to the present day, to see the home of their famous ancestors, many of whom were buried in Minster Abbey.

It seems a surprising fact that the de Shurlands and the de Northwodes were never united by marriage, the manors were adjacent, and as neighbours they must have hunted together, undertaken official journeys and met socially. Perhaps there is some basis for the story that both families come from the same ancestors, which would explain the lack of a marriage between them, as the laws of consanguinity were very strict.

Norwood Manor Farm still stands on the hill that rises from the Lower Road, with great trees round it and Choul Spring beside it. The farmer who owned it earlier this century was extremely proud of the manor's history and did his utmost to restore it to some of its former grandeur. He claimed that he could discern traces of a medieval moat, he

24

found evidence of damage done by Cromwell's men, and he uncovered several magnificent old Tudor fireplaces, complete with inglenooks, which had been boarded up and plastered over during centuries of occupation. Since he left the manor looks rather sad, as though missing the former attention.

Although the Norwoods had left the island, and Sheppey had one lord of the manor less, the Cheyneys at Shurland were thriving, and living up to the family traditions. The Cheyneys had come to England with William I, the first of the family being one Ralph de Cainito, which soon became Cheyney, Cheyne, or Cheney. Alexand Cheyney, listed in the Dering Roll of Arms as Alisander de Chene, had as a coat of arms Quarterly Or & Gules, a label of five points azure.

His son William nevertheless took the De Shurland Arms when he married Sir Robert's daughter Margaret. Their son, Robert was three times Knight of the Shire for Kent, in 1348, 1351 and 1357.

His grandson Sir William represented Kent in 1416, he was called 'Searjeant-at-law' in 1410, appointed to Justice of the King's Bench in 1415, and Chief Justice in 1424.

The Cheyneys seemed high in the king's favour, but they were content to remain in Sheppey, with Shurland Hall as their home.

His son Sir John Cheyne, sat for the County in 1449 and then left the paths of law and justice his immediate ancestors had followed to join Jack Cade's rebellion. It is doubtful if Sir John was violently anti King Henry VI, and his son was a staunch Lancastrian, but the Kentish people were sure that Kent was about to be destroyed by royal power, and made into 'a wild forest' in revenge for the death of the Duke of Suffolk, who had been captured and killed at Dover. There were also many complaints of unfair taxation and representation in Parliament.

Sir John must have felt strongly about this, or he would not have listened to an impostor like Jack Cade.

He was the ringleader of the revolt in his part of Kent, and rode off to join the rebels taking many island people with him, among them John Cokeran, a merchant and Mayor of Queenborough, John Swalman, a yeoman of Queenborough, a baker, ten fishermen or boatmen called 'maryners' also from Queenborough, two brothers named Symond, husbandmen from Minster and many others who were not named.

He stayed with the rebellion until they had entered London and beheaded James de Fynes, Lord de Say, the owner of Says Court at Harty, amongst other lands in Kent, and his son-in-law William Crowner of Tunstall and Borstall hall in Sheppey. The Lord of Say and Sele and William Crowner were two of the most hated men in Kent, and Sir John must have been convinced that there was good reason for this.

Once the rebels' Bill of petitions had been accepted, and pardons negotiated, Sir John brought his Company home, apparently having done what he set out to do, leaving Jack Cade to besiege Queenborough Castle unsuccessfully before he was caught and killed.

After this we hear little more of Sir John but his son, another John, was more prominent and just as headstrong. One historian writes of him and his brother William, 'the taste for rebellion may have been hereditary, as their father had been the most prominent gentleman in Jack Cade's rebellion'.

Sir John started conventionally enough, sitting for the county, and becoming Speaker of the House of Commons. Then, in the Calendar of Patent Rolls, 4th year of Edward IV 1464 is recorded the following:

Pardon to John Cheyne, Knight, late of the Isle of Sheppey, Kent, late Sherriff of Kent, late purveyor and buyer of victuals for the town of Calais and the marshes of the same, and keeper of the habiliments of war and ordnance of the same, surveyor of works of repair of banks and town, and purveyor, buyer, receiver and keeper of the victuals, artillery, armour and equipment for the defence of Calais, of all treasons, felonies and other offences committed by him and all debts, accounts and arrears due from him.

That is a formidable list, and may account for Sir John's Lancastrian preference. King Edward IV was 'bought off' and left France, and on this money lived in comparative financial comfort for the rest of his life. His reign was anything but comfortable, as the English nobles disapproved of his marriage, and the influence that his wife's relatives wielded.

The Wars of the Roses were a campaign of plot and counter plot, with much deception, cruelty and turning of coats. John Cheyne was chosen as one of the leaders of the rebellion, but after two attempts at rebellion that misfired, he and his brother William were forced to flee the country, to Brittany.

Richard III issued a proclamation offering three hundred marks or £10 of land to anyone capturing six of the rebels, and William Cheyne was named as one of them.

For the others he offered £100 or 10 marks of land. Kent was forced to take an oath of allegiance by the king, and this was followed by an act of attainder, with thirty-six conspirators named, and the chief rebels, and again William Cheyne, brother of John Cheyney of Shurland was named.

John, meanwhile, had been leading a rebellion in Wiltshire and it was after this that he and William, with another brother, Humphrey, escaped.

Two years later he returned in the Earl of Richmond's company to fight at Bosworth, and it is said he was knighted on landing at Milford Haven. King Richard unhorsed him during battle, not a mean feat, as it is claimed that 'he was a person of great strength'. He retaliated by killing King Richard's standard bearer. There is an odd story arising from this battle. At the height of the battle when the fighting was hot and furious, Sir John had his helmet knocked from his head and broken beyond hope of repair. Not wanting to fight uncovered, or to leave the field, he slew a bull in a field nearby, and fastening the animals scalp, complete with horns, on his head, he fought on wearing that. True or false, a bull's skull is the crest of the Cheyney's, and can be seen on Lord Thomas Cheyney's tomb in Minster Abbey.

Sir John was made a Knight Banneret for his gallantry at the battle of Bosworth Field by Henry VII, and two years later was made a Knight of the Garter and Baron Cheyney of Shurland, the first baron since the time of Sir Robert de Shurland.

His brother William was the first Sheriff of Kent under Henry VII and Constable of Queenborough Castle. Naturally the brothers required the lands that Richard III had deprived them of.

Sir John died without an heir, in 1509 and was succeeded by his nephew Thomas, son of William. Sir Thomas Cheyney was the greatest of them all in material gain, whether he was the best is another matter, but it needed guile to negotiate the uneasy reigns of the Tudor Kings.

Many people ask how the islanders lived in those days. Despite the law of gavelkind, which allowed land to be bought and sold without the Lord's permission, there were few freeholders in Sheppey. Most of the people were attached to one or other of the manors, or the priory. There was a vast gulf between the employer and the employed. The rich clothes, the furs, the armour and fine caparisoned horses were for the nobles only.

In the fourteenth century laws were passed regarding

clothing. The wearing of silks and satins was forbidden to anyone below the rank of gentleman. Yeomen and servants might not wear silver buckles, and peasants were not allowed to wear anything scarlet, or any fur except sheepskin.

For all that, famine and plague affected rich and poor alike, if the crops failed everyone in the manor went hungry. Neither were the fleas and other vermin, that were common enough then, any respecter of persons. The lady in her rich flowing gown was as good a hostess to them as her kitchen wench in her rough dress.

When Shurland and Norwood were first built they were simply the Lord's Hall, a big hall made of lathe and plaster and wood. There was no stone or brick in Sheppey. When Archbishop Corbeuil rebuilt the priory all the stone was fetched by ship, sailed up Windmill Creek, and then hauled across the fields to the abbey by ox cart. The new Lords of Sheppey could not afford this.

Shurland Hall stands on an eminence that appears to be man made, probably part of the old earth works and earlier fort. There is a large pond at the front of this hillock, and there is a theory that there might once have been a moat there. Early halls usually had some form of defences.

Norwood also stood on a hill, with a wide view of the countryside all round, and a spring by the farm. The basics were the same for both.

In the hall the Lord, his family and his retainers all conferred, made merry and slept together. The fire was in the centre of the floor, smoke hopefully escaping through a hole in the roof, the beaten earth floor was covered in rushes, and everyone slept where they could. Kitchens, stables and out houses provided shelter and sleeping places for the serfs who served in the house. The lord's hounds usually shared the hall, fighting for scraps and bones from the big table, and a favourite hawk was not an uncommon sight. It was cold in winter, hot in summer, and very unhygienic.

That was in the earliest times. Over the years the halls improved, extra rooms appeared; one, the solar was for the lady and her maids in waiting; great fireplaces in the wall with chimneys to take the smoke away, an upstairs room, which started like a loft, for the family to retire to, with beds, mattresses stuffed with feathers, and blankets and covers. In the castles of the highest barons there were luxurious wall hangings and other refinements, and a dais at the top of the hall for the family's table — the high table. Quite often the manners of the occupants did not match their surroundings. Each generation made some improvement, but there was no plumbing, water or sanitation. Lighting was by cresset, candles, and later, lamps, and the servants slept where they could, often on straw-filled sacks.

There is little said about the women of the times. Marriages were arranged, every father had an eye on a rich dowry coming with a son's proposed wife, and the girl's parents looked for a man of assured position who could keep their daughter in reasonable comfort. Workers on the estate could not marry without the permission of their lord and often had to marry whom they were told to. The task of importance for wives of any class was to produce an heir, preferably several, as infant mortality was high. She was subservient to her husband, and expected to run the home, be it manor, farm or cottage, efficiently and to her lord's liking.

This wasn't easy. For the poorer classes, a cottage was little more than a hut, draughty, cold and lacking in all comfort. The small farmers were little better off. A manor had to be self supporting, a little village on its own. There was a chief steward, but he had to be trustworthy, and overseer. There were bakers, brewers and butchers to direct. Cattle had to be killed and salted for the winter, and hence the great winter feasts — it was the last fresh meat until next summer.

This also explains the importance of poultry and eggs. There would be enough food to keep them through the dark winter, unlike the cattle.

Sheep were easier to feed, and could be milked to provide butter and cheese.

There was the washing, cooking, spinning and weaving of cloth and child rearing. There were also candles to make, herbs to dry for the winter, and the lady of the house or manor was responsible for nursing her household, growing the necessary herbs and distilling and mixing medicines and remedies.

As women of all walks of life were usually pregnant for most of their lives, they could not have had an easy time. When the lord of the manor was away, which was frequently, his wife had to be able to take on the responsibility of the estate, manor courts, farms, legal problems and anything else that might arise.

When the lord was home he attended to his land and farms, sorted out problems in his manor court, hunted, hawked and trained his horses. This last was of great importance. A good horse could mean the difference between life and death in battle, or even in a local skirmish. The noblemen spent much time in the stables, overseeing the breeding and management of their animals. Without horses they could not travel or fight.

The de Shurlands had the right of collecting wreckage, and so their horses had to be taught to swim, as well. It was not mere greed that made Sir Robert so keen to claim wreckage; many things came in wrecks beside wood, many could be valuable, or provide extra food for his hungry household.

The children stayed with the women, the boys at least until they were seven years old. They were dressed like miniature adults, and taught how to behave and deport themselves.

They had toys. The boys were taught in the martial arts from an early age and had toy swords, hobby horses and bows and arrows. As soon as they were old enough they were put on a pony and taught to ride, and when they reached the age of seven or eight they were taken over by the men of the family.

The girls had their dolls, and were taught to sew and how to run a household. They all played the usual singing and dancing games of childhood. In fact their games were popular with the adults too.

How much conventional education they received depended on their father's outlook. Many knights were almost illiterate, while others were more academically inclined. Usually a priest was employed to teach the children their letters, figures, Latin and perhaps other accomplishments.

A boy's ambition was usually to be a knight, a horseman, a fighter, not a scholar. Strangely enough, the girls were often better educated than their brothers, as they would have to keep household accounts and teach the children, and should they be destined for a nunnery a good education would be essential.

Like the dwellings, education also improved over the centuries, for the ruling classes at least.

The children of the poorer classes who showed any inclination towards learning could be sent to a monastery, where the monks would educate them. Most of the scholars of the time were in the church and monasteries and many had come from humble families.

So the Normans ran their manors in the middle ages, defended the island, and gave protection and care to their people in return for the manor work the majority were obliged to perform.

CHAPTER VIII

The growth of an island

While the Norman lords built and settled in Sheppey, the island was developing in other ways. For the first two hundred years or so after the Conquest (and this it must be remembered is only a rough estimate) there appear to be records of fines and inquisitions regarding relatively small amounts of land, disputed about, as owned by people whose names seldom reappear in later years.

A branch of the Peyforer family was settled in Borstal Hall and remained there until 1360, and their name occurs frequently. In 1202 Gunnilda, the widow of Godwin, and Robert her son, quit-claim land in Minster to Richard Fitz Dereman. The name Godwin, or Goodwin, is still common on the island, but Fitz Dereman vanished long ago.

Thomas de Stodele and Paulina his wife, Philip de Borstall, William de Codstede and Philip Burnel all appeared to own or hold of the king varying amounts of land on the island, and they faded out completely. Nicholas Malmaynes also held land in Sheppey, but his name is now far better known elsewhere, together with William de Bothmeshelle and Peter de Peckham.

The church at Warden was presented with a chaplain early in the twelfth century; a priest named William de Wrotham. The chaplains did not stay long, and William was followed by Thomas de Gillingham, who resigned and was followed by his brother John. Philip de Wigental was another; perhaps they found Warden too isolated. The church there was granted to one of the many monasteries, who were in a position to supply chaplains as necessary. Henry III had a great interest in the welfare of the Maison Dieu in Ospringe, a small hospital he is thought to have founded. There is a list of grants in the charter rolls relating to this, dated 1247, and the island people seem to have been very involved.

Richard, son of Richard de Neirford, made a gift to the hospital of all his land called Rid' in the Isle of Sheppey. There is a previous record of a Robert de Neirford claiming this ground, 20 acres of land in Ryde, from Alan son of Adam and his wife Margery, in 1222.

Margery de Hobelinge gave three acres in Sheppey, and there is a long list 'Grant to the Master and Brethren of the Hospital', which includes the gift of Geoffrey de Stonington, all the land in Scapey called Hocklinge, for a chapel. After this, Hocklynge disappears, and there is no clue at all as to where it was in Leysdown, or of another family called Picot who claimed a part of it. The list continues:— of the gift of Roger Godebold of Scapey seventeen shillings rent in Scapey of the gift of Hugh, son of Bodeget, nine acres of land in Eastchurch. Of the gift of Philip de Tunstall, three shillings and twopence in rent, in Leysdown.

All these people must have been 'freemen' of greater or lesser degree; they rented or owned small farms or holdings. The gift of greatest interest is that of Adam de Tamie, release of twelve pence yearly rent due to him from a holding in Scapey and Bobbing. Adam gives no hint as to the name of the holding, neither does he give his opinion as to the foundation date of the Maison Dieu. The charter is brief, merely recording the gift of twelve pence rent yearly, but the story has grown that Adam stated the name of his farm, and the date of the hospital's foundation. The date usually given in this erroneous tale is incorrect. The farm attributed to Adam de Tamie is Tam's Farm in Minster. Adam is not heard of again and Tam's Farm is seldom mentioned in any records through the years. In the tithe records of 1848 it is referred to as 'Farm and Outbuildings'.

It was a pleasant red brick house, probably late Tudor, situated on the outskirts of Minster village at the point where Chapel Street becomes Windmill Hill. The house was demolished in the early 1930s to make way for a small private estate aptly named 'Tam's Gardens', which is still thriving. Tam's Farm achieved more fame at demolition than it had ever done during its working life, for behind one of the fireside cupboards so common in old houses the workmen discovered a small secret room, just large enough to hide a man in. By that time it was not possible to tell where the entrance had been hidden, the demolition work had gone too far, but the village was intrigued. Sheppey people are fascinated by any sort of secret hidy-hole or tunnel, and many went to look and wonder.

Some little distance along the road are Tam's Cottages. They were a pair of cottages and have survived, and although they have been converted into one house now their outward appearance is unaltered, and they look to be at least two hundred years old. Over the next three centuries this almost over-generous granting of land to the Church by the king and his subjects gradually ceased.

From the various records it is interesting to notice the Christian names in use in the Middle Ages. The boys' names are little different from today, although the spelling varies, but the girls seem to have had a wider choice. Margaret, Elizabeth, Catherine, Alice and Joan are quite common, but Dionisia, Alianora (Eleanor perhaps) Thomasine, Affray, Rabege, Benet and Hawise are frequently found. There does not seem to be any truth in the assertion that many girls in Sheppey were christened Sexburga in honour of the island's saint. The name never appears in charters or registers.

In the fourteenth century the Bishop of Rochester, 1353–60, was John of Sheppey, said to be of the Northwood family. Rochester seems to have had an attraction for Sheppey clerics, for the prior in 1190-9 was Osbern of Sheppey. Bishop John was an active worker and builder, responsible for building a large part of the old cathedral wall, amongst other things. His tomb, walled up, was discovered during alterations in the cathedral in 1825. It is considered to be the original tomb, with a painted effigy, and despite the many years since it was carved and painted, and the unknown length of time it was walled up (perhaps to save it from Cromwell's men) it is still full of colour. The face is supposed to be a likeness.

In King Edward II's reign, in 1326, an order was issued to many counties regarding the maintenance and firing of beacons. That the beacons were no new form of warning is evident from the order, which referred to instructions given in an earlier commission. 'That certain men should be assigned as a watch of foot soldiers, and that the said watch should have a sign of fire.' Whenever danger threatened, which was frequently, as raids on the Kent coast by French and other foreign vessels were not uncommon, the beacons were to be manned. The men living on the sea coast were to light such signals 'when necessary', so that others could arrange 'for the safety of these parts'. From this time similar orders occurred frequently, as danger often threatened.

In 1338 Edward III warned that 'certain aliens, having collected an immense multitude of galleys and ships, both on the sea and in foreign parts, to do upon us and ours what evil and harm they can . . .'. The islanders were told to 'cause to be made the common signal by fire upon hills — as has usually been done in such cases'.

Edward III was constantly at war with France, and by 1354 a sophisticated beacon defence system was in operation. There were thirty-three men detailed for the beacon duty in Sheppey, twenty-five of whom came from the mainland, in the Hundred of Milton. The men of Milton were exempt from all Watch and Ward duty, excepting that in Sheppey.

The list is recorded in the *Textus Roffensis*, the 'Monks' Book' of Rochester Cathedral, and it gives the beacon sites and the names of the men, as follows (the original is in Latin; this is a free translation):—

1) Ward of Sheppey, near the Swale.
   (This beacon was probably at Harty, or Shellness Point.)
   The man in charge was Humphrey de Northwode, and he had to find and equip two men with arms. Thomas Rokesle, the constable, also had to provide two men at arms and John de Morston was responsible for one. They were not named.
   The Hobiliers, armed men who rode light horses (hobby horse is derived from this) were Lawrence de Otteringden, Bernard Ponch and John son of Richard Graveney.
   Total: five men at arms and three hobiliers.

2) The watch and ward at Rodmer was the responsibility of the Prioress, as already stated.

3) The Watch and Ward at Warden was the Abbot of Boxley's problem, as he had been granted land there.
   He had to provide two men at arms, and Margaret the wife of William of Ore (Oare) was obliged to find one man at arms, as was Robert Cheyne.
   No names for the men, but the hobiliers were Stephen Bec, John Frendested (Frindstead) and Henry Joh . . .
   Total: 4 men at arms and three hobiliers.

4) Watch and Ward at Mousehole. The Prior de Ledis (Leeds) was responsible, and had to equip three men at arms.
   The Hobiliers were Robert de Folgstone, Bartholomew Sauvage and John Donkyn. Three men and three hobiliers.

5) Watch and Ward at Ride.
   Here Matilda del Idle and Dame Joanne de Boctone were each required to provide one man at arms.
   Hobilier, John de Bladechylde, Walter de Wyse and Roger de Northwode.

The beacons were large iron baskets on tall posts, usually roughly trimmed tree trunks, in which easily lighted faggots were piled, and lighted with a torch or flare. Alternatively, pitch pots were used. The men at arms were on permanent duty at the beacon, while the hobiliers were kept busy patrolling, and they were responsible for relaying messages. Local landowners and the Church had a duty to equip and maintain the foot soldiers, while the hobiliers appear to have been the knights and esquires who were wealthy enough to keep homes and arm themselves.

All the beacon sites were on the island, and are still there, with the exception of Rodmer, which has long since 'gone to sea'. The watch by the Swale may well have had a beacon at Shellness Point, as there was a beacon there until the late 1950s or early 1960s when someone removed it. Children were always told that the beacon had been there since the time of Elizabeth I, when it had been erected to give warning of the Armada coming.

The Watch and Ward at Warden. Warden Point was an obvious place for a beacon, it is one of the highest points on the cliffs, or was, for acres of land have 'gone to sea'.

The Watch and Ward at Mousehole. No-one has heard of Mousehole in the last hundred years, but it is still there, a manor between Leysdown and Shellness. Local speech has

reduced it to 'Mussel' and Mussel manor is now a hotel for holiday-makers. Ride is still there, too, split up into different farms all known as Rides, Great, Little, Old and New.

This beacon system was in operation for centuries, and there are repeated orders about it in different reigns. Beacons had to be watched by day and night, and in an age full of superstitions and fears of ghosts, devils and witches the men must have endured some terrifying hours, especially when the night was dark and the wind moaning eerily. Luckily the Watch and Ward was discontinued in winter. Wars were more civilised in the Middle Ages, they were arranged for the summer time, when travelling was less difficult.

Edward III took the defences of Sheppey seriously. In 1360 he visited the island, and decided to rebuild the old castle there. In order to do this he bought land in the Manor of Rushenden from Sir Walter Manny, and land from the Sauvage family, who owned land in Rushenden and Warden. Part of Minster Marshes was also taken, and William of Wykeham was put in charge of the building. Henry Yevele, the King's 'Master Mason, or director of works or devizer of masonry' is credited with being the architect.

It is said that the castle was built in six years, but not without problems. Stone had to be fetched with which to build, and it had to come by sea from Caen in France, and from many places in England. At one stage six hundred and eighty-nine oaks were used, and some of these were trees from Norwood. Charles II is always blamed for the lack of trees in Sheppey, but the depredations started in Edward III's reign.

Many people have claimed that John Gibbon built the castle, and given him a long and illustrious pedigree for good measure, but his name does not appear anywhere in the records. Skilled men were brought to the island to do the work of building. At one point there were sixteen hundred people on the site — masons, carpenters, smiths and carters, plus labourers. A master mason, like John Box, received one shilling a day. Lesser masons, John Rook, Richard Gosling and John Suchlynge to name three, earned fourpence a day. Doubtless Bynne supplied some of the labour force, but there was only a handful of fishermen and farm workers living there.

In 1362 the king sent an order to the sheriffs of London 'to make proclamation forbidding religious persons or other masters to hire masons or any other craftsmen without the king's command, and to take and put them in Newgate prison until further orders, as excessive gain and gifts taken by such men for salary and wages in divers parts of the realm contrary to the statute, almost all the men hired for the king's works (Windsor, Sheppeye and Haddeley) have secretly withdrawn and are retained with religious persons and other masters, to the king's hurt and hindrance of his works, whereat he is moved to anger'. The tenor of this proclamation sounds as though the king was in a right royal temper when he issued it, and the Plantagenet kings were renowned for their temper.

Despite labour problems and the fact that everything had to be carried to the site by water, or across the ferry by cart, the castle was finished by 1366 according to report, but in actual fact it was nearer 1377 when the finishing touches were completed, and this included a garden carefully landscaped and planted. The keep was finished in 1368, and there is a copy from a patent roll of a warrant for the appointment of Richard de Blore, Richard Cok and William Chaundler as paymasters for work done. These three were island men.

The castle was unique; it was built in the shape of a rose, a beautiful example of a medieval castle. The king announced that he had placed it there 'for the strength of the realm, and the refuge of the Islanders', praiseworthy sentiments. It is described as having twelve rooms below stairs, forty rooms from the first storey upwards, being circular, and built of stone, with six towers, and certain out-offices thereto belonging, all the roof of lead. Within the circumference of the castle was one little round court, paved with stone, and in the middle of that one great well, and without the castle was one great court surrounding it, both court and castle being surrounded by a great stone wall, outside moated round, the said castle abutting to the highway from Queenborough to Eastchurch. It occupied over three acres of land. The few pictures there are show that it was an imposing castle, and pleasing to look at. Now there is nothing left of it, no ruins, stones, or even the suggestion of a moat, only the well remains, owned and used by British Rail.

The king was anxious to promote his latest castle. He renamed Bynne 'Queenborough' in honour of Phillippa his Queen, declared it a free borough and in 1366 he granted the town a charter. He wanted to attract people to come and live there, as he needed a town round the castle walls that would be able to supply the garrison. Queenborough was granted the right to elect a mayor and jurats, and the townsmen were regarded as burgesses; the mayor took oath before the Constable of the Castle. The town had two markets weekly, and two fairs, one on the Eve of Our Lady, and one on St. James' Day.

He ordered a chapel to be built, a daughter church of the abbey at Minster, and gave the new town many other privileges, including the staple for wool, which he took from Sandwich. This meant that the town was one of the few allowed to export wool, which was a lucrative business. The king visited Queenborough frequently, and did everything in his power 'to allure men to live in this place'.

For ten years Queenborough was a boom town, but it was a false prosperity, for then the king returned the privilege of the Wool Staple to Sandwich, and after that the town failed to develop. It became a small borough of fishermen, boatmen and oyster dredgers. Despite that, Queenborough retained its status, and has a wonderful collection of charters and records and a history that deserves to be recorded more fully than can be done here.

The first Constable of the Castle was John Foxley, 1362–3. The list of constables is far from complete, for there is a gap until 1376, when the king's son, John O' Gaunt, the Duke of Lancaster, was in charge. John O' Gaunt owned a considerable amount of property on the island. Part of this was the farm known as Danley Farm, which is situated on the Minster to Halfway Road. Originally it was called Dandeley, the name of one of the first farmers who lived there. A William Dandele is listed in the Kent Lay Subsidy Roll of 1334–5, where he is assessed for one shilling tax, and he is presumed to be one of the family from the farm, probably the actual tenant.

John O' Gaunt received the land as a gift from his father, and Dandeley Farm he granted to the Hospital of St. Katherines in London, on certain conditions. From 1392 the farm remained the property of the hospital, who leased it to a succession of tenants, until they sold the property in 1898. The gentleman who purchased it discovered that there were no deeds, and the sale was agreed to as follows:— The buyer states he purchased Danley Farm from the Master, Brethren and Sisters acting as the Chapter of the Royal Hospital and Collegiate of Saint Katherine. The agreement for purchase provided that the title should be 'the grant by John of Gaunt and others, dated the fourth of February 1392–1393 A.D. of the Manor of Rushenden and certain other lands in the Isle of Sheppey'.

That was the only title to the property. The hospital escaped suppression at the Reformation, and at the time of the sale Queen Victoria was the patron, and her consent to the transaction had to be obtained. The buyer related the conditions outlined in the grant, as he felt his title to the farm was unusual, to say the least. Apart from agreements relating to leases there had been no other dealings with the property in five hundred years.

The Grant is as follows:— 'To all who shall see or hear this writing John Duke of Aquitane and Lancaster (John) by divine permission Bishop of Lincoln and Henry by the same permission Bishop of Worcester greeting in the Lord Everlasting. Whereas John Kent holds the Manor of Ryshenden in the Isle of Sheppey with the appurtenances and one messuage sixty acres of land, two hundred acres of pasture, one hundred and twenty acres of salt marsh and three shillings and eight pence of rent with the appurtenances in the Parish of Minster for his life by the lease of us and Sir John de Ispre Knight and Nicholas Carrew now deceased ...'. He explains here how the land was gifted to him by the late King Edward III, and after the death of John Kent, Danley Farm and land should revert to him, John of Gaunt, but 'it was to be granted to Saint Katherine's Hospital near the Tower of London, and they were to find another Chaplain with the rents thus gained to celebrate services for the late King Edward and Queen Phillippa, the present King Richard and consort, and for himself, and their souls when they departed this life.

'And to celebrate the Obit of the late King and Queen, and himself, every year forever in the Hospital aforesaid.

'And the same Masters, Brethren and Sisters shall enter the Manor aforesaid after John Kent's death but they must find a Chaplain as aforesaid to celebrate divine services for the estate and souls aforesaid every year, in the same Church in the Hospital.

'The lands and tenements must not be put in mortmain, saving always the chief lands of those fees the services therefore to them due and accustomed.

'In testimony to this present charter we have set our seals, there being witnesses: Thomas Percy, John D'Eyncourt and others.'

This must surely be one of the most unusual deeds by which anyone has bought and owned a farm in the last hundred years! Danley Farm is still an agricultural holding, albeit reduced in size, as Danley Middle School is situated on ground that was once the farm's land. It is an attractive farm, lying back from the main road, reached by a tree-bordered lane. The house is one of the few left on the island built of wood, it is constructed of weatherboard, and as far as anyone can tell was last rebuilt, or renovated, in 1788.

The Subsidy Roll lists the names of all the landowners in Sheppey whose incomes were large enough to tax. It is an imposing number, but many of the people named did not live on the island, they owned personal estate in many of the Hundreds in Kent, and their names appeared in the Rolls of every Hundred where they had property. However, Sheppey names can often be recognised because there are farms and places on the island today that still use these names. Other names are familiar from charters relating to land on the island. Richard Bode is one of these, and the family of Douledames, William, John and Thomas, is another.

John Bele de Ossendone, John and William Holteman and Adam de Holte mean nothing in Sheppey now, but Ossenden and Holt, names that keep appearing so oddly and have left no trace, were the names of two of the boroughs into which the island was divided for administrative purposes. There does not seem to be any record, or map, to show exactly where these boroughs were, but other borough names are self explanatory. Alic' de Rissendone and John de Bynne are obviously from Queenborough, and so possibly is John de Lok, as his name occurs in Queenborough records. John and Richard Wardone and John de Herteye had to come from Warden and Harty, and Joan Ward from that area of Minster now known as Wards Hill. John Peyforer came from Borstal Hall, and John de Kyngesberche was probably the farmer at Kingsborough farm, a farm that is still very much alive today and has a most interesting history attached to it.

There are three Gerards, Thomas son of John, Thomas, and the widow of Robert Gerard. One theory is that Gerard was the origin of Garretts, as in Garretts Farm. This may be questioned, as there was a family named Garrett farming in Elizabeth I's reign, unless they were descended from the Gerards, in which case the story is probably true.

The Abbot of Radegund paid eight shillings and the Abbot of Boxley ten shillings. Respectively they had been granted Leysdown Church and Eastchurch Church, and lands. Unlike the prioress of Sexburg Minster, they were not exempt from tax. Thomas Troutes belonged to the first family at Trouts Farm, which is an old farm round Water Lane at Eastchurch. The house is of indeterminate age, has been added to from time to time, and then covered with pebble dash in places, plaster in others, so from outside it is difficult to estimate in what year it was built, or rebuilt. There are two local stories about this farm.

One is that originally it was a hunting lodge belonging to Shurland Hall. As it is no distance from the Hall, a mile at most, this does not seem very likely. That it was a small farm belonging to Shurland many years ago is true. There is a brook running by the farm called Hensbrook, older people insist that 'once upon a time', trout could be caught there. The second story about Trout Farm arose during the 1914–18 World War. A strange officer was billeted there, a foreigner. He kept to his own quarters; his own batman, and no other, waited on him, and he did not mix with the other officers. Everyone in the village was convinced that he was a foreign prince, or at any rate a person of very high standing. How much truth there was in these conjectures is never likely to be known, and the story is still believed locally.

Roger de Northwode was 'cessed' for ten shillings. The Cheyne name is not on the roll, perhaps as they had the Liberty of their Manor they were not subject to assessment. Simon de Swanley paid two shillings and five pence. Swanley Farm is on the Warden Road, where the road turns sharp right. The house was demolished by the Army as they considered it was too conspicuous, and during the Second World War an anti-aircraft battery was stationed there. A picture of the house shows it as a typical, and attractive, Kentish farm house, rather oblong in shape and comfortable to look at, probably late eighteenth century. There is no farm house on the land now, although land and buildings are still in use, and the old army huts serve as store houses.

Sir Ralph de Sauvage was taxed for four shillings. His manor was at Bobbing, where he paid more tax, but he owned land at Warden and Rushenden. He was a well known and respected knight. Robert and Richard de Ryde come from the family from whom Rides first obtained the name,

but it could equally well have been the other way about, that the family took their name from the estate, as Ryde, or Ride, simply means a clearing.

Thomas de Napleton may or may not have lived on the island. Napleton was the name of a large marsh in Harty. Bartholomew de Wattone, taxed at three shillings and fourpence, raises a query. There is a farm called Wootons, and the local pronunciation is not easily conveyed by spelling, whose name is alleged to have come from Sir Edward Wotton, who in 1548 was granted land in Sheppey. The origin of the name could only be verified by seeing how far the farm could be traced back through the centuries. The house gives nothing away, as it looks like a Victorian effort, and probably is. 'Little Woottons', a small house half a mile along the road, is far older, but how long it has had the name is hard to ascertain.

John Cokil had a high cess, twelve shillings and sixpence farthing. On early maps, one of which is a survey made in Elizabeth I's reign, there is a farm, or place, marked Cockells. It is no longer in existence, but the name is, as there is still a family named Cockle on the island.

Gilbert Alte Watere could have lived anywhere locally, but Robert Elys, taxed for eight shillings and ninepence farthing, and the widow of John Elys, taxed eight shillings, are interesting people. The Elys farmed a large estate in Leysdown, and in 1389 one William Elys became involved with a ship from Durdracht that was wrecked, and wares and goods stolen. The prior of Canterbury had twenty-eight pieces of wax in his possession, plus other things, and was ordered under pain of king's wrath to make restitution. William Elys received the same warning, which ended darkly with 'the King marvels and is wrath'.

It appears then that in less than three hundred years Sheppey had acquired a rebuilt monastery, two great manor lords, a castle, a new town, several small churches, an effective beacon system to warn the islanders of dangers from the sea, and farms were becoming settled and named all over the island. All this at a time when no journey could be made faster than a horse could travel and there was nothing mechanical to either build or farm with, everything being done with manpower. How many people today could cope with the sort of situations that arose then? It is frightening to think about.

Even so, the island was not heavily populated, as no-one would, or could, live on the marshland. With all this activity access to the island was becoming an increasing problem. It was obvious that sooner or later the ferry would prove inadequate for the increased traffic, and something would have to be done to facilitate the awkward river crossing.

CHAPTER IX

Reasonable access

The history of the first ferry is lost in the mists of time, they obscure the beginnings of it as thoroughly as the notorious mists of Sheppey frequently obscure the Ferry Road.

There is a muddled story frequently repeated that once there was a bridge. It was washed away by a great storm and after that the channel was too deep and wide to allow of another being built. The same tale is told of the fleet that once separated the Isle of Harty from Sheppey, so there is a choice.

There were some great storms in the eleventh century, in which Sheppey suffered considerably, so there may be some truth in both stories.

Tremhethe was certainly the old name for the King's Ferry, and is also put forward as the name of the bridge at Harty. However, Harty had ceased to be an island before the Middle Ages, and unless Capel Fleet flooded was accessible by road. There is another side to this which is frequently overlooked. Capel Fleet and Capel Farm derive their name from 'Chapel'. There was no chapel in Harty until William the Conquerer's coming and by that time attempts had been, and were being made, to drain and 'in' some of the marshlands. Early Normans had probably gained some control over the Fleet that separated Harty from Sheppey.

By Henry VIII's time the Ferry was officially known as Trinhide, or Trimhide, which sounds suspiciously like a corruption of Tremhethe. Throughout the centuries the people spelt as they spoke and pronunciation could vary considerably from one century to the next. Working on all these assumptions, Tremhethe was the ferry between the road leading from Key Street, via Bobbing and Iwade, and the island.

Key Street has nothing to do with keys or quays. The name goes back to Roman times when a Roman Officer, Caïus, owned land in the vicinity.

Tremhethe is claimed to mean 'beam landing place', a landing place made of logs or beams. Now known as King's Ferry, even when there is a queen on the throne, and spanned by a lifting bridge, it has had a chequered history.

There were two other ferries onto the island; one from Oare to Harty, for foot passengers only, as a rowing boat was the only means of transport. There was also a row boat plying between Elmley and the mainland. Cattle could be swum over when the tide was right, and for farmers with grazing in Elmley or Harty it was cheaper than paying ferry dues to have them ferried over. Both these ferries have now ceased to ply, although in recent years there have been attempts to revive Harty Ferry.

From the earliest times Tremhethe Ferry would have had a large boat with a flat deck in use, in order to transport to and from the island horses, cattle and sheep, as well as people and luggage. The road into the island from the ferry was a narrow bank, four feet wide at the top. What the approach from the mainland was like is not clear, but from contemporary reports it was a disgustingly bad road, to say the least. It must be remembered that this bank, also known as a 'bridge', was built across the marshes, which were more subject to flooding and wetter than they are today. Roads across marshland are notoriously difficult to build, and even with the present day facilities there were delays in construction. Before the present, relatively straight road was built from the ferry to Cowstead Corner the old ferry road was a narrow highway full of twists and turns. It was thought that the road had grown by following the tracks made by sheep and cattle, who instinctively chose the driest ground on which to beat a path. Many people thought a straight road over the marshes was an impossibility and no attempt was made to build one until after the Second World War.

However, as most goods in early times were carried by baggage men or carriers, or on the panniers of pack ponies, the bank answered well enough for foot passengers or ridden or loaded horses. Anything too large or too heavy for a pack pony went by sea, or came up Windmill Creek. When carts and wagons became more widely used, the bank soon proved inadequate.

Increased traffic was the immediate result when the king started building Queenborough Castle, and Edward III ordered that this bank should be enlarged to thirty feet in width. The bank ran from the ferry to a place called Cothelles, but its whereabouts on the island is not known. Once the bank was enlarged, it was possible for carts and wagons to carry loads to and from the castle. Obviously it was not convenient for everything to come and go by sea.

There are records which give an idea of some of the loads that were brought from the castle along the new bank. In 1369 a cart full of armour worn by the king's archers came along to the ferry. There were coats of mail (called habergeons) close fitting helmets of iron (basceriets) and others made of boiled leather (palettes). The cart passed safely over the ferry and was driven to Leeds Castle. The driver was a man called John Wautynnge, and he received the large sum of sixteen pence for the job.

After this bank had been well used for some time it became, not surprisingly, impassable, so some thirty years after it was built the islanders appealed to Henry IV for help. In 1401 he granted to the men of Sheppey the right to levy a toll upon every stranger that entered the island; they charged one penny for every stranger on horseback, a halfpenny for those on foot, one penny for every loaded horse, and a halfpenny for a horse unloaded.

Originally these tolls were granted for three years only, but afterwards they were renewed from time to time, and the tolls were extended to include all travellers, strangers and islandlers, and cattle, sheep and dogs. This created a fund which helped to keep both ferry and road in repair, but as time went by it proved inadequate, and subsequent laws granted the islanders the right to levy a tax on farmland in Sheppey. This was known locally as the 'Ferry Cess'.

Once tolls were sanctioned some kind of authority was needed to regulate expenditure and organise the work of running the ferry and keeping the road in repair. The Ferry Court, or Law Day, which dealt with nothing but the business of the ferry, probably had its beginnings at the time of Edward III. It was held at Kingsborough Farm, which until Tudor times was Crown land, and the court met under a huge oak tree, known as the Court Tree. This oak stood on a small green in front of Kingsborough.

Law Day was held yearly, on Whit Monday. The routine altered but little over the centuries. Homage was given before a steward of the king, a borsholder (constable) was chosen for the whole island, and a jury was sworn. A borsholder was responsible for each borough on the island, and a ferry keeper, ferry warden, and two ferrymen were appointed 'for the government of the ferry'. All matters relating to the running of the ferry and the maintenance of roads were settled there. The ferryman had certain rights, including that of dredging for oysters within a given distance of the ferry. It was defined as 'within the Compass of the Ferry loop, which extends one tows length, that is, sixty fathoms on each side of the cable'.

This right of dredging was recorded by several early historians, including Hasted, but the statement has been queried by more recent writers, as Hasted has been known to be in error. In this case his statement was correct, as will be proved later.

The ferry boat was worked by a long cable of one hundred and forty fathoms or more, fastened at each end and worked by hand. Over the years two ferry boats came into use, plus a skiff and a small row boat.

All this had to be recorded, and it is unfortunate, and in fact very irritating that so few accounts of Ferry Court orders have survived. These are in the archives at County Hall and it would have been helpful if more of them had been collected and deposited there.

The earliest record extant is one in the reign of King Henry VIII, and extracts from this will show how competently the islanders of bygone days managed their affairs.

The Isle of Sheppey 1546
    Kyngesborroughe. The lawday holden there the XIIIJ[th] day of June in the XXXVIIJ[th] year of our Soveraigne Lord Kynge Henry the VIIJ[th], the year of our Lord God.
    The Borough of Ossenden. John Ellyot, Borsholder there, his suters Henry Elliot and Peter Hayne. We present Edwyne IJd Passhley and Laurence IJd Short for caryinge of lod of wyne from the Ferry, we present William IIIJd Swalman for a lode of pale from the Ferry, we present Thomas Richards for a lode of stofe (stuff) wee present

John Norden for a lode of corn with a shode (shod, heavy iron on the wheels) cart unto the Ferrye.

The borough of Seden. Thomas Brodstreet, Borsholder there, Suters John Fellowe and Thomas Osborne.

The Borough of Ride. William Wreke, Borsholder there, his Suter Robert Wreake.

The borough of Holt. Thomas Collins, Borsholder there, his suters, Symon Brodstreet and Ambrose Huepse. We present Lewes Graye for making default.

Warden Borough. Richard Man, Borsholder there, his suters William Hottershad and Thomas Man.

That was the opening ceremony. The unfortunates 'presented' had broken the rules. The peculiar manner in which the amounts of the fines were written over the names of the miscreants represented the expression used then 'he is amerced for ... (whatever the fine was) upon his head'. A literal interpretation, and as few country people could read or write then, quite reasonable. The names of the jury, fourteen in number, are then recorded, written in columns of four names, with two over. They are interesting in so far as they give some idea of the families in Sheppey in that century, but apart from names like Lambe and Taylor, which are common in any age, none of them are known on the island today. John Rowhed could be from 'Rowetts', a farm just outside Eastchurch. That is supposed to date back to Thomas Rowhede of Eastchurch, 1485. The other point is the number of surnames that are alike. Everyone seems to have been related in some way, and that is usual now. An island is a small place!

Next, the Constable.

The jury present that they have chosen Richard Pawyne to be constable this year, and John Colsall to be his deputy.

[The constable had jurisdiction over the whole island, excluding Queenborough, which took no part in Law Day.]

The Ferry warden. Item. They present that they have chosen Richard Awode to be Ferry warden for the year. Item. They present that they have chosen William Hottershad and William Tersett to be Ferrymen. Sureties for the said William Hottershad and William Tersett; — William Swalman, Thomas Richards, Richard Clynton and John Taylor.

John Morris accompt. The accompt. made by me, John Morris warden of Trinhide Ferry, the XIIIJth day of June etc. 1546.

Here follows a list of rents received.

The amount received of Sir Thomas Chaine, Knight, for a parcell of lands of the Lordship of Minster is left blank. Other lands recorded give little idea of their name or whereabouts.

Rents from Sir Thomas Chayne, Knight, for lands at Shurland	IIIJ^s	0
[This was the highest rent received]		
Mr. Rodstone for Mr. Dergas lands at Elmeley	IIJ^s	IIIJ^d
Mr. Robert Harlekyden for lands late Thomas Fuller	VIIJ^s	0

Other lands referred to as Blancketts and Stanards would be difficult to trace, and John Osbornes' lands called 'Puffes' are tantalizing, who wouldn't want to know were 'Puffes' was? 'Of the heirs of William Abeylles for lands at the Harpe' is clear enough. There was a Harps Farm at Minster in living memory, to be replaced by Harps Inn, Harps Council estate and Harps Avenue. Many people would not consider this to be a good exchange, but such is the price of progress. The rents are followed by a list of debts that have been repaid to the ferry and small gifts 'received of divers men for their

goodwill', plus a note of land that has been leased out to various farmers.

Finally, charges laid out.

Paid by me, John Morris, Warden, the XXXVIIIth yeare aforesaid, for Trymhide Ferry. [Here there is a change of spelling. Trinhide becomes Trymhide and almost reverts to Tremhethe. The items John Morris bought and paid for were solely for the use of the ferry, tar, pitch, tow, rope, nails and similar things.]

IIJ littel elmes bought of Robert Fellowe for the boat cost	VIJ^d
One hundred IIIJ^d penny nails	VIIJ^d
Paid for strawe unto John Colsall	IIIJ^d

The heaviest expenses were for shipwrights, the men who 'made the walle work', their ladd, and their beds and meat and drink for five days. He finishes his account simply by writing 'Cetera desunt'.

That is the end of the Law Day proceedings, apart from the 'Ferry Feast' that followed. It is simple, and clearly outlined. Later records are not so short as highway acts were introduced in later reigns, and new regulations made to cope with increased traffic.

It seems an eternity away now, but the Law Day continued until the railway took over in 1860, and even the bridge tolls were collected until 1929.

While the access via the ferry was improving, the coasts of Sheppey were still in danger.

Richard II, in 1377, issued an ordinance

of safeguarding the Counties of Kent and Essex, and particularly the town lying on the River Thames from the perils which may suddenly come upon them from our enemies, which God forbid —

In the Isle of Sheppey a beacon, and at Showbury in Essex a beacon [and then followed a list of places needing beacons]. By especial command of our very Noble Lord the King, the sheriffs, constables and other officials in the aforesaid parts of Kent and Essex be charged that all the said beacons be speedily and suitably set up and prepared for the safe-guarding of the County and of the said Navy.

From this it sounds as though the Beacon watch had been neglected, as it may well have been under Richard II. Having ordered a day and night watch and ward on all beacons, the ordinance continued

Item. That the watchmen (at beacons) particularly in Sheppey and Shuberry, shall be from time to time warned and charged (that should they see any vessels, sail or oars) coming, the said two beacons should be set on fire, and therewith to make all the noise they can with horn and shouting, to warn all the country round to come with all their force all to help to resist our enemies.

It sounds remarkably like an early form of Home Guard, with the locals joining in the fray with whatever weapons came handiest. As the majority were farm workers, pitch forks and ox goads would have had to suffice.

Richard II was not a remarkable king in any sense. He met Wat Tyler and his following with great bravery in 1381, but subsequently the rebels were treated very harshly. He was responsible for ending the war with France in 1396, which was to his credit, but when he wanted to do without Parliamentary government, erratic as that was in that time, his days were numbered.

He appointed his friend and favourite, Robert de Vere, as Constable at Queenborough Castle in 1384, a post Robert held until 1392, with great advantage to himself. In 1382 one of the towers of the castle was badly damaged by an earthquake, but repairs were speedily done and there are no records of any other damage, or injury to the garrison.

The agitation about beacons did not affect Queenborough. One of the clauses in the Royal Charter stated that 'no burgess could be compelled to muster arms out of the borough'. Despite the loss of wool staple, the town had settled down to enjoy the privileges of a borough. They had a portfolio of charters and statutes, the latter consisting of copies of statutes made not later than 1325, among which was a copy of the Customal of Kent. This last has attracted the attention of many notable historians, and continues to do so.

The mayor was elected yearly, with two jurats or bailiffs. He also had a steward, preferably a man with some learning and a knowledge of law.

A court of record was held every three weeks, where local disputes, minor crimes, and the business of the borough were settled. There was already a limited amount of legislation regarding the oyster fisheries. Oysters were in demand by the Normans and trading with the castle would have been a profitable business for the Queenborough fishermen.

Among the borough records of 1452 there is an order referring to William Cheyne — 'no one shall drag any oysters from William Cheyne's Fleet in Ward in Holfleet on pain of six shillings and eight pence'.

William Cheyne evidently valued his oysters and would not tolerate any poaching. His oyster beds stretched from a point at sea roughly opposite Marine Parade, along to the Scrapsgate Road. There is still a point off the coast there called Cheyney Rock.

Many people came before the mayor at the View of Frank pledge, which was in fact a Court held by the mayor twice yearly, and asked for admission to the borough for various reasons. Amongst them was John Northwode Esq. in 1489.

John Northwode esq came before William Cokerill Mayor and was admitted in the presence of Richard Rand, Robert Bret and John Lecke'.

In 1459–60 one of the Northwodes, no christian name given, was recorded on the list of burgesses. There is no mention of this in the famous genealogy, and no explanation given as to why any of the Northwodes should choose to live in Queenborough, unless they wished to be near the castle for some reason.

In 1461 John Northwode esq. was constable of Queenborough Castle, but he left the post in 1462 to make way for the Duke of Clarence. He may have decided to remain in Queenborough, for that John was the last of the Sheppey Norwoods to live on the island.

The Norwoods' sojourn in Queenborough is not mentioned in any of the histories or records, and is, at present, unexplainable.

There is a will extant of a resident of Queenborough, dated May 26th, 1505, that contains some unusual clauses; it is the will of Rest Redfyn (even her name was out of the ordinary!) widow of Nicholas Redfyn, of Queenborough. She requests, among other things, 'also I will the same William Berd fulfill all my pilgrimages; First, to the Rode of Grace, a woman of wax'. This requires explanation. The Rood of Grace was at Boxley Abbey, the same abbey that owned Eastchurch church. Offerings of wax were very common, and a 'woman of wax' would be a small waxen figure of the Virgin. 'To Mr. John Shorne, in the Parish of Halstow, J^d' John Shorne was a much revered Chaplain, of Kentish birth, who was 'much saught after for the ague'. Halstowe apparently was one of the places where pilgrimages were made in his honour. He would have a special appeal for people who lived on or near the marshes in Sheppey, as 'the ague' was an accepted part of their lives, and continued to be so up to the twentieth century. The 'ague' was in fact malaria, and was common in these parts before the advent of modern sanitation.

'Item. To Sir Thomas in Harteigh, a hart of wax.' Whether this was a waxen image of a hart or stag, referring to the name Harty, or whether it had a religious meaning, e.g. Sacred Heart, no-one is likely to know now. Many people then had a 'special devotion' to places quite distant from their homes, and this illustrates that custom.

Presumably, the end of the war with France meant that Edward III's order forbidding the ringing of more than one church bell was revoked (a peal of bells signified invasion, as in the last war).

Despite rebellion in Henry IV's reign, and the renewal of war with France in Henry V's, the prioress and nuns seemed to be intent on the building of a fine church tower, and worked to this end. Many people left them money specifically for this building.

To the Tower of Minster, three shillings and fourpence. Joan Clunch, Widow. 1467.
To the work of the tower, thirteen shillings and fourpence. Nicholas at Lee. 1471.
To the reparation of the Parish Church, sixty six shillings and eight pence, and to the tower of the same church, sixty six shillings and eight pence. John Atle Hethe. 1474.

These are just a few of the bequests, and they are generous ones. The islanders evidently wanted their tower. It is notable that many bequests and gifts include fourpence or a multiple of that sum, perhaps there was a special association there that has since been lost.

Another bequest to the priory that had a note of sadness in it came from a greater distance than was usual. From Ash, near Sandwich, in 1457 Matilda, relict of Roger Clyderow, says simply 'To the Nuns of Sheppey to pray for my soul and parents forty shillings'. This is one of those little cameos from long ago that must set people wondering. Who was Matilda? It is unpleasant simply to be labelled 'relict'. Perhaps she was born on the island, and her marriage took her 'over the water' to foreign parts. For that is how Sheppey people regard leaving the island for the mainland, and it is heard even today. Her will shows she was thinking of her parents, perhaps she was homesick, and longed to die in her own part of Kent. Her will has a ring of sadness about it.

Henry V is remembered chiefly for his success at Agincourt, but he also persecuted the Lollards and this may have quietened some of the anti-clerics, and strengthened the religious zeal of the ordinary people. Few wanted to associate with a persecuted minority. It was neither wise nor safe.

Agincourt owed a great deal to the skill of English archers. They had plenty of practice, for Edward III had forbidden all village games and sport apart from archery. Everyone was to spend their free time (?) practising at the butts. In Minster a 'Butts Lane' is mentioned in the old vestry books, but with the breaking up of the farmlands and small lanes by the land companies of the late nineteenth century all trace of this lane disappeared.

Queenborough had their own butts, also long since lost. Presumably Eastchurch and Leysdown also practised, but no records mention it although there are Manor Court Rolls for Leysdown from the time of Edward III to Elizabeth I, but where they are kept it is difficult to ascertain. The chief manor of Leysdown belonged to one of the big monasteries.

Apart from compulsory archery, during the fifteenth century the lot of the countryman was slowly improving. The cottars, bordars and serfs with their boon work for the lord and the manor, were gradually giving place to tenant farmers, smallholders, and farm workers paid by wages. The trades, miller, blacksmith, baker, wheelwright, and others like them were becoming independent small businesses. In the towns the tradesmen had formed guilds to which they belonged. The richer guilds could exert quite an amount of influence when necessary.

33

Naturally, it did not alter overnight, and there was much overlapping of status, payment in kind as well as by wages, and rent partly paid by work done for the landlord, but gradually the feudal system was giving way to a society comprised of farmers, small tradesmen, and wage earners. The nobles kept retainers trained for fighting, who could be counted upon as the nucleus of an army in the event of war. The king had no regular army, and had to rely on what he could conscript in an emergency.

Minster Abbey remained the mother church on the island, to which the people came for the chief sacraments. Queenborough with its castle and charters, was still in the parish of Minster. From Shurland Hall and Norwood Manor the de Shurlands, Cheyneys and Norwoods all came to the abbey, although there was a church at Eastchurch. Eastchurch was so named simply because it was east of Minster Abbey, and was first recorded as Eastcyne in 1100.

The church there was originally appropriated to the Cistercian Abbey of Dunes, in Flanders. Pope Celestine's confirmation of that grant was made in A.D. 1196. The earliest Lambeth record was made in A.D. 1279, recording the institution of William de Wylton to the benefice. In June 1300 the Abbey of Dunes granted an endowment of eleven and a half acres of glebe land and eight shillings yearly to the vicar. In medieval times vicars were expected to produce their own food like any other countryman. They could easily starve in a poor parish otherwise.

Sir Robert de Shurland was living at Shurland Hall at that time, and William, the vicar of Eastchurch, was involved in some fashion with certain settlements in the de Shurland family. He had been trustee of the manor of Ufton in Tunstall, which he granted to Robert de Shurland and his wife Katherine in 1311.

In 1315 the Abbey of Dunes transferred the rights of the church to the Kentish Cistercian Abbey of Boxley, to make the work of administration easier. The Northwode family were also a notable family in Eastchurch at this time, and Sir Roger de Northwode's chaplain, Richard Sheme, was vicar in 1353. It was this chaplain, Richard Sheme, who testified to the extremely early marriage and equally early parenthood of Roger, so helping to record a true genealogy.

Eastchurch cannot have possessed the full rights of a parish church, as the de Shurlands and de Northwodes were buried at the abbey, to which the Northwode family were devoted.

William Cheyne of Shurland Hall was the chief parishioner in 1431 and he obtained a licence from King Henry VI to give three roods of his land (which he held of the King) to the Patrons of the Rectory, who were, in fact, the Abbot and convent of Boxley. At no time did anyone consider building a church for the parish. It mentioned in the royal licence that 'the old church had gone to ruin by reason of a sudden weakness of the foundations'.

As usual, the Sheppey Clay had shifted, and weakened the foundations and structure. Nothing is known about the earlier church, or where it stood. There have been many guesses, the most popular choice being 'somewhere near Parsonage Farm', which stands on the right hand side of a small road which joins Eastchurch main street directly opposite the church gate.

The new church is said to have kept and used some of the windows from the old church, namely those in the western porch, and the west windows of the two aisles, but nothing else was retained.

The abbot was determined that there should be no weakness in the new church, so deep, solid foundations of chalk were laid. The chalk had to be fetched from the mainland, and as it was not permitted to fetch building materials over Tremhethe ferry, the chalk, stone for building and anything else needed would have to come round by the Swale in a barge, and then up Windmill Creek to the quay nearest to Eastchurch. Once unloaded there it would finish the journey by cart-horse or bullock drawn. Local men were probably detailed for this job, but it is unlikely that they received any extra pay. Hopefully, beer was provided. This was the usual custom.

The church was built with diagonal buttresses at every angle, and three porches, north, south and west, with buttresses at each of their angles. That way there was support for the walls and western tower. It has been remarked that few parish churches have so many buttresses in so small a space. Naturally, the church was built of stone.

It was a grand church for such a small village and the royal licence stated that it had at this time all the privileges and rights of a parish church. The vicar was a monk sent from Boxley Abbey, but at the beginning of the sixteenth century the abbey's income had diminished, and Archbishop Warham allowed the abbot to send him a secular chaplain to act as vicar.

Pope Sixtus IV permitted the appropriation of the vicarage in 1472, and in January 1511–12 John Crambroke, the Abbot of Boxley, received the licence for this. After that the church was served by a curate, there was no vicar.

This meant, in effect, that all tithes that would have been due to the vicar were claimed by Boxley Abbey, so the curate was the loser.

Parish church with all rights or no, William Cheyne chose to be buried at Minster Abbey, as his will proved, and there are no records of any other of the Cheyneys or any of the Norwoods requesting burial at Eastchurch.

Eastchurch cannot have had many residents at this time. In 1670 it is estimated that Minster, Eastchurch, Leysdown and Harty had fewer than fifteen adults per square mile, so in 1470 there would have been very few cottages in Eastchurch and the villagers must have been tenants or workers of the Cheyneys for the most part.

Despite this, in 1473 Robert Manne of Eastchurch left directions in his will he was to be buried at Minster.

The bequests he left sound distinctly odd now:—

To the Church of Eastchurch. To the light of our Lady in the High Quire [the spelling is his] a moder [mother] sheep and to the High Cross Light one moder sheep.

These ewes were to be hired by a farmer in the parish who would pay for the use of the sheep an annual rent sufficient to supply with oil one lamp in the church throughout the years. 'Also a moder sheep to the Brotherhood and light of "Seynt Jamys" of Warden'. There is no record of what he left to Minster Abbey — probably more 'moder' sheep. Like many Sheppey men, before and since, his wealth lay in sheep.

After the death of Sir William Cheyne there is little mention of the new church, apart from the Abbot of Boxley's appropriation, until the dissolution.

The Norwoods left Eastchurch, and the Cheyneys that followed William were too occupied with rebellions to have much thought for churches.

It must have been in these early years of the new church, which was, and still is, called All Saints, Eastchurch, that the rood screen was carefully carved from oak and placed in position, where it still is today. It extends across the nave, and both aisles, and has many unique features.

It is said to show traces of once being surmounted by a rood loft. Mr. Dickson, the rector in 1882, felt it looked unfinished and showed the lack of the rood loft, so he had a small cresting fixed to the top beam.

There are no records about this, and how it managed to escape destruction at the time of Edward VI, or later by Oliver Cromwell's men, is a mystery.

In fact there is very little recorded about All Saints at Eastchurch, or the village, until the time of Sir Thomas Cheyne at the end of the fifteenth century.

CHAPTER X
The great days of Shurland

Henry of Richmond lost no time in consolidating his position after winning the Battle of Bosworth. He had himself crowned king as quickly as possible. The following year, 1486, he married Elizabeth of York, King Edward IV's daughter, so uniting the Lancaster and York factions, thereby putting a decisive end to the Wars of the Roses. He ruled firmly, and the country prospered. He encouraged ship-building and voyages of discovery, and apart from two minor insurrections he kept clear of civil and foreign wars.

In one of these insurrections Lord Lovell took part, and he had inherited a small manor in Leysdown from Lord de Grey's family. The chief land-owners in Leysdown were the Church. Following his mistaken support for in impostor, Lambert Simnell, he was killed in battle and his lands attainted. His property in Leysdown was granted to the Cheyne family, adding to their estates in Sheppey. In spite of a peaceful country, the beacons were kept in order. In 1468 Edward IV ordered the watch and ward be kept, and the beacons kept in repair, with provisions of new ones as necessary, as the truce with France had expired.

Henry VII endorsed this order early in his reign, sending an order to the sheriffs of the counties 'to put coast watch and Beacons in order because there is like to be open war — between Charles VIII of France and Maximillian, King of the Romans'. Britain did not become involved, but the people of Sheppey must have been relieved to know that the new king was aware of the dangers coast-dwellers were exposed to. Henry VII left the churches and prelates in peace. He ratified their charters and did not interfere. The leaders of the Church were great land-owners, rich, powerful men. At this time the discipline in monasteries and nunneries was becoming lax; few religious communities lived in the austere conditions they had committed themselves to.

Among the higher prelates dress was rich and costly and material possessions great. In the smaller foundations plentiful food, and comfortable lodgings were the norm. Only the parish priest was poor, and often uneducated. In Sheppey the small churches, Harty, Leysdown, Elmley and Warden, were poorly served, and often had periods with no priest in attendance. Eastchurch was a new church but that made little difference. Queenborough was slightly better treated, as it was under the walls and supervision of the castle. William Cheyne was Henry VII's Constable in 1485, and he remained in charge until 1488.

Apart from squabbles amongst inhabitants, Queenborough had settled down to fishing, dredging oysters, and making ordinances for the borough. In 1527 one quarrel was serious enough to make it necessary for a certificate of agreement to be drawn up between the mayor, Richard Rand, and one John Allen. They were to 'Abide the Arbitrament' of Richard Taylor, Robert Bolton, Thomas Hewet and Richard Cokerell, 'the elder Burgesses' on pain of a fine of £12 by the parties breaking the award. It would be interesting to know the causes of such a serious disagreement, unless, as it is described nowadays, it was simply a 'personality clash'.

At the priory the abbess and the nuns appeared to be making the best of life. From the archbishop's visitation in 1511 it was evident that the nunnery was not well run, but the old zest to improve seemed to be missing. The tower seemed to occupy much of their thoughts, and up to 1530–2 bequests were still coming in. There was one of especial interest in 1479.

Peter Cleve's legacy contained money for the repair of the Chapel of St. John the Baptist, and two bequests of £40, one for a 'campanile on the Priory side' and one for 'that on the side of the Parish Church'. It has been suggested that the intention was to have a beacon tower on the church, with the bells on either side, but this was never achieved. The Chapel of St. John the Baptist raises a point that has never been settled satisfactorily. It was said to be on the north-east side of the churchyard, not a clear description, and very little is known about it.

John Cheyne, made Baron Cheyne of Shurland by Henry VII, died in 1496. His place of burial is not mentioned, but he was in fact buried in Salisbury Cathedral, where his tomb can be seen today (not all the Cheyneys were buried in Minster Abbey: one has a tomb in Salisbury Cathedral, another in an old London Church, and the family spread considerably over the years). The Baron had no son, and his property descended to his nephew Thomas. Many people are under the misapprehension that nephew Thomas came of a different branch of the family, but this is not so.

Thomas was the son of William, who was as deeply involved in the rebellion as his brothers John and Humphrey. As William was a younger brother he had left Shurland Hall and moved elsewhere, married well, and started another family of Cheyneys. He had been born and brought up in Sheppey though, and doubtless his son Thomas knew Shurland Hall quite well. Baron John's title died with him, but Thomas took possession of Shurland Hall and the Sheppey lands, in addition to which he inherited property at Patrixbourne, and he also owned Chilham Castle. Sir Thomas was in good favour with Henry VII, and when Henry VIII succeeded to the throne he rose rapidly at court.

Many histories have criticised Sir Thomas Cheyne, comparing him to the Vicar of Bray, and referring to 'his plasticity of character', for he survived 'three difficult reigns', keeping his head, literally, and acquiring land and power to the last. One look at his elaborate tomb tells that he did not lack ostentation, but to survive the erratic and hot-tempered Tudors was a feat in itself, and presumably he felt he had plenty to be proud about. Basically he seems to have been a level-headed officer who refused to become embroiled in court factions or arguments, religous or otherwise. He was flamboyant, but that was a Tudor characteristic. At all times he appears to have been wise with it, and not a little cunning, or he wouldn't have lived so long.

Sir Thomas Cheyney was evidently not happy with Shurland Hall. Although it must have altered since the first of the de Shurlands built the great hall, it was still an old building, with the original hall as the focal point, and over the centuries, rooms, hearths, staircases and chimneys had been added to it. There are houses in Kent now that can be identified as old 'Hall Houses' and although it was a larger building Shurland Hall would have developed on the same plan. Sir Thomas had attended court, he had lived in more prosperous places than Sheppey and he required a more up-to-date residence. So he demolished Shurland Hall, the old home of Baron Robert de Shurland his ancestor, and between 1510 and 1518 built a new and splendid mansion on the site. Amongst other things he used material from Chilham Castle, removing most of the building and leaving only the keep. As a note of interest, the keep of Chilham Castle, now converted into a 'desirable residence' was advertised for sale in one of the London papers this summer,

1981. In the accompanying write-up, it was explained that the rest of the castle had been removed by Sir Thomas Cheyney to rebuild his mansion in Sheppey, but the keep had proved too strong for him to demolish so he left it! There is a local story that he rebuilt Shurland Hall with material taken from the priory, but this cannot be so, as the dissolution of the monasteries had not yet begun.

The new hall was described as a 'stately residence', 'a manor comparable to that of any gentleman in Kent', and other grand things. Certainly Sir Thomas spared neither trouble nor expense. There is a plan of the hall extant showing it to be a mansion that lacked nothing. There were twelve walled quadrangles, and half of them were occupied by the mansion itself. The remainder were used for domestic offices, stables, gardens, kennels, a mews, and a well house. In the centre was the great gate house, built of red brick and battlemented. There is a suggestion of Hampton Court in its appearance. Sir Thomas probably studied the current trend of architecture, before he undertook the actual building work.

The Great Hall was situated on the opposite side of the first big quadrangle, and ran parallel to the gate house. Behind this were two smaller courts, and beyond them three small courtyards. In the corner of the furthermost stood the private chapel. Flanking these principal courtyards were other large walled courts. The one on the left is clearly a huge stable block. The rest contained stores, kitchens, offices, and anything else necessary to the running of a large, isolated manor.

Sir Thomas's lands in Sheppey were extensive, and the manor park was impaled. Once the park was enclosed, all wild life there, including deer, would be strictly preserved and kept for the lord's pleasure. On his marshes, Sir Thomas kept great flocks of sheep. They were a paying proposition, for in 1527 he obtained the royal licence to export, out of England, five hundred sacks of wool 'grown in the Isle of Sheppey'.

By 1520 he had been appointed as one of the six Gentlemen of the Privy Chamber. This meant that Sir Thomas had to spend most of his time in personal attendance on the king. The Gentlemen-in-Waiting spent their nights on a palette inside the chamber, and were warned not to be curious, or gossip about anything they saw, but to keep all things secret. If these orders were disregarded, they would incur the king's displeasure. Sir Thomas rose to be a Privy Councillor, and in 1539 was made Treasurer of the Royal Household and Knight of the Garter, Warden of the Cinque Ports, Constable of Queenborough Castle and Lord Lieutenant of Kent. It was an awe-inspiring list of honours, and as they say in Sheppey 'he never put a foot wrong', though he came very near to doing so at times.

There are differing opinions about his rise to power. One historian says that he was a favourite of the great Wolsey. Another says that Anne Boleyn interceded for him when Wolsey drove him from court. There may be truth in both. Wolsey fell from grace, and by that time Anne Boleyn was, in the king's eyes, queen. The Boleyn family were related to the Cheyneys by marriage, so perhaps that prevented Sir Thomas from sharing Wolsey's fate.

With so much important work to attend to Sir Thomas must have spent much of his time in London, but he was greatly attached to his new-built mansion in Sheppey, and came home whenever he had the chance. He must have seemed a very great man to the islanders, and, what was more important, a very rich one, capable of providing employment and a measure of security in an area that was not over-endowed with wealth. Never had a mansion such as he had built ever been seen in Sheppey before, nor was there another to compare with it for many miles around. He employed at least one hundred and sixty serving men, and in addition his tenant farmers and their men were part of the estate. Some of them were directly in his service, for the home farm had to be run. When he was at home, with his retinue of gentlemen, retainers, and personal servants it has been estimated that there were at least three hundred attendants at the Hall.

It was a really eventful day for the island when Henry VIII visited Sir Thomas at Shurland Hall in October 1532. He was on his way to meet the French King, Francis I, and he brought with him Anne Boleyn, who had recently been created Marchioness of Pembroke, Anne was related to Sir Thomas by marriage, not by blood, but the connection was there, and she was apparently interested enough to wish to see his fine new mansion.

The local version of this visit is that 'King Henry VIII and Anne Boleyn came to Shurland Hall for their honeymoon', and nothing will shake this belief. If they did, it was an unofficial honeymoon, for the king was fighting hard to get a divorce from Queen Katherine at the time, but even so, there could be a grain of truth in the story!

Theoretically, the kings of France and England were meeting to finalise a treaty, regarding the expulsion of the Turks from Europe. Private dispatches to the Emperor Charles V told that Imperial Majesty that King Henry was thinking more about his divorce than the Turks. The dispatches also said that the Lady Anne Boleyn had done much to bring about the meeting between the kings, and would be accompanying King Henry.

Anne Boleyn was happily employed in ordering for herself the most magnificent wardrobe, and the king supplied her with jewels to match it, including poor Queen Katherine's personal gems. Lady Anne's dresses were commented upon at court, so the effect they had on the unsophisticated islanders must have been remarkable.

The journey from London was scheduled to start on October 4th. Plague had broken out in the city, and as the king wished to avoid Rochester and any other towns where people might be dying of the plague, he was to go from Greenwich to Gravesend by water. There he was to board the *Minion*, and 'sail to an Isle in the Thames where he will feast for three days at the house of a gentleman called Cheyney'. From there he was to go by land to Canterbury and Dover, and cross the sea in the *Minion*.

Those were the arrangements as announced, but for some reason the royal plans were changed, and the journey did not start until October 7th, which meant a shorter visit to Shurland Hall. The king left Greenwich in the royal barge, with another vessel in attendance. It may have been the *Minion*, but it was in the *Swallow* that the king crossed from Dover to Calais.

King Henry, Anne Boleyn and an untold number of attendants arrived at Shurland Hall late in the afternoon of October 7th. One theory is that he landed 'somewhere near Shurland', which could be one of several places where there are no cliffs and a boat could put in to shore. Another version is that he landed at Queenborough, and took stock of the Castle and defences before he made his way to Shurland. There is no proof either way.

The following day was devoted to entertaining the king and his lady. They spent their day enjoying all the sport available in Shurland Park. There are no particulars recorded, so it is only possible to surmise that hunting the deer and hawking would have been prominent in the day's programme. The king was fond of coursing, betting on the result (and losing frequently), so perhaps coursing matches were arranged. Sir Thomas spared nothing to entertain his king nobly, it is said that the visit cost him dearly, and Henry seemed pleased enough, he left 'for the Keeper of Mr. Cheyney's park' seven shilling and sixpence, which was worth far more than it is now. Sir Thomas summoned every man and woman on his estate as attendants for this visit, and probably had at least four hundred people busily employed.

Men-of-War afloat and in dock at Sheerness.

Navy ships at anchor off Garrison Point.

SHEERNESS DOCKYARD, LOOKING UP THE MEDWAY.

The entrance to the dockyard with steam vessels much in evidence.

Hasted's late eighteenth century map of Sheppey when Sheerness was hardly as big as Minster.

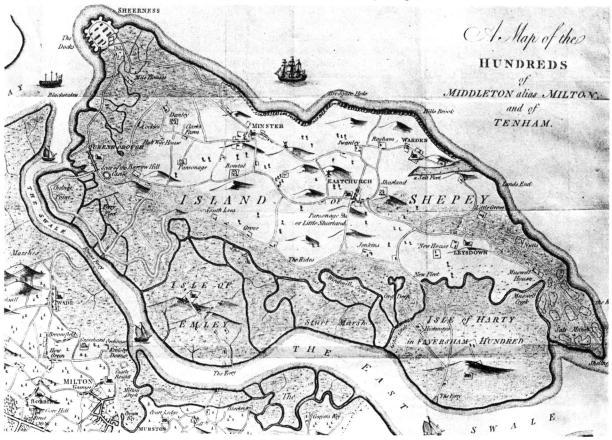

A picturesque view of Minster Abbey, from an old print.

The waterfront at Sheerness, a hive of activity.

The Eastern end of Minster Abbey today.

The Abbey Gatehouse, now carefully restored, and used as a Local History Centre.

Together with the king's retinue, there was a large enough gathering to strain the resources of even this grand new mansion.

When he left Shurland the king gave £6 13s. 4d. as a gratuity for the servants. Considering their number it does not sound much, but money was worth far more then. On October 9th, as far as can be estimated, the king and Anne Boleyn left Shurland Hall and rode across the island to Tremhethe Ferry. It must have been a glittering cavalcade of royalty, nobles, and attendants who jingled across the island on their gaily caparisoned horses, and it is a certainty that the islanders lined their route to gaze open-mouthed, and to wave and cheer. Despite his shortcomings, the king was popular. Never had there been such a sight on the island, and who would ever have believed that Good King Hal himself would visit Sheppey, certainly no one watching him ride by on that memorable day.

That brief period, the first twenty-odd years of Henry VIII's reign, must have been the greatest, and even the best time in the island's history, before or since. For just a little while Sheppey had everything, or at an rate, everything it needed and valued in an uncertain age. The priory was there, not very well staffed perhaps, but it owned a farm that gave work to local people, and nuns were there to help if anyone was sick, or in need. There was the castle at Queenborough, and although the Queenborough folk kept themselves apart because they were a borough, they were still fishermen, no different from other island men, and with the beacons Sheppey was well defended against invasion by sea, or so the people thought. Best of all, there was the great new mansion, Shurland Hall, making the island important, providing work for many, and bringing news from London, strange stories, and in fact a breath of excitement to brighten humdrum lives. However, this satisfactory state of affairs was not to last for long.

In 1536 Henry VIII decided to dissolve the smaller monasteries and priories, and the Sheppey Priory was among these. Sir Thomas Cheyney was one of the commission ordered to value the contents of the priory, and he and his colleagues did the job thoroughly — or so they thought. Prioress, nuns and chaplains were dismissed, the prioress with a small pension, and the priory left empty.

Sir Thomas was high in the king's favour, and he received the abbey and land to hold *in capite* as a gift from the king, and bought the farm stock at the nominal fee of £198. Sir Thomas appears to have performed whatever task he was given without question, and there is never any hint as to what he actually thought. That he had religious beliefs is evident from the fact that he had a small private chapel built at Shurland, but what they were is never disclosed.

As well as the priory lands, Sir Thomas acquired the lands and churches in Leysdown, Eastchurch, Harty and Elmley, which had all belonged to religious houses. As though that was not enough, he was also given lands belonging to Faversham Abbey. Some of this property he sold to Thomas Arden, the Arden of Faversham who was murdered by his wife and her lover, and later immortalised in a play. Thomas Arden appears to have been on friendly terms with Sir Thomas Cheyney, for in the play a visit to Shurland is mentioned (which caused Arden to brave the 'fogs and mists of Sheppey'). Another scene relates how Arden fell in with Sir Thomas and his company and rode from Chatham with them, and two rogues discuss a robbery at Shurland, in which silver plate was stolen.

By this time Sir Thomas had become a very rich man, with a large rent roll. In actual fact he was lord of almost the whole of Sheppey, excluding Queenborough, and later he was to own part of Rushenden marshes, and hold the lease on Dandeley Farm. Bluff King Hal evidently valued his Treasurer of the Royal Household.

To be fair to the king, he is always remembered for having six wives, separating England from the Pope and putting himself at the head of the Church in England, and dissolving monasteries. His private life apart, the reformation would have happened anyway, the religious houses were very lax and many of the people were tired of Church rule and ready for a change.

Henry VIII was not a bad statesman, he kept the peace with no regular army, he built great ships and laid the foundations of the navy, and, as far as Sheppey was concerned, he was a king to be grateful to. He refortified Queenborough Castle, of which Sir Thomas was constable for much of the time, and he installed the first garrison at Sheerness. This was a small gun battery on the point at Sheerness, which has been known ever since as Garrison Point, and it came into being long before the dockyard was even thought of.

In 1542 King Henry applied to the country for a loan. Sir Thomas was 'Treasurer of the Kinges Majesties mooste Honourable Household' at the time, and with the Lord Archbishop of Canterbury he appointed collectors for Kent. John Norton esq. of Norwood was the collector for the Hundred of Milton; he was related to the Norwoods of Milton. The only contribution from the island was from 'Richard Hayway of Sheppey, yeoman, XI's'. Presumably as chief land-holder Sir Thomas had to make up the difference himself. Much the same thing happened when Edward III sought contributions when his son Edward the Black Prince was knighted. The only contributors listed from Sheppey were the Norwoods and Cheyneys.

Early in his reign Henry VIII had had a taste of war with France, but it did not drag on and the dispute was quickly settled. Now, in later life, he had a sudden urge to reconquer England's former possessions abroad. As he was fighting the Scots at the time it was 1544 before he crossed to Calais, and captured Boulogne. After that the war fizzled out, mainly for lack of money, but not before it had involved Sir Thomas and hurt him badly. Sir Thomas was fighting with the king in France, and with him was his eldest son John. When Boulogne was attacked the army also laid siege to Montreuil, a town twenty miles from Boulogne. It is recorded: The Duke of Norfolk commanded, and with him was Sir Thomas Cheyney, Warden of the Cinque Ports, and his son John, who was about twenty nine or thirty years old'. At this siege, called by the Tudors the siege of Mutterel, John Cheyney was slain.

John was Sir Thomas's son by his first wife Fridwith, who was the daughter and co-heir of Sir Thomas Frowyke, Chief Justice of Common Pleas. There were also three daughters, who married well, and John was married to Margaret Neville, daughter of George, Baron Abergavenny, but there were no children. It is not certain when Fridwith died, the women had scant mention in olden days, but Sir Thomas remarried to Anne, daughter and co-heiress of Sir John Broughton of Toddington, Bedfordshire. She produced a son for Sir Thomas whom they named Henry, perhaps in honour of the king. Anne's father died in 1517, and then her brother died in 1529, so Anne inherited the estate, which was added to Sir Thomas's other riches. However, the death of his eldest son and heir must have been a sad blow to him, and may also have been instrumental in altering the island's history.

King Henry VIII died in 1547, and Sir Thomas by then was a powerful man, rich in lands and money, and with a high position at court. He kept his position throughout the reign of Edward VI and contrived to stay in favour when Queen Mary came to the throne, when he was again made Warden of the Cinque Ports and Treasurer of the Royal Household.

During Henry VIII's reign the beacons had been maintained, and the king had shown a great personal interest in them. A complicated system of beacons on hills and valleys was evolved, with strict instructions as to who was to fire them, and how many were to be fired at once. At times these plans went wrong, and in 1545 the south coast defences were cautioned not to play games. No beacons were to be fired unless at least ten hostile French ships were sighted who meant to land. At one point Sussex called out Kent on a false alarm, which led to much recrimination. Sir Thomas must have been well aware of all this, so perhaps that is why Queen Mary appointed him as Warden of the Cinque Ports once again. She issued no orders about beacons, leaving their management to the officers in charge.

Despite this apparent harmony, it was in Mary's reign that Sir Thomas almost came to grief. Queen Mary was determined to re-establish the Roman Catholic Church in her realm. When she chose to marry the heir to the Spanish throne to help consolidate this plan her advisors and the Commons were not a little worried, and begged her to reconsider, but she refused to listen. The people of England were against the marriage, and did not hide the fact.

Early in 1553–4 Sir Thomas Wyatt of Allington Castle in Kent collected troops and rebelled against the Spanish Philip, making it quite clear that he meant no harm to the Queen, but wished to prevent the marriage. He had many wealthy and noble supporters, among them William Cromer of Tunstall, who also owned Borstal Hall in Sheppey.

As warden of the Cinque Ports and also Constable of Queenborough Castle (although this latter is uncertain, as there are no records of constables between 1512 and 1588) Sir Thomas Cheyney's duty was to the queen. The rebels marched into Rochester, where they were met by the Duke of Norfolk and his men, from London. Evidently the plan was for Sir Thomas to collect his armed retainers and march on Rochester from the Kent approach, where he would be joined by others who had arrived by sea. Had this plan materialised, the rebels would have been caught between the two armed forces and the uprising finished there and then. In the event, the reinforcements did not arrive, the rebels worsted the Duke of Norfolk and then marched on to Cooling Castle, where they captured Lord Cobham. From there they moved on to London, where the rebellion was soon crushed. Sir Thomas Wyatt and William Cromer were tried, Wyatt was beheaded and Cromer was imprisoned for life in the Tower.

Not surprisingly, the queen's supporters wanted to know what Sir Thomas had been about while this was taking place, and the best thing to say is that the accounts were very muddled. Lord Norfolk wrote to Sir Thomas, but complained that he had received no word in reply. Lord Abergavenny, who was supposed to join forces with Sir Thomas at Rochester, found himself 'unable to follow Wyatt up' and advised calling upon the Lord Warden, Sir Thomas Cheyney, from whom he had not heard.

Sir Thomas protested to the Privy Council that he had sent several letters to the queen and received no answers. He devoutly prayed that no harm would come to her majesty, and remarked on the wickedness of the rebels. He adds that the treason of those 'whiche came with my Lord Norfolk' had turned his serving men against him, and they had all run away. As Lord Norfolk and his men were supporters of the queen, their 'treason' comes as a surprise, and Sir Thomas's letter shows much ambiguity.

He received an answer to this letter, and apparently sent copies of the Proclamation that arrived with it to Dover and other towns, as ordered, but still he did not appear at the trouble spots, his excuse this time being that he had no men

he could trust to follow him, he had been forced to leave the best part of his horses, 'on the waterside, at the coming out of the Isle of Sheppey'. He did, in fact, arrive at Rochester too late to be of any use, and then followed the rebels to London, where the insurrection ended. There is always doubt about all this, for the rebels were his friends in Kent, and it is probable that in secret he sympathised with them. At the same time, he was not a man to risk his name and his neck by joining them. They were not a safe enough bet.

Sir Robert Southwall, the Sheriff of Kent, helped to suppress the rebellion, and a deposition made afterwards by Anthony Norton throws much light on Sir Thomas's activities.

Anthony was called to Allington Castle by Mr. Wyatt 'ye Monday before ye trowball (trouble) began'. Anthony thought that they might get help from the queen's ships, and Wyatt was asked if they (the rebels) could not send men to Sheppey, where they might get horses and 'other necessities for wars'.

Wyatt answered thus: 'that ye house of my Lord Warden have much coin and treasure, at the syte whereof ye men would not abstayne their hands from robbery, whych he would not have committed'. He then continued: 'When my Lord shall come down to take up men, he shall perseve ye half of his own men to be against him, whych when he perceiveth he will undoubtedly kepe his land and not stir'.

This sounds as though a previous arrangement between friends had been made, for Wyatt appeared certain that Sir Thomas Cheyney would not interfere in the rebellion, even if he refused to join it. As always, Sir Thomas remained neutral. However, he still had to explain his lack of action to the queen and Privy Council, as it looked remarkably like disloyalty, and that could have cost him his life. Sir Thomas's defence was that his neighbour, William Cromer, had intercepted letters from the queen and Privy Council, thereby keeping him in the dark as to what was happening, and preventing their orders from reaching him.

It was evident that his story was believed, and indeed it may have had some truth in it, as when Cromer was imprisoned his estates were confiscated, and Sir Thomas received the Manor of Borstal from Queen Mary. He survived the rest of her reign uneventfully, and when Queen Elizabeth I came to the throne he kept his post as Treasurer of the Household, and was given a place in the Privy Council once again. This was the fifth monarch he had served, and he must have been possessed of a pronounced strength of character, and perhaps, personal charm, to be able to hold his own so capably.

Sir Thomas died in the first year of Elizabeth's reign, in the Tower, where he had living quarters when he was in London. Presumably he could have been buried anywhere he chose, for he was a powerful man, but his will was decisive. 'My tomb to be made nigh to the place where my late wife Frydeswith do lie in my Chapel at Minster'.

So in death he was honest, and chose the island he loved and a burial place in the abbey near his first wife, in 'his' chapel. He had a magnificent funeral, and a wonderfully emblazoned tomb. From his effigy he appears as a short, dapper man, in full court dress and wearing the insignia of the Garter, not at all like his lanky, armoured ancestor, Sir Robert de Shurland. His second wife outlived him by two years, and he was succeeded by his younger son, Sir Henry Cheyney, known as 'the extravagant Lord Cheyney'.

For the first time in centuries Sheppey was to know what a bad lord of the manor was like.

CHAPTER XI
The great Reformation

To obtain his divorce from Queen Katherine Henry VIII had flouted the Roman Catholic Church, and placed himself at the head of a newly established Church of England. To do this had been very expensive, and cost Wolsey his place in the king's favour, where he was replaced by Thomas Cromwell. Cromwell had provided the force and the arguments that brought about Henry's supremacy. He had also reorganised the system of government, bringing it up to date, to suit the times.

All this cost money, and the king needed little encouragement from his minister Cromwell to dissolve the monasteries and take their riches for himself. His position as head of the Church was ambiguous. He was definitely no reformist, preferring the old religion, and sensing that his subjects felt the same way, but the Church had to be run as he wished. The Archbishop of Winchester, Stephen Gardiner, was one of the king's chief advisers on Church matters, as he was not so inclined to Puritanism as Cranmer and Latimer. Another strong reason for the dissolution was the king's not unfounded suspicion that if the monasteries survived they would become the breeding ground for Roman Catholic discontent and scheming, thereby creating disaffection and trouble amongst the people. The king felt his way warily, starting with the lesser monasteries whose income was under £200 yearly. His task was made easier by the fact that some smaller foundations had declined and were now abandoned, and so automatically reverted to the crown.

The net value of the Priory of Saints Mary and Sexburga was said to be £129 7s. 10½d. annually, besides £10 for a marsh in dispute between them and Sir Thomas Cheyney. This must be recognised as a very rough estimate. Figures had to be manœuvred to suit the occasion.

Certainly the list of lands and possessions so carefully recorded seems worth far more.

It was detailed as follows:

The Monastery of Saint Sexburg in the Isle of Sheppey 27–28 year of King Henry VIII

Upbury, Manor of
Rector of Upbury, alias Gillingham.
   Rents in.
Pystock, Manor of
Perquisites of Courts.
Le Mynster, Lordship of.
Rents of Leysdown, Redmore, Mynster, Crekyndenn, Wardenn, Eastchurch, Copydenn, Spynbroke, Hotchekyns, Napletoun, Westfelde, Wattoun, Horsmanfeld, Barton Hyll, Le Verywall End, Rysshenden, Danley Marsh juxta South Cliffe, Watermyll, Insula de la Grayne, Beggarsthorne in Sydyngbourne Parish, Newyngtown, Bobbing, Courtfields, Boresdenn, Ossenden, Deanes Hyll, Warren Mayle, Watergore, Sowthe Clyffe, Katenden, and Longcrosse and several weirs in the sea. (gurgite in mare).
Perquisites of Courts.
Swall and Talnashe.
Farm of Reade with the appurtenances.
Mynster
Windmill in the Manor of.
Caunt (Canterbury)
Tenements in Estbridge in the City of Kylburne, Grene etc.
Kylburne for certain lands there.*

Rents in Grene, Bobbyng, Newington and Sydingbourne†
Minster Lordship
Bobbing, Rectory of.
   Salt Marshes called Grymborow and Walathorpe.
   Minster. Demesne Lands.
   Rectory of.

* No account rendered because suppressed.
† Accounted for in account and folio.

It was an imposing list for a small priory.

Very few people realise that Minster Abbey once had jurisdiction over the vicarages and churches of Gillingham and Bobbing, and collected rents from Newington and the Isle of Grain.

The list of rents in Minster is formidable, and many of the places named are now unheard of and cannot be traced. Some can be guessed at — Crekyndeun might be the area around Windmill Creek, and Horsmanfield was still the name of a marsh on the tithe map of 1848. Others are still in existence. Until recently Napleton was one of the areas of marsh in Harty, and Ossenden was one of the boroughs mentioned in the Rolls of the Ferry Court. Le Verywall End might well be Wallsend Farm, which is set back from the Lower Road at Cowstead Corner, and is still being farmed today. No-one has heard of a water mill on the island, but on a survey map drawn in Elizabeth I's reign a water mill is shown on Windmill Creek. By the eighteenth century there was a windmill there. The windmill, 'in the Manor of Minster', was on Windmill Hill, just outside Minster village. By the eighteenth century there were two windmills, one known as the New Mill. There are no mills there now, only a housing estate. All the monastery lands on the island were acquired by Sir Thomas Cheyney, which swelled his income considerably.

On March 27th, in the twenty-seventh year of King Henry VIII 1536, the Commissioners were sent to take an inventory of the contents of the church and priory. They did this thoroughly, omitting nothing, and a complete list here would be tedious. The treasures found in this 'less wealthy' monastery are surprising, and warrant mentioning, for the tales of the Abbey Treasure have never been forgotten, and legends about it continue even now.

The Commissioners were Sir Thomas Cheyney and Sir William Hawle, Knights, and Anthony Sent Leger esq. (Saint Leger). They started their inventory in the church, and there is a long list of pyxes, silver and gilt, of different designs, silver and gilt crosses and crucifixes, chalices, sensors, altar basins, and servers, all made of silver and gilt. The 'High Aulter' had three embroidered altar cloths, with red and blue crosses for Lent. A painted cloth of the resurrection 'to hang afore the Rood'. Altars were large stone blocks, but they were covered with costly hangings, and 'fronts' were made for them. The altar in the abbey had a vast supply of cloths, curtains, and fronts made of timber gilt.

'Pendants' for the altar are listed, some embroidered with arms. There were thirteen candlesticks in the 'quiyer, for wax great and small' (candles), and a great desk with an eagle of timber, gilted, and a great cloth of linen 'to draw athwart the quyer in Lent'. In the 'Nether part of the Quyer' there were more altar cloths and painted cloths, and one of damask work. Six images great and small of timber, gilt, and one image of Our Lady in alabaster.

43

Candlesticks, more cloths, a desk with a cloth painted with the image of Our Lady, and the list continues with a shrine (un-named) more cloths and altar fronts, 'one of green satin embroidered in gold a foot broad'. The contents of the shrine were listed separately, and provide a glimpse at the beliefs and customs of the times. 'In said shrine 1 little coffer of timber-gilt, and another little shrine of timber gilt full of old relics in purses of silk, one little plain coffer of wirye (wire) with lyke relics, a box of bone with relics, an old sleeve of saint Sexburg with eight pieces of silver therein.' Those were the relics the pilgrims journeyed to see, and they were all scooped up in the net of the dissolution. There were many more hangings listed, and the sides of the 'quyer' were lined their whole length with hangings emblazoned with the arms of the Norwood family. There were numerous books with silver clasps, and one cloth was described as 'verders with white rosys'.

In 'the Vestrye' they found an old pax of timber silver-covered and set with old stones, and many more altar cloths and hangings, made of 'blew velvet', red silk, and other rich materials. Copes and vestments were also luxurious, one being of red taffeta. There were eight more books, including 'one good Mass book, in parchment'.

Saint Katherine's Chapel contained relatively little, but the altar of St. Katherine had a 'front' of alabaster, and the two rood cloths were of crimson velvet and red silk. Our Lady Chapel was overfull in comparison with St. Katherine's. Two altar 'fronts' of painted timber, and cloths, curtains, coverlets for the altar, carpets of tapestry, and other tapestry work 'making twentytwo'. Even the commissioners seem to have thought this an unnecessarily large number. *Fleurs-de-lis* were embroidered in gold, 'carpet cushions' some in red silk, and once again the Norwood arms, this time worked in tapestry and used as kneeling stools, described as 'iiiy old tapestry cloths'.

Again there were innumerable vestments of all colours, some made in silk, velvet, and 'Bruges' which was a rich tissue. Then, strangely, a 'coffer of stuff belonging to Saint Johns Chapel in the Churchyard, the coffer in Our Lady's Chapel'. This sounds as though St. John's Chapel was no longer in use, and by that time perhaps it was in ruins, as although it was mentioned in 1488, there are few other references to it.

The list of hangings, some painted with the life of St. John, altar cloths, vestments and yet more hangings, is interminable. There were 'ij old myters for Saint Nicholas', and this may refer to the old custom of crowning 'a Boy Bishop', chosen from the choristers, who held office until Holy Innocents Day. Then comes an amazing reliquary, a half arm and hand of wood covered in silver. To whom the hand belonged was not specified. A sad note follows, 'a box of books, no value'. The commissioners were men of action, not scholars.

The body (nave) of the church contained more alabaster and painted fronts, nine alabaster images, fifteen great images painted and three small, and again, yet more cloths and hangings.

In the chamber in the dorter were even greater treasures. Starting with still more cloths and 'houselling towels', the list moves on to 'a prayer book in a white handerchief'. A Cross cloth in colour with the image of St. Sexburg, a pyx of silver gilt with stones, containing relics, several more pyxes, one containing a relic of St. Thomas of Canterbury, and one made of horn, four small crosses of silver gilt with stones, and a 'bone of Saint Blase sett in silver gylt'. Coffers of ivory, eleven brooches of silver gilt set with relics, tables, one of ivory, finely wrought, and more hangings, cloths and vestments, embroidered and some 'set with stones'.

It is a bewildering list of treasures, some of great value, some of great beauty, and they all vanished, leaving no trace.

It is small wonder the king regarded the monasteries with envy. If this was the treasure of a small priory, the bigger houses must have supplied wealth untold.

The commissioners missed nothing. Once finished with the church, they started on the priory, and the nuns had to account for all their belongings, some of which seem quite out of place in a nunnery. The nuns' explanation was that 'it was stuff given by friends'.

As all the chambers were much the same, a description of one should give a fair idea of the contents of them all, and show the life of comparative comfort and luxury these ladies enjoyed.

Dame Agnes Brown's Chamber; 'Stuff given by friends'. 'A featherbed, a bolster, ij pillows, a pair of blankets, ij corse coverlets, iiij pair of sheets good and bad, an old tester and selar of painted cloths, pieces of hanging to same, a square coffer covered with bad cloths on it, in the window a cubbord carved and ij little chests, a goblet with cover of silver parcel gylt, a littel maser (cup of maple) a goblet with silver brim, piece and spoon of silver, candlesticks, fire pan and tongs, dishes, porringers, basins, skyllots, a brass pot, a cawdyron, and a pewter drinking pot.' (ij is two, iij is three, etc.)

So there it is, much as the commissioners described it at the time. All the comfort possible, and a collection of bits and pieces such as any well-to-do spinster might have in her apartment. What the nuns thought and felt when they knew the commissioners were coming can only be imagined. Fear, apprehension and sheer disbelief must have been uppermost in their minds, for nothing had disturbed the tenor of their lives so greatly before. The priory was their world, they knew no other.

The rest of the chambers were much the same, only details varied, but in Dame Margaret —ocks (the name is part missing) there was 'a chamber hanging of painted papers'. That may seem of little consequence, but it is the earliest known reference to wall-paper in England, and papering a room. It is unfortunate that no-one knows more about it, whether Dame Margaret thought it out herself, or where she copied the idea from, but there it is — the first papered room known was in Sheppey. Dame Dorothy Toplove was no different from her companions, apart from 'a casket covered in leather', while Dame Anne Loveden had collected 'corse coverlets belonging to Saint John's Chapel', which sounds as though the chapel had gone by then.

Dame Elizabeth Stradlynge owned some painted hangings, and had a liking for 'a lyttel silk cushyn'. Dame Anne Clifford was not so well off: she had 'some bad sheets and an old coverlet of tapestry broken' but she appears through the years as the only nun with any personal religious feeling, as she had in her chamber a table with a painted wooden crucifix, and an image of Our Lady.

Dame Margaret Ryvers was a past abbess, but her chamber was little different from the others. Dame Ursula Gosborne, Suppnor, also had a table with a crucifix.

That was the full complement of nuns, respectable single ladies living comfortably, rather lacking in the objects of religion one would expect to find in their 'chambers', and due for a nasty shock when the Commission had finished with them.

The remaining rooms in the priory are also carefully listed.

The Frater. Apart from a silver maser with a silver-gilt brim, and silver spoons (one broken) there was little of value. 'Old platters, dishes, porringers, candlesticks, tongs, chafer, a little spit, 'borde cloths, cushyns, and a lyttle Fraterbed'. Beds appear everywhere, nearly every living-room had a bed in it.

The Hall. Four dormant tables (a fixed table at the end of the hall), then a list of trestles, forms, a long table and a high desk, hangings, naturally, a leather chair and other items of furniture.

Then, strangely, a great draw net, and 'ij great powletery baskets' (fowl coops) and a hook of iron. A hen coop in the hall of a priory seems distinctly out of place, but presumably they had their reasons for it.

The Parlour. This room contained several tables and chairs, carpets, cushions, a desk to write on, 'a table of Epiphany in old colour', a little clock (which is unusual, not many people owned clocks), a book of Saints Lives and several cupboards, with locks. Some of the chairs are described as 'turned chairs', and one table is a counter table, used for accounting, often supplied with the counters used for reckoning.

The Second Parlour. Curtains, cupboards, hangings galore, a 'trussynge bed' (truckle bed), a leather chair and a feather bed.

The Botre within the Parlour. A cupboard, chafing dishes, platters and such like things.

My Lady Prior's Chamber, Alicia Crane. This was hung with green sage, and had a trussing bed and a feather bed, with all the hangings and bed linen. There were the usual cupboards and basins, 'towells and napkyns, a ewer of silver', and a goodly collection of chalices, goblets, Apostle spoons (silver), masers 'great and less, with roses in the bottom', and four pairs of coral beads (rosaries). Dame Alicia Crane had collected more of value than her nuns.

Chamber within My Ladys Chamber, called Styling Chamber (Still Room). This was fitted with frames, had the usual cupboards and cloths, an oak chest, and a feather bed.

The Maydens Chamber. This was furnished with two beds and bolsters, coverlets (old) chests and a broken cushion. The chests are interesting. One is described as a carved chest 'with old evidences', the other, a 'shyp chest'. It might be possible that the famous carved chest at Harty came from the priory, but there is no way of knowing.

Great Bath. Basons, ewers, pewter pots, and old pewter salt, chests, hogges heads, a leather pot, a wood tankard, and a great butter knife. 'A lyttel Bell.' Anything but a bath.

The Nether Kitchen. This is a fine example of a Tudor kitchen, and was as well furnished as any to be found at that time. Brass pots, all sizes, poss-nets with long brass handles, a great brass chafer, hanging brass kettle, 'ij great punnes', 'ij mean pannes', a lesser pan, a good dripping pan, four great spits, two bird spits, brass mortar and iron pestle, 'nineteen great hogges in the roof (bacon) twelve cople ling, five cople of haberden (fish for table) besides salmon, eels and herring (not a full barrel) and two cades of red herring (6d a cade)'.

The list finishes with trivetts, pot hooks, pot hangers, three cobyrons for spits to go in, and the grid irons and tongs used then.

'Upper Kechyn.' Two great pots standing in lead to boil beef in. Then a list of plates, dishes, porringers, saucers, a ladle, mortars of stone, big and small, a frying pan, a long trivet to set (sethe) fish on, a good bucket to the well and a short chain of iron.

The chamber over the gate house called the Confessors Chamber. The origin of this name is unknown. It is a large room and was more likely used as a guest house by the priory. This had a good feather bed and a low bed, with blankets and bolsters, the usual hangings and curtains and a 'cressar of iron' for the 'chymneye'.

The chamber next to that. A feather bed, with bolster and 'image' coverlet.

The steward's Chamber. This was as the others, with two beds and with blankets etc., and a square carved chest of oak.

The next chamber the same. A sparvar of dornax, all broken.

The chamber under the same. Bed, bedding, and hangings of painted cloth.

The 'Portars Lodge'. Bed and bedding, an old coverlet broken.

Store house by the Chese House. By guess, ten cloths.

Chese House. By guess, VIIIc paving tyle.

The 'Vycars Chamber'. Feather bed and bedding, a 'covering of corse imagery'.

The chamber next the same. A mattress (no feathers) bolster and coverlet.

The chamber at 'Preston Hawle'. Which part of the priory was called 'Preston Hawle' is a complete mystery. It contained little beside feather beds and bedding, and that not in very good condition.

The Lade Chamber. Three flock beds and bolsters, coverings, and in the Rotten Row, more bedding. Rotten Row is another puzzle. In some cathedrals there was a 'Ratten Row' where inferior members lived. In Hyde Park the ride known as Rotten Row once belonged to Westminster Abbey ground. It is an ecclesiastical designation, so far not explained.

The Bakehouse. 'A horse mill with one pair of stones and other apparell to the same, a great cistern of lead to water malt, a great hogges trough, and two old hoggesheads.'

The Brew House. Apart from two new coopers for the brewing of 'vior', and seven quarters of malt, there seemed little but several large pieces of lead, and the use of these is not clear. There were three small 'tubbys' and a new 'oste-cloth' (oast, hops), so the nuns or their maltster, knew about the use of hops in brewing.

The Bultynge House. A moulding board, kneading troughs, 'bowtinge Wyches' (sifting chests) meal tubs, etc. Everything needed to sift flour and make bread.

The 'Mylke House'. A pan set in stone work, and 'other great pans', a tryvett, cheese presses and board for same, shelves round about a half tub, eight cheese moots (? moots = fats), many bowls 'great and small' and milk sieves.

This is followed by an inventory of grain 'in the garners'. Malt, barley, wheat, oats, some threshed and some unthreshed, all are carefully measured and recorded. Tares for horse-meat, and the number of acres sown with different grain, seed, and beans, and what is left fallow. The amount of hay stored and stacked is also estimated. The commissioners were more at home with the farm inventory; it is stated far more concisely and with undoubted authority.

'Catell belonging to the same House.' This started with the oxen, 'contre oxen and western oxen' are mentioned 'Whereof IIIJ contre oxen sold for VIIIJ£ xs. and thereof 1s payed, the rest to pay, the sayd oxen not yet delivered.'

Then the contre oxen, workers, on to steers, kine and heifers. There was a large herd of cows, of which ten had been sold 'for XIIjs IIIJd a pece, and not delyvered, whether the money he payd or not is unknown'. This year's cattle are counted, then the horses described: 'an horse: one old bay, a dun, a white and an ambling grey, six geldings, and horse for the plough and harrow, with five mares'. This seems a big string of horses, but they were the only transport available, and horses had to be provided for the hobiliers if they were required. The average riding horse was small, today it would be classed as a pony, and the priory had plenty of grazing and food for their stock. There was a large number of 'hogges and divers sorts', then 'wethers, ewes, twelve monthyngs and lambys of this yere'. There followed a complete inventory of a really huge flock of sheep; and their estimated worth.

The farm stock finishes with 'Plowes, waynes, and other stuff of husbandry'. Farm equipment was simple then, and the list is of ploughs, harrows and carts, and whether the carts had 'shod' or bare wheels.

'The Belfree.' One bell standing there on the ground belonging to the priory. The tower never did get built.

Names of servants now in wages. This again is a long list, and extracts will suffice. They are of interest because they show the rate of pay, and the number of different ways in which payment was made.

'Mr. Oglestone', taking wages by the year. There is no explanation as to who he was, or what he did.

'Mr. White, taking XXXVI's IIIJd. by the year', and 'Lyvere' (livery).

'John Coks, butler, livery XXXVIs VIIJd, whereof to pay one quarter and livery.'

'Alyn Sowthe, bayley, taking by year for Closure (clothes) and his servant £VJ x IIIS IIIJd and two liveries.'

'John Musterde by yere XXs, "Kowes pasture" and livery.' It is interesting to note that there is a farm called 'Mustards' at Leysdown now.

'William Rowet, carpenter, by year XLs and livery.'

'The Carter (no name) by year XXXIIJs and no livery.'

'Robard Welshe, brewer, by year XXs and no livery.'

'A Thatcher, by year XXXIIJs IIIJd, a horse cloth and no livery.'

'Jhon Putsawe, by year XIIJs IIIJd and a shirt ready made.'

'Jhon Hurryes, Frenchman, by year XXXIIJs IIIJd a shirt and no livery.'

'Jhon Giles shepherd, by year XIIIJs a pair of hoses, a "payre of shoys" (shoes) and no livery.'

'Ales Barker by yere XIIIs IIIJd and livery.' There were seven women employed on those terms.

'Sir Jhon Lorymer, Curate of the Parish Church, by year III£ XIVs VIIIJd and no livery.'

'Sir Jhon Ingram, Chaplain, by year IIJ£ IIJs IIJd, no livery.'

'Jhon Marchant, by year XIIJs IIIJd a pasture for XL sheep and no livery.'

'Jhon Helman, by year XVIs and X sheep pasture, no livery.'

'Sir Thomas Kellow, Chaplain by year III£ IIJs IIIJd no livery.'

How wages, livery (which is board and lodging or keep), and the various privileges were worked out is not known. The parish priest and the chaplains were not as well paid as the bailiff, which may explain why Sir Jhon Lorymer felt impelled to turn informer, or perhaps he had an eye to the future and wanted to stand well with the right people, but inform he did.

'Sir Jhon Lorymer, Parish Priest, sayeth that upon Ascensyon day last past, there was sett upon the High Altar of the sayde Monasterye VIJ chaleses, whereof is lacking IIJ at the day of takying the Inventorye, also he sayeth that upon Relyke Sunday there were worren (worn) VIJ copes, whereof one of blew velvet bordered with sterrys (stars) of gold, whycht is lacking, and not mencyoned before. Item, he sayeth that the same day was borne the head of Mary Magdalen, sylver and gilt which is lacking, and not hereto before mencyoned. Item. There is fownede, syns the day of the Inventorye, a playne piece of silver with a cover, the top thereof gilt, and a dozen of silver spoons with myters, the myters being gylt.'

So there was the inventory, meticulously recorded, but even so some treasures went missing, and no-one ever said if they were found or not. It would have been easy for someone to hide them, perhaps for personal gain in the future, and Sir Jhon Lorymer sounds rather unctuous in his denunciation. Perhaps he suspected someone, and wanted to be sure that he would not be accused.

Whatever happened to the treasure, the story is still very much alive in Minster today, and local people talk about the Abbey Treasure and regard it as a real hoard, hidden away somewhere, that someone will be lucky enough to find one day. The tale has been handed down since the time of the dissolution. They are equally sure that it might be in one of those tunnels that many of them believe in, but which have never, as yet, been found.

After the inventory, everything of value was removed, and the priory was closed. It is said that the records and books kept by the abbesses and nuns were destroyed. Certainly there is no record of the day-to-day running of the priory, or any notes on current affairs that abesses through the years might have kept. Even the list of past abbesses is far from complete.

As far as is known, they were:

Abbesses
  Saint Sexburg 670–675 A.D.
  Erminhilda 675–699 A.D.
Prioresses
  Agnes 1186
  – de Burghersh 1343 (Sister of Bartholomew de Burghessh)
  Joan de Cobham 1368
  Isabel de Honyngton elected 1368
  Joan Cobham 1446
from another source,
  Constance Septvans late 15 cent.
  Agnes Ryvers or Rivers 1504–11
  Alice Crammer or Crane, there at the dissolution.
Obit list of Prioresses
  Joan de Badlesmere died 2nd March (No years given)
  Eustachia died 12th May
  Agnes died 4th October
  Christina died 13th October
  Gunnora died 11th December

Dim figures from the past, of whom little is known.

The prioress in office when the inventory was taken was Alicia Crane; she was dismissed with a pension of £14 yearly, and the nuns had to fend for themselves. After such a sheltered life it must have been difficult and frightening for them. It is hoped that they were allowed to keep some of their personal belongings, but their fate is uncertain. It is said that England had a roving population of impoverished monks and nuns for many years.

Sir Thomas Cheyney acquired priory, land and farm stock all for £198. It is most likely that he kept the farm-workers on — the farm had to be run.

The church remained as the parish church, but without the images, hangings and other valuable objects. The priory vanished, it was removed and the stone used for other buildings, and nothing of it was left except the gate house, which is still there today. Saint John's Chapel disappeared altogether.

There is a saying in Minster that one can find stones from the priory in all sorts of odd places on local sites. This was illustrated recently when a lady found an unusual piece of masonry propping up part of the garage on the property she had bought. She could not identify it, and luckily, before she threw it over the cliffs (where many things go in Sheppey), one of the island's rectors saw it and recognised it as a Holy Water stoup. It is now safely in his church. It is very old, and the priory seems the most obvious place of origin.

How the people reacted to all this no-one bothered to ask. They had been used to having the priory to turn to when they needed help, and they must have felt the loss of it deeply. Sir Thomas was a good Lord of the Manor, and the farm should not have suffered, but there must have been some unemployment, and the villagers must have felt shocked and bewildered, unable to comprehend what had happened.

The church services altered radically once the Reformation got under way, and that would have seemed a shattering thing to simple people who had been brought up, and lived, with religion ruling their lives.

Although Mass was still said, English prayers were introduced in 1536. The rector had to preach against the 'pretended power of the Pope' every Sunday, for three months. This was followed by the Lord's Prayer, the Creed, and the Ten Commandments in English, which had to be taught to the congregation. The churches were provided with Bibles in English and Latin.

Some of the monks banished from the monasteries took posts as curates, and many of them married. They were drawing pensions of £4 and £5 yearly as 'retired' monks and they took care to retain these, which made them considerably better off than the average vicar or curate.

In 1538 Thomas a Becket's 'saintship' was annulled, which put an end to the Canterbury pilgrimages, and wayside chapels built for the pilgrims fell into disuse, and disappeared. In 1538-9 the king directed that a register book for baptisms, marriages, and deaths must be kept. This has been continued ever since, and the registers in Minster Abbey date from the sixteenth century although the early ones are difficult to decipher.

All churches were ordered to obtain a copy of Archbishop Cranmer's bible, printed in 1539; it was to be set on a desk so that anyone could read it who wished to do so. It is unlikely that many people in Sheppey were able to take advantage of this, as few of them could read at this time. By the time of Henry VIII's death the greater part of the service was in English, monasteries, chapels and chantries were gone, and no masses for the dead were held. Minor holy days were not recognised, and all saints shrines had been destroyed. All this must have left a big gap in many people's lives.

—Edward VI was a determined Protestant, and took his father's reforms even further. He replaced the Mass with the Communion Service, and introduced the Book of Common Prayer. Clergy were allowed to marry, and surplices were worn, instead of the elaborate vestments used formerly. The churches were ordered to remove the stone altars, which were frequently used as paving stones and so desecrated, and replace them with Communion tables. The Bible stories painted on the church walls were covered with white-wash, and texts, the Commandments and the Creed printed clearly in their stead. The defaced, faded picture of St. Nicholas can still be seen in a niche on the eastern wall, behind the high altar, in Minster Abbey. Old wall paintings were found in Harty Church in the last century, but workmen covered them with whitewash. Many of the congregation must have missed the images, the candles, and the colour of earlier services, but it was best to obey.

Edward VI was not satisfied with the closure of chantries, and ordered that particulars of sales of obit and chantry lands should be recorded. The reason for the enquiry was alleged to be the 'need to correct the superstitions and errors about purgatory and masses for the dead that held sway ...'. It was a long-winded explanation, and the lands and money were to be converted 'to good and Godly uses', which included money for the king.

The Act required information about endowments for obits, lights and such matters if used for five years previously. Old traditions were proving hard to eradicate.

A Commission of Knights, Esquires and Gentlemen searched Kent for details, and in Sheppey they discovered that at Harty an obit rent was given to the parish church by the last will and testament of one Thomas Mett, for one yearly obit to be kept in the church for ever. The rent was 10s. yearly, the poor were to have 6d. and that left 9s. 6d. clear. Thomas Mett died in 1512, and ordered that the obit of 10s. be kept with eight priests, each to have for diridge and Mass 9d. and four clerks 6d. each, and in bread and drink 20d.

That certainly would not have pleased King Edward! In Leysdown William Fayer had left three shillings and four pence 'for one yearly obit to be kept for ever'. At Minster Peter Wyse bequeathed obit lands 'for one annual and yearly obit to be kept within the Parish Church of Minster in the Isle of Sheppey forever'.

The yearly value of the land was fourteen pence. If these obits were still being observed yearly, they were soon stopped and the rents appropriated by the king.

During Edward VI's short reign the country became accustomed to the new ceremonies, and then Queen Mary succeeded to the throne and a process of re-conversion started. King Edward died in July 1533, and there was a minor upheaval during which the ill-fated Lady Jane Grey reigned for nine days, to be rejected by the country, who preferred a Tudor on the throne.

This Tudor was not a success. By Christmas of that year an Act decreed that no form of public worship was to be used but what had been used in the last year of Henry VIII. Villages that had become used to hearing a church service in English now found themselves attending Mass again. Married clergy found themselves out of a job, celibacy was once again the rule for priests. Despite her religious zeal Mary was unable to replace the monasteries, or to deprive the new owners of their Church lands.

The public became tired of Mary's enforced re-conversion and her persecution of non-Catholics. The deaths of Bishop Latimer and the old Archbishop Cranmer made her feared and disliked, and she was given the nick-name 'Bloody Mary'. Sir Thomas Cheyney retained his powerful and lucrative posts, but how he managed to avoid the queen's wrath will always be a matter for conjecture.

The queen also found it difficult to alter the internal arrangements of the churches: she could not wave a magic wand and replace the lost images and costly hangings. Saint Paul's regained a great rood in the late summer of 1554, where it remained for five years, and no longer. Sheppey's attitude to all this religious turnabout is shown in the report made by Archbishop Harpsfield after his visitation in 1557.

At Queenborough the archbishop wrote a memorandum. 'They have no font, for as they say they did nevery marry, bury nor christen but at Minster.' Apparently they had no rector or curate either, for none is recorded. The church wardens were Christopherus Robinson and Johannes Noki. Two parishioners' names follow, and then the commands.

There are many commands, and some have 'non' written by them. In short, they were to paint the communion table, make 'fronts', for it, and provide curtains and altar cloths by Christmas. Many other cloths were ordered to be provided and a Holy Water Stocke (stoup). Banners and streamers to be ready by Whitsun week.

There is another memorandum. 'They have no Roode, Mary, nor John, but of painted cloth for they say they never had other. This to be allowed for a time.' Finally, 'ye Church was robbed and they lost two chalices and a pax of silver'.

Obviously Queenborough had not been greatly disturbed about re-conversion.

At Minster the rector, basically the proprietor of the church, was Sir Thomas Cheyney. There was no vicar, and the curate, John Shaife, was shared with Queenborough. The church warden was Thomas Brodestreet, and the parishioners names are interesting, because they occur frequently in the sixteenth and early seventeenth centuries. William Swalman, Thomas Rycharde, Richard Patryn, John Cotsall, Henry Creke, William Greyne, William Carden and Robert Edmonde. All these men were tenant farmers with reasonably large holdings, and appeared at courts, in subsidy rolls and other local institutions.

Minster was ordered to 'provide furniture for the Altar at All Saints Queenborough' among other things. An order for an inventory of Church goods 'not sold' was rejected, as was the order to provide a silken canopy with fringes by Lent.

Once again cloths of silk and other hangings were to be obtained, but when it came to supplying a Mass book, again 'non' is written. 'More for All Saints' is also vetoed. The order to provide 'a fair register book and a book for Churchwardens Accounts' was accepted, as were 'the convenient banners and streamers for Whitsun', but the abbey did not appear enthusiastic.

Warden also belonged to Sir Thomas, and, in fact, was almost in ruins. Robert Segar was the nominal church warden, his parishioners were John Ruffyn, Philip Raynes and Robert Wilde, which was about the number of families in the parish. Warden, it was remarked, 'being distant a little mile from Eastchurch'.

There are no orders, only a memorandum.

'My Lord Warden (Sir Thomad Cheyney) is contented to endow a Vicar at Eastchurch (which Church is very commodius) so that this be united to the same. Also at Eastchurch there is a Vicaredge House.' The 'Vicaredge house' was little more than a cottage, Sir Thomas having acquired Parsonage Farm and all the lands belonging to it.

Leysdown had as propator the Reverendissimo Dom Archpiscopo. The patron was the Abbey of Saint Radigund, who supplied the curate. A church warden is named, Simon Clinch, and three parishioners. There are no remarks made or orders given. Leysdown Church drifted into a poor state by the eighteenth century, derelict and falling down, like other island churches.

Despite her efforts, Queen Mary did not make much headway, and her persecution and burning of so-called 'heretics' made the English people rally to the Protestant faith. In 1558 the sad, misguided queen died, leaving England and Sheppey, in chaos.

CHAPTER XII

The last of the Sheppey barons

Queen Elizabeth I succeeded to a 'shaky' throne. The country was divided by religious differences and felt the lack of former Church authority, the treasury coffers were empty, Queen Mary's ineffective handling of affairs had resulted in the loss of Calais, and to cap it all, many people disputed Elizabeth's right to rule.

The Queen chose her statesmen carefully, and she was not a woman easily fooled. She retained Sir Thomas Cheyney as Privy Councellor, as Treasurer to the Royal Household, and confirmed his other appointments. He had collected several more estates during the last two reigns, including Holme Place and the lease of Danley Farm, plus their land, when the Duke of Somerset, Thomas Seymour, lost his head in Edward VI's reign.

Sir Thomas's friends nicknamed him 'Strenuus Miles', the Energetic Knight, and he lived up to this even to beyond the assumed time of his death, for when he died in 1559 a contemporary historian (Baker) reported 'for certain, that his pulse did beat more than three quarters of an hour after he was dead, as if he had still been alive!'

After his magnificent funeral, all his estates, both in Sheppey and other parts of the country, passed to his second son Sir Henry Cheyney. Sir Henry had married a wealthy heiress, Jane, the daughter of Lord Wentworth, and he was also the Lord of his mother's manor at Toddington. Sir Thomas had been devoted to Shurland and Sheppey, but Henry preferred Toddington, and determined to build a great mansion there that would eclipse Shurland Hall. He wasted no time about this, but moved to Toddington straight away, leaving Shurland empty. Some historians claim that he built his new mansion with materials from the priory, but this is open to doubt, as the priory had been demolished soon after the dissolution, and in any case it would have been a long and difficult journey to Toddington with cartloads of stone, neither practical nor economic.

He alienated his lands in Sheppey piece by piece. As they were held in capite he needed the queen's permission to part with them, and properties were sold direct to the Crown or exchanged for land elsewhere. He was frequently in Faversham in 1563, seeking to raise money, using anticipated rents as security. Not surprisingly he was successful, as among other places he had the rents from the Manor of Patricksbourne to offer, but he was not so lucky with his servants, for in November of the year they caused a disturbance, and were gaoled for brawling.

He must have built quickly, for in 1563 he was able to entertain the Queen at Toddington. He repeated this again in 1573 with such good effect that the Cheyney title was revived, and he was made Lord Cheyney of Toddington.

To pay for all this manors and farms on the island were sold piecemeal, and Sheppey suffered. To add to other troubles, the defences had been neglected and the island was frighteningly vulnerable, and the churches were in chaos.

Early in her reign the queen ordered that the beacons should be repaired and kept at the ready. The historian Lambarde made a 'carde' showing all the beacons in Kent, and so brought a great deal of criticism on himself, as people said it would give information to enemies.

The Lord Lieutenant of the county, Lord Cobham, who was responsible for the watch and ward, had found that people 'not only the common sort, but men of place and honour' were running all ways when the beacons were fired, and often went away from the scene of the trouble, so he had the beacon sites mapped out 'plotted in Carde' showing how each one depended on another to spread an alarm.

This firmly rebutted the criticism, as increased speed in mustering outweighed other considerations.

Seamen suggested to the Privy Council that navigation lights in the Thames estuary should be removed, as they could be of help to enemies, it was termed 'A suggestion that Showe Beacons to be removed'. The advice was welcomed and acted upon. The Watch and Ward was regarded as an emergency measure, discontinued when no invasions threatened, and in winter, when the sea was considered protection enough and the roads were impassable anyway.

It is unlikely that any of this helped the unemployed islanders, the desertion of Shurland Hall had left many of them badly off. Sir Henry had levied fines on all his lands in the third year of Elizabeth's reign, and he repeated this again three years later, which made matters worse.

The Manor of Minster was regranted to Sir Thomas Hoby, who was later succeeded by his son Edward. The abbey gate house was sold to the unlucky Sir Humphrey Gilbert. As his lands were regranted or sold, Sheppey was broken up into smaller estates owned, for the most part, by absentee landlords. As many of them were the nominal rectors of the churches, which meant that the 'living' was in their hands to dispose of, the churches were often badly neglected. From church court records of 1559–65 the result can be seen. At Minster the complaint was 'Curate Sir Charles Askew has two wives, if not three; and, John Clarke will not contribute to the poor box, repairs or Clerk's wages (two pence a quarter) having land of fifty two shillings a year. He said he has offered a penny a quarter, according to the custom of the house. He is to appear at the next general chapter'.

The complaint against John Clarke shows that Minster had already replaced the priory with some sort of system for aiding the poor at parish level. It is possible that the loss of the priory initiated a system of parish government more quickly in Sheppey than in other parishes that had not been used to help the sick and needy, so close to home.

At Eastchurch, where it was a known fact that due to the Cheyneys' indifference the parish often had no curate for quite long periods, Thomas Kingsdowne was accused of withholding sixpence a year given for finding a dirge. 'It has not been paid for two years'. That is marked 'non est', and, to be cited. Poor Thomas probably could not afford the sixpence as things were. The vicar of Leysdowne, Robert Halman, produced letters of dispensation in May 1561 which allowed him to hold other benefices besides Leysdown.

Later he was asked to produce letters of institution and induction. He did not appear, and so he was excommunicated. At Warden the statement was brief. 'The Church of Warden is ruined.'

These complaints were common to the whole country, and left the people with little religious help or guidance.

The Queen was far from happy about this, and in 1573 accused the bishops of neglecting to keep the churches 'in one uniform and Godly order'. Once again the question of wearing surplices, and the unsanctioned retention of images and vestments arose. The Queen herself was a Protestant, disliking extremes, but she was firmly resolved that the people must attend church, and they could be fined for not doing so.

Archbishop Parker made a visitation in 1573, and found that things had not improved since earlier days. At Leysdown they had had 'but one sermond this twelve month', and 'the end of the Chancel lacketh reparactions'. The Chancel was, indeed, falling down, and continued to do so for many years.

An interesting point is the spelling of 'sermon' as 'sermond'. Sheppey people frequently used to put a 'd' on the end of certain words, the baby wore a 'gownd', and the price of something was 'half a crownd'. It is not heard so much now that there are so many incomers on the island.

At Eastchurch John and William Segar appeared to be arguing over what was due to the church from their father Robert's will, and Walter Sutton was doing the same about his father William's will.

Minster parishioners, or 'moste of them' had only received communion 'but once in the year'.

Harty bewailed the fact that

our Churche is in ruyne and decay, but they intend to repair hit with speade.
Item. They had had but three sermons this whole year.
Item. For lack of a mansion house for their curate they be off times destitute of a minister.

Finally, they accused people of not contributing to the assessments, for lack of which the church cannot be repaired.

It was a sad story, and Sir Henry Cheyney was partly responsible. He had left the island, rejected his responsibilities, and people who had depended on the family for centuries were left in poverty and want. They did not know it at the time, but the island would never be quite the same again. As the estates were split up and bought as an investment by strangers, or added to the lands of gentlemen far away, Sheppey became an island of tenant farmers. Very few of them owned their own farms. It is a comfortable thing to hear of a family farming the same land for generations, but

this did not happen on the island, neither was there ever a resident lord of the manor to replace the De Shurlands and Cheyneys. This in its turn had led to a dearth of records. There has been no family, of high or middle class standing, who have lived in one, or maybe two, manors or farms on the island and who therefore have estate maps, accounts and maybe diaries or other useful data concerning the growth and development of the place. As can be seen, most families came and went in the space of one hundred years, and seldom stayed on one farm for a lifetime.

By 1570 Shurland Hall stood empty, deserted, and fast going to decay. The population had decreased, large tracts of land were uncultivated, farm houses were derelict, and the island's defences weak. The tenantry complained, and finally took their complaints to the queen.

Elizabeth realised the dangers of an undefended Sheppey exposed to enemies and pirates, and she was deeply concerned about the plight of the inhabitants. In May 1572 she had the island surveyed, and maps drawn. Queenborough Castle was also surveyed, and many plans drawn. The commissioners were William Hombertson and Thomas Fludd.

They surveyed Shurland and reported; 'The Manor of Shurland taking the name of Sir Robert de Shurland but inhabited for sometime not only by Shurlands but by Cheneys'. This was followed by a list of tenants, who had yearly leases. Unfortunately only the tenants' Christian names are given, so Anthony, John and Robin are listed, and Richard 'who had land in Minster'. Few of the farms were given names, apart from Norwood and Shurland, although Clarke's Farm was mentioned. On the map that accompanied the survey there is a little more information, although what appears to be the name of the farm is often merely the name or initials of the tenant. Most of the properties have a large circle around them, with L. Ch. written in it. The Cromers did manage to own some land in Elmley, but no other landowners are apparent. The tenant farmers were Osbornes, Segars, of whom there were many, Cardens, Thomas Kingdom, Haynes and Suttons, to name most of them. The farms named were Kingsborough (crown land until Sir Thomas Cheyney acquired it) Norwood, Foxendale (now gone to sea) Nutts and Mousehole, Netts Court (Neats Court). A barn and ground belonging to Saint Katherines, Garretts, Scockles, Old Hook, and a new house at Bells. There is also a watermill indicated at Windmill Creek, which was then called Watermill Creek, which may be the one on the inventory of the priory lands. It was later replaced by a windmill. Apart from the Abbey Farm, and several that have 'gone to sea', all the farms on the map are still there in Minster and Eastchurch, but in many cases only the farmhouse remains, the land having been sold and built on.

Queenborough Castle and the fort at Sheerness point were also surveyed together with plans for a fort at Swaleness, a point opposite Queenborough. The rents of the Lordship of Queenborough were recorded, but there were no great names there, it was a list of messuages and cottages, all with negligible rents. The Lay Subsidy Roll in the eighteenth year of Elizabeth's reign provided seven names only from the island.

'At Mynster' John Ascough was described as 'generosis in terris'. He was evidently the gentleman of the party. Thomas Kingsdowne, Robert Edmonds, William Carden, and John Swalman were farmers from Minster.

From Eastchurch and Warden came Stephen Osborne and Robert Pyme, farmers. There were fewer tax payers than in 1334–5. At that time at least two thousand acres, out of approximately twenty-two thousand on Sheppey were unoccupied. Commissioner Thomas Fludd was of the opinion that the decreased population was caused by heavy rate demands.

Elizabeth was a resourceful lady, and full of ideas for Sheppey. She had heard of leather production in Flanders, and considered making use of the island's famous sheep, using the skins as a source of revenue, and with them establishing trade with the continent, which would in turn bring more ships and seamen to Sheppey.

The island was also noted for honey. In 1466 William Sygor had bequeathed bees and hives for the upkeep of a light of the Virgin Mary, and seemingly the local honey had acquired some fame since then.

The Queen considered licences and monopolies, which might bring traders and more inhabitants to Sheppey, and who could also be useful in times of crisis when forts needed manning. In that way the island would be strengthened, and the revenue helped with export dues. It was recorded 'to transport, subject to payment of custom, not more than four thousand sheep-pelts, two thousand sheep skins and four thousand lamb skins'.

However, all this was only ideas, and something definite needed to be done, and quickly. Thinking on these lines, the queen granted a lease of Shurland in 1580, with the stipulation that the tenant farmer 'shall convert ten of the outer chambers or rooms into tenements, and in them to place ten able men to serve with caliver, pike, bow and such other like weapon for the defense of the Island — and in the residue of the house some honest and sufficient person with his family to dwell, and it shall be lawful for her Majesty, if she pleases, to take down and sell certayne of the outer houses there, being superfluous'. So Shurland became a farm and a barracks, and much of it was demolished. In Eastchurch the same thing is said about Shurland as Minster said about the priory, namely, that bits and pieces of masonry from the hall can be found in many unexpected places in and round Eastchurch, and doubtless it is true.

Earlier in this century a farmer at Shurland found several interesting items in and around the remaining walls of the hall, and they are now in the museum at Maidstone.

Amongst them is a head, presumably of the Madonna, which was turned face inwards in the wall, and partly covered with bricks. It had been hidden to prevent destruction, probably in Cromwell's time.

That was the finish of Shurland Hall as a grand mansion. The grounds were 'disparked', although parts of the railings and fences could be traced for another century, or longer. Once again it was a look-out post, and a farm. The tenant farmers gradually improved the empty acres, and some of them were capable enough, and lucky enough, to do very well out of it.

Peter Heayne (Hayne) of Eastchurch, yeoman, died in 1565 leaving personal property of over £90. His seven children had bequests amounting to £190, and his farm stock was worth over £300. He made his money from sheep, but it does not say if he participated in any export schemes. He left a ewe lamb to each of his godchildren in Sheppey, and the same to each of his servants.

He owned one thousand two hundred sheep, and fifty seven cows and horses. Pigs and poultry were not mentioned, but they were usually kept by the farmer's wife, for home use. The name of his farm is not revealed, but as Groves Marsh and grounds are mentioned, it seems that he farmed Groves, a farm on the Lower Road just outside Eastchurch village. Groves has no farmhouse now, only two cottages. It is owned by farmers 'from the other side' (the mainland) and all the ground is down to plough.

There is a note that Peter died with money owing from Thomas Carden, Stephen Osborne, and Thomas Rychards, all fellow farmers who dealt with him, and J. Sherpy of Cranbrook, who was in the cloth trade and may have bought wool from Peter.

There were others who prospered like him, some did even better.

Shurland was not the only problem in Sheppey to trouble the queen. Sir Humphrey Gilbert and his family were living in the abbey gate house. Sir Humphrey had married Anne Aucher, a rich heiress, and they had five children. He had used his own fortune, and his wife's, to finance an expedition to discover unknown lands. He received letters patent from the queen authorising his voyage, and he set out from Plymouth in 1578 with seven ships, one of which was commanded by his half brother Sir Walter Raleigh. His venture failed, and he returned to the island, where he tried to raise money for another voyage.

The State Papers Domestic, July 1581, contain the following:

July, 11 Minster.

Sir Humphrey Gilbert to Sir Francis Walsingham.

I desire money owing, for service of three ships in Ireland. It is a miserable thing that after seven and twenty years service, I should now be subject to daily arrests, executions and outlawries, and to sell my wife's clothes from her back.

By 1583 Sir Humphrey had collected enough money for another voyage, and heartened by the queen's good wishes, he left Plymouth in June with five ships, one of which returned home on the second day.

He arrived in Newfoundland in August, where he sent one ship back to England, and remained himself to explore the coast. On the return journey home at the end of August he lost his principal ship in a storm, and with it all his papers and records.

In September Sir Humphrey's own vessel was wrecked, by storm, and he was drowned — lost at sea. Only one ship won back to England to tell the tale.

In January 1582–3, before Sir Humphrey left, the State Papers Domestic record that the queen is concerned and asks

remembrances for the Lady Gilbert, touching the Manor of Minster, purchased of Sir Henry Cheyney by Sir Humphrey Gilbert and conveyed by him to Sir Edward Hoby, it being the only stay left for her to live by in her husband's absence.

From this it would appear that Sir Humphrey had sold the gate house to finance his voyage, hoping to return with at least some riches. It was a bleak outlook for his family, and after his death his wife returned to her parents. It is hoped that she received some token of gratitude from the Crown.

Sir Henry Cheyney spent his money fast, when he died he had dissipated all his father's lands in and out of Sheppey, his wife's fortune, and his mother's estate. Toddington deteriorated rapidly, and became little more than a ruin very quickly. Sir Henry, his wife Jane and his mother, Lady Anne Cheyney, were all buried there, and the remains of their tombs may still be seen. Locally, Sir Henry was known as 'the extravagant Lord Cheyney'.

Before that happened, everything possible in Sheppey had been sold or demolished, even to the chapel that housed his father's magnificent tomb. Lord Henry had sold the Chapel of Saint Katherine to Sir Humphrey Gilbert, who wanted to demolish it in order to use the materials.

The application for removal is in Grindall's register

There is a small Chapel near unto the Parish Church of Minster — buried the father and divers of the ancestors of Lord Cheyney, which Chapell is with other lands there — about lately sold by his Lordship unto Sir Humphrey Gilbert for as much as he is desirous to remove the cophins and the bodies of the said ancestors out of the said Chappell —.

The Archbishop granted the licence for removal in 1581, but the peculiar thing is that no-one is quite sure where the chapel stood. It was once thought that it might be the Chapel of Saint John, but that was said to be in the churchyard, and the Cheyneys always referred to St. Katherine's as 'their' chapel. It is now generally considered that the chapel stood at the east end of the north aisle (the nuns' chapel) and when it was removed the east wall was built as it is now, with miscellaneous pieces put in, and doorways bricked up. All the licence says is that it was a 'small Chappell near or adjacent to the Church'.

The whole affair raises many queries, not least about the character of Lord Henry. He must have been completely unfeeling and cold blooded to sell the chapel in which his father had so recently requested burial. His attitude to his father and ancestors is one of complete indifference.

Sir Thomas was removed, complete with emblazoned tomb, to the chancel of Minster Abbey. His tomb stands in line with the arches that separate the nuns' chapel from the parish church.

He has been there since 1581, getting more worn as years go by, the graffiti of centuries disfiguring his armour and insignia of the Garter. His feet have been damaged, and the coats of arms decorating the sides of his large, oblong sepulchre are defaced. Every coat of arms in his family was represented here, De Shurlands, Cheyneys, his two wives and the families his children married into.

What happened to his wife Fridwith he asked so specifically to be 'laid near', has never been discovered.

Sir Robert de Shurland's effigy was also moved, and placed under a beautiful canopy wrought in stone, probably built for someone else, on the south wall of the parish church. What was done with all the other Shurlands and Cheyneys who had been buried there is not known.

The 'Knight with the Soul in his Hands' dug up in the churchyard in 1833 may well be one of them, and the unknown Yorkist another, for he was transferred onto a 'sepulchre tomb' in the eastern corner of the north wall of the nuns' chapel, his brass inscription was long since removed, and his coat of arms has worn away.

It was a callous act of desecration, and had the chapel been left undisturbed, with the tombs and effigies lying peacefully, posterity would have had one of the best representations of dress and armour through the centuries to be seen in Britain.

As it is, the island has been left with a legend from the fourteenth century and a whole lot of unanswerable questions.

While Sheppey was drifting into a minor recession, the queen was trying to avoid war with Spain. She did not want war, the country could not afford it, and was not armed for it, but it seemed it was inevitable. The younger men who surrounded her, courtiers, adventurers, and sea captains who did not scruple to become pirates on occasion, were all only too ready to take on Spain. The threat of invasion from King Philip was grave, especially as the queen had been excommunicated, and Philip was supported by the pope, and other Catholic countries.

Constant reminders were sent to the Lords Lieutenant of counties to look to their beacons.

There was a commission by Lord Cobham, the Lord Lieutenant of Kent, to Nicholas Gilbourne of Charing. Nicholas was reminded of the importance of the beacons 'for the service of Her Majesty and defence of the country against attempted invasion', and he was authorised and nominated to be Scout Master in the Lathe of Shepway, the Hundred of Scray annexed to it, and the seven hundreds.

He was to order and oversee all the watches, to remove unsuitable watchmen, and to order beacons and watchhouses to be repaired and built as necessary. The Constables were to find armour and weapons 'for all and every watcher'. It would be lawful for him to put his retinue of servants and horse 'in armes should enemies approach, and do whatever

was to be done'. He was also authorised to 'take up' any horses, geldings, hackneys or nags he might require for his use, to enable riders to carry intelligence about enemy movements quickly. Men were to be told 'to forbeare making of fire, flames, smothers or smokes or ringing of bells in any such place as shall be near the beacons', to avoid 'raising the country'.

Things were looking serious, and the beacons on Sheppey were kept ready for action. There were more of them than in Edward III's day, along the coast and inland. Until several years after the Second World War there was a beacon standing at Shellness point. It was a tall pole, with a triangle of wood fastened on the top, from which the pitch pot would have been suspended. Children were told that the beacon had been there since the time of the Spanish Armada, and it was regarded with awe and curiosity. What reason there could be for removing it is hard to fathom, but it is gone now.

While the abbey at Minster was being taken apart at Lord Cheyney's whim, the church at Eastchurch was frequently without a curate, and the records for this time are obscure. In 1580 Thomas Webb was the curate, and it was recorded in the Archbishop's Ecclesiastical Court that John Saunders of Eastchurch had been condemned to excommunication, in May 1579, for fornication. He ran away to Sturry, but it was not far enough for the courts censures caught up with him, and he was made to return and do public penance in church.

This he did on Sunday January 31st, 1579–80, and the curate certified the fact. Public penance was a nerve-racking experience, as the penitent had to stand up in church, often barefooted, sometimes in a special 'penitent' gown, and declare his sin and his sorrow for it in front of the whole congregation.

Stephen Osborne of Nutts Farm, Leysdown, died in 1581. He styled himself yeoman, and his will was detailed carefully. He actually owned his farm and land. All wills then commenced by 'bequeathing my soul to Almighty God' and requesting pardon and peace. Stephen left to the poor of Eastchurch, Warden and Leysdown parishes fifty-three pounds, to be bestowed upon lands for them forever. 'Whereof my will is that warden shall have yearly eight shillings, and the other two parishes the residue between them.'

He then detailed bequests to his family, with a stern admonition about his daughter 'if she marries without the consent of my wife and my brother Harry Osborne, she gets nothing'.

Having dealt with his son John and his guardianship, he continued 'If I can be justly accused of any wrong, for every penny of wrong proved I give them tuppence'. He then allowed eight pounds 'to two young occupiers for four years, then the amount to be repaid in four years for another two, and so on, forever'. This must have been one of the earliest attempts to help youngsters make a start in life. It became known as Stephen Osborne's Charity, and is still distributed in some form in Eastchurch now.

Stephen was the son of William Osborne of Hartlip, his son John grew up to run Nutts Farm, and John's grandson John was styled 'Gent' of Sutton in Surrey, and he sold the estate to a merchant in London in 1661.

Later Nutts was to belong to Edward Jacobs of Faversham, the historian, geologist and naturalist. In the decade before the Second World War Nutts Farm house was derelict, and falling down. The barn and lodges (farm buildings) were in little better condition. Now it is a holiday camp and only the name survives.

William Cromer of Tunstall owned land in Elmley. Rent was supposed to be paid toward the upkeep of Rochester Bridge from this property, and there were frequent disputes about it.

In 1586 Cromer, in his capacity as a J.P. was investigating

a riot in Sheppey, and Richard Askew, bailiff to Thomas Randolfe, was examined about goods found on the beach and other places. There is no further explanation, but it suggests that either a wreck had been robbed, or there had been some smuggling afoot, both quite usual happenings on the island.

When Richard Askew of Minster died in 1602, he left corn on the ground and in store worth £15 3s 4d, livestock valued at £75 0s 2d, and personal estate of £138 14s 2d. Where he lived is not named, but 'The Hall' was well furnished with tables, stools and chairs, and hanging on the walls were a picture of a ship and six escutcheons of arms, which, it is commented 'were unusual in a Farm House'. He had plenty of pewter dishes, saucers and salt cellars, the parlour was luxurious for the times, and, of course, contained a bed with a vast amount of feather bedding, as well as the chairs and tables one would expect to find in a parlour. There was a determined attempt made there towards comfort and the good things of life, and it might well be asked where all this luxury came from, it seems a great deal for a man who had earlier been a bailiff. Richard Askew's activities would bear looking into, there might be a good story there.

Harty, which was once a small island of two miles by one and a half, and had been for centuries a part of Sheppey, seemed to attract more muddle and trouble for its size than all the rest of Sheppey together. It was once called Harteigh, allegedly from the Saxon words Heord-tu, meaning land filled with herds of cattle, as it usually was.

There has never been a village there, in 1780 it was recorded that there were six lookers' cottages, about twenty inhabitants, as the marshlands deterred people from living there.

Most of the land was divided between different monasteries until the reformation, when Sir Thomas Cheyney became the owner.

Mote Farm was part of the Manor of Sayes Court. Sayes Court is now being restored, after a period of dereliction. The Mote Farm passed through a Champion daughter to the Chevin family, and in the reign of Elizabeth, John Chevin sold the farm to Mr. Thomas Paramour. John then declared that he was under age at the time of the sale, having resold it to John Kyne and Simon Lowe. In the thirteenth year of the reign those two gentlemen brought a law suit, called a 'writ of right', against Paramour for recovery of the land, but they lost the case and Paramour was given possession. Upon receiving the writ of right a trial of battle was demanded by Paramour, and awarded by the court. This has been described in many books, as it was the last time this particular form of deciding a legal action by battle was engaged in. The queen intervened, and ordered that they were not to fight, but the formalities had to be observed. The champions chosen by each party, properly accoutred in full armour, met at Tothill Fields, Westminster, on the appointed day.

The trial by battle had stirred the curiosity of the public, for it was estimated that four thousand people had gathered to watch.

The Justice of the Common Pleas were present as Judges of the Duel, and when after much formal ceremony, and making of proclamations and declarations, the non-appearance of Kyne and Lowe was recorded, a non-suit was requested and made, and the land judged to belong to Thomas Paramour. So the battle fizzled out tamely, and the onlookers were doubtless disappointed. Eventually the land came to the Cheyneys.

During this period, while the lands of Sheppey were being bought, sold, and made productive again, and the defences and watch and ward guards were being strengthened, Queenborough was living a separate existence as a borough, but it was not escaping the queen's attention.

CHAPTER XIII

Queen Elizabeth slept here

Queen Elizabeth I regarded Queenborough as one of the more important coast defences. All the fortifications at the mouth of the Thames were surveyed, and plans drawn of them, during her reign. Upnor Castle was built, and the fort at Garrison Point, Sheerness, strengthened.

The defences at Queenborough Castle were improved, and a fort built at Swaleness, a point opposite Queenborough. A large sum of money was expended on the castle in Elizabeth's reign. Queenborough was used as a harbour for the fleet, a fact that is frequently overlooked. During the war with the Scots and French, it is recorded that on December 27th, 1579 'the fleet left Queenborough for Berwick, in heavy weather. Admiral Winter was in command'.

It is hard to picture the great men-o'-war at anchor off Queenborough, trying to set sail on a rolling grey sea under a lowering grey sky — pennants flying, seaman shouting, and the creak of timbers and ropes. Yet it all happened there, four hundred years ago.

Despite the castle's importance, the borough had not grown very quickly. In 1566 there was one main street with twenty-three inhabited houses, and one person homeless. There was a quay for the town, and some of the men were employed in shipping cargoes from port to port. There were

twelve boats, or little ships, of varying sizes from three to sixteen tons, although only two were really large. Forty-five of the men of the town, and that must have been nearly all the male working population, were engaged in oyster dredging, fishing, or coastal trading.

However, they took their position as a borough seriously, and everything was entered in the appropriate book. There was a comprehensive set of bye-laws, which included the regulation of grazing on the common, and who was allowed to turn horses out there, and many other things. If anyone exceeded their 'stint' they were hauled before the Mayor's Court and duly fined.

The mayor's salary was set at twenty pounds yearly, and a lease for grazing twenty sheep on the common. A jurat refusing to accept the office of Mayor stood to be fined fifty pounds. A bailiff refusing to become a jurat was fined twenty pounds, and a free burgess declining the office of bailiff was fined twenty pounds. It was better to accept gracefully, and economics probably settled the question for most of the small community.

The cost of being admitted as a freeman was forty shillings for the sons of freeman and apprentices, but a fearsome six pounds in the case of 'Foreigners'. Foreigners in this sense were anyone not from Queenborough. The term is still used in Sheppey, and means anyone who comes from 'over the water' (The Ferry) or 'the other side', unless they happen to come from an island family, in which case someone is bound to remark 'Sheppey folk always come back!' which was often true in days gone by, but is not such a certainty now.

With such a sound foundation in correct book-keeping, the charters and folios of the borough were usually up to date and in order.

Thomas Robinson, described as a 'singleman', left a minutely detailed will in 1557. It starts with the old formula 'I give and bequeath my soul to God Almighty, and my body to be buried in the Churchyard of Mynster, to the Parish Priest of same IIIJ^s IIIJ^d to the Chappell of Queenborough XX^s'.

He continues naming all his friends and leaving them small sums of money and various articles from his wardrobe. 'To Gilbert Amore, one doblett. To William Howke, one shirt and my best breeches.' Friends' children are not forgotten, and 'To each house XIJ^d.' There was to be a Funeral Feast. 'To be bestowed at Mynster at my buryall one ewe sheep with as much brede and drynke as shall suffice, and at my months mind at Queenborough.' The 'month's mind' was a small feast a month later. His executors were directed to sell his house to the best advantage, and to devote the money to making a well in the middle of the town. It is doubtful if this was done, as there was no further mention of it. He ended 'To every pore house in the town XIJ^d and all the rest to be bestowed in dedes of mercy and pyttie'. The will was witnessed, and proved before Robert Colens, Mayor, in 1558.

In 1571 the queen granted to Queenborough the privilege of returning two members to Parliament yearly. The first two elected were John Cobham and John Parker, esqs. This made the borough a place of importance to would-be Members of Parliament striving for a seat in the house, and led to many abuses later. It also added to the paper work, as the records show.

It did not appear to worry the Mayor's Court in 1573, when the mayor, bailiffs and burgesses 'ordained' that 'every Baker in ye town and liberty should sell to every victualler thirteen loaves 'to the dosson'. If anyone 'offendeth to the contrary' he was fined three shillings and fourpence.

In 1575 they presented that the butts (for archers) were in decay, and 'willed that they be made up this Week'. The 'said jury' also ordered the town to clear up round the churchyard and church.

Seven years later. Item, we present that we think it is expedient to have a ducking stoole made in the towne 'for the punishment of scoulds and unquiet.' It sounds as though they had a form of 'womens' lib.' in the sixteenth century, but the men took good care it did not prosper!

Two years on and all the inhabitants of the said Town were presented for Bowling and other unlawful games, and ordered to pay two pence into the poor mens' boxe, refusal to pay earned a fine of tenpence.

The 'poor mens' boxe' suggests that Queenborough had started to take responsibility for the poor of the town, a responsibility formerly left to the church.

Also in 1584 Richard Higat, Fleming, was ordered to pay dues to the church and the town clerk. It was also agreed that 'Richard Higat, Fleming, shall provide one caliver furnished, to remaine in the custody of our Chambers for ever, upon payne if he does not provide it by midsummer next twenty shillings'. (A caliver was an early type of hand gun.)

It was a Fleming, Mathias Falconer, a man from Brabant, who started the first *copperas* works in Queenborough in Elizabeth I's reign. Copperas is stone containing iron pyrites which was used to make dyes for various industries. This was the first industry to come to Queenborough, and it continued until the early years of the nineteenth century. Richard Higat

was, in all probability, a member of the copperas works.

Four years later the court was presenting 'privy tipplers not licensed to sell malt' for which they were duly fined, and Robert Lulley Clarke for selling a black mare of three years old in the market for the sum of fifty-three shillings. Why Clarke was at fault in selling his mare is not clear, but only certain people had the right of turning horses out on the common, and perhaps Clarke wasn't one of the elite.

In October 1565 the mayor and corporation were informed that they were avoiding customs duty and smuggling ('conveying secretly') dutiable goods into the town. All vessels to be searched and 'tried out', and kept in safety until passed. The town was undoubtedly doing just this, and somehow they managed to avoid being caught. It was not the first nor the last time they had been under suspicion, but smuggling was a way of life to all Sheppey men, and providing they escaped conviction they were not unduly worried.

However, they were annoyed when Mr. Burlacey, the Constable of the Castle in 1573, passed a letter to the mayor regarding hulkes carrying salt that were berthed at Queenborough. They replied indignantly 'this town will utterly decay if ships may not harbor here as they have done'. There was an enormous amount of letter writing going on at this time. A letter from London to Queenborough possibly dealing with smuggling and allied subjects, bore the superscription 'Haste, Haste, for Lyefe, Lyefe, Lyefe. Post at Sittingbourne see this sent away with all possible speed'. This is one of the earliest examples of an Express letter.

The following year they were defending their liberties, when they were accused of taking a prisoner away, pointing out that they were out of the Lord Warden's jurisdiction, and could deal with their prisoners themselves.

More serious was the accusation of 1574–5.

'To The Mayor
My Lords of her Majesties Council are informed that there are certain Pirates ... that use the harbor and various creeks and some of the town deal with them and furnish them with victuals ...'

My Lords demanded to know the truth of this, and warned the town to be more careful, and more watchful. The mayor's reply was plaintive and conciliatory. 'They were but a poor weak town' and, of course, they wouldn't dream of doing such terrible things! 'It was in no way trew, but they would take better watch.' Which they did, to their own advantage. There were no gangs of smugglers who terrorised the countryside, as happened at Romney Marsh, but the islanders had no conscience about smuggling, they regarded it as a right, and they were all involved in it to some extent. Not only Queenborough Creek, but Windmill Creek, the other small creeks round Harty and Eastchurch, Warden Point and Barrowbrook were all ideal places for smugglers. Left to themselves they hurt nobody except the excisemen.

That is but a small selection of Queenborough records in Elizabeth I's time. There is also a muster roll for 1574, as although they could not be called upon to serve out of the borough, they certainly had to be prepared to serve in it. Walter Wheatley was the mayor, and had to provide two calivers, furnished. The land bailey and the water bailey had to provide the same. Eli Graff had to provide one caliver and one corslet furnished. There were eighteen men named, some called upon for a bow and sheaf of arrows, others for a sword and dagger, or 'a bill, sword and dagger'.

All of them were warned to keep their weapons ready for use. For a small, not very wealthy borough, Queenborough had a great deal to live up to, and judging by the records, did it very well.

There is a description of the hall of the castle as it was seen in 1629. It was described as a noble room, and round the top were placed the arms of the nobility and gentry of Kent, with the arms of Queen Elizabeth in the centre, and underneath the following verse:

Lillies the lion's virgin breast explain,
Then, like a virgin and a lion reign,
Pictures are pleasing, for the mind they shew,
And in the mind the Deity we view;
May she who God in life and empire shews,
To me the eternal Deity disclose,
May Jesse's flower and Judah's lion deign,
Thy flowers and lions to protect, Great Queen.

The original poem was in Latin, this is the translation.

The reason for this rather sycophantic verse, and the arms in full colour round the hall, has often been pondered over. It could have been displayed in honour of a visit from the queen, or it could have been simply tudor ostentation.

Whatever the true reason, it is confidently asserted, and the island firmly believes, that Queen Elizabeth visited Queenborough in 1582. Not to be outdone, Minster also insists that the queen came 'up the Island' to visit and view Shurland, passing Minster on the way.

The stories told are charming, but not very convincing. It is best to start in the time-honoured fashion, so, —

Once upon a time, in 1582, Queen Elizabeth stayed at Queenborough Castle. She arrived in Queenborough unannounced, and the mayor, a thatcher by trade, slid off a roof and tore his breeches in his haste. The queen laughed and said that it showed loyalty, and thenceforth sent a pair of breeches to the mayor yearly, on that date. Eventually Queenborough wrote to the queen, saying that they had enough pairs of breeches, thank you ma'am. The queen replied that she understood, and in future would send - - - - - - the word was unreadable, and looked to the Queenborians like 'Elephant'. So the corporation hastily constructed a pen to put the animal in. No elephant arrived, but instead came a sum of money in lieu of breeches, which was reputed, in 1860, to still arrive regularly. The pen was left *in situ*, and for centuries people believed it could still be seen there.

It is a good story, there is no argument about that. It is unfortunate that a similar story was circulated about Queen Phillippa's first visit to the new borough named in her honour in 1366, and again a sum of money was sent yearly to replace the torn nether garments.

Minster's story is more prosaic, after all, they were earthy country folk. Queen Elizabeth came to visit Shurland Hall, to try to sort out the problems there, as the tenants had applied to her for aid. She left the Lower Road at what is now called Scocles Road, presumably to view her 'new brick built farm of Scocles', and left Scocles Road at Stickfast Lane. In actual fact, until 1900 Scocles Road went no further up the hill to the village than the Stickfast Lane turning. The road ended there, and a footpath led across farmland called Joynters Hill up to the village. To go back to the story. She turned right up Stickfast Lane to get to the Minster to Eastchurch Road, as that was the way to Shurland Hall. Along Stickfast Lane she stuck in the mud, herself and the whole cortege, and her language was worth hearing! That is why it is called Stickfast Lane, generations of children were told, because Queen Elizabeth got stuck there.

Sadly, it is no longer Stickfast Lane, winding from Scocles Road past old farms to Pigtail Corner, where it meets the Minster Road. Some years after the war a tidy-minded council, who obviously had no knowledge of local history, decided it would be 'nicer' if the lane was renamed Elm Lane, and so it now is.

Sheppey residents who have been on the island for many years still call it Stickfast Lane though, and the noticeable thing is that their young children do the same, so the name won't die out for a few generations yet.

The trouble about all this is that despite the assertions, and the definite date given, there is absolutely no record extant of the queen's visit to Sheppey, and therefore no way of proving the truth.

With Queenborough's talent for recording everything that happened, it does not seem possible that they would have omitted to record a visit from the queen, but there is nothing about it in their records at all. Neither is any of the correspondence re breeches and elephants to be found, and surely a letter from the great queen herself would have been carefully preserved. It may have been lost during the intervening years, someone could have quietly annexed it for their private collection, many things could have happened, but it is certainly not there now.

As for her visit to Minster, well, if she tried to take her mounted retainers round Stickfast Lane she did get stuck there in all probability, for until quite late in this century it was a notoriously boggy lane. Nicholson's 'Progresses' do not give any account of a visit to Sheppey. That the queen visited Faversham and Sandwich is documented, and her visits to Lord Cheyney at Toddington, but not Sheppey.

So while no-one can say, on the face of such unquestioning belief and strong local stories, that the queen did *not* visit Sheppey, with such a complete lack of recorded evidence no-one can say positively that she did. One thing is sure. Whatever anyone says Minster people will always believe that Queen Elizabeth got stuck in Stickfast Lane — after all, that's why it was called that, and to them that's proof enough.

The threat of a Spanish invasion was growing. Beacons were in readiness, and local men had their arms prepared. Queenborough was one of the naval ports where England's great ships were anchored, and this is something not often remembered. In January of 1588 twelve of the fleet were in Queenborough harbour, where they were scraped and tallowed. Drake was at Plymouth with more of the fleet, and another detachment of vessels was at Dover, hoping to block the Duke of Parma at Gravelines. This was the Channel Fleet.

Drake was sent to Queenborough in January to assist in reducing the crews while the ships were laid up. He had orders from the Lord Chancellor to pay the five thousand three hundred men under his command at Queenborough 'as the winter had tried the men severely'. A wooden ship, in a north east gale, anchored off Queenborough, can't have been exactly a fun place.

Lord Admiral Lord Howard of Effingham was in command of the ships at Queenborough, Lord Henry Seymour was Admiral, Sir Henry Palmer Vice Admiral and Sir William Winter was Rear Admiral. They played a big part in the defeat of the Spanish Armada.

The Lord Admiral was aboard the *Whitebear*, a vessel of one thousand tons. There were some well known battleships in the fleet there, *Triumph, Ark Raleigh, Lion, Bonaventure* with John Hawkins in command, *Vanguard*, which was Sir William Winters' ship, and *Dreadnought*, to name some of them. They left Queenborough in April or May to join Drake's fleet at Plymouth.

The *Bonavolia*, a galley, lay off Sheerness with three small ships from Queenborough, Minster and Leysdown, to give warning of the approach of enemy ships.

Sir Francis Drake was Vice Admiral of the Fleet. He was well used to sailing on the Medway and the local rivers that run into the Thames mouth, as he had left Devon when he was a small boy, and for a time lived with his family in a hulk in Gillingham Reach. His father, Edmund Drake, acted as a chaplain to the seamen, later when he became the Vicar of Upchurch he and his wife and their eleven sons had a more comfortable residence. Vice Admiral Drake learnt his trade as a seaman on the Medway, sailing in a coaster.

It is said that the Spaniards planned to invade Sheppey as early as possible in their campaign and then use the island as a naval and military base. Their plans were discovered, and every precaution was taken to thwart this scheme. Guardships were placed at strategic points round the island, and Sheppey had more men posted on defences than anywhere else on the coast.

The British scattered the Spanish armada, and returned to port victorious. No-one thought to record if the Sheppey beacons were fired at the approach of the armada or not. During the battle a Spanish general, Signor Jeronimo, was captured when his ship was taken. He was put ashore at Queenborough, where he was kept as a prisoner in the castle by the constable, Sir Edward Hoby. In December 1591 he died, and was buried at Minster Abbey. His burial is recorded in the church register, and can be seen as it was written at the time. For many years the Unknown Yorkist's tomb was regarded as that of the Spanish prisoner, until someone with knowledge of the subject took a closer look at the armour and the Yorkist collar. The true site of poor Jeronimo's grave is unknown, it is doubtful if any stone or memorial was put up to remember him by.

Sometime in the second quarter of this century, the tenants of a small cottage called Bath Cottage had a fire in a beam above the hearth. Bath Cottage was one of the old wooden buildings, made of shipboard, and was situated at the bottom of Windmill Hill, lying back from the road. When the occupants had extinguished the fire, which was in reality more of a smoulder, they found behind the fire-place a small, hidden room 'just big enough for a man to stand in'. In this hidy-hole was a pair of very old shoes like none they had ever seen, with silver buckles. There were also old maps 'on funny paper', with pictures of 'old fashioned' sailing ships. As they didn't want their landlord to hear about the fire they burnt their finds under the copper, so that there would be no evidence. Later they confided all this to someone they could trust, a man who would have dearly liked to examine these things, and who never ceased to wonder if they had any connection with the armada.

Once the armada was routed there was general rejoicing in England, but the wars were not yet over. Beacons still had to be manned, and riders at the ready.

The master of the Queen's Horse, the Earl of Leicester, had been having difficulties in getting enough suitable horses. He decided that too many were being transported, and wrote to the town of Faversham complaining

of the transportatione of the beste geldings and horses of the Realm out of the Creeks and Portes that lye next France and that in a greate parte under the colour of transportynge unserviceable horsses jades titts and mares which by statute are permitted to be transported, that I am dryven to take specyall and stricte order for restrainte thereof in all other places so in the Countye of Kent and in all the Portes and creekes thereof . . .

He ordered that no 'horse geldinge mare jade or titt etc.' should be exported without special licence, and all masters of vessels had to give bonds of good behaviour. If they broke their bonds, the consequences were dire. It is hoped that his measures were effective, and that the Sheppey mariners took note. The illegal export of horses is nothing new, evidently.

His wording may sound strange, but horse dealers in Kent frequently called inferior horses 'tits', and the older ones may still do so. It was often heard in Sheppey.

The people of Kent became disillusioned with continual taxes and 'mustering' for war. There was a second alert in 1592, when Spain threatened again, and troops were sent to fight in France, the Netherlands and Ireland, to keep Spain out of these places. Men were sometimes levied and then

disbanded, and they objected strongly if they were mustered at harvest time, which wasn't really surprising. Desertions were frequent, and often arms and armour went home with deserters. It is estimated that there was an average of three hundred and thirty-eight 'muster men' sent from Kent annually.

The county set up a fund for disablement pensions for those 'hurt in wars', and there was a commission to examine vagrant and maimed soldiers.

Sir John Hawkins founded Chatham Almshouses for sailors, and in 1593 an Act of Parliament ordered the Justices to levy rates to provide for the relief of war casualties. There was a general feeling of apathy and discontent in Kent, military taxation was heavy, and the people were tired of foreign wars. There was also a growing concern about the number of vagrants, beggars and poor people wandering the roads. Despite laws ordering that vagrants be whipped, and returned to their place of origin the numbers were increasing, and in some cases proving a danger to orderly communities.

The queen was troubled about this, especially the plight of the poor and the homeless. In 1598 and 1601 the first Poor Laws were passed. These laws made the parish responsible for its own poor, and ordered them to provide work for the able-bodied poor. This was the start of the House of Correction, the Poor House, and the enforced return of vagrants to their place of origin, plus a whipping to remind them not to stray again. To move about the country poor people needed a pass, signed by Justices of the Peace and Overseers of the Poor. These acts also confirmed Government by the Vestry, and villages were administered by Churchwardens, Overseers of the Poor, Borsholders and Waywardens elected by the people of the parish at a vestry meeting.

The church no longer doled out charity and the Manor Courts had almost disappeared — the worthies of the village took over. In this case Britain was in advance of the Continent, the queen had laid the foundations for a system that continued until late in the nineteenth century and although it is now considered that it was a brutal and harsh system it was in tune with the times it served, and the country was never to see the beggars and poverty that was the norm in other countries. To beg in England was unlawful, unless the unfortunate person had been granted a licence.

Despite wars, vagrants and poverty the country as a whole prospered in Elizabeth's reign. It was a busy, adventurous time, new lands were discovered and colonised, merchants prospered, and the arts took on a new life. Sheppey was no exception. As the manors were broken up and sold tenant farmers expanded, they rented extra land and many grew wealthy. A new class, the yeoman farmer, came to the fore. Their houses became more comfortable, they no longer lived in a labourer's cottage and slept on boards, their wealth was in household goods as well as farm stock and land.

The largest owner of sheep in 1602 was Henry Harris, yeoman. There were Harris's as tenants at Danley Farm, and he may have come from their family. He owned two hundred and twenty ewes, one hundred and forty lambs, one hundred and nine wethers and tegs, and twenty 'calling ewes'. The rest of his stock is not enumerated, but he was a man to be reckoned with. In many cases the yeomen farmers rose in the social scale to become the gentry of the next generation, as John Osbornes' grandson did.

The queen was interested in every aspect of government, and another act passed was the Highway Act. The results of this can be seen in the account of the Ferry Court in 1596.

The boroughs are recorded as before, and the borsholders and their suters. A few of the family names are the same as in Henry VIII's time, although spelt differently. The Bradstretes, the Passhleys, Manne or Munne, and Ruffyn; then new names appear, John Long, Elex Dirkin, George

Fox, William Cowshole, Thomas Kingsdowne, Mathew Sampson (of Sampson's Farm, Eastchurch) and others.

The Constable was John Brayles, his deputy Thomas Keynes. Henry Harrys (of the sheep) was appointed Ferry Warden, with John Wood and Mathew Sampson as ferrymen.

Following that, the operation of the Highway Act can be seen. No longer was the Law Day held under the Court Tree ever again to be a short and simple proceeding.

Also the said Jury do assess and appoint to be taxed for this year toward the maintainance of the Ferry called Trinhide alias the Kings Ferry every twenty acres of fresh marsh and upland six pens, and every twenty acres of salt, one penny. Also we appoint the Ferry Book to be made at the house of Richard Smythe in Minster and therebe Robert Allen, William Richards, and Thomas Keynes for Minster, and Henry Smythe, Richard Glover and Mathy Sampson for Eastchurch, and Gysemer, John Wyly and Thomas Ruffyn for Leysdown and Warden, and if (either) of them make default to forfeit to the use of the Ferry and Ferry House, two shillings.

Also we appoint the ffere Warden to go and to make survey of the ferre house and lands belonging to the ffere on this side, and before the Feast of Saint Michael 'th archangell' next upon payne of forty shillings to be had and levyed to the use of the ferre and ferre house aforesaid. And we appoint the said ferry warden to warn two out of every parish at his election to ryde with him to survey the said lands, and if 'any of theym refuse to goo' he or they to forfeit to the use of the ffere three shillings and four pence apiece.

Itm. We appoint the ferre warden shall trim and dress the boats and ferry house on this side and before the Feast of Saint Michael 'th archangel' next upon payne of five pounds to be levied to the use of the ferre.

The Law Day finishes with the account of William Brown, the present Ferry Warden, delivered and taken at Kingsborough on the day and year aforesaid.

This account started with a list of people who 'demandeth to be abated' for amounts of land 'sett down upon his head' which was more land than they had. Sir Edward Hobye, Richard Askew of riot fame, and Stephen Awgar were amongst these.

William then lists the money 'laid out by me' which includes twenty shillings for the steward, fifteen shillings spent at dinner at the making of the Ferry Book, and expenses for new oars and other gear for the boats.

Cetara desunt. Fifty years separate the Law Days of Henry VIII and Elizabeth I. There are no records for that period and during that time the taxes allowed had been increased and regulated. The steward's name is not disclosed, which is a loss, as he was usually a person of standing locally.

It is noticeable, too, that Trinhide, or Trimhide, has now become the Kings Ferry, and King's Ferry it has remained, even when a queen is the reigning monarch. The making of the Ferry Book must have taken much thought and nail biting, and probably took several people most of the day. They needed that dinner! There is not another Law Day account for seventy years, by which time King Charles II was on the throne, and the orders had multiplied still further. The only names that re-occur then are the ubiquitious Smiths, and John Ruffin, now styled 'Gent' — another yeoman farmer who had made it.

So in Elizabeth's reign Sheppey settled down to a way of living that was not to alter appreciably, apart from the intrusion of the Civil War, until the late nineteenth century. When the queen died in March 1602–3 she left a secure and prosperous country. The people were deeply grieved by her death, and mourned sincerely; it was said that they loved their ruler 'in spite of her being a woman', and the islanders mourned with the rest of Britain.

CHAPTER XIV

The calamitous Stuarts

After the lively, bustling reign of Elizabeth I, the accession of James I of England, VI of Scotland, was rather an anticlimax, and Sheppey didn't appear to have been unduly impressed by him.

The Manor of Shurland had been leased to Sir Edward Hoby, but on the expiration of this lease James I granted the estate to one of his favourites, Sir Philip Herbert, elevating him to a baronetcy, Baron Herbert of Shurland. For many years the manor remained with this family. In 1630 Baron Herbert succeeded to the title Earl of Pembroke, and the Sheppey title became merged with the senior title. Baron Herbert was also appointed Constable of Queenborough Castle; he was the last man to hold this post.

Sir Edward Hoby had sold the Manor of Minster, and that came into the possession of the Levesey, or Livesey family. Gabriel Livesey was the youngest son of Sir Robert Livesey, a former Sheriff of Sussex and Surrey. He acquired several estates on the island, and the family played an important part in local affairs for some years. He bought the lease of Danley Farm from Sir Henry Cheyney, and re-sold it to Sir Julius Caesar in 1604.

Sir Julius Caesar was the Master of the Rolls and a Privy Councillor to Elizabeth I. He was an Italian, and it is said that Julius Caesar was not his real name, but that the queen gave it him as a nick-name, and then he changed his name legally, presumably because he though that would please her, or maybe he decided he was better known as Julius Caesar. Sir Julius settled the lease on his eldest son Charles Caesar, esq. Needless to say, none of these Privy Councillors lived on Sheppey; the farm was let to farmers who worked the land and ran local affairs on the island.

Robert Livesey also acquired Parsonage Farm with the land and titles at Eastchurch, where his son Gabriel actually lived and brought up his family. He was Sheriff of Kent in 1621, and he either built or rebuilt Parsonage Farm, Eastchurch. In the late nineteenth century two stone chimney breasts were uncovered during alterations at the farm. They were carved with fruit, flowers, and figures of birds, together with the Livesey coat of arms and the arms of Gabriel's second wife Anne, who was a daughter of Michael Sondes.

The Parsonage Farm has been in private hands for many years now, and it is impossible to say if the great stone fireplaces are still *in situ*.

All this annexing of Church property left the curate of Eastchurch with no parsonage, little land, and no titles, but no-one seemed to worry about that.

Solid Georgian architecture in Queenborough High Street. The building on the left is dated 1706.

Queenborough Town Hall still retains the dignity of its former importance.

Norwood Manor — now a somewhat faded shadow of its former self.

The Baptist Chapel in Sheerness — recently demolished.

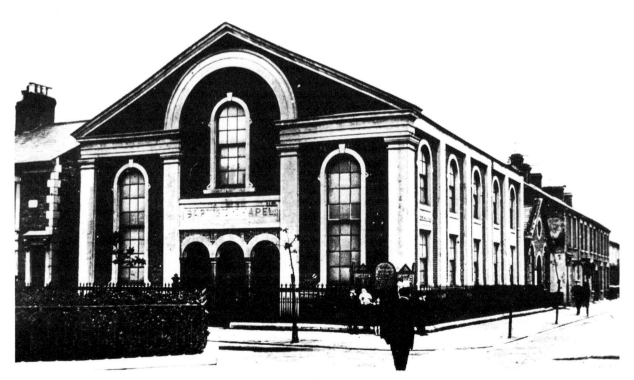

Leysdown Church stands aloof from the vulgarities of the seaside resort down the road.

Holy Trinity Church, Sheerness.

The road to Warden Point. Part of Sheppey's lost land.

Tudor grandeur still clings to the crumbling remains of Shurland Hall.

Sir Gabriel and his wife have a large and rather lovely tomb in Eastchurch Church, in which their children are represented, Michael kneeling and the baby lying dressed in a gown, and the family is commemorated in verse. Unfortunately the Livesey family fell out of favour in the island because of Sir Gabriel's son Michael. The effigies of Sir Gabriel and his wife Anne lie on top of the tomb, dressed in Elizabethan court dress.

Norwood Manor had also been granted to Baron Herbert, and was let as a farm.

The Parsonage Farm at Minster was owned by Sir Gabriel Livesey, complete with titles and land, and once again the vicar of Minster Abbey received nothing from it, a fact that was noted and complained about in a later century.

Calehill was a mystery manor, of which no trace can be found. The redoubtable Hasted says it was there in the time of Henry VIII when it came to the Cheyneys, and was then alienated by Lord Henry Cheyney; it was owned then by the Crown until James I granted it to Baron Herbert, but its precise whereabouts remains unknown. There has been no mention of it in any rolls, deeds or property transfers studied so far.

Sheerness was still an area of marshland. The foreshore was a famous place for gathering mussels, and arguments about who had the right to collect mussels abounded.

In Henry VIII's reign a legal action followed one of these disagreements, and as a result only certain people were allowed to gather mussels, and intruders were warned to keep out.

At Warden the church was in a bad state of repair. The church had once belonged to the Maison Dieu, together with land given by Simon de Wardune in Henry III's reign, but now it all belonged to Sir Edward Hoby, and remained in his family for some years. The church, St. James, was combined with Eastchurch Church, but it wasn't a good partnership. Warden Manor had changed hands many times since the Savage family of Bobbing owned it, and it was usually leased to someone local. Later it was to gain a certain notoriety as the Smugglers Headquarters.

At Leysdown the manor that had once belonged to the Church of Holy Trinity in Canterbury was confiscated by Henry VIII and transferred to his new Dean and Chapter of Canterbury. In Edward I's time the prior had claimed all manorial privileges, and a Court Leet and Court Baron were held there. The Leysdown Court Rolls are scattered, a few in the archives, the rest at Lambeth Palace. They ended in Elizabeth I's reign. The manor was leased, and there is no trace of the house now. In earliest Norman times there was a special rent paid in this manor called weregavel, for wears or kiddels, which the local fishermen were allowed to set in the sea coasts to catch fish, but later this practice was stopped.

The second manor, which William Cheyney had been granted when Lord Lovell lost his estates, Lord Henry Cheyney alienated. In this manor was the farm of Nutts, whose name was said to have been taken from a family named Notts. In Elizabeth's reign the Sampsons owned it, later selling it, with St. Bartholomew's Farm and Churchfield, to Stephen Osborne. Churchfield now has caravans and chalets on it, Bartholomew's Farm has disappeared, and there is a camp on ground called Priory Hill. When William Cheyney was the owner, he granted the Wardens of Rochester Bridge four pounds annually out of the rents towards the upkeep of Rochester Bridge, and to maintain three chaplains in the chapel house near it for ever.

Leysdown Church, St. Clements, was also in dire need of repair; it belonged to the Archbishop of Canterbury. There was no village at Leysdown; it was empty of all but the farms and a few cottages. From Leysdown to the point of the island was nothing but empty marshland. The marsh, now called Shellness beach, was called Schotton, and this name was still in use earlier in this century. Shellness was an empty area of marsh and shell beaches. Samphire grew there, it still does, and the samphire gatherers used to go out there to pick it.

Elmley was used for grazing, and had descended through Peyforers and Potyns by devious ways to the Cromers of Tunstall. The church, St. James, had little more than walls and a roof. Once belonging to Leeds Priory, it later belonged to the Crown, and the advowson was granted to All Saints College, Oxford. They still own much of Elmley today.

Harty, also with no village and much grazing land, had also passed through Lord Henry Cheynes' hands, as most of the land there had formerly belonged to the church. The church, St. Thomas the Apostle, once belonged to Davington Priory, and in King James I's time was in the king's book, the 'tenths' being paid to the king.

The land belonged to different owners, as Lord Henry sold it to Richard Thornhill, esq. who later disposed of the various farms and land separately. Again, there was no village, just the church, the farms, and lookers cottages. Farm names changed. Abbat's Court, once belonging to the Convent of Faversham, became Hall Farm. The Mote was known as Hall Farm, Long House has now gone, but Elliot's Farm, Mochett's, Pery Marsh and Napleton's Marsh still keep their old names.

So in James I's day the inhabited parts of Sheppey were still chiefly in Minster, with Eastchurch a close second, and, of course, Queenborough.

Queenborough was going along steadily, holding a court, imposing fines, and complaining when necessary. In 1607 the mayor and corporation sent a petition to the king complaining that although King Edward III built them a chapel of their own, and that they provided a convenient curate, yet they had to pay tithes to the parish church of Minster.

It was probably in Elizabeth's reign that they were granted a licence to bury, baptise and marry people.

Queenborough's earliest church registers were accidentally destroyed, so no early records are available for study. There are Chamberlain's Accounts for 1611 onwards.

In 1613 was paid to Mr. Lee (steward) for his fee £2

Item. Paid for the vane and setting it up 8s. 4d.

1623. For gaging four hundred and ten barrels of beer at 4d. per barrel £6 17s. 4d.

Paid to Mr. Pretchett for making of a sermon ye 4th of June 6s.

For repairing the Court Hall and building of a prison under the same and for repairing of the cage and pillory £15 12s. 3d.

Paid for chardges in going to the Burgesses to London and for lobsters that were given to them £1 0s. 0d.

Small accounts, but revealing. They had a new vane on the church, and liked to hear a good sermon there. Beer had to be 'gaged' presumably to make sure it was of the right strength, not watered down or adulterated. It had to be good, and plentiful.

They had laid out money on a prison, and repaired their 'cage' and pillory. The cage was a small lock-up, and previously they had ordered a ducking stool for scolds. Were they really such an unruly borough, or were the mayor and corporation just being on the safe side? It is hard to tell.

In 1623 Baron Herbert of Shurland was writing to the borough about the Parliamentary Elections, but he was not chosen as Member for Queenborough until Charles II's reign.

The elections led to many acrimonious exchanges; they were considered a source of wealth for Queenborough.

The way the island was shaping was going to be the pattern until the end of the nineteenth century.

The rurals areas remained practically unchanged for centuries, and it has been remarked that the villages in 1890 were little different from the villages in 1590.

Until well into the nineteenth century the Kentish 'turn wrest' plough was still in use, a clumsy plough described as looking more like a cart than a plough, which laid all the furrows one way, unlike the ridge and furrow of other ploughs. In the hands of an experienced ploughman it could be used to make ridge and furrow, and this was done on wet land, when added drainage was necessary. Oxen were used for ploughing into the eighteenth century and oxen shoes have been turned up by later ploughmen in many island fields. The number of fields called Oxen Pasture, or Ox Marsh, are proof of the widespread use of the animal for work as well as meat.

It would be safe to bet that there are two things James I will always be remembered for in Sheppey. One is the Gunpowder Plot in 1605, which had repercussions in more ways than one for centuries.

For some unknown reason the islanders developed a passion for fireworks, and not just the children, either. In the mid-eighteenth century there are court records of fines imposed on people for 'throwing fireworks and rockets in the main street' at Minster. The Constable had been warned to watch for this. One unlucky youth blew himself up in his attempt to produce fireworks.

In the earliest records of Minster Primary School (that is 1872 and onwards), there are references to 'Pupils preparing for Pope's Day', and it is obvious that teacher is as enthralled as his pupils. Why 'Pope's Day' no-one can explain, but that is what they called it, and reading between the lines one has the impression that an effigy of a pope was made for burning. Throughout the centuries local events of any importance have ended with a firework display, which seems to have been the highlight of the evening in every sense.

The second thing King James I is remembered for is, of all unlikely things, mulberry trees.

In the gardens of some of the older houses on the islands there is a mulberry tree, an odd tree to find in what is often a desolate place, and there is no logical pattern in their distribution. At 'Fig Tree' house in Queenborough there is a huge one, and this is understandable for Fig Tree was one of the 'better' houses in the borough. There is another in the garden of Cheyney Rock House, a large residence, now flats, where different families 'of quality' lived in bygone days. Once the oyster fishing was run from there, later a surgeon lived there, but the house is on the sea front at the end of Marine Parade, hardly a place for a mulberry tree.

Yet another is in the garden at New Hook Farm, looking rather wind-torn out there on the marshes, but surviving. There may have been others, that is not a complete list, but they were certainly planted in some unlikely spots. The local people can give the reason for it. 'It was King Charles, or James, one of that lot' they will tell anyone who asks, 'they had mulberry trees planted to try and start silk making, to make work, and try and give folk something to do.'

This time the story is correct — this is no local legend. When Lord Edward Wotton was Lord Lieutenant of Kent, 1604–28, James I wrote long and detailed letters to him with instructions 'for the making of silk'. His majesty gave repeated warnings against the dangers of idleness, the ills of poverty that resulted, and the honour that honest labour brought to a country. The point of all that was that he wished to have mulberry trees planted to encourage the silk industry around Maidstone, the plants to be sold in the fair at six shillings per hundred and they would be chargeable in a levy within the county. This was written on November twentieth in the sixth year of his reign.

Lord Wotton dutifully wrote to the deputy lieutenants and the J.P.s 'concerning the encouragement to be given to the silk industry in the county, to set the common people on worke to prevent them from idleness (the mother of all vices) and also to bring general profit and gain to them. At the next quarter sessions they are to debate on how to implement his Majestie's instructions. He desires them to buy Mulberry plants themselves to give good example. (Myself intending to invest in one thousand plants).' From the court at Whitehall 1608. Hence the mulberry trees, which were widely distributed. The king's intentions were good, but the scheme itself was rather a hare-brained effort. There is no record of silk being made in Sheppey, but the old trees bear witness to the attempt.

James I gives the impression of being a somewhat ineffectual sovereign. However, he was a Protestant, and was as intolerant of Puritans and Calvinists as he was of Roman Catholics. Conversely, he believed implicitly in witchcraft, and during his reign a witch hunt was a usual occurrence. Everyone believed in witches and magic, not only the peasants and labouring classes, but the yeoman and aristocrats as well. Many harmless old ladies, and some not so old, found themselves in trouble, perhaps over nothing worse than a spiteful look or remark. There are no records of trials of witches on the island, but several Faversham women were accused and tried. There are stories of witches and wise women, especially one that lived at Warden. She was well known for her powers of healing both people and animals, and would do no-one any harm unless she was crossed. Unfortunately there is no date for this little story — it is one of those 'a long time ago' tales.

The islanders have always been inclined to superstition. The reason why the 'Cottrells' have never been excavated is proof of this; no-one would chance bringing so much bad luck on themselves.

Until quite recently many of them believed in the 'evil eye'. It was possible for people to wish 'bad' on you, and if anyone suffered a noticeable run of ill luck he or she would be certain that someone had ill wished them.

There was a recognised spoken formula that anyone so ill wished could employ to 'turn it back' on the person who had cursed or bad wished them. It was perfectly in order to do this, a form of self-defence in fact, and it has been known to be used.

Naturally enough, people ask if this really works, and the only answer is that no Sheppey man would commit himself to an answer, but he certainly would not risk saying that it *didn't* work.

There were also the Good Luck charms that were carried, hares' feet having an especial attraction and a magic of their own.

There was a big emphasis on 'being fair', and a marked injustice would be met with the odd remark 'it's not fairations'. If people didn't believe in 'fairations' and were repeatedly unjust, everyone was certain that 'it would come back on them'.

Basically, it was the ancient belief in Divine Intervention that most oppressed classes have resorted to when not in a position to tackle the oppressors.

There was also local belief, in Minster at least, in signs, portents, the powers of people who could 'dream true', and 'see' into the future, or had a sixth sense that warned of impending trouble. By and large, Sheppey folk probably had a certain amount of sympathy for the king in his fear and horror of witches.

Witches or not, James I was largely responsible for the publication of the Authorised Version of the Bible in 1611. Ordinary people were allowed to own a copy and read it for themselves, the drawback to this being that so few could read.

A copy was in every church, and James I's Bible, that was in use for generations, can still be seen in Minster Abbey, worn and somewhat battered but quite readable.

The vestry meeting and election of officers by the parish was an established fact by this time. No records as early as this remain, but early records that are available give the impression that this form of administration had been established for many years.

James I was succeeded in 1625 by his son Charles. King Charles I was continually at loggerheads with his government, largely due to his own obstinacy. He attempted to govern by personal rule, and found that without Parliament there was no money. He raised funds by the sale of monopolies, which upset the balance of the many new ventures that had begun to prosper, and not surprisingly this incurred the merchants' wrath. Another very unpopular measure was 'Ship Money', which was demanded from seaports and coastal towns.

This fell heavily and unfairly on Kent, and small towns suffered, including Queenborough.

The farm called Netts, or Neats Court, had always been Crown property. In Elizabeth I's time it had been let at an annual rent of £10. Charles I settled it on his new bride, Queen Henrietta-Maria, as part of her dower. In the fourteenth year of his reign a lease of the Manor of Neats Court was granted to Sir Edward Hales, Knight and Baronet, for three lives, in consideration of a fine of four hundred and fifty pounds, and other conditions.

There is no explanation of the name 'Neats', but a Neat was another name for an ox, it was used frequently in the Middle Ages, and the name may be derived from that.

Neats Court, on the Queenborough to Eastchurch Road, is a large Georgian house with several large yards beside it, and is still used as a working farm. It is said to have big double doors in some of the rooms, a gun room and a cellar filled with water. It has several cellars, and the water-filled one may be nothing more than an underground water tank, quite a number of the older farms have them. The water was pumped out with an old-fashioned hand pump, and used for household purposes; it was not supposed to be used for drinking.

At Harty, the coat of arms of Samuel Hayward can still be seen. He owned land there and was buried in the Church of St. Thomas in 1612. William Hayward shared his father's resting place on 'March ye sixteenth, 1679', while Elizabeth presumably Samuel's wife, mother, or sister, was buried in 1610. John Cuslocke, who was twice Mayor of Faversham, took as his second wife Alice, one of the daughters and co-heirs of Samuel. There are so few burials of note recorded at Harty in early days that it is pleasant to think that someone there had enough land and prestige to be courted by the Mayor of Faversham in 1651.

Throughout the reigns of James I and Charles I the beacons were kept in readiness, and various orders were issued regarding them. They were allowed to lapse after 1640, with frightening results.

One of Charles I's early Acts was to rectify the Queenborough Charter. This had been confirmed by previous kings, but the new charter issued by Charles, based on the original granted by Edward III, was preserved and used as the basis of Queenborough law until the Municipal Corporation Act of 1835. Extracts from it show how the borough was run and governed.

1) The Former Charters were recited.
2) The present Charter granted on petition of the Mayor, bailiffs and burgesses in order 'that there shall be continually had in the same borough one certain and undoubted mode of keeping the peace, and for the good rule and government of our people there . . . and that they shall think themselves more strongly bound to serve us and our successors.'
3) Deals with the limits of the Borough by land and sea, 'saving and reserving nevertheless to us, our successors our Castle of Quenborowe and all the waters

and lands within the liberty, circuit and precints of the same Castle and of the Constable thereof'. There is a note here that the Castle well is, and has been Crown property.
4) Grant of liberties of piscaries and fishings, power of making laws and imposing penalties.
5) A list of the first Mayor, jurats and bailiffs.
6) Mayor to be chosen each Michaelmas Day by the jurats and bailiffs, and 'to take his corporate oath upon the Gospels before the Constable of the Castle'. Jurats and bailiffs to elect their successors. A jurat to be chosen as Deputy Mayor.
7) A court of Record to be held every third Monday.
8) Jurats to elect 'one discreet man learned in the laws of England' as steward of the Borough.
9) 'Two officers called Seargeants-at-Mace to execute the processes of the Court, and to carry silver or gold maces with our arms before the Mayor.'
10) Refers to the twice yearly holding of Frank Pledge.
11) A grant of common gaol. The Mayor to be keeper of same.
12) Parish Constable to be appointed to take corporate oath etc.
13) Grant of fines in the Courts to the Corporation.
14) No burgess to find arms out of the Borough, but 'all to be always ready and well armed and accounted to defend the Castle and Borough'.
15) A long list of 'freedoms', including Tallage and Kayage.
16) General grant of all manner of liberties and franchises except accustomed services.
17) 'To be held as our Manor of East Greenwich, as in free and common socage, and not by Knights' Service, paying to us and our successors ten shillings at the Feast of Saint Michael the Archangel yearly and forever.'

It was a grand-sounding charter for a small borough.

Sir Edward Hoby died in 1616, it is said at Queenborough. Before that time he had disposed of most of his property on the island, and the Manor of Minster, including the site of the monastery and other small estates, was sold, and came to Sir Michael Livesey, the son of Sir Gabriel from Parsonage Farm at Eastchurch.

Sir Michael in his turn conveyed the manor and lands to Sir John Hayward of Hollingbourne, the son of a London alderman. When Sir John died in 1636, he left the Minster state in trust, the money it earned to be used for charitable purposes. This became known as 'John Hayward's Charity'.

In later years many people imagined that John Hayward was a local man who had desired to do something effective for Minster, but the truth was that he barely knew the island, and most of the money provided from his 'charity' left the island to aid other areas.

By 1636 the steeple of Queenborough Church was in such a state of ruin that it had become a danger, as it was more than likely to fall. The residents of the town had attempted to repair it, but found the expense too great. Accordingly, the mayor and corporation obtained a certificate from Quarter Sessions at Canterbury Castle signed by the knights and dignitaries of Kent, Isaac Bargrave the Dean of Canterbury, and the local J.P.s. This certificate they sent to the king, together with a 'humble supplication' for aid.

The king obligingly granted them 'Our Letters Patent of Collection under the Great Seale of England, that so they may be enabled to ask and receive the charities of well disposed people . . .'. The right of collection so granted allowed Queenborough to send the brief to every parish in England.

The king's description of Queenborough Church's distress

was detailed and calculated to inspire pity. After the usual formal greetings, and a recital of the borough's certificate and their petition, he continued:

That the steeple of the Church aforesaid standing open to the sea, and being a common land mark at sea, to which place Mariners and Seafaring men in time of foule weather or danger make for shelter, which said Steeple is now by the extrodinarie violence of Tempest become so ruinous and in such decay, that it is very likely to fall to the ground, the Fall whereof will be very dangerous and hurtfull to the body of the Church. Upon the repairing and beautifying whereof the said Inhabitant have of late expended and disbursed a good summe of money, but are no wise able to new build the said Steeple, which being viewed by well experienced workmen, must of necessity with part of the Church be taken down to the very foundation, the charge whereof as the said workmen doth affirm, will Amount unto the sum of six hundred pounds at the least, which charge the said inhabitants are no ways able of themselves to undergo, the whole Towne and liberty thereof consisting but of two hundred acres of land, with two and thirty households, and the most part of them very poor Fishermen, whereof our subjects the Inhabitants of Queenborough aforesaid have most humbly besought us, that we would be graciously pleased to grant unto them Our Letters Patent of Collection . . .

So there was Queenborough, about ten houses more than in the time of Elizabeth, a town of poor fishermen with a wellnigh ruined church.

They were not very lucky with their collection, as from one thousand four hundred and seventy-six parishes the receipts show that less than a total of one hundred and thirty-five pounds was collected. Four hundred and twenty-eight parishes collected amounts varying from one penny to eleven pence, and sixty-two sent the brief back with no money at all. Somehow they rebuilt their tower, but it must have been hard going.

While Queenborough steeple was in danger of falling and Minster was being bought and sold as though the priory had never existed, or been the chief point of importance on Sheppey, Thomas Johnson, an apothecary with a shop on Snow Hill, was seeking fresh places where he could find plants for his pills and potions. In 1629 he ventured as far as Sheppey, where he found the local people hostile and suspicious, so suspicious that they arrested the unfortunate plant hunters and locked them up. Later the mayor questioned them, and released them. Whether they had to pay for their release, and whether they continued their search or took the next boat back to London, isn't told, which is a shame. Presumably the explorers had left London by ship, and come ashore at Queenborough.

For many years Sheppey has been accused of disliking strangers, and the accusation is not altogether unfounded. In defence of the islanders, it is only fair to point out that 'foreigners' have not always been kind to them, as history shows.

The king's relationship with his Parliament and advisers was deteriorating, although it is unlikely that at that period Sheppey was much affected. There were no big landlords resident, except for Sir Michael Livesey, and the farmers, small-holders, village tradesmen, and their men were too busy to worry about what was happening in London, which seemed long miles away to them.

When the Civil War started in 1642 the fighting passed Kent by. The county families were involved, joining either the king or the Commonwealth, but at that stage the local people were not greatly affected. As the war progressed, this altered. Kent was considered 'malignant', supporting the king, apart from the dockyards at Greenwich and Chatham.

Sheppey, it is thought, had royalist sympathies, but Sir Michael Livesey was a leading Parliamentarian, and the islanders soon knew it.

It is unfortunate that records of the Civil War are so scarce and unsatisfactory. Church registers have great gaps, and those that are available are frequently ill kept, as many of the Commonwealth incumbents were lacking in education.

Archbishop Laud was arrested and imprisoned in the Tower in 1641. Most parish priests' entries ended in 1642, and then there was a break of twenty years. The Church was never again to have the same power in lay affairs.

Michael Livesey enforced the Commonwealth regime in Sheppey, and replaced the curates in the churches. Marriage was regarded as a civil contract, and Sir Michael's signature can be seen on marriage certificates of this time, as he frequently acted as magistrate for the occasion himself.

In the sixteenth year of King Charles' reign the Members of Parliament for Queenborough were Sir Edward Hales and William Harrison, esq. They were turned out to make way for Sir Michael Livesey and Augustine Garland, esq., who were the choice of the Commonwealth. From there it was not long before Commonwealth soldiers were billeted on the island.

They came to Queenborough, and from there spread over to Sheppey. Much of the damage done to Minster Abbey is attributed to Cromwell's soldiers, and a farmer who once lived at Norwood Manor said that the destruction they caused there was easy to identify. They were billeted at Shurland, and what was left of the great Hall suffered under their hands. In an attempt to enforce their form of religious belief, they defaced and wrecked anything of beauty that they considered was High Church or 'Popish'.

To this day people speak with disgust of 'what Cromwell's men did', and Cromwell was, and still is, hated on Sheppey.

So deep did this bite that when Queenborough was offered a portrait of one of the Commonwealth M.P.s, in the years following the second world war, they refused, saying that no-one who had anything to do with the death of Charles I was going to have his portrait hung in their guildhall.

Queenborough had good cause for complaint. King Charles I was beheaded in 1648, and Queenborough Castle was promptly seized by the State. It was surveyed, and the report was brief and concise.

Survey of the Castle.

It was built in the time of bows and arrows
There are no platforms for cannons.
It does not command the sea.
Not fit to be kept and restored but to be demolished.

As the castle had been refortified, at great expense, in Queen Elizabeth's reign, its uselessness is open to doubt. It was a strong castle, and there is no proof, so far, that cannons could not have been placed there. As usual, the islanders have their own story about the demolition. There was nothing wrong with the castle, they said, but old Cromwell was afraid that the islanders would take it over and stand out against him, so he had it taken down, which is exactly what he did. He sold it to Mr. John Wilkinson, who demolished and removed it — completely. Only the well was left, which the town was then allowed to use, provided that they maintained it. The materials, excluding demolition costs, were worth £1,792 12s. 0½d. It is said that at the same time all the records and documents stored in the castle were destroyed, and certainly very little remains to tell anything accurate about life in the castle, not even a complete list of constables.

'Neat's Court' and 'a tenement called Hughes', both 'lately belonging to Queen Henrietta-Maria', were also surveyed. The tenement called Hughes has long since disappeared without trace. It was a small farm, the house consisting of a hall, kitchen and buttery, one little barn and one stable, a garden and a fold yard. Various other small pieces of land are surveyed and valued, the whole amounting to £32 2s. 0d. Neat's Court was much larger, a small manor house. It had a hall, a parlour, one larder, a buttery, two other rooms, and four chambers (upstairs) with garrets over them. Four great barns, one being new built of brick and roofed, buildings with bays (for storing hay and straw), and a large stable, several out-houses, one garden and four yards, two fold yards, all two acres and a half value two pounds and two pence. John Tise was under-tenant. The Hill field of forty-four acres was valued at forty-five pounds. All the land was surveyed, including a field called Joan's Field of thirty acres, and Joan's Field Marsh. These names appear again on the tithe maps of 1848.

There were thirty-two acres called Queenborough Marsh, and Henry Segar was the under-tenant. Furze Field was estimated as sixty-seven acres, and Furze Hill is still a local landmark.

Sir Edward Hales was named as chief tenant of the Ferry Marsh, worth one hundred and ten pounds. After the survey, the Queen's lands were leased to John Show, or Snow, of Minster, with the proviso that the rents were to be paid yearly, the sum of ten shillings was to be allowed towards the Ferry maintenance, and the sea walls and hedges were to be maintained.

It was a sad end for a castle that had once been an important military base, and the islanders found Commonwealth rule a hard yoke to bear.

CHAPTER XV

The troubled times

Although there is a gap in the church registers, the Minster registers commenced in 1569, but they are difficult to decipher. Eastchurch registers commence later, which isn't surprising as Eastchurch was frequently without a curate. Their Overseers of the Poor accounts commence in 1667, and the first Overseers accounts from Minster are 1694–5, but they are not available for inspection. The point about the accounts, and the vestry reports which date from the early eighteenth century, is that they seem a recognised institution, they have been compiled in this way, and the work carried out as stated, for many years. Although no earlier parish records have been retained, it is evident that this had been the recognised method of parish government throughout the seventeenth century and at least part of the sixteenth century, and the Civil War had not interfered with the parish's administration.

In a record of the Courts Archdeaconry and Consistory of Canterbury, under Presentments, the churchwardens of Harty made the following charge against their curate in 1637.

> Our Minister useth to wear a short Priest's gown but hath no gown.
> We present our Minister for that since Michaelmas last he hath been divers times to an alehouse in our Parish (namely John Osbornes') at cards and useth sometimes to swear more than is fit, as fame goeth.
> Our afternoon sermons (which we have twice or three times in a quarter of a year) are not turned into catechism by question and answer, as is required, but usually performed as at other times.

To the first the curate replied that 'he is a poor man and not able to buy him a gown, but weareth a short coat in performing his duty in the Church and a surplice over the same, but graduate he is none'.

To the second 'That he hath been at the house detected and there sometimes played at cards at Christmas time with one of his neighbours in friendly sort and some small matter, and not otherwise, and unawares an oath might fall out of his mouth, but he is heartily sorry for the same, and promises seriously hereafter to be more wary in giving occasion of offence of that kind'.

Records for the church at Harty are scant, and the officious churchwardens were not named. It was a hard life being a curate on about £20 a year, often he was little different in kind from the farm workers he ministered to, but they obviously objected to him living as they did.

Records for Warden Church are also few, apparently their early registers were burnt in a fire.

Minster registers tell a good deal about the people living in the village. The burial registers record that in 1614 Alexander Sampson of Eastchurch was buried, but there is no explanation as to why he chose Minster. In 1637 Sarah, wife of Richard Barefoot was buried. Thomas Barfoot was one of the jurors at the Law Day at Kingsborough and must have been some relation.

Also a Chrysome of the Widdow Richards. There is much debate about 'chrisoms'. A chrisom was a baptismal gown, and the expression seems to refer to a baby that died within a month of birth, not necessarily unbaptised, and the christening gown was then used as a shroud.

A Northman, a stranger from the Widdow Woolet's, was buried. So strange that no-one bothered with a name for him! In February 1639 Phillip Wyborne and 'Old Mother Willis' were buried, so the name Wyborne had survived from the thirteenth century. In 1642 Sarah, daughter of Thomas Woollet, 'with one arm' was buried, and then there are no records until 1660, when 'Charles, son of Samuel and Elizabeth Carden', and on December 31st 'Susanna ye wife of Adam Segar' were buried. The comments in the old registers make them far more interesting than the more conventional entries of today.

The Cardens and Segars were island farmers in the time of Elizabeth I, but after the seventeenth century their names gradually fade out, and there is no way of knowing what happened to the families, whether they left the island, lost their money and local standing, or simply died out.

That gap of twenty years must have seemed a long time to the people of Sheppey. The Commonwealth rule grew harder and meaner as the years went by. Taxes were imposed on the export of wool in 1640, which led to more smuggling in Kent, as, if wool could be taken quietly overseas the profit was far greater than when it was shipped out lawfully. May Day was abolished in 1644. No more May Day dancing or going to the woods early to pick green boughs and flowers to festoon the houses with. That was all forbidden. The Constables were ordered to remove the Maypoles at once, and there was a fine of five shillings imposed for every week they remained up. So that was one much loved county celebration killed outright (and it never really came back in the same way) and the people were angry and resentful. No-one in Sheppey has any idea where the Maypoles stood. At Minster it is thought somewhere in front of the abbey, perhaps in the southern corner behind where the King's Arms stands now. Eastchurch has no idea, and an old Queenborian once heard that there was 'somewhere called Maypole Hill in Queenborough but no-one knew where it was'.

By 1647 the Puritans were well in command and decreed that there was to be no Christmas Day, or Christmas celebrations. The day to be kept as a fast, shops to open; if it happened to be a market day, as it was in Canterbury, the market was to proceed as usual. There were no church services, and anyone hanging holly, rosemary or bays on their door would be penalised. Plum puddings and nativity pies were also forbidden. Not suprisingly, Canterbury rioted, and this was the beginning of the Royalist rising of 1648. After the usual committees and petitions, fighting began, and there were battles at Aylesford, Rochester and Maidstone. Sheppey escaped, but there are local stories of the aftermath.

There were a number of Roman Catholics in the area, as the Roper family of Teynham were Catholics, and headed the party. Some of the Sheppey people, most of whom were Royalists, were sympathetic to them, and when the king's men were beaten in the fighting around Maidstone many came to the island for sanctuary. Their luck was out, for Michael Livesey knew the layout of the island's hiding places, and soon flushed out the defeated Royalists. It is only a local story, but there is probably some truth in it. There is no record of which houses they went to for help, but there is proof of a hidden room at Tam's Farm (now demolished) Borstal Lodge, Warden Manor and Whybornes Farm, and there must have been others.

Then, of course, there were the tunnels. The islanders were, and still are, obsessed with tunnels. There is no place of any historical interest that is not credited with a tunnel. Tunnels ran from the abbey to Borstal Hall and to Parsonage Farm at Minster, from Warden Manor to Shurland Hall, there is an opening to a tunnel in Back Lane, Minster, in fact there were no end of tunnels. If only someone could actually discover one of these old tunnels and explore it, everyone would be satisfied, as it stands at present there is no conclusive evidence.

To start with, the ground is unsuitable for digging tunnels. It is heavy clay, and a tunnel would need to be brick lined or it would collapse in on itself very quickly. Tunnels from the abbey are not very likely, if there were any they would have led from the priory, and during all the foundation laying and road digging that has taken place none have been discovered. Beneath the abbey floor are many graves, it is impossible to do any work to the church floor without disinterring old bones.

Beneath the gate house a small cellar was found and cleared of rubbish, but there was no sign of a tunnel opening. The low cellar walls were lined with old tombstones, and nothing more. There seems no reason for a tunnel to Borstal. It was a minor Manor, usually leased, and rebuilt in the eighteenth century. Under Borstal were cellars, with, it is said, openings bricked up 'that could have been tunnels', and could equally well have been disused cellars. As Borstal Hall was burnt to the ground in 1948 no-one will ever know, unless they do a lot of digging. Plenty of reasons can be advanced for a tunnel to Parsonage Farm, as that was where visiting monks were lodged, and the populace is completely convinced that there were 'goings on' between the monks and the nuns. Even today people will swear that there is an opening in a road near Parsonage 'not long filled in' which led to a tunnel. Looked at squarely, the length of such a tunnel would make it an impossibility.

The distance from Warden Manor to Shurland Hall makes it again rather a long tunnel to construct. Shurland Hall was rebuilt 1510–20, and was deserted by 1570. Warden Manor has had a chequered history, and the cellars have been filled in because they flooded, preventing any investigations there.

Shurland has always been the biggest 'tunnel' attraction. Before the Second World War a young man went down what he thought was a tunnel and had to be hauled out, overcome by foul air. Since then it has been verified that there are numerous large vaults and cellars under the Hall, or where the Hall stood. There is yet another Shurland story. Earlier this century a young farmer was ploughing there, he is an elderly man now and tells this story himself. His tractor was large and probably rather clumsy, and it went through the top soil. Delighted, he rushed to investigate, thinking that he had plunged into 'The Tunnel.' It turned out to be the remains of an underground store, or cellar, of great age, complete with wooden pegs for hanging food on for storing.

The latest tunnel has an opening somewhere near the old people's bungalows in Back Lane. There is an opening there, now covered up by the council, but no-one seems in a hurry to go down and look. There was once an old row of terraced cottages there, on the corner of Back Lane and Scocles Road, situated at right angles to them in Scocles Road a similar row. They were referred to as Malt'us Cottages although the row in Back Lane was formally named Swale View Terrace. The tunnel was originally in the kitchen of one of these cottages, and a man went down it and returned clutching an old sword, white faced and unable to speak. The sword has disappeared, and presumably the hero of the day has recovered his voice, but no-one seems to know what he saw. The family who once owned the property says that there was a huge cellar beneath the cottages, and if they were originally built and used as a malthouse that would be a reasonable explanation. So the tunnels remain unverified, but people are unshaken in their belief in them, and everyone locally would be delighted if one was actually found, and the beliefs confirmed. Tunnels or no, the Royalists were caught, or kept moving, and the revolt, with its rallying cry of 'For God, King Charles and Kent', failed.

The people endured until 1660, and then King Charles II returned and England rejoiced.

Queenborough has a small account of events in a record of 1653. There were the usual payments for mending windows and roads, and they were then having stocks erected, to add to the other correctives. A poor man needed a sheet and socks (for sockinge of him) for burial. Then comes:

For lobsters for Colonel Kenniwicke	15s. 6d.
To Weldishe and William Helowe for fetching back the souldiers	3s. 0d.

So Commonwealth Colonel and Soldiers were well looked after.

The other item of note is the money paid for 'cleaning of the well', and work done around it. This was the castle well, and the town now had access to it, for which they must have been grateful, for fresh water was not plentiful.

In 1654 the mayor received a letter telling him that 'His Highness the Lord Protector and the Council have thought fit that at the time and place where proclamation shall be made for the election of the Burgesses, the instrument entitled Ye Goverment of the Commonwealth shall be read'. Of course the mayor read it to the borough, he had no choice.

On King Charles' return it is said that Queenborough was illuminated that night, and there were celebrations and rejoicing. Minster and Eastchurch would not have been far behind, the rejoicing consisting in those days of bell ringing, bonfires and beer. In 1664 Queenborough paid a cess of £37 for renewing their Charter. Sir James Herbert was M.P. with Sir James Wheler—Livesey and Garland had fled. A certain Mr. Richard Thompson was presented at the Court Leet in

1660 for breaking down the cage and stockhouse, for detaining money given to the town by James Herbert, esq., and for detaining the plate taken off the town mace, whereon was engraved the last Pretended State Arms, and they order it to be delivered (as before) on penalty of forty shillings.

Victuallers were ordered to sell a full wine quart of strong beer (to anyone who asks) for one penny, penalty twelve pence for default, not exceeding two quarts in one day per man.

There were the usual complaints about people keeping more hogs than their stint on the Common, and not coming to church, and then 'the Register Book not kept properly, (several persons uncapable of keeping the same) several persons who have been born and buried have not been registered, to the great dishonour of the town and these born therein, so the Minister shall have it, or someone capable'. That seems to say it all.

By 1661 Minster Abbey had a new curate, Samuel Symonds, followed by Thomas Brocklebank in 1664. At Eastchurch the curate had been sequested in 1640, but at the restoration Michael Livesey's lands were granted to James, Duke of York, and the king was the patron of the church. He presented Robert Wilkinson, described as clerk, in 1660, and in 1666 he presented the reverend Thomas White, who stayed until he died in 1682. The large silver paten dated 1675, a smaller decorated paten also dated, and a silver cup, all inscribed in Latin, are attributed to the Reverend White, who presented them to the somewhat denuded church. Charles II granted the church and rectory to Sir Henry Palmer of Wingham and eleven other men, and to their heirs, in trust. They were to find a fit person to present as vicar, and the vicar was to be allowed to enjoy the titles and profits. Forseeably, that didn't work. The vicar served the church, but Parsonage Farm (Eastchurch) tithes and profits, somehow found their way to another owner. This continued until all the trustees had died, then their heirs carried on the good work. Until 1827 or thereabouts, the vicar lived in a tumbledown cottage at the west end of the churchyard.

In spite of these difficulties, Eastchurch was happier now the soldiers had left Shurland and Sir Michael had gone, and some of their entries in the church register were original to say the least, and sometimes not very pious.

Baptisms start conventionally enough with; '1678 Elizabeth, daughter of William and Elizabeth Love, December 5th'. There are still many Loves living and farming at Eastchurch and Leysdown, and if Elizabeth is a remote ancestor she can also claim to be ancestor to Beals, Mounts, Ingletons and other local families.

Thomas, son of John and Mary Greengrass, October 2, 1690. The Greengrasses were mentioned in Elizabeth I's reign, one of them farmed Stonepit Farm in the eighteenth century and then the family seemed to fade out. Stonepit Farm was later farmed by Harold Ingleton, before becoming the R.A.F. station and aerodrome, and now the prison at Standford Hill. Another entry is sad. In 1693 William, 'ye orphan of William and Elizabeth Couchman, baptized at ye interment of his mother, November 15th'. His father must have married again, it was usual, and hopefully she was a good step-mother.

In 1700 comes a down-to-earth entry, not likely to be seen today. 'Elizabeth, second bastard of Joan Gold, poor whore. October 27th.'

Burials are as descriptive. '1677, A stranger, threshed for Thomas Higgins.' No name, no bother, just nothing. He was 'a foreigner'.

In 1678 it is recorded, tongue-in-cheek fashion: 'Captain John Ruffin of Newington. Buried in woollen, on account of Act of Parliament proved September 19.' Following this reads; 'Bastard child of Anne Bullowe, John Dowing a poor boy, and Mathew Holmes an old man'. They wrote so little,

yet it told so much. In 1683 Damared Young, servant maid, was buried, in 1684 Mrs. Bridget Dade of Borstal, in Minster. Mrs. Bridget Dade left money as a charity for poor women, it is still distributed, and known as Madame Dade's Charity. Her husband owned property in Eastchurch, although she lived at Minster.

The entries continued in this manner, one burial was 'A stranger come from Warden' in 1685, and there were 'poor maids', 'poor orphans', 'poor parish maids and widows', plus a good sprinkling of bastard sons and daughters.

At Minster the registers were much the same. The plague visited Minster in 1644–5 and nineteen people died, six from one household. It did not spread any further, for once the under-population was beneficial. In 1654 Ann Allan was buried, killed by the fall of a water cart.

In the following century the vicar of Minster Abbey was to become busier than any previous incumbent, but that was still in the future.

Charles II's reign had started merrily enough, but he was not to have an easy time. He had come to a kingdom that had very little money, Cromwell and his army had accounted for most of it. The king was accused of extravagance, his court was superficial and amoral, but there was little cash in the Treasury to start with. The Great Plague and the Fire of London shook that city in 1665 and 1666, and then, to shame everyone, the Dutch sailed up the Medway and caused chaos. There is really no better account of this time than Samuel Pepys' Diary. He was in London, and recounted vividly the horror of it all. He also made quite clear the lack of money for defence purposes, and the poor, literally starving plight of the unpaid dockyard workers. The king had quarrelled with the Dutch, but as there was a conference arranged to be held at Bredon, in March 1667, he hoped that the Dutch would keep an unofficial truce. There were no beacons, no soldiers or hobiliers, the fort at Sheerness was obsolete, and the castle was gone. Never had Sheppey been so defenceless.

'King Charles II started the dockyard' is the story told in Sheppey, as though he had dropped it there, complete, overnight. He didn't, and the story of Sheerness dockyard would make a book in itself, so this of necessity will have to be an outline. In 1665 ground in Sheerness was surveyed, with a view to a dockyard. The king's opinion of the marshy waste was not complimentary. In 1666 a fort was decided on, and in 1667 the king and the Duke of York arrived at Sheerness, (and there was nothing there at that time but Henry VIII's small outdated fortification) to 'lay out the design' of the proposed Fort.

Following that, for many reasons, but mainly lack of money and men, very little happened. 'Pressed' men were employed as unwilling workmen, and working conditions were very bad.

The Dutch were preparing for invasion, and the English chose to ignore this. English men imprisoned in Holland volunteered to act as pilots for the Dutch, for the rivers were known to be difficult.

By June 5th the Dutch were off the North Foreland, but when the reports reached Whitehall, the government remained unperturbed. The Duke of York ordered the yards to 'stand by', but when the Dutch landed on Canvey Island looking for food the panic started. The local militia drove the Dutch off, and the people in charge rushed about looking for fireships.

Prince Rupert went to Woolwich, the Duke of Albemarle to Chatham, and Samuel Pepys was at Deptford with Sir William Coventry, still searching for fireships. On Monday, June 10th the Dutch ships were off Sheppey. The only British ship was the guard ship Unity. Sir Edward Spragge was in charge, and he sent for Scottish troops who were at Margate. After much dithering only one company was sent.

The Clerk of Check at Chatham was ordered to send men

from the 'Monmouth' to Sheerness, when the ship had been brought above the chain. Ships were going aground in the panic, the 'Monmouth' amongst them, and the men deserted. The army went to the Isle of Grain and didn't return, and the Kentish Militia at Sheerness were useless.

Admiral Van Ghent's squadron reached Sheerness at 5 p.m. The Unity, with fireships and ketches, was in their path, standing off Garrison Point.

The sixteen guns in the fort were so insecure that firing them was well nigh impossible. Some were made serviceable by putting planks under the carriages, but they could not stop the Dutch. The Unity tried to distract the enemy by firing, but she was chased by a Dutch fireship and so she withdrew, taking her ships with her. The Dutch opened fire on the fort, and some of the defending gunmen were badly injured. The rumour spread that there was no surgeon (and it was probably no rumour) panic ensued, and all but seven men deserted. These had to give up as the Dutch had come ashore, and they were rescued by Edward Spragge's yacht.

Troops were stationed at the ferry to guard it, and it was debated whether or not the marshes could be flooded, to prevent the Dutch crossing to the mainland. The Dutch fired on the fort for some time then captured it, and hoisted the Dutch flag in place of the British flag. The Dutch found timber, masts, tar, gunpowder and other stores, and what they couldn't take with them they burnt. Luckily for the island, they hadn't enough troops to garrison the fort, or to venture far inland, and they decided not to ravage Sheppey.

According to a Dutch report, some of the ships' crews ventured into Sheppey, found that everyone had fled, and returned with booty.

Another report states that Dutch troops marched to Queenborough, and the inhabitants paid them to go away, but the Queenborough records do not mention this. There is absolutely no record, either Dutch or English, of the Mayor of Queenborough hoisting a white flag, or of Queenborough being captured, so where that story came from is anyone's guess. By the 12th of June the fort at Sheerness had been demolished, and a few embankments had been destroyed for good measure. The Dutch knew all about embankments and flooding.

Troops arrived in Sheppey, English and Scottish, and had a fine time looting and vandalising abandoned houses. The Dutch sailed up the Medway as far as Gillingham, capturing and destroying British ships. It is an unpleasant story to tell, but many English men deserted to the Dutch, where they were fed and paid well. That was the attraction, and the reason for deserting. The Dutch fleet lay off Sheppey, and on June 19th went ashore for food, where they met with no resistance and took what cattle and sheep they needed.

There was no violence or bad behaviour, and sailors were punished severely if they disobeyed this order. The punishment was hard. They were thrown into the sea three times from the end of the main yard, and then received one hundred and fifty lashes. Looting soldiers received the same treatment.

After coming ashore for food, the fleet left Sheppey and did not return. They continued to harass English ships in the Channel until July, and cruised around being irritating until well into August, but there is no truth in the statement that they were around Sheppey and coming ashore for three months.

The action was all over in ten days, but that was long enough for the islanders. After this the fort at Sheerness was rebuilt, and thirty guns placed there. There was some question of re-erecting the beacons, and a survey was started, but it came to nothing. The repairing of the Sheerness Fort started the following January, as the Privy Council Committee for Fortifications determined to see it finished after the previous delays.

A further scare occurred in 1692 when French and Irish forces collected in France to invade England, but the French Fleet was defeated by Admiral Russell at La Hogue, ensuring peace for a while. The Government still felt unable to relax even when the peace treaty was signed, and all the Medway forts were repaired.

The estimates for Sheerness came to three thousand four hundred and forty one pounds, and eight shillings. For that money parapets were repaired with brickwork, floors were raised, thousands of feet of platform were paved, and other improvements made. Even this was not considered enough, for under 'more for Sheerness', there is another estimate for eleven thousand pounds. This was to include building lodgings for the officers, thousands of yards of paving, again, for the fort, and the most important thing left to the last, 'for supplying the guns with standing carriages' five hundred pounds. Much of this work was done with Kentish ragstone from Boughton quarries, which was shipped to the fort direct, just as had been done when Queenborough Castle was built.

While all this was taking place ground was bought by the Crown for a dockyard. It was described as 'an unhealthy marsh of little value', but there was the usual skullduggery when it was purchased, and there was much hidden about the various deals. At the time of the Dutch raid the dockyards were almost useless due to lack of money, but by the end of 1667 a small yard was in course of construction. At that period the yard men were owed a year's wages, they were starving, and even marched to London to complain and beg for assistance and pay. By 1672 some ground with a store house had been enclosed and the following year Prince Rupert was ordered to send ships that only needed minor refits to Sheerness. Back wages were still owing, the workmen were weak from lack of food and some died of starvation. An attempt to stop them taking 'chips' proved useless. Everything they could remove they classed as 'chips', it was all they had to live on.

Men were fetched from Chatham by boat to work at Sheerness and returned the same way. There was no accommodation at Sheerness, and no fresh water, that also came by boat from Chatham. As a temporary measure shipwrights and other Chatham men lived on hulks on the foreshore, but like many temporary things this continued all through the eighteenth century. They petitioned for houses, a market, and a minister, saying that they were 'living in a manner like heathens' without a padre. Houses built for them were taken by the Military, and for the next century the yard took second place to the garrison. In 1686 the yard was closed for a period, it was decided that it was too expensive, and of little use in peace time. This, then, was the start of the dockyard, and a complete and full account of it is not possible here.

Once the initial scare was over, and the Dutch gone, it does not look as though the rest of the island knew or cared about what was happening at Sheerness. New farming methods were becoming known, although not yet widely adopted. Sheppey had had none of the enclosure problems that beset other counties, as for centuries it had been an island of small enclosed farms, apart from marsh grazing. Neither was there any lord of the manor enclosing land to enlarge his estate, in this case it was the reverse, as Shurland had been 'disparked', and was tenanted and run as a farm. Potatoes and turnips had arrived in England, better methods of cultivation were being discussed, and many of the farmers in Sheppey were making a good living. In spite of this, there were very few big houses on the island. The lists of houses compiled for the Hearth Tax, which was levied from 1662 to 1689, show that in 1668 only two houses paid this tax. The house had to be worth over twenty shillings a year, before paying tax, which was set at two shillings for every hearth in the house.

Many people made a little extra money killing vermin, and Eastchurch Parish Records list the payments.

- 1667. Seven shillings and six-pence was paid for a number of hedgehogs and sparrows.
- 1669. Twenty five dozen of vermin cost the Parish six shillings and eight pence.
- 1676. and an otter killed, one shilling, but nine years later an otter earnt half a crown. Rooks heads were presented for payment, and two polecats.

Hedgehogs were killed in large numbers, twenty-seven and forty-five at different times. It seems strange and cruel now, hedgehogs are harmless creatures, but in 1700 the country people were convinced that hedgehogs sucked the milk from cows in the fields.

The parish clerk received ten shillings as one half year's wages for whipping the dogs out of church, and four years later the beadle received a shilling for keeping the dogs out. Eastchurch was never without a curate now, for as one died another was presented by the patrons. In 1684 the trustees presented Dr. James Jeffries as curate, he was the brother of the ill-famed Judge Jeffries, but there are no horror stories about him.

Minster was running smoothly enough on the same lines. The Abbey Farm was leased, it belonged to John Hayward's Charity, and remained in the hands of the trustees until 1800. Farm workers lived in the abbey gate house, and continued to do so until 1921–2. Various extensions were built around it over the years, and it was divided up in various ways in order to get more families in there.

At Queenborough the courts were being held and the records kept, although without the castle there was little for the town except fishing, and the small copperas factory. Queenborough quay was the landing place for anyone or anything that came to the island by boat, and the garrison and dockyard made no difference to this.

Sir James Herbert was M.P. until 1679. He was genuinely interested in the borough and in agriculture, and he helped the island in many ways.

In the latter part of the seventeenth century a silver mace was provided as a ceremonial badge-of-office for the town. It was inscribed Charles Rex, 1670. R. P. Mayor. The church was presented with a large silver flagon, a paten and a cup by Sir Joseph Williamson, one of the M.P.s in 1674. The Williamson arms were inscribed on the gift, and it is now in the chapel of Leeds Castle, for safe keeping. The court of Queenborough made a ruling that no-one with under a certain income could keep a horse, except 'Ye Mayor, jurats and bailiffs, and ye two butchers', on forfeiture of three shillings for every day. Then they must have relented a little, for they added 'The Hoymen and bakers admitted to keep a horse on the green'. At this court session, Stephen Morris was disfranchised until he had paid five pounds for contempt 'in sliteing and undervaluing ye charter'. Queenborough valued the charter above all else, but noticeably took no part in the lawday, or the management of the ferry.

There is a record of a lawday held in the reign of Charles II in 1679. There are no known records of the Interregnum, and in the seventy years since Elizabeth's reign the rules and regulations had multiplied. The format had not altered, it started with the details of the place Kingsborough, the date, and the king's titles. Henry Whitlocke was the Constable for the last year. The boroughs were listed, Ossenden, Seden, Holt, Rydes, Warden and Leysdown, and their borsholders. None of the names had appeared before, they are all unfamiliar. The jury had swelled to twenty-nine men, and of these Adam Segar, Thomas Hobson, John Greengrasse, John Ruffingent, John Garrett, and Thomas Barfoote are all that we recognise from former days. Among the new names Chidwick Silver is of interest, and Thomas ffort and Robert

Fort appear in years to come, or the name Fort does. There were, inevitably, two Smiths, John Smith and Thomas Smith of Mustards Farm, Leysdown. 'Mustards' is still there, and being farmed in a small way. Henry Harrison was chosen as the new constable, and Thomas Hopson as ferry warden. The name Hopson appeared frequently in the following two centuries. The ferrymen were Joseph Templeman and John Baker. Then the jury settled down to the business of the orders. The warden was to 'cause the Ferry boat to be dressed' before Michaelmas next upon pain of five pounds. They confirmed Peter Theobald, gent. Steward for the term of his life. He was evidently a man of some standing locally. There were new regulations, many of them showing how the islanders regarded Sheppey, and the care they bestowed on the general wellbeing.

The ferry warden had to pay twenty shillings for gravel to repair the ferry way and 'let out the water', and another twenty shillings for 'below the ferry wall if need require'. The order regarding viewing the ferry lands included lands on the mainland, Iwade, Halstow and Upchurch, and it had to be done before July 25th 'upon payne of two shillings in case he make default'. As before, the warden had to take house-holders from Minster, Leysdown and Warden with him, and refusal incurred a fine. The ferry keeper's wages, and his duties regarding ropes and cables were set out in detail.

The occupiers of Land in Harty were ordered to 'pay for importing their cattle as followeth':

For every horse two pence. For every bullock two pence. For every score of sheep and every score of lambs eight pence, to the use of the Ferry Keeper.

All rents, assessments and fines had to be collected, and any owing could be recovered by distraint on the owners goods if necessary, all to be accounted for at the next court. The next order seems hard, and there is no explanation for it. 'They also order that every householder of the Isle of Sheppey not being sick or otherwise hindered by urgent occasions allowed by the Ferry Warden, shall appear at the next Court to be here holden by eight of the clock in the morning under payne of three shillings and four pence.'

A solemn order was made regarding inhabitants who refused to take office, or did not appear to take the oath 'bee not present in Court to take the Oath according to the ancient custom ...'. Refusal could have a fine of up to five pounds, at the jury's discretion. The Ferry Book was to be made at Eastchurch in July, fresh marsh and upland taxed at twenty pence the score of acres, and salt marsh two pence for every score of acres, for the maintainance of the ferry, the boats, the Ferry house and the roads and all else necessary 'as of long time hath been accustomed, and by the statute of the eighteenth year of Queen Elizabeth they are enabled to do'. Anyone refusing to pay 'the cess' was fined. Men from each parish were nominated to make the cess. Here they refer to parishes, not boroughs. Adam Segar was one of the men chosen for Minster. All persons, whether strangers or inhabitants, had to pay for the ferry keeper's help when boating cattle. For every pasture horse and bullock one penny, for every score of sheep and every score of lambs four pence, that shall be exported out of this island.' It sounds like home rule for Sheppey!

There was a long order about disbursements, receipts, and recovering unpaid taxes. Selling the debtors goods to pay the fine was quite in order.

The borsholders were to give in writing the names of all the householders in their respective boroughs by Whitmonday next, or be fined for not doing so. There are instructions to the executors if 'the Warden now elected should happen to dye in the time of his office'. The jury were not taking any chances.

They do also order that 'the Ferry Keeper shall not carry over the said Ferry any manner of cattell on the Lord's Day, neither at any time sett or ferry over any Rogues, vagabonds or wandering people under the penalty of ten shillings for every such offense.' This last refers to the Act of Settlement made by Charles II's parliament. This act allowed a parish to refuse to take anyone who might become a charge to them, they could return them to their own parish, and this they did. They had to keep the rates down! The ferry keeper was allowed to keep the toll for his own use from anyone using the Ferry on the days of Saint Thomas the apostle, All Hallows Day, Palm Monday and Whitsun Monday, the toll being tuppence for a horse and one penny for man, woman or child. The days named were all fair days in Sheppey. Anyone bringing a packhorse with merchandise or 'victuals' for sale on to the island was to pay tuppence to the ferry keeper for his help in loading and unloading. The ferry keeper was not allowed to carry lime, brick, tiles, bushes, timber 'or any other stuff whatsoever' in any of the ferry boats unless it was for the use of the ferry. He would be fined for such offences. Many people may wonder how building material ever reached the island with this rule in practice. It had to come to Queenborough by boat, where it was unloaded and fetched by horse and cart, or it came to one of the farm quays up Windmill Creek and was collected from there.

The ferry keeper was not to make 'any hogstie' in the ferry stable, and he had to keep it clear, or again he would be fined.

The ferry warden was allowed to 'present' anyone who dredged or gathered oysters in the ferry lock, and his expenses would be met.

There were orders regarding the ferry ropes, the times carriages were allowed to 'come or go laden in the Ferry Wall', which was only in May, June or July, and then only if the ground was dry and hard and would not be damaged. Neither could they go below the ferry house with a laden carriage. All these offences were subject to fines.

Vessels unfortunate enough to run aground were fined, and failure to pay meant levy by distress warrant or court action. The remaining orders dealt with the court books, bonds for them, and the steward's duties.

Legal matters were mentioned (but not explained) and Peter Theobald was referred to as an attorney, which places him on the island.

That is a shortened account of the lawday, but it shows how the islanders attempted to foresee any and every eventuality. The lawday was still held under the Court Tree at Kingsborough Farm. The paper work had increased over the centuries, but luckily it did not continue to do so, and records of the eighteenth century had very little added, and the language became somewhat simplified.

Charles II's reign was coming to a close. The farming community on the island was running smoothly enough, with a little smuggling on the side, Queenborough was becoming poorer, and Sheerness had acquired the beginnings of a dockyard, with many stops and starts. Although the rural area had nothing in common with the dockyard, Sheerness was in the parish of Minster, and that was going to cause administrative problems in the future. Before that happened, Sheppey was to know the excitement of James II's short reign.

CHAPTER XVI

An inglorious end, and the eighteenth century

Charles II had not been an unpopular king, despite his addiction to romances. King James II was heartily disliked before he came to the throne. He was militantly Roman Catholic, and due to this he had been debarred from holding any government office, and so was forced to give up his position at the Admiralty. Following a plot attributed to the Pope in 1678 there was an upsurge of anti-Catholic feeling in England, and James had quietly gone abroad for a while. There was a move to prevent James succeeding to the throne, but Charles II would not agree with this, and so in 1685 James became King James II. He was never a success, he made every mistake in the book and the biggest of all was his attempt at crushing the Protestant religion.

He had only been king six months when one of Charles II's illegitimate sons, namely the Duke of Monmouth, attempted to gain the throne, backed by many Protestants.

The Battle of Sedgemoor crushed this attempt, the duke was executed, and the 'Bloody Assizes' of Judge Jeffreys followed. Many men were transported, two hundred and thirty were executed, hundreds died in prison and many more were fined or flogged.

Therefore, when William of Orange landed in Devon, at the invitation of Parliament, men were slow to join him, deterred by memories of the last uprising. William of Orange was a solemn Dutchman, he had married Mary, daughter of King James II and his first wife Anne Hyde. However, as he

marched on towards London men rallied to him, and James II, in terror and despair, decided on flight. In this he was helped by Sir Edward Hales, a Catholic convert and a favourite of the king. With two attendants they left London at two a.m. on the morning of December 10th, 1688. Sir Edward held Neat's Court, Sheppey, of the king, and he had instructed his steward, Mr. Bannister, to have a boat waiting at Elmley Ferry. This was an easy task for Bannister for he could cross the fields from Neat's Court to Windmill Creek, and take a small vessel down there quietly enough, and so enter the Swale and slip round to Elmley Ferry. There he was met by the king and Sir Edward Hales. The king was disguised in clerical clothes, with a simple wig that matched his dress. They boarded the waiting hoy and dropped down on the tide to Shellness Point, where, it is said, they waited to take on ballast.

The attendant Labadie was seen returning from the ferry with two led horses, caught, and taken to Sittingbourne. The people of Faversham and Sittingbourne were on the lookout for fugitives, and seeing a man wearing Hale's livery they concluded that Sir Edward was trying to leave the country. He was not a popular man, and a detachment of militia quickly went in pursuit. At eleven o'clock that night the hoy was seen off Shellness, and boarded. To board her they took three smacks with forty men, and three files of the Faversham musketeers with William Amis as captain.

On board they found three 'persons of quality', one being Sir Edward Hales. They did not recognise the Jesuit priest, and so they stripped and searched him, somewhat roughly. They unclothed him to the point of taking his trousers down, and seized three hundred guineas, a gold watch and two medals, one commemorating the birth of James' son (later the Pretender) and one made at the birth of Charles Ii. Somehow the coronation ring remained undiscovered.

It was late at night, and the fugitives were brought back to Oare. It is claimed that James spent the night at Kingshill Farm at Elmley, and the next morning they crossed the Swale again and were taken by coach to Faversham. Here the king was recognised. There is a story that the local fishermen were embarrassed and rather apprehensive when they realised that they had de-bagged the king!

The Lord Lieutenant of Kent was summoned, but he didn't want the errant king, and so James was lodged in the mayor's house for three days, and then sent back to London, where he was received politely enough, but it was made clear to him that William was now the king.

James was still determined to escape, and two days later he went to Rochester by barge, where he stayed for several days with one of the local J.P.s. From here he crept away early one morning, and with his illegitimate son the Duke of Berwick he boarded a pinnace and made for Queenborough. At Queenborough he managed to obtain a smack, and he crossed to Essex, then sailed on to France. After several attempts to regain the throne and being finally beaten in battle in Ireland, he died in France in 1701.

His attempted flight must have been known about on Sheppey, and doubtless gave the islanders something to talk about for months.

William and Mary were crowned in 1689, and Sheppey approved. Eastchurch has a record of it. April 11th, 1689. King William and Mary's 'crownation'. 'Twenty three shillings on ye ringers and for beer at ye bonfier.' If records were available for Minster they would probably be much the same.

During James II's reign the abbey at Minster had been presented with a silver cup, and a flagon cover. These were inscribed 'de Minster in Insula Scapoi', and were the gift of Adam Segar and Thomas Vidgin, church wardens. Adam Segar's gravestone can still be seen in the churchyard, but it is so worn and marked that little more than his name and parish (Minster) are visible.

Under William and Mary Sheppey settled to a reasonably steady rural existence. Poor Mary died in 1694 of smallpox, and William reigned alone until his death in 1702. He was a king chosen by Parliament, and tried to do his duty by his adoptive country. He involved Britain in wars with France until 1697, and then the wars of the Spanish Succession followed, with John Churchill, Earl of Marlborough, in command. The island seems not to have been unduly troubled by these wars, apart from the problems that disabled and impoverished soldiers and sailors brought on their return.

The first records available from the parish of Minster are those of the Overseers of the Poor, 1694-5. There is a gap then until 1714, when the Churchwardens Accounts begin. There are accounts and records for the whole of the eighteenth century, but unfortunately, not all are in a condition for inspection. There were not too many impotent poor, and the parish appeared to look after them quite well and kindly. In these records is found the first mention of the Poor House. By this time all villages had a poor-house, usually a cottage where homeless and destitute people were allowed to live, often with an attendant, usually one of the village women, to look after the elderly. In Eastchurch there were several cottages that were rent-free to widows, and

sometimes families, that were unable to earn a living for themselves.

The poor-house at Minster always seemed to have a hint of mystery behind it, for repeatedly throughout the years all anyone could say was 'A person unknown gave for the relief of the poor a house and some land, containing about three acres (this is sometimes estimated as four acres) it was last rented at £4 per annum, but is now in the possession of the Parish'. That is Hasted's account, and he has been repeated ever since. In the Parliamentary returns of 1786 the same statement occurs, i.e. 'Land of the annual value of £4 was left for the relief of the poor etc.'.

A small estate map of Sir John Hayward's land in Minster, dated 1700, shows the poor-house standing squarely where Sheppey General Hospital stands today. Two titles were conferred in the seventeenth century, the century in which Sir John Hayward's charity commenced.

In 1680 Elizabeth, widow of France's Lennard Lord Dacre, was created Countess of Sheppey for life. She died in 1686. In 1689 Henry, the youngest son of Robert Sidney, Earl of Leicester, was created Viscount Sidney of the Isle of Sheppey, Baron of Milton, and in 1694 Earl of Romsey. He died in 1704 and the titles became extinct.

It is doubtful if the islanders knew or cared about any of these things, and the only one of the three that affected them in any way, and would continue to do so for many years to come, was the Hayward Charity. Sir John had bought the Manor of Minster with the rights of the Lord of the Manor, and he left it for charitable uses. The capital was large, and the trustees were to use the endowment for building poor-houses and providing work for the poor in places they decided upon, the only condition being that St. Nicholas Parish in Rochester should be one of them. A portion of the property which earned £50 annually was used to provide a workhouse in Rochester, and later, provision was made for one at Crediton in Devon. There does not appear to be a complete list of all their grants. In view of this, it looks as though Minster Poor House and land were provided from the Hayward Charity, as they were originally on his land. There are many local stories regarding the origin of the hospital. The most usual is that it was once part of Wards Farm, and the 'Lodge' and offices were once Wards farm-house. This does not tally with the history of Wards, although at one period there was a cottage and garden belonging to Wards behind the hospital.

There are papers relating to the charity in the archives, collected when it ended in 1800, and the map is amongst them. As records they are far from complete, but they explain several things about Minster. From 1623 to 1800 the Manor of Minster belonged first to Sir John and then to his charity, administered by trustees. This ensured that for a period not far short of two hundred years the farms and lands belonging to the Hayward Charity were virtually untouched. Farm-houses were not pulled down and rebuilt, as so many were, and estates were not split up or sold away. By the mid-eighteenth century there were several people owning large estates in Sheppey, nearly all of them absentee landlords who had either inherited land or bought it as an investment, but the Manor of Minster was left untouched.

Among the papers collected is a record of Dorothy Franklin's papers, which came into Sir John's hands. Dorothy Franklin's papers were kept in a little black box, that is how it is told. There were letters, accounts and receipts which belonged to the Liveseys, and, a fascinating thought, copies of indents made between Henry VIII and Sir Thomas Cheyney, including a copy of the grant of the monastery, dated the twenty-ninth year of Henry November 12th. Also a livery grant by James I to Sir John Hayward, by letters patent, the documents concerning the Abbey Lands, and papers concerning the charity. Unfortunately, there is no clue given as to the whereabouts of the little black box.

The Abbey Farm was leased by the executors; Thomas Forte was an early tenant. In 1723 Thomas Dyer rented the Abbey Farm, his father Thomas had recently died, as Thomas junior was an executor. The Dyers were a local family, and had been on the island for at least a century. A seventeenth-century token for a halfpenny stamped with the name Dyer has recently been found, during renovations on the gate-house. Over the years a number of such tokens have been discovered in different places, but never kept for further inspection. Designated as 'local money' by the islanders, little notice was taken of them. There were several families who minted their own tokens in Sheppey. There was a shortage of small change after the Great Fire of London because the Royal Mint was destroyed, and many places had permission to mint their own tokens.

The trustees of the charity employed a steward, who sent them reports. One concerns the Abbey Farm and the farm under the hill, which was apparently part of Abbey Farm. Half a year's rent was fifty pounds.

There was a tenement adjoining Minster churchyard, and ground and stables opposite the tenement. Whether this tenement included the gate-house is impossible to say. There was another house somewhere near the abbey where Widow Winter lived, and in 1722 some work was being done there. There was also a meadow, a place called 'Shodds', and several other houses 'near the Churchyard', probably some of those in the village street.

The forge belonged to the charity. It stood in the same place as it does today, and William Winter had been there for the last twenty-one years, from Michaelmas 1692. Later it was Smith's 'forge and backside with appurtenances' next to Faulcon yard and 'west' of Minster Street. The 'West' is confusing, as it appears to lie more to the east, but that is how it is described. The forge was in use until 1939. After the war it was used as a greengrocer's shop and store. It has massive oak beams in the roof, and a vertical beam from floor to ceiling with pegs and holes chiselled and gouged in it. This was known as a 'restraining beam' for restive horses, and there are very few such left now. Ropes could be put round the horses legs and attached to the beam via the various slots, pegs and holes, which allowed for adjustment. Recently it seemed likely that both the forge and the farrier's house next to it were for demolition, but thankfully they have been reprieved. Of Faulcon Yard only the name remains; it is now a small estate of houses called Faulcon Gardens. Somewhere among the gardens is a well, now covered in, said to be a well that once belonged to the monastery.

The other farm of note belonging to the estate was Whybourne's Farm on Wards Hill. Now a private house, without land or buildings, it has retained all its character. Archaeologists who examined the house surmised that it was an old Hall House, with Tudor additions. Modernisation has not destroyed it, well into this century the back of the house was one large room with a gallery round it, and this is still easy to see, although now divided into smaller rooms. The basic structure is unaltered. The study, a room at the front of the house, has massive oak beams, and a burnt patch is discernible on one of them. In the time of the depression in farming in the last century, the resident farmer there was in financial trouble, and decided to set the house afire and so claim the insurance. He started the fire in the study, and left the place, but he had not gone far up the hill when a friend came chasing after him to tell him the house was afire, so that scheme was thwarted. Behind one of the big fireplaces is a small, hidden room. It was found by a curious owner who thought the wall in a cupboard sounded hollow. They made an opening in the wall, which was built of 'daub and wattle', and found the room. It is probably a relic of the days of religious persecution. Daniel Broadstreet lived at

Whybournes for eleven years, from 1702. If the harvests were bad his rent was reduced for that year, and in 1722 the rent was twenty-seven pounds for half a year.

Later, Mary, the 'widow of Broadstreet' was mentioned, and then Edward Philpott was tenant for seven years. At the Abbey Farm, William Burgess was ordered to 'leave fallow when he comes out'.

That was not the whole of the property. The weirs were let for fishing, to Nathaniel Webb (whose tomb can be seen near the church), John Gold, Thomas Norrington and William Smith. From other sources of information it is clear that they were not very successful, as their weirs were regarded as fair game for poachers.

The oyster grounds were let, and kept stocked, tended by fishermen who knew the job well, and made the fishery pay. The copperas grounds were leased to Mr. John Crisp and his partner for ten pounds the half-year. Copperas stones were the iron pyrites that abounded on the beaches from Minster to Warden, and the lord of the manor had the rights over them. There was a copperas factory at Queenborough, where the stones were treated. The best stones were described as a bright, shining silver, and they were used for wheel lock pistols and fuses, after treatment. The others, of more mundane colouring, were used for wool-dying, making clothes and hats black, for ink, for tanning and dressing leather, and for oil of vitriol and Spanish brown for painters. They were even used to produce a dressing for sheep. Their value varied; in 1634 a ton was worth five pounds at Queenborough.

The gentlemen who rented the copperas grounds would pay poor people to gather them. They would be piled in heaps, and when enough had been collected a hoy would come to the beach, and the stones would be loaded and transported. This was regarded as an occasion for merriment and horseplay, and it was not unknown for all concerned to get happily drunk, and who could blame them — collecting cold stones on a wet, muddy beach can't have been an inspiring job at fourpence a bushel.

A small map shows the various properties. Minster Street is drawn, with ten or twelve houses, actually more than there are now. The forge is shown (it hasn't moved since then). Sixteen ninety-two is at present the earliest date known but it was probably there long before that. Almost opposite the forge is a tenement, stables and slaughter house, built on waste ground by Mr. Richard Chalke; he paid ten shillings rent. The waste ground was a small triangular piece of ground in front of Streetfield. There was a slaughter house there, in use, until the decade 1930–40, and the building is there still and used as a store house. The road called Minster Street passed round the churchyard, and it was a proper dog's leg of a road, past the forge, and on to Windmill Hill. There was no 'Chapel Street' in 1700. Back Lane was a narrow lane that turned sharply out the end of Minster Street, just before it reached the slaughter house. The turning has been widened considerably since the war, and the 'dog's leg' has been partially straightened. Leaving Minster Street at the northern end, where it starts to descend the hill, and passing the abbey and the Abbey Farm, the road, if at that time it could be so described, led round the poor-house, and so down Wards Hill to Whybourne's Farm. As vestry and overseers records show, the poor-house had been part of village life for a long time. It is likely that it was established at an early date, for the village would have felt the loss of the priory keenly. In the poor-house the old and homeless were lodged, and the sick nursed. There are references to payments for doctor's accounts. The first overseer's accounts of 1694–5 show that the farms were assessed on their rentable value, and the Poor rate was one shilling in the pound. The names of householders considered to have enough property for tax purposes are all recorded. The minister heads the list, and

Thomas Hopson, gent. is prominent. In the early list no farms are identified. Many of the people named are familiar, Thomas Barfoot (originally that was Barefoot, it alters through the years to Burfoot, then Burford), Thomas Head, John Samson, John Garrett, John Greengrass, and William Bull among them. Many of these appear at the Law Day Court, and in church records.

The Hopsons were a local family, unusual because they had risen from tenant farmers to become landowners. The accounts for this first record are not very clear, but it is apparent that the overseers had obeyed the rules and tried to find work for the able-bodied poor. Hand-made 'stockons' (stockings) were paid for and 'shoos' bought for children when necessary. The money allowed to the poor was referred to as their salary. Children were boarded with local families, who were given an allowance for their keep. 'Paid to Thomas Forte for his half year's salary for keeping Richard Marshall, £2.' Later records show both kindness and understanding — an overseer's job cannot have been a pleasant one at times, and some of them found writing difficult, into the bargain. Many of the parishioners could not sign their names, someone signed for them and they made their marks.

Sheppey was living reasonably well in the rural areas. William's reign gave way to Anne's but the islanders did not seem interested. It was a time of good harvests, which meant that food wasn't too dear and on the farms there was work. The wars on the Continent continued until 1713, but apart from paying the land tax that financed the military operations, and grumbling about paying it, the country people took little notice. Farming had not altered much from earlier days. Cattle and sheep were still small, and most of them were killed and salted in the early winter, as there was no fodder for them in the bleak months after Christmas. A tax on salt in 1703 led to a protest that the poor would suffer, as they were dependent on salt for preserving their food for the winter.

Areas with large communal fields were at a disadvantage as new crops could not be tried, everyone had to sow the same seed, and reap it, at the same time. Sheppey was lucky here, for the small enclosed fields and small holdings of the 'Uplands' (the hills) meant that different crops could be grown, and by the middle of the century most vegetables, including recent importations, were grown and enjoyed.

Although the farms were leased, many landlords owned large estates. Baron Herbert of Shurland's descendants still owned Shurland, Norwood and other farms round East-church. Sir Edward Hales had owned Elmley, and later sold it to the M.P. for Canterbury.

A family called Thornhill had become possessed of most of the land in Harty; they sold it to a London merchant whose heirs, in their turn, sold it again to a Faversham family. The remainder was bought by Mr. Jacob Sawbridge, and was owned by that family until the early nineteenth century.

A farm known as Bilsington Farm at Harty was bought, mortgaged, and then resold to a Mr. Gore, who owned several large estates in Sheppey in George II's time. Bilsington Farm has gone, and its whereabouts is not known now.

At Minster the manor rights and farms were kept together by the charity. There were many other farms that had passed through Lord Henry Cheyney's hands, and one of the most interesting is Ripney Hill. It is interesting because the deeds date from 1664. Many island farms are sadly lacking in records: Lower Wards goes back no further than 1859, Upper Wards, now a small housing estate, lost its deeds when it was demolished, and there are others similar. Warden Manor, one of the most interesting old houses on the island, has no deeds at all — they were accidentally burnt. Warden belonged to the Sawbridge family in the eighteenth century, except for one tenement and six acres of land. The church

had somehow come into the possession of Vice Admiral Francis Hosier, who also owned other property.

When deeds are complete and carefully kept, it is not always possible to research them, and it is only due to the kindness of the present owner, Mr. William Mills, that the story of Ripney can be told.

It starts in 1636, when Edward Appleford's last will and testament contained a contract for £400 relating to Ripney Hill Farm. He left the property to his son Daniel Appleford; it was to be sold and the mortgage paid. In 1668 James Browster was the tenant, and nothing further happened until 1679, when the question of the mortgage arose once again. Samuel Durrant was by now the tenant. In 1686 Daniel Appleford and executors sold the farm of two hundred and forty acres to Alexander Saunders, citizen, haberdasher of London. The tenant was Thomas Mills, and under-tenants were James Stiles, Stephen Salmon, Robert Marr, Joseph Templeman, Thomas Barfoot, Thomas Nutley, Henry Jarvis, and Thomas (?) Sidge. They all rented grazing land.

In 1687 there was another indenture about £400 lent by a William Pott in 1679. There are many repetitions of the conditions set out in the will, and in 1684 there was an official acquittal of the original debt. There is a gap until 1712, when Sarah Sanders 'and others' allowed Sarah Toswell of Ripney Hill a mortgage of £200 in English money. Another gap to 1783, when the question of letting the farm to William Hopson arose. His father John had rented and farmed the land and he wished to continue to do so. By this time the property belonged to Sir John Lade, who had recently died, and his son John Lade II wanted to sell the property. There is a curious note here that John Lade was formerly John Inskip but took the surname of Lade, but it does not make it clear which John Lade, father or son, effected the change of name. There is an inventory of his property, most of which was in Sheppey. 'Ripney Hill' was let to John Hopson at a rent of '£42 yearly for eighty seven acres, and seventy acres at £28 yearly. Several pieces or parcels of meadow land, eleven acres two rods, £15 yearly. Also Horse Marsh, ten acres at £5 10s. yearly. Stable, orchard and garden let to Edward Bigg, £3 10s. yearly. Barn, stable, close converted into garden ground, three acres let to James Hall, £8 10s. yearly. Ripney Marsh, sixty five acres at £42 yearly let to John Hopson.' Other pieces of land were let to other tenants. Some of this land, and other land off the island, was sold to Sir Philip Jennings Clarke and Henry Smith, esq. but in return they had to pay Sir John's debts.

In 1780 various properties in Minster were rented by John Cradock, yeoman. Pieces of land are described by their boundaries, one called Pinns Yoake and Spring, but as both land and boundaries have disappeared it is hard to know where they were. There were other properties and occupants listed, too. In 1780 it was recorded: 'and also all that messuage and tenement known as Wards, with barns, stables, outhouses, gardens, land, etc. which included nine closes or enclosed grounds and all the rights thereof. Isaac Fort was the tenant. One hundred acres more or less.'

Powers alias Poore's Farm, three score acres, tenant Daniel Turner. There were other pieces of ground in Minster, Richard Chalke the butcher was tenant of a field near the church, and two pieces called Crumps Croft and Long Croft, long since gone beyond recognition. Churchfield Farm in Leysdown ends the list, and it was all sold to Mr. Bateman Robson to sort out.

In the ensuing redistribution, William Hopson son of John, somehow contrived to raise over £3000, and to buy Ripney Hill, Wards Farm and Powers alias Poore's Farm, and other smaller properties. That was a big step up for a tenant farmer, and later he bought Parsonage Farm, Minster, to add to his property. Parsonage Farm had been part of William Goris' estates in Sheppey; he died in 1768 and left all his property to his relations.

William Hopson had married Elizabeth Ongley, widow of a Queenborough man, James Ongley. The Ongleys were a well-known family in Queenborough — one of them was mayor for a year. That may have been Elizabeth's husband. Elizabeth already had a family by her first husband, but she and William Hopson had no children of their marriage. When William died in 1817 he left instructions that if Elizabeth's son William changed his name from Ongley to Hopson he would be permitted to inherit the estate. Elizabeth died in 1823 and was buried at Milton, and in 1824 William Ongley became William Hopson II. William Hopson II had married Mary Meade of Islington in 1820. They had a fairly large family, and the children were all given the name Ongley as a second name. Mary died in 1851 and was buried at Kensal Green; William died in February 1855.

By the end of the year all the property was on the market. The eldest son was a captain in the Army, and decided it would be wise to sell the estate and divide the proceeds amongst the family, so ensuring that his sisters were provided for in the event of his death in action. For some reason the family had to be identified, and this was done by a farmer named Charles Lake, who had once rented and farmed Poore's Farm, and also acted as agent for the Hopsons on the island.

At the time of the sale the tenant of Ripney Hill was John Chambers, and the executors of Richard Ingleton deceased. Parsonage Farm was left by William Hopson to his friend and former agent, Charles Lake.

It is noticeable that the farms often used to have more than one tenant, but this happens repeatedly and was a normal occurrence in Sheppey. Quite simply many of the farmers were not wealthy enough to run a large farm, and would rent grazing land, or a 'garden', so dividing up the farm. The farm was sold and relet, but the new tenant could not make a living, and had to give up his stock, crops and household effects to pay his debts in 1891. The farm was resold, and empty for a time. This was a very bad time for farmers, and many farms were empty. It was let again later in the year, on a seven years lease. (Names are deliberately withheld here, as this is fairly recent history.)

This left the Hopsons far behind, and brought the farm into the twentieth century. The farm remained with the same tenant for many years. After the second world war William Mills, esq., the present owner, bought it, and his family farm it. The acreage is less than in William Hopson's day, as some of the land has been sold, some of it to the golf club, which has made the golf club one of the best for many miles around. The farm cottages, once a pair, are now converted into a pleasant and attractive single dwelling. They were built roughly two hundred years ago.

The farm-house was built early this century, after the former house burnt down. The cellars of the old house are now under the lawn in the garden and there is an amusing, and rather macabre, tale about them. Somehow the story has arisen that 'sometime in the old days' one of the farmers who lived there murdered his wife and buried her in the cellar. The present mistress of the house admits that she doesn't like to think about it too much, especially when she is there on her own!

Ripney Hill is fortunate in having such a complete history, and the deeds give some help with the history and age of other farms in Minster.

The Hopsons, John and William, the original father and son, were evidently hard workers, good farmers and good business men. The name will not be forgotten in Minster, for although he may not be remembered as a farmer, William Hopson I will always be remembered as a benefactor of Minster School. In his will of 1817 he bequeathed £700 to be used for the education of poor children. In this he was ahead of his time. Education in the eighteenth century and early nineteenth century was very hit and miss. Tradesmen and the better-off farmers paid for education for their children. There were small village schools, and later, private schools in Sheerness.

The 'Parish', later 'workhouse' children, were taught at the parish's expense. In this they were more fortunate than the children of the poorer agricultural workers, who received no schooling at all, or very little. William Hopson's bequest altered this for Minster children. A schoolroom was made in the north aisle of the Abbey Church, in what is now known as the Nun's Chapel. A floor was built to divide the schoolroom into two storeys, and here the children of the village were taught. It would be interesting to know who taught them, but there does not seem to be any records. When the national school was built in 1872 the school in the church ceased, but the bequest was carried on to the new village school, and awarded yearly as various prizes, known as the Hopson prizes. This was in operation until well into this century, and is probably still carried on in some form now.

For the rural area the eighteenth century was a reasonably comfortable time, and not until the end of the century did troubles threaten.

For Queenborough it was a different story, and Sheerness, struggling to get a footing as a town, was the nearest to the descriptions given of the Wild West towns one can imagine.

CHAPTER XVII

Growth and development

While the farming community was experimenting with new crops, and pulling down and rebuilding houses and barns, the Queenborough people were having a hard time. The copperas factory was a small one, and did not employ many local people. Most of the inhabitants were fishermen, and the oyster grounds were not providing enough work or money to support the town.

In 1724 there was a minor war going on between the fishermen of Queenborough, Milton and Faversham with Southend. The Southend men had thrown the small, useless oysters overboard, and they had subsequently grown and made a good profit. The Queenborough men, led by the mayor, took one hundred smacks and six sloops and raided these 'between the tide marks' beds, claiming that these were a common fishing ground. The Southend men were unable to resist this onslaught, and in roughly ten days the Kentish men had gathered thousands of bushels. Five sloops rushed them to London, but this caused a glut and they had to be sold cheaply, or not at all.

The Southend fishermen started a legal action over this, and won it, and were awarded seven thousand pounds in damages, plus the costs. It cost the Kentish men over seven thousand pounds, and Milton, Faversham and Queenborough all had to pay their share. It took many years for the companies, or fraternities, of oyster fishers to pay this bill, and this did not help Queenborough's situation. In Sheppey there used to be a feud of long standing between the island fishermen and the Essex fishermen, and it could have started here. In 1724 a long and complicated list of rules and orders for the working of the oyster beds was made, with heavy fines imposed on those who dredged more than their stint. Everything had to be overseen and checked, and three and sixpence was deducted from every bushel to repay the money borrowed in order to stock the oyster grounds. No freeman or widow could begin dredging before the gun fired. Money was made from the elections, and there are many letters relating to this. George II had caused the original act to be altered. When the borough was authorised to send M.P.s to Parliament, all freemen could vote for the M.P. of their choice, but now the right to vote was restricted to the mayor, jurats and burgesses. This led to all kinds of sharp practice. In 1731 the Assembly Book records that 'God's penny raised on every oyster voyage for the poor be increased to two and sixpence because of the great poverty'.

There was a happier note in June that year, when the town paid the ringers, and for bonfire, beer, etc. upon his majesty's coming to anchor within Sheerness, one pound, thirteen shillings and six pence.

The next day the mayor, jurats and bailiffs waited on his majesty on board the *Carolina* yacht, and the boats crews were paid one pound. His majesty was King George II.

Queenborough needed the occasional festive day. In 1734 a plague of vermin, called Five Fingers, partially destroyed the oyster beds. 'Five Fingers' was the local name for starfish, and they had to be collected, brought ashore and destroyed. In spite of poverty and worries, the usual rules and regulations were carefully followed. The school house was repaired, and a bye-law introduced to prevent any letting of common rights to nonfreeman.

The castle well had been neglected, which seems strange when fresh water was at a premium, and it was cleaned and re-opened in 1720 by order of the navy, as there was no fresh water in Sheerness. The well was two hundred feet deep, and Mr. Peter Collinson F.R.S. bored another eighty-one feet down before the well filled. It was soft, sweet water, and came from one hundred and sixty-six feet below the deepest place in the adjacent seas.

The highway was repaired, and a case was brought about people who stole fish from the ponds on the green.

By George III's reign the town was in such a bad state that an act of parliament was passed to help the townspeople in their poverty. The borough had sent a petition to parliament asking them to bring in a bill for the relief of the poor.

During this time the quay and wharf at Queenborough was the port for all local trading, loads were brought by boat and then collected and taken to places all over the island, and goods were despatched in a similar manner. It seems incredible that on such a small island the only town could be in dire need, whilst the rural areas were comparatively comfortable. The bi-weekly markets had deteriorated but many people still went to Queenborough Fair. It seems that apart from meeting for business purposes, the communities did not mix much.

The painter Hogarth and two friends visited Queenborough in 1732 while they were on a short holiday in Kent. Hogarth sketched the Market House, which was in the main street, and it is claimed that his sketch shows it back to front. They wrote a hilarious account of their adventures, they ran into trouble over lodgings, but kept out of the trouble that was brewing between naval midshipmen and local girls. The next day they walked to Sheerness and then Minster, stopping for refreshment at the 'George', a public house on Minster Hill now called the 'Prince of Waterloo'. The 'George' alehouse was sold for £75 in 1754, and the name was changed after the battle of Waterloo, and no-one is certain who the Prince of Waterloo was meant to be. One hundred and ten years later it was advertised in the local paper as empty, then it boasted five bedrooms and a butcher's shop at the back.

One of Hogarth's friends wrote a burlesque account of Baron Robert de Shurland, in which the bold baron is made to swim out to a ship with Queen Elizabeth on board — it is amazing how the centuries become confused when people look back, 1300, 1500 or 1700 — to most people it makes little difference.

There was no landing place at Sheerness, apart from a bank of shingle at high tide, and supplies such as grain were usually unloaded at Queenborough and transported by land. The yard men were still owed fifteen months' wages in 1693, but it is stated that their condition was better than in 1691, when, living on bread, cheese and water, they were too weak to work.

The day wages for workmen were from one shilling and sixpence to three shillings, and by the end of the seventeenth century they were running a profitable smuggling racket.

When George I came to the throne in 1714 new Admiralty and Navy Boards were introduced. Up to that time the Navy Board officers had taken everything that wasn't nailed down, as well as official papers. During the reign of William and Mary the yard men had been regimented and drilled, but they were hopeless. In 1715 an inspection found the arms useless from lack of attention.

The yard was growing. The first dry dock was built in 1708, although it is not shown on a plan until 1725. The storekeepers were taking bribes, and men were building houses of 'chips', short lengths of wood under three feet long. The houses looked like patchwork log cabins, and they were all painted the same dark grey-blue colour, dockyard paint. It is hard to visualise now, but at that time they were built in the yard itself, all around the docks and buildings.

In 1715 only single men were sent to Sheerness, as there were stores around, which afforded opportunities for thieving. They were to live in 'Garrison', and lodge with the troops, but that didn't work for long. Any houses that were built for them were commandeered by the Army, and for the greater part of the eighteenth century the yard was a poor second to the garrison. Most of the workmen lived in the hulks. Old men-of-war were laid up by the dockyard in such a manner that they would break by force of the tides, which were especially heavy when the north-east wind was blowing. Here the yard workers lived, they made streets on board the ships and built bridges between the vessels, with entrances on the landward side. There were quarters for a midwife on every 'street', and the men and their families made the best of things. Indeed, when the time came to do so, they refused to leave.

From the early eighteenth century new entries appear in Minster Abbey Church records. Marriages take place at Minster, the bride and groom coming 'from shipboard'. Children were buried 'from shipboard', and also 'found drownded'. Many pathetic little bodies were washed up on Deadman's Island. Anyone suspected of dying from an infectious illness was buried on Deadman's Island, with little ceremony, hence the name.

From 1730 onwards the christenings and burials came from 'The Blue Houses', the local name for the houses built from chips. By 1712 there were one hundred and sixty-two men and sixty shipwrights working in Sheerness yard. There was a public house nearby named 'The White Horse', where young women often stayed when courting a sailor, and sometimes this was their address when they married. Young women stayed there for other reasons, too — there was never a shortage of camp followers.

By now the water shortage was acute, and so in 1720 Queenborough well was reopened. The Admiralty ordered lodgings to be built for the men in 1730, but they were slow to materialise.

In 1739 there was a fire, due to the gate porter selling spirits. The order prohibiting the sale of spirits was read, as only small beer was allowed, but no-one had bothered to enforce that. A war with Spain was threatening, and at that point Chatham yard mutinied, winning their case and keeping their right to 'chips'. Sheerness was restless, and the authorities were nervous, but nothing dramatic occured. A Naval hospital at Queenborough was suggested, but nothing further was done about it. Sheerness at this time was out of favour once again.

They tried drilling the men again in 1744, but the master shipwright and clerk of the check quarrelled over who should be captain, and the drilling came to nothing. In 1760 'Shereness' is described as a strong and regular fortification, with apartments for officers or Ordnance, Navy and Garrison. The town consists of three little streets. By now, nearing the end of seven years' war with France, there were four hundred and fifty-five men there. The regiments were revived once again, and Sheerness managed to raise two companies. The yard was spreading 'river ward', for as the old breakwater ships broke up they formed extensions of made ground. Cornwallis Jetty is said to be built over the old wooden man-o'-war H.M.S. *Cornwallis*. There is a block of new flats in Sheerness now named Cornwallis House.

Sheerness was in favour again, as between 1759–63 the yard had proved useful for docking and supplying cruisers of the North Sea squadron. It was around this time that it was labelled 'Sheernasty', not only by the Navy, but by the Army as well. A certain lady who grew up in the Army at the end of the nineteenth century had always heard it referred to in this way, she didn't visit the island until she was an adult, but her ideas of Sheppey were always influenced by the description heard when she was a child.

In 1765 plans for dry docks and an extension of the yard were considered, and then they realised that the port was infested with *Teredo Navalis* (ship worm), and malaria mosquito. They attributed this to the old hulks, full of mosquitos from all over the world, and the vessels in quarantine in nearby Stangate Creek. The nature of the ground made construction of dry docks a problem, so the plan was shelved.

In all fairness, Sheppey was notorious for its marshy ground 'full of evil humours', and the ague (malaria) was an accepted part of Sheppey life. The undrained marshlands, complete with pools of stagnant water, made it an ideal place for mosquitoes — the hulks cannot take all the blame. Some of it was indigenous.

Wages were still in arrears, and there was a spy scare on, as foreigners could enter the yard at will; there was a public road running through it. When war with Spain was once again feared, in 1770, a police system was organised, and the yard watchmen were replaced by Marines, day warders and night watchmen.

There were sixty ships in dry dock by 1774, but the workmen couldn't be persuaded to come, or to stay there. There was no accommodation, and the district was reputedly unhealthy. So privileges were granted, together with some housing, and more breakwater ships. The place was disgustingly overcrowded; there were four hundred and twenty-five people living in one hundred and ninety-two rooms, and five hundred and fifty-one in two hundred and fifty-eight cabins on hulks. It is small wonder that the infant mortality rate was high. Water was being fetched by boat from Chatham again, as Queenborough well could not supply enough, so a well was dug at Fort Townsend, at a place now known as Well Marsh. The men digging the well had to dig through a layer of what is described as 'petrified forest' before water was found. This caused general interest, and samples of the old petrified trees were sent to museums and various scientific institutions.

The end of the eighteenth century abounds in scares and regulations. Standing orders regarding fires were issued, as up to that time no system of firefighting had been organised, and Sheerness yard was supplied with fire engines, hooks, and ladders. Another order prohibited workmen from wearing overcoats and wide trousers, an attempt to cut down the thieving that constantly took place. That was the idea, at least. There was more talk of enlarging the yard, the war with America had highlighted its drawbacks, but again nothing was done. A government enquiry into 'fees' charged, hampers of wine, and other bribes in yards was carried out. Following this, in 1794, 'great Alleys', a form of housing, were built near Garrison Point, but the men preferred the hulks.

In 1800 the dockyards were investigated yet again. Grain was suggested, and rejected, but then Sheerness was not recommended either. It was unhealthy, there were doubts about the ability to build strong foundations, and the north-east winds continued to cause trouble.

By the end of the eighteenth century there was a dockyard, a garrison, and very little accommodation to serve them. A small chapel had been built over the gateway that led from the dockyard to the garrison. In 1767 Mr. Wesley preached there, but after he had preached there a second time he was forbidden by the authorities, to use the chapel again. Both Mr. Wesley and Mr. Whitfield preached in the yard, holding services out of doors, and standing on jossing blocks to preach. From this beginning the Congregational Church in Sheerness started. By 1755 Blue Town had a few buildings and services were held in a carpenter's shop there. Later in 1763, a small meeting-house for the Bethel Chapel was built there, followed by a larger chapel, school rooms, and a minister's house in 1784. Mr. Shrubsole was the preacher and guiding light at this time, and his vault can be seen in the churchyard at Minster.

So the dockyard grew in squalor and poverty. During George III's reign acts were passed ordering that a certain number of men should be 'raised' for the Navy from stated districts. Sheerness was one of those named. If the men weren't forthcoming, the press gang was there to bring them in.

Convicts were drafted into the Army or Navy if they were willing, and their sentences commuted. This practice grew after the loss of the American colonies, as for a time the courts were left without anywhere to transport convicts to. There was also an increase of drafted convicts in time of war, but drafting men in this way did not guarantee they would make good sailors.

There is an old saying on the island that 'Minster and Sheerness don't mix', and until quite recently Sheerness people had no idea about Minster and the countryside around, and Minster people knew little of Sheerness outside the High Street and the Broadway. The Sheerness folk implied that this was a form of snobbery, but that wasn't the case.

As Sheerness developed, its growth outstripped both manners and cleanliness for a time. With the press gang on the prowl for likely victims, and Navy and Army men on the lookout for likely female company, the farmers and other

The interior of Eastchurch Church showing the famous rood-screen.

The finely proportioned Eastchurch Church.

The interior of the Dockyard Church as it was before being gutted. It is now used as a sports centre.

Still imposing, although redundant, is the Dockyard Church in Sheerness.

78

Above: Harty Church stands prettily on its lonely site overlooking the Swale.

Left: Sayes Court at Harty, at the time of writing, being restored, and in the foreground the remains of an ancient moat.

Sheppey Court from a Victorian print.

The Georgian Terrace by the dockyard in Sheerness, formerly for the use of officers of the yard.

countrymen took good care to keep their sons and daughters up the island, as far away from harm as possible. Later, this division was exacerbated by the attitude of the townspeople, as early local papers show.

At that time in the eighteenth century Eastchurch and Minster seemed oblivious of what was happening in Sheerness. In 1797, as England was threatened with invasion from both Holland and France, a large part of the fleet stationed at Sheerness mutinied. The revolt was led by a seaman named Richard Parker, who sounds like a typical lower deck lawyer. Parker incited the crews to rebel against their officers, and the twenty or so ships involved were seized by the ratings, and taken from Sheerness out to the Nore. The seamen had many just grievances, for sailors were scurvily treated, but Parker overstated his case. Parker and his 'delegates' came to Sheerness daily to make their plans and discuss future moves, and any hint of interference with them was countered with threats of blowing up Sheerness and sacking Sheppey. The officers were put ashore, or held hostages in their cabins. The Admiralty sent a deputation to reason with the men and to attempt to pacify them, but Parker refused to accept what was offered.

Some accounts say that the men terrorised Sheppey and looted and devastated Sheerness, but a contemporary account written by the Parish Clerk of Minster does not confirm this. The mutiny started on May 17th, and Sheerness was kept in a state of siege, but after ten days or so the men tired of Parker's domineering ways, and fighting broke out among the crews, and between the ships. They all mistrusted each other, and after refusing the concessions the Admiralty had offered they were afraid that their demands would not now be met. One by one the ships sailed into Sheerness and gave themselves up, Parker on the *Monmouth* last of all. Parker gave himself up to escape his fellow sailors, and was sent to Maidstone gaol, out of harms way.

The usual arrests, trials and punishments followed, and Parker was hanged from the yardarm of H.M.S. *Sandwich*. There has been much written about the terror and helplessness of the islanders, and how some of them left the island for Chatham, but the parish clerk and his friends did not seem unduly perturbed.

On May 14th he records that they were looking at the revolt of the sailors from the Nore to Sheerness. During the next two weeks they frequently went 'on the hill' to watch the gun boats, and the shipping. On June 9th, having been to Shurland Farm to 'settle with Mr. Pratt', he returned to the hill to watch the ships 'get away from the delegates' before going to his son's public house ('The Highlanders') and then 'in bed by 10 o'clock'. For Minster it was business as usual, with the mutiny thrown in as free entertainment. On June 17th he was up between five and six o'clock to see the Light Horse go to guard Parker, the pirate, from the Ferry to Sheerness to be tried for piracy. That was evidently the day Parker was returned from Maidstone gaol. Several days later he wrote coolly, 'Buried Joseph Putmore who was drownded and supposed to be a Dillegat'. On June 30th 'Up and about and spent all the forenoon to see Richard Parker hanged in the Sandwich for mutiny'. For the local people the hanging was a day out. The clerk records the names of the other seamen hanged, and on the first of July goes again to watch four men being hanged on the *Sandwich* at Blackstakes. The next day he buried William Gregory 'who was hanged yesterday on board the ship *Sandwich* for Mutiny in May last. He was a cabinet maker aged thirty three years.'

These outings to watch the hangings continued for several days, and John Down and Richard Browne were buried at Minster 'that was hanged for Mutiny at the Nore'. Following the hangings, there was another excursion to see the men whipped for mutineering. There was no trace of fear or undue worry in that account, just the morbid curiosity of the age and satisfaction at justice done.

Richard Parker's body was taken to Minster for burial, but, so it is said, his wife and some friends removed it that night, and took it to London, where they planned to put it on show and thereby earn some money. This was quickly stopped by the magistrates, and Parker was buried at St. Mary's, Whitechapel. After the mutiny conditions in the Navy started to improve. It was a slow improvement, but for the ratings things were at least going in the right direction.

Queenborough still had dealings with the ships, because in 1798 William Holland from the ship *Spanker* died, and on examination was found to be a woman. Smallpox was prevalent on the island, and caused numerous deaths in Queenborough in 1776–7. It was not smallpox that killed the infant John Jones, however; he died from drinking oil of vitriol. This poison was often kept in the house, as it was sometimes used in the treatment of sick horses. Henry Pennal (no age given) accidentally drowned himself in a pond on Queenborough Green, and in 1794 the unfortunate William Indell 'died of a mortification' after having his arm amputated. The doctors weren't quick enough with the hot tar that time.

Then back to the Forces, for in 1801 Lieutenants Joseph Carnol Minster and Christian Lesching killed each other in a duel. Duelling had been made legal in Charles II's reign, as had the Game Laws.

The pursuit of game had once again become important to the landlords of large estates, and no-one was allowed to kill game of any sort, even on ground he rented, unless he was worth one hundred pounds a year at least. This made life miserable for the ordinary countryman who liked a chase after a hare, rabbit or game bird, and valued the dinner it provided.

Warden had its own connections with authority, and was well known to the Riding officers and other excisemen. The coastguard cottages that were to encircle the coast of Sheppey in the following century were not yet built, but preventive boats were in use; one was moored off the beach between the 'Ship on Shore' and Scrapsgate. At this time John Sawbridge, esq. owned Warden Manor, and his son Samuel Elias owned it after him. As Sawbridge was once Lord Mayor of London, Warden Manor and land were simply an investment, neither is there any available record of the tenants who lived there. The manor has been so altered around and built upon over the years that it is difficult to trace the original building. The stables are now a dining hall, many hearths have newer models superimposed, stairs are walled up, and it is possible that behind and beside some of the fireplaces there must be hidden spaces, or rooms. A stone overmantel was found in two pieces, it is now back round a hearth, but the coat of arms is too worn to be identifiable. Rooms have been divided, new ceilings built, and generally 'tidied up', but there are still great beams to be seen in many places. There are shutters outside the windows, and there are also shutters inside, that spring into place at the touch of a lever. In an upstairs cupboard is a small hatchway opening onto the outside world; it has a firm base and an easily opened little door. The cellars were vast, with openings leading off them — tunnels, of course. They are filled in now, to prevent flooding, openings and all.

In Warden Manor, or Warden Court as it has been called, it is claimed that the smugglers used to meet. Certainly there was a family of smugglers at Warden — their name was Gold. In the manor all the shutters would be closed, and the lawless band would await the arrival of a pigeon at the hatch in the upstairs cupboard, for the 'hatch' was a pigeon door. The bird would have the details of the next run strapped to its leg, and the smugglers would collect ponies, horses and carts, and go down to Barrows Brook (a small valley that opened onto the beach) at the appointed hour to collect the contraband as it floated, or was rowed, to the shore. There are tales of wild night chases as the smugglers fled the Riding men, but no word of them ever getting caught.

In the early part of this century writers, artists, and ghost hunters used the manor as a meeting place, and there are many ghost stories of dark figures galloping along the Warden Road to the Point, followed by ghostly excisemen on horseback. The manor is alleged to be haunted, too, by strange figures and weird sounds.

Only recently a man was working in one of the rooms when he saw a lady 'in old fashioned costume' come in, walk across the room, and disappear through the wall. He was too startled to say anything, and later asked the caretaker who else was in the house. When told 'no-one', he related what he had seen. The caretaker wasn't surprised. There was known to be a ghost, and the wall she had vanished through had a flight of stairs behind it. The man who tells this story is a matter-of-fact, level-headed man, and until that day he didn't believe in ghosts. Now he is not so sure.

It is a great misfortune that the deeds have been burnt, and that there is so little record of what happened there. The openings said to lead from the cellars may well have been hiding places, or even sally ports, leading out to somewhere safe in the neighbouring gorse coverts.

Eastchurch seemed untroubled by wars or smuggling at this stage, although it has always had its quota of ghost stories, especially regarding Shurland Hall. They come later. The church was, and is, large, and was not elaborately furnished. Outside, water barrels collected rain water from the roof via water pipes and spouts, and each barrel was locked, the owner keeping the key. This was an attempt to overcome the shortage of fresh water in the village, but it did not improve the appearance of the church. The church warden's books and accounts illustrate the kind of problems that faced Eastchurch.

1703 Paid ye Apparitor for ye Service Book for ye Tempest. One shilling and sixpence.

The Apparitor was the official messenger from the Archdeaconry Court, and the fast and service was kept on January 19th, 1704, by proclamation of Queen Anne. This tempest was the worst ever known in England, for no other tempest had ever occasioned a Parliamentary address, or a public fast. The hurricane, for that is what it was, lasted nearly a week. The Eddystone Lighthouse was washed away and twelve warships were sunk off the coast. Houses, barns and trees were blown down, there were floods in the Thames Valley, and casualties were heavy. In 1707 William Barrow of Borden gave the church a 'great silver flagon' and also left land for the use of the parish. In 1702 Mr Robert Eaton, Vicar of Leysdown, was buried, also T. Jordan (a poor Anabaptist), Susan Wide (a poor old maid) and —— Thomas Stevenson, yeoman, renting about six hundred per annum, together with Thomas Stevenson his nephew, a youth of about fourteen years of age, died in ye house called Parsonage House within three quarters of an hour of each other, December 15th, and were both buried in a grave December 18th. There is no reason given for these two deaths, and it is the sort of account that evokes fresh curiosity every time one reads it. In January 1747–8 the legitimate and illegitimate sons of the same man were baptised together, and in July 1756 William Johnson, Sexton, being lunatic hanged himself. In 1754 George Marsh was found dead on the marshes due to the inclemency of the weather, while in 1791 Thomas Hammond was found drowned in the hog tub, supposed to have been blown in by ye wind.

Seventeen thirty-nine produced an entry of note in the Marriage register: 'Edward Jacob married Mrs. Margaret Risdon of Canterbury (by license)'. Now Edward Jacob was a well known Faversham business man, mayor of the town at least once, a writer, and a historian. He later bought Nutts Farm at Leysdown, and did a great deal of work digging out fossils from Warden Cliffs, preserving them and then classifying them. Nowhere in his book on Faversham is any indication given as to why he should steal away to Eastchurch to marry by licence. His reasons are hidden, and likely to remain so.

Two other marriages took place, in 1705, that caused some conjecture. Thomas Dilly, labourer, and Susan Wilkinson, poor whore, married May 13th. Perhaps that was a shotgun wedding — the comment is cruelly frank. Then came a man of courage, if not sense. John Davis, labourer, and Elizabeth Smith, widow aged eighty-one (he being her sixth husband). For the record, she outlived him! In 1797, on June 9th, a man was buried on the beach, supposed to have been killed on a ship at the Nore mutiny. So that was Eastchurch's share of the mutiny. Drowned men were buried on the seashore in those days not fetched to the churchyard. In 1771 a man unknown was found drowned on the beach and buried in the churchyard, but it was unusual enough to warrant an entry. In 1798 two men 'supposed to be Russians' were found on the seashore, and were buried in the churchyard. Why they were supposed to be Russians no-one explains.

An inventory of All Saints, Eastchurch, was made in 1773. There was nothing outstanding mentioned: a reading desk, a pulpit (which is late Tudor or Jacobean, and very beautiful), a table (communion) and a chest with three locks and keys for alms. This chest is still there, although it is too battered now to be usable.

There was a Bible, two common prayer books, a Book of Martyrs and one of homilies, the registers, and the church plate. A list of prohibited degrees hung in the church, it states, and the commandments and chosen sentences were 'fairly written' on the church walls.

In 1762 William Mantle and Sarah Oast married. There are descendants of the Mantles still on the island, but the Oasts, and they were a large family, have disappeared.

The Gold family, of smuggling fame, was quite extensive. One Gold married a girl called Hearsey, and their son was christened Hearsey Gold. In the register of marriages 1785, there is a large notice, later crossed out, regarding John Roberson, curate. Notice to say he went before the archbishop on account of the 'enormous vile crime' of having carnal knowledge of Elizabeth, the wife of William Brett of Minster. The writer continued with a long and irate dissertation about the curate and his 'vile crime'. In 1794 the deputy registrar scored it out, saying that it had no place there, and unfortunately making it difficult to read.

There are the usual baptisms of bastards and base-born children, the book-keeper was nothing if not honest, and then in 1718 is written Anne, daughter of Francis (and Anne) Cull, curate. The curate's poor wife evidently put in as an afterthought, or perhaps he did produce the baby by himself.

In 1769 Grace, wife of Isaac Davis, affidavit, who drowned herself in the Old House Pond. This is one of the last times the affidavit was used, and it is not made clear where the unlucky Grace was buried. Well into the middle of this century there was a tale that the pond was haunted, and that the drowned woman walked at night. Some said that it was because she was buried in unconsecrated ground, or that a full burial service was not read. Latterly, the pond has been filled in, and no more has been heard of the ghost. In 1728 the vicar, the Reverend Richard Forster, died after twenty-nine years in office. He was a very good vicar, and the parish appreciated his concern on their behalf. The Reverend Forster left to the patron of the time, Thomas Palmer, a deed of gift of a house and orchard in Leysdown, as a perpetual endowment for teaching poor children to read, write and learn the catechism. A small school room was made in the church, and the children were taught there. The next vicar was the Reverend

Alexander Young, and he was succeeded by Dr. Thomas Hey in 1755. These vicars were related to the patrons, and Dr. Hey became both rector and vicar, as the patron, Miss Frances Palmer, bequeathed the advowson to him. This ended the rule of the twelve trustees and their descendants.

Moving from Eastchurch to Warden, it is found that the Warden records are scanty, but it is surprising how many Minister people are buried there. The truth was that Minster had very little room left in the churchyard, and with the influx from Sheerness, space was becoming a problem.

There is little about Leysdown. As one historian said 'there is no village, or anything there', just the farms and the cottages of the workers, and much of the land belonged to the Sawbridges. From a Leysdown rate book of 1760 came the following account, and the explanation. The historian who first recorded it suppressed the surnames, as their descendants were still living.

Paid license for Richard P. and Catherine G.

for their marriage	£2 5s.	0d.
Ring for Catherine to be married with	14s.	0d.
Expenses of keeping Richard in hold	9s.	0d.
Paid for Richards examination, his oath and dinner	3s.	0d.

Married by licence at Leysdown. It sounds like a rush job, and it was. Richard and Catherine had been keeping company, with a view to marriage, then suddenly Richard cooled off. Catherine had problems that needed solving quickly, so she confided in the Overseer of the Poor, Mr. Hickmott. Richard was ploughing quite happily when the irate overseer appeared, put him under arrest and kept him in hold, while giving him a stern lecture at the same time. Mr. Hickmott then saddled his horse, rode with all speed to Harty, where he swam the ford (so it said) and hastened to Faversham for a licence and a ring. On his return, he released Richard on the understanding that he would marry Catherine, and no nonsense, which he did. It is hoped that they lived happily ever after. Let no-one make the mistake of thinking that Mr. Hickmott was full of moral indignation. He may have been, of course, but his aim was to get the pair respectably married, and so prevent Catherine and the expected baby becoming a charge on the parish. That was his duty, and he did it thoroughly. Richard must have wondered what hit him!

At Harty, the landlord of Sayes Court made a charge of twenty pounds to whoever rented the farm, in order to pay the incumbent. Mr. Sawbridge devised this scheme, for he found that the curate had lost glebe land of sixty acres, also land at Hoo, but was still obliged to pay the tithe. Mr. Sawbridge was known for his concern about his property, and was a reasonably kind landlord. The tenant of Sayes Court also had a clause in his agreement that he must put sheep to graze in the churchyard. This was an obligation, not a privilege, and it prevented the churchyard becoming overgrown and full of weeds.

In 1756 a whale was washed ashore at Minster, causing great excitement. At least, everyone thought it was a whale, and so it was recorded. It was thirty-six feet (and over) long, twenty-two feet around, eight feet from its eyes to the tip of its nose, and it yielded twenty hogsheads of oil. How they disposed of the carcase isn't revealed, but it seems to have caused more excitement at the time than the dockyard or the wars did.

This could not last. Eastchurch, Warden and the other small hamlets might remain untouched by the brash new town growing, but it was in the parish of Minster, and Minster's peace was bound to be shattered by it.

CHAPTER XVIII

A period of comparative calm

Queen Anne's reign did not seem to impress itself on Sheppey very deeply, but once the continental wars ended in 1713 England enjoyed a peaceful spell. The Act of Union between England and Scotland had been signed in 1707, and Great Britain was a reality. One thing the queen was remembered for was her creation of 'Queen Anne's Bounty', which gave back to the Church a fund raised from titles which Henry VIII had appropriated. Amongst other things it was used to increase the incomes of poorer clergy, which badly needed a boost.

It is a sad fact, but true, that by the end of the eighteenth century every church in Sheppey was in need of repairs, some urgently. The Minster Vestry Reports and Church Warden's Accounts that are available provide evidence of care for the abbey, but they couldn't keep up with all the necessary repairs. Hasted described the other churches on the island, and they were in a pitiable condition. Minster Abbey was under the jurisdiction of Canterbury, and seemed to be reasonably well cared for. What was then termed 'the ville of Sheerness' was regarded as part of Minster parish, which added to the number of burials. When the tombstones in the old churchyard were more legible than they are now, many children wondered why so many people from Sheerness were buried there, and today people do not realise that Minster Abbey was the church for Sheerness until the late nineteenth century. The chapel over the dockyard gate, previously referred to, was solely for the use of the garrison, for services. Queenborough's church, Holy Trinity, had been a chapel of the abbey, and the living was in the gift of the corporation. It had one aisle, one chancel, and a painted ceiling. There was a high, raised seat for the mayor and bailiffs, and it had been 'paved and ceiled', and a gallery built at the west end by Thomas King, one of the M.P.'s in 1695. The tower steeple at the west end appeared older than the church and there was a small wooden turret with five bells.

Eastchurch church, All Saints, was described as large and handsome, with three aisles and three chancels, and a flat roof surrounded with battlements. Eastchurch had more charities than any other village in Sheppey.

Warden church, Saint James, was described as a poor, mean, plastered building, with one aisle, one chancel, and a small turret at the west end. It had not been used for a long time, but had recently been repaired, although it still was not really fit to hold services in, and was so dilapidated that it was not expected to stand for much longer.

The church at Leysdown, Saint Clement, was just as bad. The tower, described as ancient, hung towards the south, seven feet out of line. The body of the church had fallen down, so services were held in a shed. This shed was simply a room with an aisle and a wooden turret at the west end, with one bell. The tower had been taken down to within eight feet of the ground. At Elmley the church had no pavement or ceiling, although the walls and roof were intact. There were no doors or windows, and it was used as a storehouse.

Saint Thomas at Harty was surviving, a small building consisting of a body, chancel and two side chantries with a pointed turret at the west end. There was, and still is, the remains of a flight of stone steps that led to the rood loft, which was erected in the fifteenth century with money left by a bequest for that purpose. Service was once a fortnight except in severe weather.

It looked as though the churches had been neglected since the dissolution, but the fact was that apart from Minster and Eastchurch the villages were only sparsely populated, and they did not have the wherewithall to keep up the necessary repairs.

For many years the islanders were not renowned for regular churchgoing. Of course they had a reason. After the religious disturbances of the Tudor reigns, they were just settling down when along came old Cromwell wanting to alter it all again. This was too much for Sheppey, enough was enough, they said, in future no-one was going to tell them how they should worship, and if they could not do things in their own way then they would not go to church at all. It is still possible, when asking what church a person belongs to, to be told 'Church of Sheppey'!

The Church Wardens Accounts for Minster commence in 1709, and like the Overseers Accounts, they start with a list of people who farm or rent enough land to be taxable. Burford, Silvester, Thomas Salmon, all names that occurred in the previous century, are among them. William Burgess and William Chalk were church wardens for the year. One was chosen by the Minister, and the other by the Vestry and called the People's church warden.

There were several Chalks in the family, one was the butcher who had built his slaughter house on the 'waste', and the name occurs frequently until well into the nineteenth century.

William Burgess (the Minister's Warden) and Will Chalk. Account.

For bread and wine at Easter	7s.	2d.
A warrant for Amy Nare's husband (and a horse)	2s.	6d.
Spent at ye visitation	£2 6s.	8d.
To a souldier to bury a man	1s.	0d.

There is more bread and wine at Whitsuntide, which suggests the communion was for special occasions, not a weekly service. A prayer book costs 1/- and 'ffor to fetch a load of sand' 6s. Lime also had to be fetched, and two barrels of water.

Paid to Mr. Woolett, for gaol money   £2 12s.

This gaol money had to be paid, by order, for the upkeep of prisons.

These accounts were presented yearly, and are all much the same. The total was in the region of £8, and as that was not the only bill the parish was liable for it is easy to see why churches with no village to support them suffered.

The following year, 1710, there was an assessment bill for church repairs and fences.

Uplands and fresh marshes at 1½d. per acre, and salts 4d. per score of acres for one half year ending at Michaelmas 1710. This was made by the minister, the church wardens and the rest of the inhabitants of the parish. Nearly every farmer is listed, and his farm. Some of them farmed two holdings, like Henry Garret, who farmed Scockles, Parsonage, his own land and Cheney Marshes.

Thomas Dier (or Dyer) for ye Abbey

	— 320 acres	£2	
him more for ye field	— 006 acres		9d.
Him more for Lady Manuels land	— 40 acres	5s.	

This expression 'him more for' occurs frequently as do references to Lady Manuel's land, but the odd thing is that none of the old historians or chronicles mention Lady Manuel. William Chalk farmed somewhere called 'Friends' often spelt 'ffriends' of one hundred acres, and it has since then lapsed into obscurity, and so far cannot be traced.

Not all the farms are named, but nearly all the ones that are can be identified. Sometimes only the landlord's name is given, so that James Stamp for Borstal, only 75 acres, then becomes 'him more for Sir Thomas Culpeppers' which is tantalizing.

In William Chalke's account for 1710 there are the usual payments for bills, books, and burials, more lime and brick, to be fetched from Queenborough, and the collar maker was paid one shilling for five bell ropes. Widow Winter was paid seven shillings 'for beer to ye workmen'. There was also a list of rents due from 'outdwellers', the absentee landlords and farmers. Here Lady Manuel figures frequently, also the 'the Hon. the Lady Gernsey!' In 1714 William Chalke is still church warden, and Mr. Goodyear is doing ye register.

The ringers on Thanksgiving day were paid six shillings. Gaol money was paid, the Poor House is mentioned. To Mr. Bork, or Bock, a quit rent for ye Poores House, 2s 6d. It looks from that as though Mr. Bork was the steward for the Hayward Charity. All the vestry signed this, including William Appleby of Ripney Hill deeds, and Thomas Burfut made his mark. In 1711 Henry Garrett, of Scockles Farm, was also church warden.

There was a visitation, on April 20th, which cost £3 4s

For ye Churchwardens and sidesmens' oath and for the ministers dinner	5s
For burying seven men by the seaside	7s
Gave to a poor man with a wife and five children	2s
Given to eight poor seaman in distress	1s
Given to Thos. Jenkins for killing two otters	1s

(In 1566 a statute was made enjoining church wardens to destroy vermin.) Washing church linen cost 10s. to John Davis, and more for his wages, 10s. There was 'oyle for bells', and the 'Glaser, his Gill' which was 13s 9d. In 1713 Arden Rafe, at the mill, is mentioned.

In the accounts there were many sailors in distress, and some French prisoners, who received 8s. This was the result of the continental wars. In 1714 the accounts included eight soldiers with papers, 5/- The 'papers' were permits to allow them to travel back to their native parishes. Poor people were not allowed to wander around the countryside without a pass. Eight seaman who suffered shipwreck were also helped. More drowned men were buried 'by the seaside', at the cost of one shilling each, and persons who had suffered by fire (poor distressed persons) were aided.

| To Brissenden proclaiming King George | £5 10s | | |
| William Brissenden when King George was crowned as ye bill | £3 | 5s | 2d |

And more bricks and lime and sand for ye church repairs.

Sheppey accepted King George as placidly as it accepted anything else that was at a distance. King George spoke no English, realised he had only been nominated as king to keep the Catholic Stuarts out, and spent much of his time in Hanover, leaving the Government to rule. Apart from a Jacobite rebellion that failed, England was at peace for a time.

This routine of assessment and accounts was clearly well established, and carried on with nothing to disturb the routine for many years. In 1716 Thomas Saywell paid to a poor woman and children with a pass, half a crown. Without the pass she would have been in trouble.

There were the usual distressed seamen, three poor sailors with passes, and building materials. They also splashed out on a cloth for the communion table and two napkins, £1 9s., and a flagon, two plates and a basin, 14s. 8d. When these accounts were audited, there was a triumphant declaration 'So it does appear that the accountant is in purse'. Usually they were not!

In 1717 Thomas Dyer recorded expenses 'at ye visitation. and Sittenbourne, and at the Ferry House £2 19s 6d.' The Ferryhouse was also an ale house and victuallers, as well as the residence for the ferry keeper. There was another ale house on the mainland side, where previously a little stone house had stood. This little house was built by George Fox, who had to wait there a long time in the cold one day, which decided him to build a small house for shelter so that other people would not suffer. The Ministers dinner that year cost 5s. 6d. and Expenses for King George's birthday 5s. Quite how the birthday was celebrated is not explained, and the rest of the account was the usual bills and poor sailors, apart from paying William Augur to clear the churchyard of stones and rubbish, one and six-pence, and expenses concerning the clock, six shillings.

There is an Overseer of the Poor's account for 1715, written in beautiful handwriting, but very blotched with age. Once again all the farmers and landowners are listed, including the elusive Lady Manuel, and as the cess is based on rents, houses are included. Ripney Farm has several different tenants, and there are numerous signatures, headed by the minister; Isaac Skilder and Nathaniel Webb were the overseers, and the Webb vault is still clearly 'readable' in the churchyard. At that time 'Nat' Webb farmed Tadwell Farm round Stickfast Lane. The account is hard to decipher. Not many people were kept in the Poor House, the 'Workhouse' days, of which so much has been written, had not yet arrived.

The people relieved, mostly widows and the old, received a 'salary' of one and six or two shillings a week. Five shillings and eight pence was paid for shirts for the Warren boy at Milton.

Stakes were bought for making weirs, which suggests that work was found for those capable of doing it. Someone named Bills needed a chain, three shillings, and then had to be chained down, watched, and boarded, and it all cost. Then his wife needed help, half a crown.

The Halloway boy was boarded at Benstead's, and needed two shirts and stockings, ten shillings, and 'paid for coat for Ladd child, three shillings and nine-pence'. Robert Wilkens had been 'boarded' costing three shillings and a penny. Then comes 'paid for Goodman Wilkins coffin, eight shillings, to Mr. Chalk for meat in Mr. Wilkins sickness, one shilling'. There are bills for the expenses of having indentures made out at the sitting at Sittingbourne, one of five shillings, and one of ten. Children needed shoes, their board paid, and boots mended. 'Paid to Michael Codd for mending for ye poor 13s 6d. Paid the King's Tax for ye Poore House 1s.'

Various Doctors bills are met, yarn is bought for 'Widow Coombers boy', so he was evidently given something to work on. The widow was allowed '£7 5d. for keeping the Butler boy'. The total amount spent was £76 7s 4d, and the overseers 'were in purse'. Out of this money they had kept the very poor fed and warm, boarded out and clothed orphans, provided work where they could, attended to the sick, providing doctors, medicine and attendance where necessary, and arranged apprenticeships for children when they were old enough. They collected the 'cess' and kept the accounts, and all this was unpaid, the duty of the parish.

Eastchurch was run on the same lines, but having less inhabitants the job was easier. The Poor House there was in the village street, and Queenborough also followed the same procedure, with a Poor House and parish relief.

Minster was still the largest village, and was vulnerable because the priory had gone, and they had always been used to having help at hand. It is unfortunate that the items about Mr. Bills are badly blurred and obscured. He had to be watched, and chained down, which suggests that he was deranged, and in the Poor House.

It was seldom that the ill, or mentally unsound, were sent off the island. Sheppey, they say, looks after its own.

The geographical situation of the island did not lend itself to easy transport. Even letters were difficult. In 1672, when there was a garrison at Queenborough, offices were requisitioned for the mail. In 1673 the 'letter office' was at Nicolas Badcock's house. Mr. Gascoigne was post master at Sittingbourne, and letters arrived there quite safely by the Royal Mail coach. The post then went to Sheerness, but this part of the journey was neither regular nor rapid, and letters took even longer to reach Queenborough. Boats took mail to and from the Fleet, and the obvious thing would seem to be to send post down river from London by boat, but once the Royal Mail was in operation that was the way it had to travel.

The church wardens accounts continue, and the names become familiar. Isaac Skilder, Thomas Greengrass and their contemporaries appear to undertake all the different parish duties in turn, and the accounts contain many records of 'burials by the seaside', money given to poor people, and bills paid.

There was a memo in 1720 that the pales at the east end of the churchyard between the Faulcon Yard and the churchyard belong to Mr. Garrett, and are to be by him maintained. In July 1722 the parishioners agreed to an assessment in order to take down a part of the old roof of the church. This is followed by a large memorandum written by the curate, Richard Tysore, in which he claims his right to all 'wood chips, etc.' from the repairs. 'My predecessor, Mr. Broadbank, and others did carry it home, I have claimed it as mine, it has been unanimously acknowledged by the Parish to belong to me as my inherent right ...' he then makes a present of it to 'Mr. Richard Chalk ye present Church Warden' and he was recording the fact 'for the benefit of those that come after'. In one account are the expenses £1 3s. 6d. for William Brisson 'going ye bounds', which suggests that the parish boundaries were walked at that time, but there is no indication of when 'beating the bounds' ceased in Minster.

New names appear, Mr. Potter at Wybornes, and Thomas Suffling at Pigtail. There has been much surmise about Pigtail, a small piece of ground on the corner of the road where Stickfast Lane meets the Minster to Eastchurch (Chequers) Road. The 'British Queen' stands on the other Stickfast Lane corner. Pigtail is a corruption of the word pightel, which means a small piece of land in the open fields, or a small enclosed plot, other spellings are Pightle or Pingle. It describes the corner field exactly.

There is a bill for shingles, and for money paid 'when ye part of ye Church roof was raised'. The next year in the church cess Lady Manuel's name is coupled with esquire Herbert, which suggests she was one of the descendants of Baron Herbert of Shurland. Also included is a list of 'Intruders in the Parish of Minster', meaning the out dwellers.

Expenses were incurred for taking Rebecca Mornington to 'ye justices', and a horse had to be hired, but her crime is not revealed. There is a quit rent for several years for the Poor House, this time for a Mr. Chapman. The Sparks family appear as owing five shillings, this family became big landowners in the following century.

In 1723 another Poor Law Act was passed, in which parishes were to provide Workhouses, and encouraged to form Parish Unions.

In that same year the redoubtable Elizabeth Davis died 'widow of the Parish of Harty aged one hundred and five, out of this island but two years in her life. She had six husbands whose names were recited at her funeral.' If there had been a

Book of Records published then, she would surely have been given a place in it. In 1724 there was a widow Skilder of Wallend, perhaps Isaac's mother. The church clock was cleaned, and Mr. Woollett was paid four shillings for drink 'for the men that took down ye dial board and put it up again'. There is still a dial board over the main door at Minster Abbey, but it is not very likely that it is the same one.

The accounts vary little from year to year. An odd entry in 1726 is 'Fetching the capilace £4 2 6'. This is the local spelling for Capellanus, meaning the vicar. The following two years have no extraordinary entries.

In 1729 William Brissenden cut down the weeds in the churchyard for half a crown, later there was a visitation, and new bell ropes were purchased. 'For a leather Batherick, as of bill £1 5s 6d.' Again an odd spelling, and baldrick was the word they were looking for, the leather belt or thong which suspended the bell clapper. There was also a bill for fetching a load of board and shingles from 'Windmill Key 7s. 6d'.

In 1730 John Gransden of Ghost Farm is mentioned, but the farm has lived up to its name, and cannot be traced. Expenses for putting up the vane, 6s. This was the famous weather-vane with a horse on the top, and a horse's head in place of one of the arrows. It was fashioned so in honour of Baron Robert de Shurland, and the church became famous for it. Many different historians and writers remarked on the 'Horse vane', and the church was known to mariners as the Horse Church. This weather-vane remained on the Church steeple until the decade following the Second World War, when it was replaced by a more conventional one. It was renewed during the intervening centuries, and the rather battered metal horse, now tailless, that is still kept on show in the Abbey is dated 1813. There was a memorandum in 1732 that settlement certificates and papers delivered 'to ye Parish' were in the Parish Chest. These certificates had to be produced by newcomers to the village, to prove that they could return to their own parish should they be in need, or that they were wealthy enough not to become a charge on the parish. To be able to rent property worth £10 a year entitled them to become residents.

Work on the church, mowing the churchyard and all the usual outgoings continued for the next two years. Ghost Farm was still running, and Richard Duffy had taken the Mill. In 1735 the parish staged a minor rebellion, and the 'cess' list is heavily crossed out.

Memorandum. This cess was of no use for whom it was made. The parishioners thought it too big so that they ordered another to be made, at three pence in the pound which begins on ye next page, and that is all ye cess there was for the year 1735 and that was from Easter to Michaelmas 1735 and that page and ... was none afterwards.

In the expenses, Mr. Sharpe was paid 'two years quit rent for ye Poore House, Ten shillings', and there were the inevitable distresses and buryings.

In December 1734 Thomas Webb (probably brother to Nat) was buried in the Churchyard 'killed by firing his fowling piece', and the next year in February John Perry was drowned by high tides at Elmley. Mr. Segars brewhouse was 'cessed', so there were still some Segars around, but where the brewhouse was built is not known.

From 1737 vestry orders are available for a number of years. Minster Vestry Book bought at the charge of the parish and cost one shilling. Richard Tysore curate. Thomas Randall church warden.

Vestry meetings were open to the parish, and church wardens, sidesmen, overseers, surveyors, waywardens and borsholders were elected there. Frequently one man held several posts. In July the Poor Rate was agreed at Threepence, which was not high. The keys of the parish chest were entrusted to Mr. Randall, Mr. Chalk and Isaac Skilder. Mr. Thomas Randall was also a sidesman, and overseer. He had either inherited or bought Borstall Hall, sometimes called New Hall, and he was one of the wealthier men in the parish, and rented and owned a large amount of property. Newly elected church wardens were William Dobson, and Daniel Turner.

There was a list of children kept at parish expense from Easter 1736, and poor women. A few examples show how things were run:

At Mrs. Hodges, William Holloway for his board and Susannah Bones at half a crown a week.
At Mrs. Pain's the Izzard girl at half a crown.

There were others, and the list ended with Dames Augur and Bromley, two shillings. These two old ladies lived in the Poor House, and Mrs. Bromley was described as 'lunatic'. In 1740 the poor rate rose to fivepence in the pound. Repairs to the church were again mentioned, and it was agreed with Mr. Beal that the parish was responsible for S. Bones, paying one shilling a week, and taking her away 'at their pleasure'. Church wardens accounts for 1741 record that Mr. Jowell was paid four shillings, for burying four men in Chetney Salts. There are a larger number than usual of buryings 'at the seaside' that year, and it is no wonder that old skeletons are sometimes found on beaches and marshes.

All through the accounts there are references to shingling the church roof, and other repairs, shingles were fetched from Windmill Quay, and 'the Apparitor' was paid for a book, one shilling. It was all recorded faithfully. In the accounts for 1743 there were expenses for 'Doctor Hicks, the Hospitall', one shilling, so the Poor House obviously tended the sick.

One of the biggest problems with 'Parish' children was finding them work, and apprenticeships were arranged for them when possible. In July 1743 there is such a record:

To put John Hunt apprentice to Henry Lee, Barber, to serve till he is one and twenty years, Officers of Parish to provide two suits of apparel both linnen and woolen, and to give the Master Henry Lee for taking said John Hunt as apprentice £6. viz. £3 at binding, and £3 more a six months after, and the said Henry Lee to find the boy in two suits of apparel when he shall come to the age of one and twenty; and to find him in all necessary clothing during his servitude.

This was signed by all those present at the vestry meeting.

They were still making church 'cesses', and received quit rent for ye Poore's Meadow, which was leased. The quit rent they paid for the Poor House seems perplexing at first glance, but quit rent was paid to the Lord of the Manor, in lieu of duties, and as the Poor House was on land belonging to the Manor of Minster, the trustees of the charity would receive the quit rent as a legality. They also paid Mrs. Austin 'more' for schooling, one shilling and threepence. Seventeen forty-five and 1746 contain nothing new. The accounts were unvaried, and the vestry meetings were mainly concerned with the keep of the poor children. Mr. Beal kept D. Kidwell at two shillings a week. The Beals are a large family and have been prominent on the island since, roughly, that era. It is in the later eighteenth century that the names of families still here today first appear. An interesting entry is that John Jeave was at Mrs. Jelly's, Farding Close. Probably Farthing Close, for they wrote as they spoke, and they do not say where Farding Close was. As well as John, several other children went there 'for victuals'. Where they lived, and who looked after them between meals is anyone's guess.

In 1749 the vestry 'agreed to seal the Church', and the church wardens were 'impowered' to get the same immediately done. The accounts include 'Beer for ye carpenters' and 'Mr. Roust's bill'. Mr. Rouse was a local builder, among other things. Account was taken of the all important certificates 'though there may be more in the chest'.

At another vestry meeting that year they agreed to employ Mr. Chapman the attorney to sue for the houses left to the parish by Amy Paine's will. (Parish to pay expenses.) Mr. 'Roust's' bill for the work done in the church steeple and churchyard came to £35 9s. 3d.

In April the vestry 'unanimously agreed' by those whose names are underwritten that a Workhouse be established for ye maintainance and employment of ye poor of our parish. A long list of signatures follows, it looks as though the Act of 1723 had at last caught up with them. The poor cess was sixpence, and eightpence the following half year. George II was king now, but there was no mention of his 'crownation' in the accounts.

In 1752 the calendar altered, and the New Year commenced on January the first, as it does today, and not March the first, as it had done up till then.

The following year there is an entry 'Paid for Children's Schooling more that the common money — £5 10s. 0½d.' Here the church warden's account book ends, which is frustrating, and there is not another available for the eighteenth century. The vestry orders continue, in April 1754 they agreed to a rate of sixpence for one year for repairing the highway and each team to be paid sevenpence for the day. The 'highways' were repaired with shingle from the beach, the local farmers suplying the horses, carts, and labour. In December they agreed to another cess of sixpence for church repairs, and sixpence poor rate. The rates were quietly increasing with the growth of the local population. In 1755 it was the same story, the highway rate was continued, the church rate reduced, but the poor cess up to eightpence. There were women and children to be maintained, costing ten and six a week, with coals, 'as the officer shall think proper'. Mrs. Towndrow to live in one part of the Poor House rent free. There must have been some alteration the following year, for no church warden 'for the Minister' was appointed.

In March 1757 'Agreed not to pay for any more schooling (the schooling of any more children) than what the Schoolmaster shall produce an order signed by three of the Parish Officers'.

The rates stayed up. In April 1759 they let to Stephen Rouse the Poors Meadow to Lady Day next at £4 5s. the year. This was the highest bid they received.

By 1760 the Poor Cess had increased to one shilling, and once again the parish of Minster agreed to erect a Workhouse for the employment of the Poor etc.

In August the 'Vestry Duty' agreed that Mr. Lucas proceed to recover the legacy of a house left by Mrs. Pain to the parish. Apparently Mr. Holloway had achieved nothing in the proceeding eleven years. In September they agreed to sink a well at the Poor House for the use of the poor. Later in the month 'It was agreed' that 'Thomas Tritton, bricklayer, do sink and stean a well at the Poore House in this Parish for eight shillings per foot, finding all materials.' Thomas signed this, his handwriting was good. That well is still in use today, the water is soft, and tastes good. Until there was a water supply in Minster which was not before 1903, the villagers would fetch their drinking water from the Union Well, paying halfpenny a bucket. This charge helped to finance the Workhouse.

Their next idea, in face of rising rates, was to allow a shilling a week to persons 'that the Parish Officers think to be proper objects of charity' rather than admit to the Poors House.

There was some discussion about their legacy of Mrs. Pain's house or houses, which they were still trying to claim.

Edwin Austin donated five pounds for the poor, which was carefully shared out and the names of the recipients noted. In July 1761 it was agreed to give Jane Jones two and threepence per week for looking after and taking care of the poor that are in the Poor House.

In 1762 the even tenor of the meetings was broken when John Beal refused to be deputy sexton for Edward Baker. Despite promises of good behaviour and fair shares of anything that might come their way, John Beal refused the job. They gave up their attempts to get Mrs. Pain's house, it appeared that they could not prove any claim to it. Stephen Rouse continued to rent the Poors Meads, and in 1765 managed to get a lease for three years at a reduced rent of £4 a year, with certain conditions. The rates did not fall. In March 1767 the Officers and inhabitants of the Parish 'indemnify and bear harmless M. J. Penn and J. Rice Churchwardens and J. Head Overseer who have entered into bond and — (blank here) for a bastard child sworn to Mr. Dean and before Mr. Thomas Brown Mayor of Queenborough and witness'. This sounds odd now, but the Bastardy Act of 1732/3 obliged the mother to declare her pregnancy and name the father. The Parish Officers would either coerce the parents into marriage, or obtain a Bond of Indemnification from the father, which made him legally responsible for payment for the child's upkeep. The illegitimacy rate was rising, and the parishes could not afford too many unpaid-for children.

Here the vestry book ends, and again there is no follow up, but it gives a good idea of how the village was run. The church registers show how Sheerness was growing, and how the entries were written, as comments were allowed.

> 1776. Baptised Christopher, son of William and Alice May on board ye Conquistador.
> 1786. Francis, daughter of Henry Johnson (a black man) and his wife (fair) Martha.
> In 1788 this was repeated.
> Sarah, daughter of Henry Johnson (a black man) and Martha his wife (a white women)

Such a marriage was obviously very unusual then! 'Kezia, daughter of William Smith and Kezia, The Old Ship, The Lennox.' This was one of the hulks. Then an odd entry, and rather out of place in a Baptismal Register. 'The Late Reverent Fox's baptising children had to be received and ratified by Samuel Langley.' It is believed that the unhappy Reverend Fox went mad.

There are other entries 'from ship board' christened in church, and some were christened at 'The King's Head', an Inn of the Blue Houses, by the Garrison Chaplain.

Burials were equally descriptive. In 1770, August, 'Edith Crock, aged sixtyone years killed by falling into the dock at Sheerness'. 'Thomas Warknam who was drowned by jumping from this Hulk (Sheerness) in to sea to bath himself.' Elizabeth Thomas was buried, then William Thomas, husband of the above, who was drowned the night she was buried, near the old ships. '1771 Buried John Tapley', (an old German). In 1772 Lewis Imgar was killed by a blow from a fisherman. 1773, February, 'Buried George Hammond a wealthy farmer from this Parish, Ann Hammond who died four days after her husband'. 'December, Buried John Hunter, a very honest man.' 1774, 'Martha and her son Thomas Dunn, both in one coffin'. In 1776 they buried William Burdett, surgeon of the *Daphne*. In September, 'A stranger who was a servant of Mr. Rice for a little time but nobody knew his name'. Hiring someone to work for you was a very simple procedure in 1774, no cards, nor questions asked.

In January and February 1777 there was an outbreak of smallpox, several children and young people died, a stranger 'whose name I do not know', and five sailors at the hospital.

In March another six sailors died, presumably the hospital was the naval sick bay.

> 1781, February, Buried Thomas Bigg, is a good young man as was in the Parish.
> August, buried John Kirkpatrick, who was shot quite through ye body on ye fifth, in Admiral Parkes engagement of ye Dutch off ye Dogger Bank.
> 1782. Buried a man who cut his throat by the Blue Houses
> 1783, Thomas Malory who was hanged on board the Prince Edward.
> In April, Buried a stranger who was dug out of the cliff.

The cliffs are still treacherous now, but usually people in trouble are rescued in time. In 1786 comes one of the saddest requiems in the book. 'July 24th. Buried David Wildish, aged seventy-six (a stranger, labourer, and pauper from over the water).'

So the list continues. Many babies, young people 'in a decline', and innumerable unknown and found drowned. Queenborough was much the same. They had built a Poor House in 1761 and provided allowances for poor children, but the town itself was very poor. In 1773 they made a 'resolution' 'To take all the children that is able to be took from there mothers that have relief of the Parish and to be put in the Poor House and a fitt and proper person to look after them'. Whether they carried this out, and whether it worked, is not told. It reads like a foretaste of the next century, when the Workhouses did just this. Later, there is a memo. that Mr. Bishop had a school for the Poor House children.

Minster Parish's methods seemed the more humane, and it is a pity there are no records of how the children fared later. They were boarded out, and while it is fashionable now to say they were used as cheap labour, all children were expected to be useful in the eighteenth century, and the treatment they received really depended on the family they were living with, human nature being what it is. The parish clothed them — apart from shoes and shirts, there was mention of a linsey wolsey petticoat, and even a pair of stays for one girl! — and schooled them, and in that respect they were luckier than the average village child. When they were old enough an apprenticeship was found and paid for, failing that work was obtained. It was probably farm work, or dairy work or servants work for a girl, but that would not have seemed unusual in those days. They were nursed, and medicine and a doctor found if necessary, things could have been a great deal worse for them. The idea behind it all was to make them healthy, independent, and capable of earning a living for themselves. There was nothing comparable to this on the continent for the poor.

It was in the following century that the Workhouse became a place of terror, and that was partly due to the increase in population, the number of poor, and the agricultural depression. There are no records of 'pauper children' from Minster being sent to the mills in the North of England, as they were from Chatham. There was a story told in Queenborough for many years about a prosperous businessman who kept a shop in the town. He is said to have left instructions in his will that every Workhouse child should have sixpence for a fairing, and an orange, every year. His reason for doing this was that he had been brought up in the Workhouse, he had been fed, dressed, schooled, and sent out to fend for himself, which he had done very creditably. He felt he owed the Workhouse some thanks, he was never ashamed of his upbringing, and that was his way of showing it. He was one of the fortunate ones, for there is no gainsaying the fact that when the Workhouse system really got into its stride not everyone fared so well.

CHAPTER XIX

Country people's lives

A parish such as Minster seemed well able to run its affairs. At the same time, the inhabitants must have had some recreation; it cannot all have been vestry meetings, law days and accounts.

It is recorded that the island had a breed of horses of its own, of long standing. Draught animals were imported, but these little horses, ponies they would be called now, were used by the islanders for riding and driving. No more about them has been discovered, but as there had been small, light horses kept for the hobiliers, perhaps they were descended from those.

There are no descriptions of any sports or recreations after Henry VIII's day, but the parish clerk's diaries give some sidelights on the life in Sheppey. These diaries are an enigma: they have been lost, found, and divided by different hands, but are now fortunately safe in the keeping of the County Archives, and are of great value to anyone studying local history, as they are one of the very few contemporary records that exist.

The clerk made an inventory of many of the houses and farms as he knew them from 1745 to 1792, and extracts are interesting. He started in Leysdown, where Mussel Manor was still known as Mousehole Farm. Not all the houses are named — there were so few that everyone knew where they were! At a farm two fields from Mousehole, he wrote that 'Mr. Pullen's wife killed her infant child as soon as it was delivered from her body, and buried it with a knife behind the stable, and then went up to her chamber again, and died also'. Her husband made oath that he did not know she was with child. 'I was one of the jury', he writes, 'and heard him say it.' At another house nearby, now taken down, one Bladsole whose things were distrained for rent removed them in the night to Sheerness, and John Jones at the 'Sign of the Ship' by giving leave for their waggon and goods to stand in his open yard until the boat could take them away (only a few hours) was obliged to pay the lawyer £100. So that was one moonlight flit that did not work out! They do things more efficiently now-a-days, by van.

To go back to the writer: 'adjoining this was a parcel of Marshland which was part of Home Place Farm of Minster. On this land W. Robinson Shoemaker of Eastchurch shot John Goodchilde in the evening as he lay watching for wild fowle, supposing Goodchilde's head to be a duck. He was acquitted, but never enjoyed himself after until death.'

He relates how he was defrauded over some building by the Curate of Leysdown, and ends the tale with the remark 'worthy Clergy be hanged'. His records are full of life and give a vivid account of the farming life of the island. The present John and Hearsey Gold's grandparents at Warden were described as 'famous in the smuggling way'. Many of the houses and much of the land at Warden had already 'gone to sea'. Farmland was 'used' by a farmer who ran several farms, and then a looker would live in the farmhouse. Small houses were often left to fall down, or caught fire and burnt down, and then the land was 'used', or laid to other farms. Tenants and landowners are carefully named, arable and grazing land estimated, and the number of teams of horses noted. At Eastchurch, the round-house was untenanted and the land ploughed 'by whom I have forgot, but when we repaired the house I stood on my head on the chimneys!' A man called Boothe had a housekeeper known as 'Betty Bootshoes'. He tells how part of a field of wheat slipped down 'many yards under the cliffs', then stopped, and fourteen shocks of wheat was reaped in harvest and drawn up the cliffs with ropes, and tithed.

There was a farm called Souchens Farm, of which there is no trace now. Dr. Jacobs of Faversham bought it. All the histories, marriages, alliances and misalliances of the families are detailed. Houses were pulled down, quit rents unpaid (so the land then reverted to the manor lord) and many of the farmhouses and barns completely rebuilt. In Eastchurch, a Mr. Love bought two pieces of 'Garden Land'. That is not flower garden, it is market garden or small-holding land. The family of Loves came to Sheppey in the late eighteenth century. One of them explained it thus: The family was growing bigger, and needed more land. Land in Sheppey was cheap, it was 'four horse' land. That is, it was heavy clay and needed four horses to do the work of two, but if you were not afraid of work you could make it pay. So, in this contemporary account, one meets the Loves arriving. There were many more public houses, known as ale houses, than now, and later many became private houses. The looker who lived at 'Little Bells', George Mount, drowned in the ditch going home from the street (Eastchurch Street). He makes no comment on this accident!

In Eastchurch Street there were several ale houses, the 'Three Mariners', the 'Crooked Billet' (old and new) the 'Green Man', the 'Woolpack' and the 'Three Horseshoes'. The Widow Scoales of the 'Three Mariners' had two sons. William died in a consumption, and Richard, who was an apprentice, to Adam Smart, wheeler (wheelwright) at Minster, was blown up with gunpowder at the 'Kings Arms', Minster on November 5th.

At the minister's house the curate, Robinson, a Scotchman, 'was turned out by the incumbent Dr. Hey, for being more conversant with Mr. Brett's wife at Minster Abbey Farm than with the Church Bible'.

The Little House at the stocks was once the 'Three Horseshoes', and one of the small houses nearby was the first house the clerk lived in when he married, 'the first house I ever paid rent for!' Later, he moved to Minster. The land called Cable Hills was rented by the present Mr. Baker's father and the estate Sawbridges, esq. In this little old sheephouse lived Thomas Scales, looker over the land, and brought up a family of six children, two of which were drowned in the ditch adjoining the house, and the eldest daughter poisoned herself being in love with a man that lived at New House Farm as a servant. (N.B. The New House was built very lately.)

That was a chapter of accidents, and would probably make a splash in the papers if it happened now. The farm at 'Cable Hills', now called Caple Hill Farm, has been occupied by members of the Love family for many years now, and their descendants still farm it. Working from Eastchurch towards Minster he records an orchard and a market garden, where the produce was taken to 'Sheerness Market'. Two pieces of garden land there were recently purchased by Mr. Love. He mentions Conets Farm and Garretts Farm, at the latter

Hearsey Gold had married the widow, by name Whitehead, and so acquired the farm. There are still plenty of Whiteheads on the island — it is a very old family. One of them is a much loved nurse at Sheppey General Hospital.

Where now John Mantle lives, and here he recites the former tenants, the last one of whom left the lease to John Mantle. 'The estate did belong to Lady Finch, and by Mr. Punnet the Lawyer of Maidstone making her will', and it somehow became the Punnets' after that. It is in the Manor of Minster, but half the barn is in Eastchurch Parish. So that explains how Punnetts Farm obtained its name. He does not mention Cripps Farm, which is almost opposite Garretts in Plough Lane, and he only records Hook Farm, although now there is Old Hook and New Hook. Both these farms have land running down to Windmill Creek, and both of them had a wooden quay on the bank. Their name is said to originate from the Anglo-Saxon Hoc, a tying up place, or quay. Groves Farm also had a quay, and Windmill quay was at the back of Poore's (or Powers) Farm. The remains of these wooden quays are still evident, although the windmill has gone.

In Minster there were two fields called Drummers Land. 'This land belonged to two persons, one, an idiot from a parish in East Kent, the other a drummer in the army, from where it got it's name.'

At Chequers there was inevitably an ale house, 'the Olde Signe of the Chequers', which later became a private house. Paddy's Point was so called because an Irishman with the unlikely name of Halfpenny once lived there. Since then it had been bought by the Biggs family.

The Biggs were all farmers, they were a large family and farmed through the eighteenth and nineteenth centuries and well into the twentieth century. There are still members of the family on the island. Near the 'Sign of the Harrow', which was somewhere near East End, 'lived old Baker and wife, who made her husband believe she was delivered of a child, and that Dame Seale buried it in his wig box, although she was between fifty and sixty years of age, and they had a jovial lying in too on that account'.

There were two Tadwell farms then, Little and Great. At Little Tadwell, now gone, lived David Ansell and his wife, until he shot a seafaring man for stealing turnips out of his garden. The man fell with his head against one of the elm trees before Mr. Faulkes' gate. Ansell left Sheppey immediately, but was taken a few years after, and tried for his life at Maidstone and burnt in the hand, and came home and lived many years after. Considering the rough justice of the age he escaped lightly.

No-one has ever attempted to explain the name Tadwell. It is a farm that has several springs of fresh water, and until well into the 1930's the people of Brambledown fetched drinking water from there. As Tad is an old English spelling for Toad, it is fairly safe to assume that it means nothing more than the Toad's Well, or the Well of the Toad. It is a reasonable explanation until something more definite appears.

Poores Farm House had been taken down and rebuilt by a man from London, and 'in less than two years that house gave way and was obliged to be taken down and rebuilt —'. The 'Thatched House' was a hostelry of some sort in the Halfway area, run by many different people, including Richard Ingleton, and that is another family who appeared in the eighteenth century and is still farming on the island. Mr. Brisley was the last owner named by the clerk, and he rebuilt the house.

Mr. Hopson had bought Ripney Hill and Parsonage Farm, and there were two Whybornes, again Little and Great. Little Whybornes has vanished without trace; it was another of Hopson's properties, let to Mr. Ingleton. Dog Kennel Meads belonged to Sir John Lade's estate. Later it belonged to Lower Wards Farm, via Mr. Hopson. It was usually sublet, in two parts. The diarist says that there was once a dog kennel on the land, from where it got its name. It was grazing land until after the second war; now the new Minster Primary School is built there.

At the Abbey Gate House 'lived Parker and two children; he went away and left the two children in bed, Robert and Elizabeth, and never was heard of after, and the Parish brought up the children'. Various other farm-workers lived there, and eventually Mr. Shrubsole rented the farm 'and pulled down the house and barn', but whether that was the old priory barn is impossible to say.

Minster Street, Poor House and Meads:

He details former tenants, and then says that he rented the meads for thirty-two years, and then the parish took them to their own use. In the poor-house lived Dame Bromley, a mad woman, and Dame Augur, a widow, 'which I think was all the poor that was in the house, which was lately burnt down and the present one built'.

He says little of the houses in Minster Street, there were only fourteen in the village, sixteen at the most, except that he hired one, and that Stone Tallow, a chandler and tobacconist, was hanged with Collington.

He ends with a list of farms, fields, and beerhouses, and in his record he has compressed about fifty years' village gossip. His day-to-day diary is equally fascinating. He was a builder, he ran a school, he took out an auctioneer's licence, for a time he ran a 'collar makers shop' (horse collars, not human ones) and he was the parish clerk. He was literate, so he wrote letters for most of the village, sorted out their business and legal problems, and acted as undertaker and coffin maker, as village carpenters usually did.

In August 1777 he took his boys from the school to 'see the Feversham men play crecket with Minster', and that must be one of the earliest records of village cricket. 22.4.1773, Daniel Horn, who appeared to run a general store at Minster, died, and was buried five days later at Warden. The next day he noted 'the wife of Daniel Horn late disceased poisoned herself about two o'clock this afternoon'. He does not mention burying her, and subsequent entries do not make it clear as to whether she died or recovered. His son Stephen ran the 'Highlanders' (which was at that time built of ship board and thatched as was the 'King's Arms') and he was there frequently. He helped to collect wrecks that belonged to the Manor of Minster, taking the necessary legal steps if anyone attempted to steal them. He went to church, and commented on the sermons. Later he built the first chapel in Minster, and attended there as well. He owned a mare, which was continually being borrowed. 'Our Hills had my mare over ye water', and a hound bitch of some sort called Nimble. He went to Chatham, to Ye Gentlemen of Ye Chest, had dinner at the 'Mitre', and doubtless discussed Scockles Farm, which belonged to Chatham Chest. In 1789 he was 'on ye sand hill to see the Chatham hounds hunt'. There were many references to hunting on different farms, often with their own hounds. They were probably beagles or harriers hunting hares and rabbits.

He buried many of his family, and christened the children — as parish clerk he was allowed to do this, or help, at any rate. Many of them were buried at Warden, as he was in due course. He attended the 'Court' at the abbey, which was still dispensing justice for minor things; the solicitor in charge was Mr. Twopenny from Rochester. He helped organise, and then enjoyed, Minster Fair. One year he records 'Bought Nella a white handle knife and fork'. Fair day was a holiday, and there were stalls, and games, and fairings, and money collected, and 'making Punch at the Abbey'. One year he made a 'Plann' of Minster Fair. It was held round about the abbey, and the stalls were built in Abbey Farm barn.

There was a Fair at Queenborough, and one at Eastchurch every year, but Minster Fair appears to have been the biggest

and most popular. It was still held in the mid-nineteenth century, but there are no records of it, or when it ceased. In 1791 he had done a great deal of rebuilding at the Abbey Farm, and he noted that 'it was an exceeding dry time, no water for the stock but at Summerwell and Round Hill ponds'. He went shooting, about the Abbey Farm, on Wards Hill, and on other farms on the island.

A family named Alexander ran the Cheyney Rock oyster grounds, and he sometimes went on the 'watch boat' with them. When William Alston bought the manor from the Hayward trustees (the Charity went bankrupt) he sold it later but retained the foreshore rights. The clerk was involved in surveying the manor and marking the boundaries. There was a small map made at the time.

At Christmas, 1800, he gave away forty-eight pounds of beef and sixteen gallons of bread 'to ye necessary poor of ye Parish, by order of Mr. William Alston'. He seems to have written out accounts, Poor Cess, Ferry Books, and all manner of things for the villages. On 17.6.72 'writing ye account of the Poors Book for Mr. Berry', and in March 1789 he went to Mr. Berry's to a hunting feast. Feasts were popular. They held Copperas Feasts, Ferry Feasts, Harvest Feasts, a Feast when a building was raised called a Raising Feast, and Club Feasts, although there is no explanation as to what the clubs represented. He went shooting frequently, sometimes alone, often with other farmers, and sometimes with one or two of 'his men'. They shot mallards and grey geese at Scrap Gate, and snipe at the Harps.

In April 1770 he noted that he saw eight swallows and heard 'ye nightin-girl'. It is doubtful if a nightingale would be heard in Sheppey now, but there were still one or two as late as 1950. In December 1773 'we night catched larks', he writes. Larks were still eaten as late as 1800, possibly later in country places. In June 1776 he records 'Shot ten brand geese, and ten sea turkeys in Stray Marsh'. The list of wildfowl is never-ending, and must have kept the larders supplied for weeks.

In 1784 he notes 'This is the backwardest spring I have ever known. Scarce a green leaf to be seen out full on the white thorns on the sixth day of May. Neither have I seen, or heard, a blackbird since the frost and snow went away, to my knowledge.' There had been several very severe winters in the 1780's. The sea was frozen, and so was the Swale, and instead of coming over by ferry boat the travellers walked across the ice in 1776. It was reputed to be the worst freeze-up since 1684, when the river froze and people walked across it. The winter of 1788–9 was even worse, and the clerk described it as 'a continuous sheet of ice from Sheppey to Essex'. The Nore lightship fired distress signals, and no-one could get to them. Whelks and lobsters were frozen on the beach in the frozen sea, and were picked up by the islanders and used to make a tasty dinner. The ferry boats could not work, and the boats from Sheerness to London did not sail. The looker from Wall End Farm managed to ferry post, goods and one or two passengers in a small boat at Stray Creek, one of the creeks on the marshes, but it must have been a cold and miserable journey.

Following the bitter winter of 1776, he writes that in March 'In this, the last week, there was the most wild fowl of the vidgeon (or winder) kind about Emley (Elmley) and Sheppey and the most killed that I ever remembered in forty years. On Monday the sixth Stephen Rouse Junior shot forty six, on Tuesday ye seventh I brought home sixty three geese, duck, winder and divers and Richard brought home nineteen. John Jenkins, a looker in Emley shot the same day ninety-four.' It is an astounding shoot, and what they did with the bag, and who had the thankless task of plucking the birds, is not told. After that he went back to his building, and puts out a fire in Mr. Boarer's stables 'occasioned by lime'. Fires were common, he makes various reports on children who were burnt to death, or started fires in stables with a candle.

Mr. Brett ran several farms, and the clerk was equally at home on all of them, walking the ground and finding hares, planting potatoes 'on a ring of mould', looking at the hops (they tried growing 'hops in Sheppey, but it did not work), attending the Shearing Feast, catching fish in 'the Gutt hole', attending to leases and the poor book, altering the cesses, attending to a wreck, burying members of Mr. Brett's family, and his workmen, and finally going to the Hop Supper. His list is endless. Measuring timber for felling, and houses for building. He went all over the island, putting up pounds at the Mile Houses (a mile from the dockyard), sorting and selling household goods, and spending time with the blacksmith having tools made, and writing the smith's letters. 'Cryed a sale of Household goods of Thomas Adams at the Chequers that was stab'd with a chezel', he writes, a glimpse of violence unexplained in time long gone. He was the builder who attended to the church repairs the vestry meeting had ordered, and he lists them all. 30.11.80 'No Churching, the windows taken down.' On December 10th, 'the new clock ordered at a Public Vestry meeting in July was set going on the tenth day of December following and I heard it strike five for ye first time'. In spite of all their efforts they were still looking at the 'delapidations' in 1806. It was a never-ending tussle.

As parish clerk he assisted at funerals, and records many of them, especially those that were buried in the church. The parish were petitioning for a new churchyard, in the meantime many people were buried under the abbey floor. 'Buried Mariah Baron an officers child from Sheerness in ye Chapel, 1782!' In 1789 Mary Bensted from Sheerness was buried 'in ye chancel near ye brass covered stones'. Thomas Wilson was buried 'under Mr. Lees Stone'. In 1810 he buried Ann Pirkins aged sixteen years two months 'in ye chancel close to Lord Shurland's tomb'. There was no place in the church where people were not buried, and many of them had no stone to mark their grave. In July 1806 the Bobbing and Borden singers came to Minster Church, and it was estimated that there were not less than four hundred people at the service.

He was also involved with the workhouse. Apart from his normal work, someone called Old Vallentine was good at 'finding' gin, which was quickly removed and paid for. In 1784 he agreed to build part of a workhouse, and speaks of 'laying out the cells' for the workhouse. The foundations were laid, and a new apartment built. This was followed by a Raising Feast at Stephen's, 'The Highlanders'. He was building there until February 1785, and in 1789 he was 'at ye Workhouse with Mr. Brisley to chain the poor' which sounds sadistic, to say the least. The next day he was there again 'to make a prison'. In August 1789 the workhouse burnt down. The thatch caught fire, and the whole building was demolished. Three days later a parish meeting was called, and orders given for the poor-house to be rebuilt. Later he writes that 'he went to the Workhouse about a cradle'. There was a lying-in ward there for the destitute, and local girls who had 'got into trouble' and been disowned by their families had no alternative but to go there.

In 1897 he records that he baptised John George Bull son of Christiana Clayton for the workhouse. The church register is less tolerant, referring to John George as 'the base born son of Christiana Clayton in the Workhouse, baptised in Church'. In 1802 he 'buried Ann German, the old nurse at ye Poorshouse'. He records the smallpox epidemic and the deaths, and also tells of the different families and children who were 'given the smallpox', an early form of inoculation, and something no-one would expect to find at Minster, at such an early date.

He frequently went fishing, setting weirs in Crog Deep,

and visiting the farm ponds, which were all stocked with fish. One they visited had not been 'drawn' for twenty years, and they made a record catch, but at a later date no fish were to be found in the pond at Wooton's Farm, and he reports 'Cryed ye Robing (robbing) of Richard Biggs pond at Wooton's Farm'. He visited the poor-house and arranged for poor people to be employed cleaning oysters, which had to be done when the mussels over-ran the seashores. The poor had to scrape the oysters, which were then returned to the oyster beds, and for this they were paid fourpence a basket (half a bushel).

He went to the copperas house at Queenborough, and noted that 'the inhabitants got drunk at loading the hoy with copperas'. Another note says 'In twelve houses out of the sixteen in the street, some person was drunk'. When he attended the Copperas Feast with other men from Minster who also had dealings with the copperas pickers, he remarked that 'Greets', the Mayor of Queenborough, was present. He rented the poor-house meads and land in Stickfast Lane, kept a cow and pigs, and ran a thriving market garden. All the villagers had ground they cultivated, and exchanged seeds, plants and ideas. They grew turnips, asparagus, radishes, cucumbers, many varieties of beans and peas, and all the flowers anyone could think of, as well as soft fruit, fruit trees, and hay and corn. Peach and cherry trees were planted, the science of grafting experimented with. Herbs were grown for distilling and making ointments. They made wine, from elderberries and sloes amongst other things.

From 1779 and 1809 he rented and ran a collar-maker's shop, bought and sold hides, and often worked there with his men. With his various business interests, and his ability to write letters and accounts, he was on good terms with all the farmers and tradesmen on the island, and many of them sent their children to his school. In 1798 there was a note of cruelty when he wrote 'Buried John Crane a man from the Parish House, who perished under the sea wall near ye hundred acres after being horse whipt by Leonard Lester the Keeper of the Poor'. Lester was one of the people who brought cases against the firework throwers in 1820. He was an unpleasant man to say the least, and was 'turned out' from his place as Keeper of the Poor.

In 1777 he records, 'This second day of August the Windmill at Minster in Sheppey was finished and made fitting and did grind the first wheat'.

Two years later he is agreeing to build a house 'at ye furder Mill' for Mr. Swift. Old maps show two windmills on Windmill Hill. One has gone leaving no trace, the other was a ruined stump, little more than foundations, sited in a little shaw (small wood) on top of the hill. Both foundations and wood have gone since the last war, and there is a housing estate there now.

In 1773 he 'set out ye Malthouse — and at Mr. Bretts about ye oast'. That was in May. In July, malthouse and oast were built; oasts then were simply 'small houses', the traditional oast house had not yet been developed. Later entries refer to burying children from 'the old Malthouse'. If these malthouses are the same ones that were on the corner of Back Lane, Minster, until well after the second war, underneath which the famous tunnel is supposed to open, he certainly does not mention it. It is more probable that he built a large cellar under them; only recently a local man remarked on the 'long cellar' that was there.

In 1800 he built the first 'Meeting House' in Minster, and attended the services there afterwards, enjoying the preacher's oratory. He kept a list of all those he had heard. From this meeting house Chapel Street derived its name. The present Bethel Chapel stands a few houses further along the road than the original building. Between the present chapel and some modern houses on the corner of the road was a row of wooden 'ship board' houses, and the old chapel was incorporated in one of these. They are now demolished, leaving a gap full of weeds and a well. The well may be the one that was dug 'in Mr. Hill's garden opposite ye Smith's forge' in 1786. It was thirty-four feet and nine inches deep, and cost £7 4s. 9¼d. to dig and stean, exclusive of bricks and curb, and 'I drinked of the first bucket raised'. A new well in the village was an event to be recorded — fresh water was in short supply. He owned a house in Stickfast Lane, and he owned a property in Minster Hill, just below the 'Prince of Waterloo', with the peculiar name of Sluts Hole, This cottage he sold to Mr. James Greathead in 1808. Mr. Greathead ran a store of some sort near the dockyard. Sluts Hole was used and lived in until the last war; it has since been pulled down. Between Sluts Hole and the public house was another chapel of Methodist persuasion, also gone now.

In 1778 he wrote that there were twenty soldiers quartered in Minster Street. (He does not explain how the sixteen houses managed to accommodate them.) 'Satterday twenty-fifth of July, and went away next morning to Sheerness. That was the first, except two at a house twentyfive years before, ever known in Sheppey.' That little invasion must have put the village in a whirl of excitement for a few weeks. In 1781, there were four hundred soldiers in Sheppey, camped in a hundred acres near Sheerness. As the Napoleonic wars did not commence until 1793, it is hard to explain these troop movements, but there was often insufficient room in the Garrison for incoming draughts, so that may have been the reason. On September 10th, 1790 the new churchyard was opened. This must refer to the small burial ground in Love Lane beside Sheppey General Hospital.

In 1791 he notes floods, but there are no details. Floods were a usual event, and accepted as part of living in Sheppey, like the falling cliffs and the smuggling. In October 1797 he wrote that 'the Galant Admirals Duncan and Onslow gained the noble victory over the Dutch Fleet near the Texel' — and goes on to describe the battle. He went up on the hill in the evening to see the illuminations at Sheerness and Queenborough, and early next morning watched four of Admiral Duncan's ships come in. He buried Charles Slade Moorman, a wounded man of Admiral Duncan's (his gravestone is in the churchyard), also Mary Ann Ross, a woman who was on board ship with Admiral Duncan. It is not likely that she was actually with the admiral; the sailors used to take their girlfriends along for the trip in those days.

A month later he attended the Thanksgiving Service for the admiral's victory which was held at the Minster Abbey. He was always busy, planting, harvesting, sorting out letters, leases and other things, appraising 'stuff' for auctioning, building, shooting, fishing and hunting. It was a full life. This was the time the separate wash house began to be fashionable, complete with sink, pump, and copper, and he mentions building several of these. In November 1798 he was at the Church Thanksgiving, and he gives the text and sermon, when Admiral Nelson destroyed the French fleet.

23.12.05. He was on the hill to see his majesty's ship *Victory* with Lord Nelson's body come to the Nore. The *Victory* put in at Sheerness before sailing on to London, and this small statement, above all others, seems to bring the past

and its people clearly into focus. He was a man who thought about things, and he makes one telling observation, with no comment. 'In 1754– In the Church Book there were sixteen Blue Houses. In 1792 There were one hundred and thirty Blue Houses.' He was obviously speculating on the rapid growth of Sheerness.

There are many references to the Court Tree, choosing a Ferry Warden, casting the Ferry cess, and attending the Ferry Wardens Feast, for which he sometimes made punch. His scattered notes give the impression of a happy community, self-sufficient, independent and decidedly insular, with most of the inhabitants working on the local farms, or in trades allied to agriculture. He seldom mentions the women, unless he is burying them — even his own wife receives scant attention. The women appeared to produce a baby almost every year, and many of these died in infancy. Frequently the wives died young, too, and then the farmer would re-marry and the babies start again. It seems terrible to people today, but then it was the accepted way of life, and they expected to 'lose a few'. The last available Law Day record was made in the clerk's time, in 1795, in the reign of George III. The set-out is as it has always been, and the boroughs are listed, and there is still no indication of their boundaries. The names of the jury are familiar, both from the Vestry Books and the Churchwarden's Accounts. Among them are John Brett, John Gold, Samuel Crayden, John Head, John Featherstone, Richard Ingleton, Richard Downe and John Davis. The usual nominations are recorded, and the regulations have altered very little since Charles II's day, although the language is simplified.

Fresh marsh and uplands at one penny per acre, salt marsh at one penny for ten acres, and Elizabeth I's act is quoted. When the Ferry toll is recited, and the coaches and waggons have been dealt with, there is a new 'cess'. 'Also threepence for every dog each time of passing (except hounds) which shall pay at the rate of half a crown a pack each time of passing.' From that, it seems that hounds were regular visitors to the island. The usual rules are repeated, no building materials are allowed unless for ferry use, and two new items, 'nor let waggons be loaded in the Ferry way (except for corn and grain for seed etc.) and H.M. carriages. Penalty one pound. The Keeper must keep glass in the windows of the Ferrry House (pain of ten shillings if not).' The number of people on the jury is restricted to fifteen at the outside. Then, a very practical ruling that has not appeared before: 'If the Ferry Keeper dies, summon a meeting and elect another.' When the accounts were cast, Mr. John Brown, the last ferry warden, was in purse £105 3s. 5d. Robert Busbridge was the elected warden for the coming year.

There is an account for the year 1753–4, when John Franks was ferrry warden, and it is not different from those of former centuries. They bought loads of gravel for above and below the house, paid salaries, and bought pitch and tar and things for the boats. There is also a list of ferry wardens up to 1762. After that there are no records available, although the Law Day under the Court Tree continued until 1857, when it ceased and was forgotten as though it had never been apart from one dying kick, which will come later.

CHAPTER XX
Century of change

At the start of the nineteenth century the Napoleonic wars were claiming the nation's attention. A warning note had been sounded in 1795 when bread became very dear, and the poor could not afford it. The infamous Speenhamland system was one of the remedies tried, in which the parish and the employers made up the wages of the out-of-work men and part-timers. This did not affect the landowners, but it hit the farmers, and in many cases they ended up as poor as their workers, which helped no-one. This system was not widely used in Kent, but at the end of the eighteenth century the number of poor in Minster needing assistance had risen, and the parish was beginning to feel the strain.

There was a certain amount of alarm, as villages and towns on the Kent and Essex coasts feared invasion. There were various schemes for 'calling up' men for service, and a certain number from each parish, termed 'Quota' men, were chosen by local ballot. Minster had to provide nine men, and there were thirty-seven men in the age group liable for service. Most of them paid the overseers a guinea for exemption, and the overseers then had to find substitutes, which proved costly. William Swift of Borstal Hall was one of the churchwardens, and the hard man Leonard Lester the other. Together with the overseers, they levied a rate of six pence in the pound to meet this unlooked-for expense, citing an Act of Parliament as permission, and this rate was levied until the war ended in 1815. A similar scheme was followed at Queenborough, but there the additional rate aggravated their miseries and poverty. William Swift had inherited Borstal Hall from the Randalls, and in the late eighteenth century he rebuilt it completely, making it an extremely attractive small Georgian manor, surrounded by trees.

The rural areas of Sheppey were not too badly affected at this time. Smuggling had increased, and kept the excisemen busy, but the farming way of life continued as it had done for centuries past. They were still using the Kentish turn wrest plough, and threshing corn by hand. Mowing hay and reaping corn was still done with a scythe, but they were not afraid to try growing new crops, and there was a ready sale for fresh vegetables in Sheerness now, and for milk, cheese, butter and eggs.

In September 1803 the Sheppey Volunteers were formed, as were many other volunteer corps in other parts of England. They only lasted for a few years, and there is very little recorded about them. By 1806 their strength was two hundred and ten all ranks, and their uniform was a scarlet coat with french grey collar and cuffs, and breeches. In 1805 the Mayor commanding was Bryan Bentham, but whether he was from the local Bentham family of farmers is impossible to say. There was also an Isle of Sheppey Cavalry, and no more is known about this than about the Infantry. It sounds rather like a cross between the hobeliers and beacon watchers of former days, and the Home Guard of the following century. While the war lasted the farmers received good prices for their crops, and although food was dearer, the farm workers derived some benefit from the relatively stable conditions, and they were nearly all in a position to grow some food for themselves.

The first population census in England was made in 1801. The returns for the island are interesting, and illustrate the distribution of the local population. Eastchurch had an acreage of 7,015 acres and three hundred and ninety two residents. Elmley had 1,984 acres, and eleven people living there. Leysdown, with 2,194 acres, managed eighty-eight

inhabitants. Minster (including Sheerness) and Sheerness Ville was 7,925 acres. Minster and Sheerness had 4,139 inhabitants, and Sheerness Ville 1,422. This description of Minster and Sheerness is confusing, until it is realised that Minster included all the land and farms as far as the dockyard and Queenborough. Sheerness Ville was the dockyard itself. The population there gradually dwindled, eight hundred and seventeen in 1821, sixty-one in 1831, and then there is a memo. to the effect that all the remaining houses were demolished between 1831 and 1841, and it then became part of the dockyard. When this happened, the population of Minster and Sheerness rose accordingly. Queenborough with 302 acres mustered five hundred and forty-five residents, and this did not alter much for many years. Warden was the uttermost part of the island, a point there is named Lands End, and with 207 acres had seven residents. At that time Minster was still the chief village and centre of the island, but Sheerness was growing like the proverbial beanstalk, and before the century was out was making itself felt, often to Minster's discomfort.

In 1801 Admiral Vincent, the First Lord of the Admiralty, investigated the administration in Sheerness. The amount of thieving there was enormous, and there was a flourishing smuggling racket going on as well. Barracks had by now been built for the dockyard men, but they preferred their hulks, where, it was said 'there was no species of infumy un-practised, and they were unobserved'. In 1802, by orders of Admiral St. Vincent, and the dockyard commissioner, Sir Isaac Coffin, they were ejected from the hulks, and moved to the barracks. The following day was tense. The men rioted, and that night they attempted to kill Sir Isaac Coffin by way of revenge.

Things were restored to order, and the hulks were quickly filled with convicts. One ship, the *Bellerpheron*, was used solely for boys aged eight years and upwards. These poor lads were often nothing more than half-starved street urchins, whose only crime was petty thieving, often food. The convicts were entirely at the mercy of their keepers and had a very hard time, they were kept short of food and clean linen, and whipped at the smallest excuse. Infection was rife, cholera, malaria, smallpox, and other diseases that spring from dirt, undernourishment, and over-crowding. To prevent the spread of infection to the dockyard and town the dead were buried on Burntwick and Deadman's Island, especially the latter. Prisoners of war were confined in the hulks, too, and these floating prisons were so notorious that it is claimed Napoleon himself had heard about them. The census for Minster in 1811 states that the numbers given included five hundred and twenty convicts in hulks.

During the war, between 1792 and 1810 the yards were stretched to the limit, and could not keep up with the work required of them. In 1808 Sheerness had two dry docks and two slips. The 'Blue Houses' made of 'chips' and painted with grey-blue dockyard paint, were clustered around the yard, the number grew so rapidly that after 1800 they were known as Blue Town. The town grew outside the yard, too, although it was said, and with some truth, that every other building was a pub, and every third one a brothel. It was rough, tough and completely unmannerly. Fights were common, sailors were frequently found unconscious from drink or fighting, and with empty pockets, the morning after they had come ashore. The unluckiest ones were dragged out of the fleets and ditches that comprised the only drainage system, drowned and filthy. There was so much trouble that the courts were always full of unsavoury cases, and magistrates complained that nowhere was so bad as Sheerness.

A Commissioners report in 1808 reported that the yard's foundations were giving way, and a high tide and a heavy gale arriving together would destroy the yard. It had been built of timber, and 'thrown together as wanted'. By 1813 it needed rebuilding, it was in such a poor state it was almost useless. At this point John Rennie was called upon to design a new yard, which was commenced in 1815. It covered approximately sixty-four acres, and had dry docks, machine shops and a storehouse. This storehouse was noted for its size and construction, and recently the conservationists have been fighting hard to save it from demolition.

The yard was officially reopened in 1823, and finished a few years later. The ground was unstable, and a great deal of knowledge and skill was used in this rebuilding, which was estimated to cost three million pounds. The dock gates were of cast iron, and part of the yard was paved with iron blocks that had once been used as ballast for the men o' war. Admiralty House was built in 1827, and the people of Sheerness hoped that the Duke of Clarence would become resident there. They had a great affection and regard for this particular duke, and naturally there was an ale house in Blue Town named in his honour, the 'Duke of Clarence'. It later became a private house, and there is a lady on the island today who was born there. She is a nursing sister at Sheppey General Hospital. Other houses were built for dockyard officials — Naval Terrace is an example of the housing provided. During the Napoleonic War a twenty-eight-gun ship was brought ashore as a residence for the Port Admiral, as there was no suitable accommodation then.

The convicts were used as workmen during this rebuilding, and it cannot have been easy for them, for they had to work with a heavy chain with an iron ball on the end of it attached to one leg. They must have been a motley crowd of workmen, ragged, dirty and manacled. In fact, they were often frightened, for they knew that if they fell into the sea, or the boat taking them from hulk to dock capsized, they had no chance of rescue, the weight of their chains would sink them immediately. They were also scared that the hulks would fall to pieces in stormy weather, as they were very old and rotten.

Minster Abbey was the parish church for the whole of this area, and the burials from Sheerness far out-numbered those from Minster at this period, in some months only one or two out of the twenty or more recorded would be from the village. All the entries are rather depressing.

In 1811, May. Joseph and Rebecca Adams, twins, both in one coffin, aged nine weeks.
Mary Baker from the Parish House. (Her husband once ran the Thatched House).
Elizabeth Griffiths from Sheerness, a pauper, 17 years.
James Keeler from Sheerness who was drowned. 17 years 10 months.
James Lamb and Anne Lamb both in one grave and paupers from Sheerness.

In June nearly all the entries were from Sheerness, paupers, sailors, and 'drownded', and July was little different. August, John Carter, a soldier and a lieutenant, aged 46 years. That was followed by more children under a year old than usual, probably the hot August weather had some bearing on that, and of course, there were the usual paupers. In September, 'A drowned man, name unknown'. More paupers from Sheerness, and sailors who 'drownded', and a child from Wallend Farm, aged 6 years, (the only Minster Burial) and James Troop, who was killed on the Selecting Battery, Sheerness, by 'a gun going off unexpect', aged 42 years. In October, thankfully, there were less children dying. George Mallinger from Sheerness, a respect-

able shoemaker, aged 49. A soldier called Joshua, whose surname is illegible of Colonel Blake's Company West Yorkshire Militia, 28 years. A more interesting entry is 'Sarah Rayner, from the Old Ship House, in the Street, Minster, aged 57 years'. The 'Old Ship' in Minster Street had caused some bother in the 1780's. The landlord had left it hurriedly, and after he had gone large quantities of gin were found hidden there. There was a great to-do about it, then the 'Ship' caught fire, and was partially demolished. It had obviously been patched up by 1811, but later houses were built on the site. This list continues with little variation, paupers, children, and drownings from Sheerness.

When Sarah Adams was buried in January 1812, they thought fit to add 'A native of Minster, aged three years'. Amelia Bastard from Sheerness, being smothered, aged 6 years. This time whoever kept the register was not being outspoken, Amelia's surname was Bastard, and the name still lives in Sheerness today. In June, 'Anne Shockley who being a lunatic poisoned herself (pauper)'.

It is a sad list of servicemen, drownings, and paupers. One wonders where they had all come from, the town had grown like a mushroom overnight, and all the flotsam and jetsam from everywhere appeared to be gravitating there. Improbable as it seems on reading the large number of deaths of babies and young children, the population of England almost doubled in the nineteenth century, but it is difficult to understand how.

The town of Sheerness was growing away from the immediate vicinity of Blue Town by now. Blue Town was separated from Sheerness by a moat, and a drawbridge. The drawbridge was removed long ago, but the moat is still there, and is known locally as 'Pneumonia Bridge'.

In Blue Town itself the 'Fountain', almost opposite the dockyard gates, was one of the first hostelries. Nelson had stayed there, for he had come to the yard to inspect ships during his lifetime; his last entry 'in pickle' on the *Victory* certainly was not his first visit.

There had been a theatre there too, demolished when the yard was extended, as were some small shops and other appendages. The manager of the Sheerness Playhouse, which opened in 1803, was Sam Jerrold, who was well known on the 'Circuit' in Kent, and he ran the theatre until the end of 1815. His son was Douglas Jerrold, later to become a famous playwright and the first editor of *Punch*, and possibly best remembered by the populace for his song 'Black Eyed Susan'. Edmund Kean, the famous actor, became a member of the company in 1804, under the name of Carey, for fifteen shillings a week, and he remained there for some time. He returned in 1807, now as Kean, at one guinea a week, and became very popular with the theatregoers, most of whom came from the garrison, and the dockyard. He had been in Sheerness Theatre for about a year when he had a difference of opinion with a local townsman, and in consequence of this he was threatened with the press gang, who had apparently been bribed to take him. He asked protection from a magistrate, Mr. Shrove of Queenborough, who could only guarantee him four days' grace, so when he had played the four nights on stage Kean departed on the Chatham boat, escaping by night, and not without difficulty.

The road, if it could be called such, between the dockyard and the Mile houses, was soon built up on each side, becoming High Street, Mile Town. Some of the first houses to be built there were constructed with their backs to the road, which led to caustic remarks later about 'the view from the High Street being of the wash houses, and privies of Mile Town'. Behind these houses, on the landward side of the street, other houses quickly followed all built of wood — shipboard houses. The local story was that they were all built out of old ships timbers. Some of the houses were large, comfortable and spacious, but for the most part they were small and pokey, and some were arranged in courts, entered under an archway which had a house, or part of one, over it. None had any water or sanitation, and they were all interspersed by alleys, to allow entry via the backyards.

When the dockyard was being rebuilt, Sir Edward Banks came to Sheerness — apparently he had some part in the reconstruction work. He was best known as the builder who demolished old London Bridge, and built a new bridge which was opened in 1832. He must have liked the island, for he bought property, moved in, and brought his wife and two sons, Delamark and John, to live there.

He built Sheppey Court, now converted into an old people's home, and he made it a large and imposing mansion. It is not generally known, or it has been forgotten, that a farm stood there prior to Sheppey Court, called the Red House. The Red House had been the farm belonging to one of the Chalk family, who had prospered as butchers, farmers, and business men. In a very old copy of the *Sheerness Guardian*, 1862 or thereabouts, there is a story that Mr. Chalk, emboldened by business success and the rapid growth of Sheerness, started a private banking company. This was his undoing, in a very short time he was bankrupt, and his pound notes were selling at sixpence a piece. His son had 'taken Holy Orders', and was so determined that none of the creditors should lose their money that he worked unceasingly until all were paid in full. Sir Edward Banks acquired the Red House and a vast amount of land as a result of the sale of property.

Edward Street, now the Broadway, was built in 'Mr. Chalk's hundred acre field', and the well where the locals gathered to gossip and 'watch the buckets going up and down' gave way to houses. Boots the chemists stood on the site until recently, now it is a charity shop. Boots now occupies the site of the old 'Belle and Lion', the first public house to be built in Mile Town, although it was rapidly followed by others. In 1821 (other dates in the early 1820's are given for this) there was a fire in the dockyard, and the blue houses literally went up in smoke. After this any that remained were demolished, and the big dockyard wall was built, using convict labour. Shops, and a small market, were no longer tolerated in the yard, and Blue Town, with its pubs and alleys of small houses, grew accordingly.

So did Sheerness. Sir Edward Banks weighed in with Banks Town somewhere about 1820, a rather superior terrace, and other houses at the Minster end of Mile Town. He built the Royal Hotel, and had pleasure gardens laid out round it. Almost opposite he built Holy Trinity Church in 1836, but it was only a 'Chapel of Ease', and came under Minster Abbey. It had no licence for marriages, baptisms or burials.

This was soon followed by the development of Marine Town, terraces of large, rather superior houses. One terrace, built in a pinky red brick, has always been known as Shrimp Terrace, from its colour. Behind the terraces the streets of smaller houses grew rapidly. There was a Sheerness Development Company, and the speculators were at work. There was still no water or sanitation, but the houses were brick built and solid, and stand today, making pleasant homes still. Again, all the houses were interspaced with alleys, none were back to back. It is possible to travel the length of Sheerness via the alleys, if one knows the town, and never trouble with walking the roads.

Sir Edward's son, Delamark Banks, whose name is remembered in Delamark Road (where there was once a Delamark Primary School, always known as the jelly babies) had a race-course laid out on the marshes opposite Sheppey Court, and the Sheppey races became a yearly event. It was a great novelty at first, and well attended, a day out for the officers and their ladies, but it did not live up to its first promise and the last races there were in 1857. Details of them

were given in a copy of the *Sittingbourne and Sheerness Gazette*, July 25th. The paper stated that the races were better than usual that year.

The Stewards were: Captain Wolfe, R. A. William Coveney, esq. (A minster farmer), W. Shrimpton, esq. (A farmer from Warden). The judge was Mr. W. Hobbs, and the hon. secretary was Fred Leese esq. (the farmer who rented Neats Court). The first race was the Sheppey Court Stakes, and the five horses entered all belonged to local people, among them a Mr. Ward, who appeared to keep a sizeable stable. There were five races in all, not more than four or five local horses ran in any of them, and in the last race there was an objection and the mare 'Vestige' was disqualified. A detailed account of each race was given, but in spite of the interest the race-course seemed to fall from favour. The local horses then engaged in private wagers and trotting matches.

When the steamboats started a regular passenger service, 'a person' stood by the gate to the pier and collected a penny from everyone coming or going by boat, as toll. There was also a turnpike gate at the top of Mile Town, kept by an old lady called Mrs. Dodd, who collected the tickets. The Russian fleet was anchored off Sheerness in an effort to evade Napoleon, and the admiral's children attended a private school in Sheerness run by a Mr. Herbert, where the children of the professional classes and the well-to-do were taught. Sheerness is full of stories such as these, fascinating sidelights on a vigorous new town.

A telegraph system had been started by the Admiralty in 1795, from a plan devised by Lord George Murray. There were stations from London to Deal, with a branch line to Sheerness. Telegraph or no, there was a story current on the island at the time that a large pile of dry faggots was kept on Telegraph Hill, ready to be lighted should a French invasion threaten. The islanders had more faith in beacons than newfangled telegraphs.

When the war ended, food became scarce, and dear, and the year following Waterloo was one of great distress for the lower paid. Yard workers' wages averaged from ten to twelve shillings weekly, rents were high in proportion to earnings, and illness was frequent, partly due to the insanitary living conditions, and the lack of fresh water. The dockyard men lived in the small wooden houses in Blue Town for the most part, and the equally insanitary little wooden huts round the back of Mile Town. A group of dockyard men banded together to see if they could find some way to keep their families decently fed. There was a certain risk in these meetings, as there were laws against more than two or three people collecting together, and they could have been accused of illegal assembly, and arrested. They decided to form a society, that would buy in bulk, and then share the purchases at cost price. They engaged a solicitor to make the society legal, and had rules drawn up. 'The Society established this twenty first day of November in the year 1816, by the officers and men of his Majesty's Dockyard, Ordnance, and New Works at Sheerness, in the Isle of Sheppey, County of Kent, for obtaining for themselves and families a supply of wheaten bread, and flour and butcher's meat, shall henceforth be denominated the Economical Society.'

There it was, the first 'Co-op' started by a handful of dockyard mateys as a protest against the high prices of the local bakers. The first shop-keepers in Sheerness, were in a way, pioneers, and they could get away with charging high prices because there was no alternative shopping centre. The society contracted with local butchers for meat, and all the members shared in the work and the business dealings. Owing to transport problems, flour had to be ground locally, and the three Sheerness mills were always busy. Any member who tried sharp practice, or would not pull his weight, was quickly ejected from the society. Once the flour and meat trade was running smoothly, they added water to their list of priorities. The Sheerness people had to fetch their water from a pump at the beginning of Blue Town, near Dockyard Terrace, where a well had been dug. The Co-op men chose a site on the corner of Railway Road and Broad Street, where there was a small well, improved this well, and supplied themselves with water. The cost was a halfpenny a pail or a penny a load, which was two buckets carried on a yoke. Some members became water merchants, they filled barrels for a shilling and then resold the water, making a small profit. The water had to be hand-pumped into a cistern every night, and usually one of the poorer members, a labourer with a large family, earned a little extra doing this.

A bakehouse had been added to the flour trade, and the constant traffic of water carriers round the bakehouse and well turned the road there into a bog, so large stones were laid down. The Co-op offered to form a water company, but by 1857 the Sheerness Water Company had been established, and the society was too late. When at long last piped water arrived in 1864, the Co-op water works closed. By 1838 new rules were necessary, volunteer labour was insufficient, and paid workers were employed. The rules were very strict, and everything was sold as cheaply as possible for the members' benefit, just allowing enough profit to cover expenses. The bakehouse was enlarged and deliveries of bread were started, up to then it had been collected, usually by sending the children to fetch it.

The delivery carts were unimaginable! They were large hand barrows, with dogs as draught animals. The dogs were harnessed under the body of the barrows, between the high wheels, their stout leather collars attached to iron brackets under the floor of the barrow. A team of dogs was kept for this job, the leading animals being Lion and Joe. Each dog had its own barrow. The roads were rough, pushing the barrows was hard work, even with a dog to help, and sometimes the dogs lost their tempers and had fights with other dogs they met. It seems incredible now to think of bread being toted round Sheerness in a barrow pushed and pulled by man and dog, with no cover for the loaves but a flour sack, but that was how they did it.

Tin tokens were issued to customers with their name on, different shapes for different weights of loaf, and these were issued for cash on a Friday, bread was paid for in advance. This cut down book-keeping, and there was no chance of money going missing on the round, or bad debts. In 1849 a second Co-operative was formed, which restricted the original society's expansion, but it continued to flourish, and the members received useful dividends in bread and flour.

A steam flour mill was opened in 1875, and the original rules, current coins, newspapers and balance sheets were buried under the stone of the mill. This building is now used by the Sheerness Times-Guardian newspaper. The society branched out, with premises at Minster and Queenborough, a confectionery shop in Sheerness and even a reading room and library, and a dairy farm and small-holding. Their hundred years celebration could not take place until 1919, owing to the first world war. Then they made up for lost time; they had a procession, a feast, speeches, and made a great day of it. Souvenir trays were given, and there are still a few about these days.

Eventually they amalgamated with the Sheerness Co-operative Society, but they had done great things from a very small beginning, and whatever other claims are made they must surely have been the first organised Co-operative Society legally registered.

While Sheerness grew vigorously, if a trifle ungraciously, Queenborough's fortunes were at a very low ebb. The town was described by a contemporary writer as having grass growing in the streets, and houses with broken windows stuffed with rags and sacks. The cause of this was the failure of the oyster grounds, but the cause of the failure was more

complicated. The corporation had somehow mismanaged the oyster grounds, they were badly in debt, and they were at loggerheads with the freemen of the town. There had been some chicanery, that was certain, and the person most blamed was the mayor, Thomas Young Greets, who had contrived to keep himself and his friends in office. There was a law suit brought by the freemen, and there were stories of a lively meeting between mayor, corporation and freemen which ended in a riot. The burgesses refused to let the jurats leave the hall, the constables were called but declined to help, and the burgesses kept the doors closed and told the corporation they would have to go out through the windows, which eventually they were compelled to do.

Thomas Young Greets was certainly unpopular, and the testimony of the two luckless men he flung into Queenborough gaol in 1822 is damning. The gaol consisted of two small dark rooms, with a narrow passage of about three feet in front, which was secured by an iron fence with a gap of about one and a half feet at the top, and this small opening provided all the light and fresh air available, which was not much. Also unavailable was any form of sanitation in the two cells, and as the prisoners were not released at all the atmosphere and odour is best left to the imagination. The men were imprisoned from April 15th to June 4th, when they were released on bail by a judge. During their term of imprisonment they were not allowed any visits from friends or relatives, or any food beyond the prison diet of bread and water. Small wonder the prisoner complained that his health suffered!

Despite the poverty in the town, in 1817 the corporation added to Queenborough's regalia, and a silver oar with a long silver chain was bought, and inscribed '1817 Thomas Young Greet. James Bowton, Water Bailiff.' Mr. Greet was also chamberlain, and controlled the fisheries' finances. Fifteen years later this, and the silver mace, disappeared mysteriously, and vanished completely. Following the second world war, they turned up at a sale at Sotheby's and Queenborough was able to raise the money to buy them back and return them to the borough. Mayor Thomas Young Greet died in 1829, and according to a story in a local paper published in 1863, when Greet died a halfpenny was thrown into his grave to pay his passage to hell, his effigy was burnt on a bonfire, and anyone who did not have their windows lighted in celebration of the event was liable to have the windows smashed by other townsmen. A macabre story, but Queenborough was suffering dire poverty at the time.

The arguments over the oyster fishing continued, and in 1830 the freemen rioted yet again. In the parish books of 1799 'no more schooling for Parish children was to be paid for'.

Richard Webb left an endowment of forty shillings as a bequest for a school in 1813, and a small room was provided in the Old Town Hall, but the scheme was not a success, and by 1855 three boys and a little dog were the only pupils. A Church School was started, and failed, and eventually all were combined in the National School.

A Gas Company had been formed in Sheerness in 1833, and many of the houses in the town had gas lights. The small settlement of Westminster had sprung up as a result of this, the houses clustering near the gas works. Queenborough wanted gas laid on, and was told by Sheerness that 'they would have to fight for it'.

In 1835 the Dockyard Church was built for the use of the Fleet and the Garrison, but only for services. When Sheerness decided to build a pier in 1829 Queenborough was annoyed, and organised a petition against it. Queenborough already had a pier, and doubtless saw themselves losing yet another advantage, as many things were unloaded there for Sheerness. Prior to the pier, Sheerness had been dependent on a shingle bank only suitable for a row-boat, and then the tide had to be right. This was followed by a paved causeway

Minster Abbey Tower.

Queenborough Church amidst its crowded graveyard.

A pleasant old weatherboarded cottage in Eastchurch close to the church.

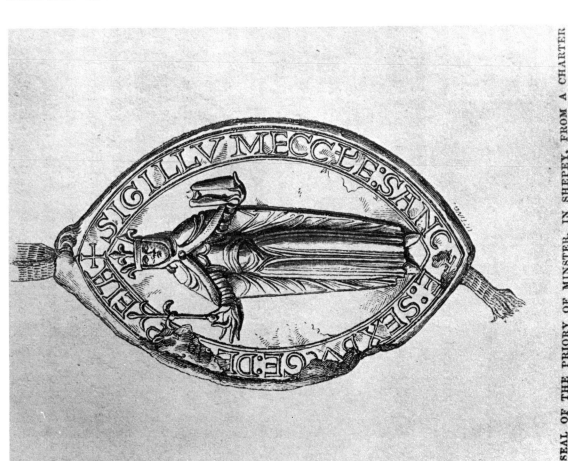

SEAL OF THE PRIORY OF MINSTER, IN SHEPEY, FROM A CHARTER
OF THE DEAN AND CHAPTER OF CANTERBURY.

The ancient seal of Minster Priory.

Right: Mocketts farm on Harty. A picturesque place.

Below: The Northwest prospect of Sheerness. A view from a famous series produced by the Buck brothers in 1739 to guide mariners around the coast of Britain.

THE NORTH-WEST PROSPECT OF SHEERNESS, IN THE COUNTY OF KENT.

on which goods could be landed, but it was awkward for passengers, and as steam boats became more widely used a pier was necessary. This was opened in 1835, it made travelling by boat relatively easy, and was the accepted way of going up river to London and Rochester for many years.

At Minster and Eastchurch things altered very little during the war with the French. A directory of 1803 shows the same names and occupations as ten or twenty years previously, but there are now Customs officers and Riding officers included.

Smuggling was prevalent. There is a stone in the little burial ground by the hospital that tells its own story.

O' Earth, cover not my blood!
Sacred to the memory of a man unknown, who was found Murdered on the morning of the 22nd April, 1814, near Scraps-gate in this Parish, by his head being nearly severed from his body.

A subscription was immediately entered into, and one hundred guineas reward offered on the conviction of the perpetrators of the horrible act, but they remain at present undiscovered! What an inscription on a stone! Naturally they never were discovered, but it is a sure bet that everyone locally knew who 'they' were.

The story, and of course there is one, is that some local lads were hauling in contraband on the beach at Scrapsgate when a stranger appeared. As the excisemen were too numerous to be healthy, they acted first and asked questions later. The stranger was unknown to them, a poor sea-faring man, and as a sop to their consciences they had a headstone erected, or at any rate subscribed to one. Who chose the wording is another undiscovered secret.

The Preventative officers were living in ships, an old hulk was stationed between Barton's Point and Scrapsgate, the officer married from there and his wife made her home on board. When the French scare was over, the coastguard houses were built. The 'Ship on Shore' was originally a coastguard station. At some time in the latter part of the nineteenth century a ship loaded with barrels of cement ran aground and broke up there. The cement had hardened, and when the barrel staves were removed the barrel shaped cement blocks were built into a shelter, called the Grotto, and decorated with stones and shells. It it still there, and patrons of the 'Ship on Shore' can sit out there in good weather with their drinks.

The coastguard houses encircled the island. They were placed on Scrapsgate Road, Wards Hill, East End (now Oak Lane) the small valley on the cliffs at Hensbrook, East-church, Leysdown, and at the further end of Shellness. One hundred years later they were all being put up for auction.

The 'Royal Oak', a hostelry at the very top of East End Lane, was a recognised smugglers' haunt. It was a mile from the cliff edge then, and started its life as a farm house, later becoming a victuallers, for anyone who liked to stroll out there. It was still used as a 'pub' in the 1950's, then one day there was a notice outside, chalked on a piece of board, which said simply 'Sorry, this ain't a pub no more.' Since then it has gone over the cliff. A smuggler allegedly lived at Chequers, in a small thatched house, where he could command the road to the 'Royal Oak', and also had easy access to Windmill Creek. It was a strategic vantage point.

Land in Minster was still changing hands, and the farmers were not quite so prosperous. In 1830 what is sometimes called the 'Last Labourers' Revolt' took place, and although there is no record of trouble in Sheppey, island men were known to have taken part in demonstrations on the mainland. Their reasoning was simple. Agriculture was in a depressed state, and with the advent of the threshing machine they could see that what little winter work there was would be lost to them. Threshing was still done as it had been done since the first farmer grew the first grain. The grain was beaten from the ear of the corn by hand, by men using a flail, usually in the barn. This was winter work, and when the threshing machine took over the same number of men were not needed. So they formed a gang, and destroyed the hated machines, and what started as an act of self-protective insurrection later developed political overtones. At first the magistrates were sympathetic, for the poor wages and rural distress were no secret, but when later outbreaks led to violence they were suppressed with greater severity. Despite their war cry of 'Bread or Blood' no-one was killed or injured in the riots, and the most severe sentence passed on the rioters was transportation. Later in the 1830's the depression eased a little, and also many people left the villages, hoping for a better life as industrial workers.

During this time the number of poor supported by the parish was increasing, and the farmers found the taxes were rising, making their chances of survival more difficult. In 1834 a new Poor Law Act ended the system of 'doles' paid from parish rates. The parishes were ordered to form unions, building a workhouse if they did not already have one, and to appoint a board of guardians, who were responsible to Government authority. Later these guardians were to have extra duties placed on them, for which many of them were not really able. The parishes on the island had formed a union several years before the Act, although there had been some objections from Queenborough, and the town refused to pay the poor rate on one occasion.

Sheerness had run its own small workhouse in the early days of the yard, and money was stopped from the men's wages to support it, but when the yard was rebuilt and enlarged the poor and destitute were sent to Minster. This was the beginning of the dreaded workhouse régime, about which so much has been written.

In 1835 Sheerness petitioned to have the convicts and the hulks removed, fear of infection being one of their reasons, and so hulks and men were transferred to Woolwich. A postscript to that petition was that some years later there was a rumour that the townspeople were thinking of petitioning to get them back, as they missed the trade! By that time it would have been too late anyway, as transportation had re-commenced, to Australia this time.

The Board of Guardians was duly elected for the new régime, and it was the usual local people who undertook the work. It was advised that 'The Clerk writes to the Church wardens and overseers of Minster and inform them that the Board of Guardians will occupy the old workhouse at Minster as tenants at £65 5s. 0d. per annum ...' There was much more work to be done, and the Poor Law Commis-sioners, who were nominally in charge, took an average of the residents in each parish in which Minster, which included Sheerness, was reckoned at forty-seven hundred people.

At the time the Church Registers still recorded that the greater part of the marriages, baptisms and burials came from 'on ship board' and Sheerness.

Some of the workhouse books that were kept by the Master are revealing.

7th October 1835 George Hodges aged 13, having left the Workhouse without permission is to be left in solitary confinement and to have bread and water only for a week and to be cleaned.

14th October. Robert Elliott married man of Minster having five children one of them lying dead appeals for the ground being allowed him to bury in having had a great deal of sickness in his family.

To be allowed the ground.

Thomas Smith a single man of seventy three years belonging to Eastchurch who left the House without permission applies to be re-admitted.

To be re-admitted and kept on bread and water for a week in solitary confinement and thoroughly cleaned.

That was the beginning of the new era. Men and women were segregated, married couples separated. Boys and girls were kept separately, they had their own schoolrooms, wards and quarters. People capable of working were found work to do, cleaning, mending, cooking, tending the union garden, and in some cases pushing barrow loads of stones for some unknown reason. It was a far cry from the old form of parish relief sorted out at the vestry meetings, but there was an infirmary for the sick, nurses and a doctor, and however bad the times the islanders knew they had somewhere to turn to.

In 1821 the Preventative men had been extra busy, and at the 'Ship Inn' at Faversham John Warren was brought to court for harbouring one quart of French Geneva. William Kemsley, one of the boat men of the prevention boat, boat number two on the Isle of Sheppey Station, said he went to the defendant's house in Minster and saw the defendant's daughter run into a room with two stone bottles in her hands. She attempted to shut him out, but he went in, turned her out, and found the bottles containing one quart of French Geneva. An empty half anchor (of gin) was concealed under the bed. The defendant said 'I know nothing about it'. He was fined £100 which was mitigated to £25.

Thomas Gooding was accused at the same court by John Claringbold, the Chief Officer, of having eleven pounds of tobacco, which was hidden under some rubbish between the stable and the dog kennel. The defendant's answer was the usual one, so was the conviction. Peter Halbert was accused by the Officer of Excise George English of having a silk shawl in his possession, which was found in a chair opposite his bedroom. The draper asked to examine and value it said he could not swear to it being foreign, but Peter was convicted just the same, for six guineas. In 1823 two farm labourers from Leysdown were brought to court by the farmer William Mantle for laying snares, both pleaded not guilty, but witnesses testified against them, and they were fined £5 a piece. The game at Leysdown, Harty, Elmley and Warden was being carefully preserved, because hunting and coursing were fashionable sports, but it was rough on the farm-workers who were at their wits end to keep their families fed.

In 1832 there was a cholera epidemic on the island — not the first or the last. Sheerness was the place most badly affected, but two harvest labourers at Eastchurch died from cholera. 'Knight Norfolk, harvest labourer, July 29th burial', and a note is added 'This person dying of the disease called Cholera Morbus, was buried in the Parish Meadow Eastchurch Street, a portion of which was fenced off for that purpose as directed by the Lords of the Privy Seal. There is a second entry for Charles Russel Yalding, harvest labourer. These were the only two burials recorded, but the fenced corner remained for many years afterwards.

Two years later in 1834 Sir Richard King, K.C.B., Commander-in-Chief at the Nore, died of cholera, but apparently the orders of the Lords of the Privy Seal did not apply to him, for he had a 'stately funeral' and was buried in a vault in the centre of the chancel at Eastchurch, with a commemorative monument on the church wall, which can

still be seen. It seems that sometimes cholera is more infectious for some than others.

In 1836 the Great Tithe Act was passed in Parliament. For a long time farmers had been complaining about the payment of tithes, and now they were to be commuted, and a final payment made that would settle matters for all time. Maps were made of the farm lands, and lists of landowners, tenants, farmers, cottages and fields compiled. Despite the break-up of large estates, or the acquiring of them, the actual layout of the island had scarcely altered since Norman times, apart from the growth of Sheerness. Fields and farms had the names they had always been known by, and the tithe maps of Sheppey of 1840 bear very little relation to the map of Sheppey today.

No one has heard of Great Wards Hill or Little Wards Hill, Summerfield, Pigeon Loft field, Pheasants Close or Witches Field. They all disappeared at the beginning of this century. Many of the marshes had names, too. Joans Marsh was still there as it had been in Elizabethan times, Horseprickle Marsh, Scotchmans Marsh, Ox Marsh and many others, but most of them are forgotten.

Of the farms that remain on the island, some do retain their field names. Round Hill is still there, out on the cliffs, but Merriman's Hill has been 'terraced' in an attempt to halt cliff erosion, and is almost gone. None of the Abbey Farm fields are left, or their springs and shrubberies. At Ripney Hill some of the names remain, but Little Ripney Hill, Great Ripney Hill, and One Tree Hill are unknown now.

Rice's Meadow remains, a reminder of the Rice family who once farmed Danley Farm, and for some reason issued their own tokens in 1750, called 'local money'. Upper and Lower Bonstans, Hollands and Shoulder O'Mutton piece, once belonging to Parsonage Farm, are gone. Rape Hill, Thistle Hill and Rag Field are still at Scocles which has been remarked on as being the best kept farm on the island, and there the land is well used. Kingsborough Farm still has Poor Dick's Field, but on another 'lost' farm Cross the Road Field, Ruffit, Foulkes Meadow, The Grove, and Jointers Hill are all gone for ever, as are Mount Pleasant, Pheasant's Close, Upper and Lower Merry, and Drummers Land. Wyborne's Farm had Jill's Slip, Springfield, Breackneck and Breackneck Hill. Breackneck and Breackneck Hill was the hill and land now called The Glen, now a public open space with the stream that ran along the bottom filled in, the children with ponies confined to one small space, and houses all round. Much of Breackneck was arable, and looking at the big round hill and the high bank at the top of the Glen opposite Wards Hill, it seems impossible that men and horses could ever have ploughed it, but Bunny Hill and Bunny Banks were man made in 1876.

The field names were the history of the countryside and the islanders, telling a story of themselves, and they vanished almost overnight, leaving a muddle of road names that can never replace them. However, they were all there in 1840, and no-one thought they would ever alter. The farming would continue, even though numerous new Acts of Parliament arrived to change the long-standing methods of rural administration.

CHAPTER XXI

The pace quickens

One thing that the Tithe Records made very plain was the fact that the greatest part of the agricultural land on the island was owned by absentee landlords: business men, usually from London, members of the nobility and gentry, and other moneyed families. It is doubtful if many of them ever visited their land; it was leased out, and they merely collected the rents.

An exception to this was Delamark Banks, son of Sir Edward. He and his brother John had settled in Sheppey, and both married local girls. Very little is heard about John, his vault and a stone monument on the north wall of Minster Abbey are all that is left to remember him by. Delamark had either bought or inherited, and the evidence is not very clear, Warden Court, the greater part of Warden, and land in Eastchurch and Leysdown. He had inherited his fathers aptitude for building, and set about reshaping Warden Court to his own design, which is one of the reasons why it is so difficult to assess it today. He also rebuilt Warden Church in 1836, which was in a very sorry state, services were not held there, and no repairs had been attempted since the latter part of the eighteenth century. He built a church tower from the stones of old London Bridge, with a turret as a nice finish, put a new stone floor, a ceiling, and sound pews in the body of the church, and made it a useful and attractive little building. He placed two stones from London Bridge in gardens at Warden, one at Warden Court itself, and one in the grounds of the house he had built for his bailey, Mr. Hughes. This stone was inscribed Old London Bridge 1176 to 1832, and it would be interesting to know of its whereabouts now.

Delamark Banks was also a sportsman, he was responsible for the making of Sheppey race-course, and he was keen on preserving game, as unfortunate locals found to their cost. The rabbits were not for them.

There were large numbers of both hares and rabbits, hawking had long since given way to shooting and coursing, and Delamark enjoyed organising hunting parties. At one such outing it is recorded that 'upwards of one hundred hares were killed by coursing, and two hundred rabbits shot'. It is to be hoped that a few found their way to the tables of the needy farm workers. At the height of his career Delamark was a magistrate, and also held other official positions in the county. He had married the daughter of Mr. Shrimpton, of Carts Farm, and his wife died before him. After this little is heard about him, and a note by an Eastchurch historian of the nineteenth century may explain this. He records that after his wife's death, Delamark 'contracted an invalid alliance with her sister, who, after Mr. Bank's death, married Fred Leese of Neats Court Farm'.

Today he would have been able to marry his dead wife's sister, and all would have been well, but such a match was unlawful in the early nineteenth century, and the society of the time would have ostracised him. Presumably his second 'wife' became respectable again when she married Fred.

His church did not stand as a monument to him, for it was taken down in 1876 to prevent it falling over the cliff. Delamark Banks' tombstone was removed to Eastchurch burial ground, where it may still be seen, and he also has a commemorative stone on the north wall of the parish church in Minster Abbey, which his wife and daughter share. He died in the late 1830's. In 1883 there was a great slip of land at Warden, and the churchyard went to sea. It was estimated in 1881 that there was one hundred and fifty acres of land at Warden Point, where previously there had been five hundred acres.

In 1840 beyond the church and churchyard there was a farm, a coastguard station, and a garden land, and a fifteen-acre field. A roadway to Leysdown ran around the outside of this field, and beyond that was the 'Smack Inn', formerly used by smugglers. The 'Smack Inn' changed hands in 1864 and for a time had a new owner, and a fair was held there yearly, in May or June, called Smack Fair, but it cannot have lasted for many years after this. Warden Point is heavily pounded by wind and tides, and continues to lose acres of ground yearly. Warden Court was further affected by fire in 1878. A Mr. Paine was the occupant at the time, and little is known about his popularity or otherwise, but the fire was so serious that incendiarism was queried.

Coursing was a favourite sport on the island, and Elmley was a noted place for it. The church there was derelict, but having walls and a roof was used as a storehouse, and cattle shelter. It belonged to a Canterbury family who owned most of the land at Elmley, and no services were held there until a descendant of this family, who was a clergyman, complained bitterly about it, and the archbishop was compelled to order a service there, weekly. At the same time, coursing meetings were being held at Elmley, and when hares hid in the foundations of the old church they were left there and considered to be 'in sanctuary', which was pretty sporting of the coursing party when one considers it. Sometimes during the century a parson, and there is no indication as to which parson, approached the coursing fraternity and asked for a donation to the repair fund for the church. The owner, or huntsman, was quite prepared to subscribe, provided that the hares would still be allowed under the church. The parson would not agree to this, and both hunters and hares were very put out, so the story goes. Elmley had a sudden in-rush of residents from 1860 onwards, and then the coursing finished.

Sport was not the privilege of the wealthy alone, all country people enjoyed a hunt, and this was demonstrated clearly in Minster in 1862. There was a meet of hounds in the village, and the villagers must have enjoyed it, because the bellringers, backed up by the church wardens, and the parish clerk, broke open the belfry and rung the bells, although the vicar had forbidden them to do this. The vicar at this date was the Reverend Willis, the clerk was Mr. Edward Jarrett, and the church wardens were probably Mr. Palmer and Mr. Ward. The vicar was furious at this disobedience and took the unlucky bellringers to court, where the judge gave them a severe reprimand, and fined them. The ringers were unable to pay the fines, and had to stay in prison for five weeks, until 'other persons' had paid them. It seems a hard punishment for what was little more than 'a bit of silliness'. Mr. Jarrett, the clerk, died in 1884, aged eighty-six. He was still the parish clerk when he died, and the vicar, the Reverend Bramston, wrote a short paragraph in the parish magazine claiming Mr. Jarrett was the oldest clerk in the United Kingdom having been appointed in 1827, assisted three vicars, and served as clerk for fifty-seven years. It sounds like a record!

There are no parish records available before 1841, and then it is obvious that the old camaraderie of the vestry meeting has gone. Very few people attended, many names were new, and little was done in comparison with the eighteenth century.

As the workhouse was now run by the Board of

Guardians, the vestry meeting did not have to consider the welfare of the poor. Mr. Thomas Burford from the Abbey Farm was present. Mr. Howe, whose first names were oddly Baldwin Duppa, who lived at the Ferry House and was the Ferry Keeper, J. Crampton, the village schoolmaster, Edward Jarrett, Parish Clerk and Shoemaker, Ralph Adams, and Frank Venable. Strangely Joseph Fairhall was present, he originated from Queenborough and there were many tales about him. He had the reputation of being something of a rogue, he ran the 'Ship Inn' at Queenborough for a time, (which was an old building in the High Street then, not where it is now) and he was not above keeping his supplies up with help from the smugglers. He was in charge of Queenborough gaol for a while, but prisoners escaped so frequently that people became suspicious, feeling that anyone could go free if the price was right.

Joseph rented Dog Kennel Meadow, 'Part of Lower Wards Farm', and ran the 'Prince of Waterloo' on Minster Hill. At different times he set up as a saddler, a builder, and was known to be a horse dealer. A man of many parts, now keeping an eye on the administration of Minster and Sheerness. Having elected Mr. Howe as chairman of the meeting, it was ordered that 'in consequence of the dampness of the Church this meeting do adjourn to the Waterloo Inn'. Safely in the warmth of the inn, they dealt swiftly with rates, and church wardens accounts.

In 1842, when the church wardens were elected, the vicar chose Mr. Baldwin Richard Duppa Howe, and the vestry chose Francis Venable.

It was noticeable that the Overseers of the Poor, whose job was to collect poor rate, were now allocated divisions: the Upper Division, Minster, and the Lower Division, which was split again into Blue Town and Mile Town divisions. The people acting for the Lower Division came from that area, apart from John Ingleton, who has a Minster name. They adjourned to the Waterloo to sort out their accounts, which included £100 for the commissioners of Sheerness Pavements. Sheerness was becoming an expensive child for Minster to rear. In April there was a special meeting about the roads, which were nearly impassable at certain seasons in the year. The roads in question were the Faustall (or Funstall, the writing is difficult to decipher) Stickfast Lane, evidently living up to its reputation, Crips Lane, a road through a marsh called Oxen Pasture, and the road over Bartons Hill. Of all these roads only Stickfast and Bartons Hill are still identifiable, and Stickfast had had its name changed. A road leading though Wattens (Wootens) to the Lower Road was to be done away with, as it had been ploughed up for the last nine years!

There was a meeting in September, but so few attended that it was cancelled. It was recalled in October, and twenty names were put forward for constables, seven of them from Mile Town and seven from Blue Town.

The question of repairs for Holy Trinity Sheerness was raised, and a proposal to consult an architect carried, whereupon an amendment was moved that 'the proposal be negatived', and this was carried so nothing was done about the repairs. This was the usual pattern for the meetings. They were often badly attended, and often acrimonious. Minster found Sheerness a strain, and Sheerness resented being in the Parish of Minster. All meetings ended in the 'Waterloo'; the church was in a shocking state of repair.

At the visitation in July a long list of church repairs was made, but nothing was done about them. In 1844 Leonard Lester died, leaving poor rates uncollected. which led to much discussion on how to recover the rates owing. The Wards, senior and junior, had started to appear at meetings. Mr. James Ward was a solicitor in Edward Street. People either liked him or hated him, and he was at the centre of many disputes.

At a crowded meeting in April 1845, Trinity Church was considered again, and then crossed out, and the following recorded: 'At a meeting of the Minister and of pew renters of Trinity Church Sheerness, being a Church without a district and built upon a site' — here it becomes incomprehensible. Nothing was decided, and the statement was signed by the Trinity church wardens, George Hogben, linen draper and Thomas Frank, grocer.

The Minster church wardens had been unable to make up their accounts 'in consequence of unforseen circumstances' so that was postponed.

In 1844 the Public Health Acts decreed that the surveyors' duties were to be transferred to a local Board of Health and the rates should be paid to them. The meeting was nonplussed by this, and adjourned.

Victoria had succeeded to the throne in 1837, and was determined to lift the country out of the rakish ways of her profligate uncles. She was well supported in this endeavour by the solemn Albert, and new Acts appeared as frequently as royal babies. At the next meeting the surveyors laid their papers before a solicitor as they considered it was an important question for the parish, and basically they were suspicious about it, and unwilling to part with their authority.

Naturally they had no case, and in December the balance of the accounts was handed to the local Board of Health. At this stage Sheerness was granted a separate Board of Health, which was a much better arrangement for all. When the constables were chosen in 1850 one was Stephen Tong, a gardener from Butts Lane, Minster. In no maps examined has Butts Lane been shown, and no-one has any idea where it was.

The County rates had been declared, and there was a new committee responsible for them. The vestry meeting adjourned, unable to cope. When they met again it was to air their grievances about the increased County rate. Their own Church rate had also increased, to threepence. A proposal that a Mrs. Cripps should have some financial help so that she could emigrate raised a storm of objections, and no help was forthcoming.

There were more new statutes concerning the Poor rate, more disagreements about electing church wardens, and still problems regarding Holy Trinity, but they refused to pay for the Church of Sheerness.

In June 1851 the whole parish turned up at a meeting to consider rebuilding the church tower and steeple. Agreements were proposed, passed, and then negatived. It became a nonsensical muddle, and Mr. Ward protested vehemently about the prevarications.

At a further meeting the parishioners decided that the repairs were necessary, and a small committee of four 'all practical men' was appointed to investigate and report. The report came back that repairs were more than necessary, and listed all the rotten beams, frames, timbers and other woodwork. Plans were produced and ragstone was recommended for the tower, but no-one could agree, and again there was an adjournment. The following week the whole village attended a meeting in the schoolroom in the Mile Town. The vicar from Holy Trinity took the chair, which nearly caused a riot, and when things had quietened down and the matter could be discussed they could still reach no agreement, so a poll was decided on, at Mr. Brightman's instigation. The result of the poll was a complete rejection of all the plans for repairs, and so the church was left in partial ruin.

The next accounts included a memo. to get surplices washed at 'as low a rate as possible'.

5/- for decorating the Church at Christmas to be disallowed.

8/- for emptying the privy (in two sums of 4/- each) and 10/- for holly at Christmas, disallowed.
Bill for candles (and Trinity) £1 13s. (Well, they did allow Trinity some light!)
All bills objected to be disallowed, except for the holly and to empty the privy, they be now allowed.

From then on the vestry meetings were one long disagreement which ended by voting, or a poll.

In April 1853 the expenses for winding Trinity clock were disallowed. 'The person who is paid threepence a week for attending the Church to wind clock.' In October they considered a poll re-making a church rate for repairs at Minster. There was much acrimony over this, and the chairman was asked to vacate the chair. Eventually they had a poll, and the vote was against the rate. At every meeting there were stormy sessions, but in October 1855 they were brought up short by the Burial Grounds Act. After much argument, and meetings, it was obvious that the Abbey churchyard would have to be closed, and a new one found. Still more adjournments and arguments, and a Cemetery Company was formed, and advised to find a new ground, as the one by the workhouse would only last ten years more.

In 1857 they wanted to redirect or stop up a road that ran from the Ferry to Neats Court by way of Cowstead and Barnland, leaving a footpath there, and they had to inform the Board of Health of this decision, but the outcome is not recorded, and the road is still there, as far as it is possible to tell. More discussion about the law on roads in 1861 ended in argument, and a poll was called for between James Ward and Mr. Brightman. It seemed they could decide nothing without resorting to a poll. The whole thing was ridiculous, the church was disintegrating around them, and all they could do was argue.

In all fairness, Minster was agricultural, and farming was not doing well. Victoria's reign saw the division between town and country intensify, and the fashion was to back industry, and regard the country somewhat patronisingly. The Sheerness people were a totally different breed from those in Minster at that time, and it was not a happy alliance that the two places had been forced into. The farmers' main concern was to keep the rates down, they could not cope with their own church and they certainly were not going to pay out for Sheerness if they could avoid doing so.

In January 1862 there was a serious meeting about dividing the upper part of Minster, described as east of Sheerness, from the lower part, under various new Acts just passed. Sheerness was to come under a separate Highway district, as ordered by the Secretary of State. So it became the district of Sheerness, instead of the district of the Parish of Minster, and was treated as a township.

All the Minster farmers signed this, Robert Palmer, G. A. Benstead, Fred Leese, James Mantle, Alfred Beal, John X his mark Beal, Charles Fox the shoemaker, Edward Ingleton, Anne Masters and others.

Nothing untoward happened after this, apart from the never-ending arguments and polls, by 1863 they had at last formed a Highway Board, and a way Warden was appointed for Minster. For the next few years they managed fairly peacefully, making and passing rates, coping with the new Acts as they came, and deciding to rate owners, not occupiers, for Poor Relief. Everything seemed quiet, and then in 1871 for some reason James Ward declined the nomination for Minster's church warden, so that year there was not one. There was no explanation given for this, but James Ward must have felt strongly about something to act in this way, he had been Minster's church warden the previous year.

At the July visitation the archbishop advised attention to tombstones which made the path dangerous, and that the churchyard be cleared of weeds, and sheep put in to graze it down as the best mode of keeping graves and grass in order.

Mr. Ward accepted the post of Church warden again in 1873, the County rate was increased and the Vestry objected, and they returned to the question of repairs and asked for voluntary contributions.

Things had quietened down in the Vestry. Apart from a poll to decide the church wardens in 1875, and Mr. Robert Brightman dying and being replaced by his brother, nothing of note was recorded. The Reverend Willis died in 1877, and there is no record for a short time, as there was no vicar. Between 1888 and 1894 the Local and Government Acts were passed, and the Vestry Authority was replaced by the Parish Council, later the Rural District Council. This severed all connections with Sheerness, who had their own Urban District Council now, and Holy Trinity was licensed to administer the sacraments. St. Paul's Church had been built in Sheerness in the 1870's and this too was granted parish status.

In 1856 the Railway decided to open a line to Sheerness and started building, and in 1859 the Dockyard Railway Station was opened. There was no mention of this in the Parish records, but it was an event of the greatest importance to the island. The Dockyard was the obvious place for the station, where it could serve both Fleet, Garrison and Yard, but the local interpretation for this position was rather cynical. 'Of course they put the station in the Dockyard, now when Jack comes ashore he can be dumped straight on a train and sent home to his family with money in his pocket, instead of being found dead drunk and penniless next day, with perhaps a dose of something worse, that is if he did not get drowned in the fleet overnight.'

The Sittingbourne and Sheerness Railway, which was a branch of the East Kent Railway, later to be bought by the London, Chatham and Dover Railway in 1865, acquired the ancient rights of the Warden and Jury of the Ferry and from then on no more were elected. After centuries of maintaining and running an adequate ferry for the island, the Law Day held under the Court Tree at Kingsborough was no more, literally vanishing overnight and nowhere, so far, has any record been found to tell how the islanders felt about it, but it must have seemed to many of them that part of their lives had been suddenly taken away. How the railway managed during the building operations is not revealed, either, and the bridge they built, a large lifting bridge to allow for the passage of river traffic, was not opened to road traffic until 1862. The ferry tolls were still imposed, all traffic had to stop on the bridge, pay the collector, and collect a ticket.

The Law Day Court did not give up without a struggle. In the August 8th edition of the *Sittingbourne and Sheerness Gazette*, 1857, there is an account of a case heard in the Nisi Pruis Court, in London. 'Action because railway is interfering with oyster beds round Sheppey.' It was alleged that the Bridge was trespassing, as the oyster men were deprived of their rights of dredging oysters 'two ropes length each side of the Ferry'. Recent tenants of the Ferry gave evidence that they could take or lay oysters with no interference from Milton ot Queenborough. Mr. Ward was the Ferry steward, and explained the procedure of the Law Day held under the Court Tree at Kingsborough, every Whit Monday. He had been elected six years ago by the jury which had been appointed by his predecessor Mr. Hinde of Milton, whose father and grandfather had been stewards for upwards of eighty years. Mr. Ward had received three books from Mr. Hinde's executor in which entries had been kept regarding the business, the Ferry House repairs, and the duties of the Ferry warden.

It was a useless plea. Lord Chief Baron Sir F. Pollock said it was all rubbish, and the defendants, the railway, won the case. So the era of the Law Day and the Court Tree was finished, and what Mr. Ward did with the Ferry books is anyone's guess.

In 1884 there was a small paragraph in the *Sheppey Church Magazine* about the Old Court Tree at Kingsborough Hill, which, it was said, was fast going to decay; it had been a great tree in its time, but the remaining stock was fast falling to pieces, and a heavy gale might 'wrench it altogether from its roots'. It was calculated to be of very great age, old enough 'for Sir Thomas Cheney to have looked on it, and perhaps even the Baron de Shurland when it was a sapling. Who can say?' No-one could say, few cared, and the Law Day was soon forgotten.

With the vestry now restricted to church affairs, there is little to be gleaned about the village, and records from the newly appointed boards are scarce. Minster Fair had died out by the middle of the nineteenth century. It was still held in 1843, but had lost its importance. Neither is there any record of the cutting dug at Mill Hill in 1876, when it was decided that the hill between Minster and Pigtail Corner was far too steep for loaded carts and so a cutting was made through the hill, leaving a high bank on either side, as it is today. It was all done by manual labour, and the earth was removed by horse and cart, and dumped at the top of Breackneck, making Bunny Hill and Bunny Banks as this century knows them.

The one windmill remaining was left on top of the high bank beside the new road, there were two in 1790, but one had disappeared, leaving no trace of its location. The remaining mill ceased working somewhere about 1882, and subsequently lost a sail and other parts of equipment in a high wind, which left it vulnerable to any breeze that blew, so that it frequently turned and the remaining sails hung across the road. Eventually it caught fire and was burnt down, leaving only the base, and that has gone now.

For several months there was no vicar at Minster, vicarage and church were both in a dilapidated state, and the stipend was so small that no-one wanted to take the job on. In December 1877 the Board of Guardians discussed the matter, the chairman Mr. Robert Palmer having already written to the Archbishop of Canterbury about the situation, and received a non-committal answer. They decided to write again, and this report, and several other letters concerning Minster Abbey, appeared in the *Times*. It appeared that the tithes were £1,800 per annum, and the vicar received £2 a week. The vicarage was in ruins, and the clergy were afraid to take the living, as they could not afford to pay for the necessary repairs. The condition of the church was as bad.

The Reverend Bramston did take the living in 1788, and his first task was to restore the church. He was granted a faculty to do this in 1880, by which time he had formed committees, raised money, and had plans approved. There was an imposing list of subscribers, headed by Queen Victoria, and on June 9th, 1881, the church was reopened, a special service being held for the occasion. Since then the abbey has been carefully tended, and it is difficult to imagine now that the roof was so full of holes that rain came in everywhere, the windows were broken, the woodwork of the turret had given way, and the walls were mouldy, with green patches of damp and fungus growing.

Strangely there was another Julius Caesar involved in the church at this period, a Doctor Julius Caesar who was the doctor for the workhouse for a time. His name appears on a brass plate on the wall of the church as one of the church wardens. It is also believed that Charles Dickens had the abbey in mind in his description of an old church in *The Old Curiosity Shop*. He liked to visit a friend, Captain Johns, who lived at Prospect Villa, a house at the bottom of Minster Hill. He used to take Mr. Burford's little daughter pick-a-back through the churchyard; Mr. Burford was church warden then, and doubtless Mr. Dickens knew the abbey well.

All the churches in Sheppey were repaired in the latter part of the nineteenth century. Queen Victoria's influence was spreading and Sunday schools, church clubs and associations and other good works became the accepted thing. This was accompanied by a distinct class consciousness, and everyone was given a place and kept in it. You performed charitable works, or you were on the receiving end and had to be duly grateful.

A church inventory of Minster in 1852 lists the communion plate, various carpets and matting, two candlesticks, prayer books, the pulpit and font, and a miscellaneous collection of blacking brushes, stoves, scrubbing brushes, lanterns, coal scuttles and other domestic items. There was a gallery, and a ladder leading to the belfry. In 1887 the gallery had gone, and the inventory included two carved oak chairs and a valuable carved oak table. Also something that is made of lead, dated 1760. By 1913 the list included old branched brass candlesticks, and a solid brass chandelier for candles, amongst other lamps. The lead tablet of 1760 is again mentioned, one carved image of the Blessed Virgin Mary, and other corbels. The corbels, wonderful little faces, are still there, the image of Mary was of eleventh century origin, made in sandstone, and was found to be extremely valuable. It was sold to a museum in 1970 for £2,000, and the money used to help rebuild St. Peter's Church at Halfway.

At Leysdown the church was almost completely rebuilt in the 1870's, and the 'small hut' dispensed with. At Harty a great deal of money was spent on the little church, and it has been cherished ever since — that is the only word for it — and is one of the loveliest old churches anyone could wish for.

At Eastchurch work started in 1871, with the draining of the church and churchyard. In 1872 they carried on with the work of restoration, at the same time ordering a letter to be written to the Clerk of the Union to demand of Minster overseers that their parish should be rated equally with other parishes or they would appeal. The screen, which is unique, and irreplaceable, was restored, by the time of the next visitation it was back in position, and the archdeacon was pleased with their efforts, his only criticism being about the weeds. In 1881 they altered the church paths and gates, to give themselves more burial ground. During the restoration the water spouts and butts had been removed, which was an improvement in itself. There is evidence that Eastchurch had 'Church music', an odd assembly of violins, bass viols, and an instrument called a serpent, all reminiscent of Thomas Hardy's country choirs.

The vestry meetings at Eastchurch had none of the aggravation of the Minster meetings. The White Post Cottages, parish property, and the alms-houses were made over to the Guardians of the Poor for letting.

According to the Public Health Act a new burial ground was needed, and they waited until the Glebe Lands Bill became law so that they could buy a nearby garden to add to their existing ground. It was all done calmly and equably, with no arguments.

In 1827 the Reverend John Barton had become the rector, he was a relative of the patron, and he demolished the tumbledown cottage that served as vicarage and built a new residence, a large and elegant vicarage which is still in use. In 1885 the tombstones from Warden were moved to Eastchurch, but the bell from Warden Church had gone to Minster Abbey, where it stood in the belfry for many years.

The cost of their new churchyard was £53 6s. 11d. and it was consecrated in 1892, but it was not all peace and happiness in Eastchurch, for in 1890 the village had suffered a great tragedy when two of the rector's sons, Thomas and Bernard, were drowned while out in a boat with the sons of the Leysdown vicar, one of whom was also drowned. There is a stained glass window in the church at Eastchurch in memory of them.

Eastchurch had other diversions. In 1880 an elephant was captured in Shurland Park. It was thought to have been lost from Sydenham, and how it reached Sheppey is a mystery. Also in 1880, Thomas Holden of Eastchurch, was killed by a drunken man on the green near the 'Wheatsheaf' Inn. Earlier in the century a small elephant had been found on the shore at Leysdown, and buried by coastguards.

There were innumerable fires. Church Farm was burnt in 1868, and John Goodwin, the farmer, lost £1,500 of stock. Old Hook Farm was destroyed by fire, Alfred Cheeseman was living there, and he lost everything. Old Hook house is now comparatively modern compared with New Hook (which is early Georgian) and the date, 1868, is inscribed on the house. The barn seems older, and has a small cat door in the big door, something that is not often seen.

Garretts Farm also had a fire that year, and Mrs. Elizabeth Benstead lost her cowshed, and hay, wheat and oats. Mr. Ingleton's threshing machine was burnt at the same time. In 1881 New Rides lost all stacks and buildings, only the house was saved. The fire was caused by sparks from a threshing machine falling on a thatched barn. For all its troubles, Eastchurch managed its affairs more reasonably than Minster did.

After the restoration at the abbey, there were more arguments about rates and valuations, and during one altercation about choosing a way warden Edward Ingleton was told that he could keep quiet, he was not entitled to vote as he had not paid his Poor rate.

Gradually things calmed down, and at the next visitation the church was declared excellent — but the fence needed repairing.

While all the churches were being restored, and Sunday schools, cookery classes and libraries organised, out at Elmley a complete reorganisation was taking place. The census of 1831 recorded that Elmley had twenty-nine inhabitants, mostly farm-workers and lookers. In 1851 the number had risen to one hundred and thirty-one, and by 1891 there was a total of two hundred and nineteen, an unheard-of population for Elmley. The reason for this sudden expansion was, of all unlikely things, cement. Up to the mid nineteenth century mortar was made of lime and sand, but then someone invented Portland cement, and the stones and mud of Sheppey were ideal for making it. So a cement works was started in Elmley in 1860 by Messrs. William Leverett and Co. for the production of Portland cement, and named the Turkey Cement Works. This drew labourers to the area, and a rather poor village quickly grew. There were no shops or ale houses, and court cases regarding people selling coal and foodstuffs and giving short weight were not uncommon; one man was summoned for selling beer from a cart.

In 1866 the Reverend Scott Robertson was appointed rector, and here the villagers were lucky, for he was a humane man, and concerned about their physical as well as their spiritual welfare. His was the driving force that had the church restored, and a school built for the children.

He lived at Sittingbourne, and he would ride to the Ferry on a weedy thoroughbred horse, cross the Swale in an open boat, and remain at Elmley for the day, bringing sandwiches that could be eaten in the vestry. He kept his pockets full of sweets for the ragged children who opened the many marsh gates for him, and on Christmas Day provided plum pudding for all and treats for the children, which would be shared out at a party in the vestry, after service. Sheppey was lucky to have him, too, for he was an archaeologist and historian of some standing; he became interested in the island's history and has left some of the best researched and written accounts of Sheppey to be found. He was Rector of Elmley until 1884, and the rector that followed him did not appear to have the same interest in the parish.

The cement works closed in 1900, the people drifted away and the village became derelict, with only the farmhouse, Kingshill, and a few cottages inhabited. In 1962 the church was demolished, and only the ruins of the school remain.

In 1872 schooling became compulsory, and the school rooms in the churches of Minster and Eastchurch were closed when the National schools were built. Schools were built at Leysdown and at Harty, too. Harty had no village, but the children from the farms and the cottages needed education. This was, in fact, a Church school. In 1853 Sayes Court was used by Messrs. Cooper as a factory, making clothing and bedding for immigrants. It is not clear if immigrants were working there, but the children of the workers would have to attend school when the time came.

The enforcement of schooling was not altogether popular as Minster school records show. Attendance was poor if work in the fields was available, and often the beginning of term was postponed in September if the harvest was late. They would lose children again at potato picking time, and if horse races were held in the locality, as they sometimes were at a place called Cheeseman's meadow, the school would close for the day, as the teachers knew that no-one would turn up for lessons.

The records also reveal the poverty of the farm workers at that time. Many children had no socks or shoes, and in cold weather they would arrive at school freezing, often without a decent coat or jacket. Illness was usual in winter, due to the cold, and under-feeding. Dirt and vermin were not unknown, either, but they seem to have been restricted to certain families, who just could not cope.

It was some time before education became accepted. Children would work to gain their leaving certificate. If they could achieve that, they were allowed to leave school at thirteen, and go to work, but if they did not make the grade they were compelled to stay until they were fourteen. The majority passed their exams, and left with their certificate, which proved that they could read, write, and do simple arithmetic. It is something to ponder about, in today's age of specialised schooling and the illiteracy that is always under discussion.

The children were also taught religion, and after the reopening of the Abbey Sunday School, the choir, and later bell-ringing were all part of the order of the day. By 1884 the number of children attending Sunday school had risen from ten to eighty. In July of that year the belfry was re-opened, and ringers went into frantic training.

Sheerness had built schools, too, of necessity. There had been a Church school attached to Holy Trinity for some time, a school run by the Bethel Chapel in Blue Town, and a number of private schools had sprung up in Edward Street for the children of the officers of the Garrison, and the Fleet, where they were joined by the families of the professional men and wealthier tradesmen of Sheerness. Other National schools were built, St. Paul's Church was built in 1873, and was made a separate parish, containing Blue Town, and in 1894, if not before, Sheerness became a parish, and Minster's guardianship ended.

The Catholic Church of St. Henry and St. Elizabeth was built on Marine Parade in 1864. Formerly the Roman Catholic Church had been a small building in Rose Street, almost behind a slaughter house, built by Irish shipwrights in 1813.

There were numerous nonconformist chapels, and a synagogue, and the Jewish burial ground is still there, behind a high wall in Wood Street.

The second half of the nineteenth century had been one of change, not only of material change, but also change of outlook, and the pious, solid Victorian way of life was now the accepted one.

CHAPTER XXII
A town growing up

Sheerness eventually shook off the ties with Minster, and became a town in its own right, but it still had a long way to go, and a great deal to learn.

In 1857 the only local paper for the island was the *Sittingbourne and Sheerness Gazette*. Their reports on Sheerness were mainly concerned with court proceedings. 'Richard Cheeseman, butcher, summoned for assault on Richard Murton, the Master of the Union.' The reason for the assault — Cheeseman had sent putrid meat to the Union, and Murton had returned it. James Ward's colt was drowned off the beach near Marine Town, while being broken in. It bolted into the sea, and the weight of the cart it was pulling dragged it down.

'The pier was re-opened, after being damaged by a barge nine weeks ago', and 'a joke that went wrong': two men were summoned by the local policeman for killing a horse by whitewashing it, while they were whitewashing the stables. They protested that it was 'only a lark', and the case was dismissed with a £2 fine for ill treatment. So far so good, but evidently someone was not happy with this judgement. The accused men and their friends stopped at the ferry house on their way home, leaving their horses and traps outside. When they were ready to resume the journey they found that 'someone', never to be named, had whitewashed the five vehicles they were travelling in, and that was how they had to return to Sheerness.

The paper remarked that the joke came back on the jokers, but it goes deeper than that. It was an example of rough justice, something Sheppey always believed in, considering, rightly or wrongly, that they had their own laws on the island. Many queer accidents have happened, and crimes never been solved, but usually the facts have been known locally, and the action taken condoned.

Sheerness was delighted in 1857 when county police were sent there. In the event, instead of the force of men they had expected, two policemen arrived. All the local constables and watchmen had been discharged, and the town was disappointed and furious, with good reason.

It was no uncommon thing for men to strip to the waist and start a fight in the High Street, loudly cheered on by a crowd that gathered rapidly, and could easily number a hundred people or more. One policeman on duty had no chance against odds like these.

In June, they reported that S. Russell, the brother of the celebrated Henry Russell, fell down a hatchway in H.M.S. *Colossus*, and died. That is all, no further explanations. Henry Russell was born in Sheerness in 1812; he later studied under Rossini and became a leading musician. He is best remembered for 'A Life on the Ocean Wave', and his name was commemorated by 'Russell Street' in Sheerness. He died in 1900, and both his sons were musicians: Henry Junior was famous in opera, and his brother, Landon Ronald, was well known as a conductor and composer.

The island has had a fair share of famous people over the centuries. The mother of D. H. Lawrence, the author, was Lily Beardsall from Sheerness. She was employed as a school teacher in the town before she married.

The paper managed to get a reporter allowed into the Board of Health meetings, although the Board was not very gracious about it. Of course, the fleet was 'lit up' for the coronation anniversary, and in the courts a dealer's 'long dog' was accused of worrying sheep, there was the usual list of petty thieving, assaults, and at least one lady who 'kept a house of ill repute'.

It reads like an account of a Wild West town in the old cowboy pictures, but Sheerness meant to establish itself creditably, and worked to this end.

By 1860 the town had two local papers of its own, and directories were being compiled and published. The directory of 1860 tells it all in the introduction.

Sheerness has no water or drains, water is conveyed in barrels drawn by donkeys. There is dirt and disease, ague and intermittent fever, the houses are overcrowded wooden hutches, the footpaths are too crowded to walk on, and the road is filthy.

The papers bear this out. The editorials were frank to the point of rudeness, but no one seemed to consider that untoward, or libellous. The Board of Health, later to include the Highway Authority, fought and called each other names at every meeting. The papers were named *The Sheerness Times* and *The Sheerness Guardian*, whichever one people chose to read. The papers and the local boards made it crystal clear that they had no time for the people in the rural areas, especially when they were voted into positions of any authority. It seems a poor way to organise a town, but it has to be remembered that the various boards and councils were all in their infancy, this type of local government was new, it had not been tried before, and the people elected were the same people that used to deliberate at vestry meetings: farmers, tradesmen, innkeepers, with perhaps a lawyer or a doctor to make up the number.

There was an inspection by the Public Health Authority in 1849, the evidence being damning, and conditions had not altered by 1860. The inspector was assisted by the usual people who formed local committees, so they were left with no illusions about the town.

He commenced with observations on the marshy condition of the ground. Farmers Till and Robinson told him that the marshes were periodically flooded, and sometimes frozen over. They were undrained, and could not be cultivated, and this state of affairs the farmers appeared to accept without argument. In 1831 there were 8,894 people in 1,617 houses. In 1841 there were 10,064 people in 1,798 houses, so in a period of ten years there were almost two thousand more people, and only one hundred and eighty-one additional houses. Blue Town was the worst off, with no less than forty-nine alleys, courts, passages, and lanes, and two hundred and sixty-three houses, with small rooms, in which lived 1,153 people. Mile Town was slightly better, with only thirty-three alleys, courts, etc., but all were grossly overcrowded. Amongst this conglomeration were thirty-six licensed public houses, and seventeen beer shops. The authorities worked out the average expenditure per week, and it was frightening. The common diseases were ague (malaria), and intermittent fever, diarrhoea, cholera, and continued fever of a typhoid type. There was a bad outbreak of cholera in 1832, in which Blue Town suffered more than any other area, and this was repeated in 1866.

It was pointed out that all this led to a loss of public money! Men were paid two shillings extra on account of the unhealthy state of the place, and they were frequently on the sick list. The diseases were accounted for quite easily. The inspector listed: Open ditches full of decomposing rubbish, including dead cats and dogs.

Alleys with twenty-six houses and two lavatories to serve them all, as a result excreta was kept in the house all day and then thrown into the alley at night. Some alleys housed piggeries for extra flavour, and in one court the privy flowed down the passage in front of entrances and windows. Some passages and courts had no privies at all, and some lanes and alleys kept tubs for 'the extra', and everything was flung out at night. Not surprisingly, the mortality rate, especially for babies and children, was higher in Sheerness than in the rural areas.

There was much more on those lines. There had been no plans drawn for drains or sewers, only for surface water, and those drains were inefficient. Some drains had been built wrongly, so that the outfall went from outlet to source, instead of vice versa. The farmers were blamed for the bad roads, as were the surveyors. The roads were muddy and holey, badly drained, and if stone was laid it shifted because the roads were too wet for it to hold and settle.

The water supply was inadequate, and main water was needed. A list of wells was included, five at Minster, three at Queenborough, and two at Sheerness, one of which belonged to the dockyard, and was not open to the town. The inspection finished with a long list of recommendations, which included 'W.C.'s and sewers'.

It is a terrifying document, but the town had grown too rapidly, the developers and speculators had rushed in for a quick profit, and there was no town planning or building regulations to ensure decent standards.

In 1860 Sheerness was a town of contrasts. It had a pier, a church (in the parish of Minster), bathing machines, the Sheerness Development Company, a bandstand, a swimming pool of sorts, and the Hippodrome Playhouse. It also had a super-abundance of pubs and ale houses. The oldest in Blue Town was the 'Fountain', where Nelson is supposed to have stayed on occasion. Long ago someone unknown wrote an imaginary tour of these hostelries. It is amusing, and provides a picture of the time. The Sheerness papers recorded it all, and extracts illustrate the general muddle. In 1862 there was a long article on some horse races held in a field at Shurland Hall. Between one and two thousand people arrived 'mounted and on foot', and there was apparently a hope of reviving the Isle of Sheppey races. There were about five races, horses had names like, Wonder, Tomboy, Taffy and Gameboy, and were ridden by farmers, and local tradesmen.

When the races finished, there were one or two private matches. The islanders have always loved a horse — the recent upsurge of pony riding is nothing new. During the races a Sheerness boy fell out of a tree, and broke his arm. A subscription was promptly raised among the spectators to pay the doctor, who, luckily for the boy, was there!

Petty sessions reports are monotonous; pubs open out of hours (George Bastard of the Medway Beer House was one of these), unlawful games of dice and similar things in pubs, payment for illegitimate babies (one and six a week) and labourers stealing turnips and potatoes from farms. The punishment for this was severe, three months' hard labour.

The admiral held a ball at Admiralty House, and one to two hundred of the local élite were present. That was the paper's description. The local élite were, for the main part, Army and Naval officers. The garrison and dockyard were drained, with all mod. cons. provided, and it is unlikely that the ladies there ever set foot in Blue Town. In 1862 the paper gave an enthusiastic description of the new Army barracks that had recently been built in the garrison, and claimed that they were the most up to date barracks in England, complete with specially equipped washhouses; a far cry from local conditions.

The Board of Health declared that Blue Town, Mile Town, Banks Town and Marine Town all needed paving, and unfit houses be condemned. Marine Town was in trouble; it had been built on a meadow, with no roads or drains. True, but at that end of Sheerness the houses were built in brick, and they

were not so poky as the older wooden houses. At County Court there were arguments over rates due on new houses, and someone's fowls were causing damage to a neighbour's garden. In between these items were sandwiched notices of shooting matches at the 'Plough Inn', and sparrow-shooting matches at Minster.

One story of note in 1862 was that Stones or Little Mill had caught fire and been completely destroyed, it was built of wood and tarred, and the barn, stables, and horses were all burnt as well, the cottage going last. Fire engines came from the dockyard and the garrison, but it was hopeless, and it was remarked that the isolated position of the mill saved the fire from spreading. The mill was built in 1810, and was the first building in that part of town. It stood roughly behind what is now the Freemason's Hall, near to the present football ground. The fire left the miller destitute, and the paper put out an appeal for help, for he was not a young man. There were two other mills, Rides, or the Great Mill, the base of which can still be seen behind a furniture shop in the High Street. There used to be a corn merchant's shop there. This mill worked until 1918, latterly by steam, and was pulled down in 1924. The walls were reckoned to be twenty-one inches thick.

The other mill was for some reason unfathomed known as the One Hundred Acre Mill, unless the name derived from Mr. Chalk's one hundred acre field, which is possible. The base can be seen in the yard of the Seaview Hotel. The mill worked until 1872, but the owner claimed that the newly built Catholic Church interfered with the windpower. It was pulled down in 1878. The mills could not keep up with the demand for flour in the earlier part of the century, but when the railway came to Sheppey, making transport of flour and other goods easier, the demand fell off.

There were always arguments about the new iron ships versus the old wooden ones, at that time both types being built in the yard. Shipping lists were published, and the number of ships in an out of the port seems unbelievable now.

A coloured opera troupe was to visit the Co-op Hall; there was no shortage of entertainment; troupes, circuses, magicians, singers, something called a diorama, and even a photographic artist in the High Street.

Someone suggested using chalk and flint on the roads instead of shingle, and the Police Courts continued with the usual run of drunk and disorderly sailors/soldiers/marines, embezzlement, theft, and robberies in houses of ill repute, and in one case robbery from a sailor who was lying unconscious in the road.

Two gypsies were arrested for obstructing the public thoroughfare in Edward Street by tethering their horses and camping out opposite the Royal Hotel for the night. For a change, there were trotting matches on the Ferry Road. If a horse galloped, it had to be pulled up and started again, rather like the present-day gymkhana race.

All the vestry meetings were commented on, and Mr. Palmer was not liked in Sheerness. 'Petty power, the overseers of Minster are notorious.' The vestry meeting fought among themselves, with Sheerness, now the lower division, wanting more say.

It was rough on Minster, because the vestry was not orientated to deal with a swashbuckling, growing town, and the farmers were struggling with an agricultural depression at the time.

There was a minor flood in April, due to rain and sea combined. The recreation ground was six feet deep in water and the sea wall was damaged, and then this was forgotten in the excitement of a prize fight on the beach near Scrapsgate. It was a poor fight, was the disappointed comment — it lasted two hours twenty-five minutes for £50 a side.

The arguments and polls at the vestry meetings were

enlarged upon. 'Mr. Palmer and co. call Sheerness "the roughs". The overseers get in by a trick, and the rates are fiddled.' The accusations were never-ending. 'It is the old system of mulcting the townspeople to ease the rates of the gentlemen farmers. The Upper Division has too much to say. Those who get no share of vegetables and fruit from the Union gardens, or butter and eggs from the Union Dairy, should take matters into their own hands. The Poor Rates are going to the Establishment, not the poor.' Cruel words, and untrue. The number of poor had risen, it was one hundred and eleven in 1845, and increasing. The house now had room for three hundred and fifty inmates. It also ran an infirmary, and admitted people who needed treatment, as well as providing nursing for the inmates.

The farm had been started to help feed the Union, and it provided work for the able-bodied. It also employed local people. An elderly man once said that he knew the Union well, he had been born in a cottage there, as his father worked as the pigman for the workhouse. His descendants still live in Minster, and they are far removed from those days.

Rude posters were displayed if someone was defeated in a local poll, and at times the friction descended to shouting and violence. In between those acid comments were accounts of running matches at Halfway, where the runners took names like Deerfoot, and the Lancashire Antelope, followed by notices about a quadrille band at the Royal Hotel pleasure gardens.

Still there was no water. The water barrel donkey was an accepted part of life in Sheerness. There were nine registered water-carriers, and they led the little donkeys around Sheerness, selling water at a halfpenny a bucket from the barrel the animals pulled.

The water company that started in 1857 would have been a joke, if it was not such a serious matter. The first plans made were lost. Eventually they started to build a water tower behind Trinity Church, where the council buildings are now. So are the wells, but they have to be looked for. The water tower fell down, literally, before it was completed. That started another storm of abuse, and heads rolled. Sir John Rennie was recalled to advise — it was a bad ground to build on — and eventually the tower was completed, but there was no water before 1864. Then there were more arguments about water rates, where to place stand pipes, and what it would cost private houses if they required a supply laid on.

At times the water was not forthcoming, and people would have to wait until the stopcocks were turned on, or adjusted. As late as 1950 some of the old wooden houses, arranged in courts, still had only one tap per court.

There was a railway station in the dockyard, and it was not long before the town decided it needed another. After much letter writing to the railway authorities, Mile Town station was opened in 1883.

By this time the regatta was a yearly event, and growing in importance, although at different times sabotage had been attempted by rival functions. It had started as a cutter race between the dockyard and the Navy, but by the end of the century there were boat races, a swimming gala, and novelty water games and contests, which the spectators loved.

The committee and judges went out in barges to watch and judge. There was, at the turn of the century, a London man deeply involved in this. His people came originally from the island, and he spent much of his time there.

He was a judge of swimming, and coach to the Olympic swimming team. His large family were all keen swimmers, and one of his sons was in the Olympic diving team. They used to swim from the beach by Neptune Terrace, and people would come to watch them. His sons entered the regatta swimming contests, but he would not allow his daughters to take part. His reasoning was simple. 'If the boys win, and someone says "you only won cos your Dad's on the committee" the boys can put their fists up, but I will not have my girls fighting in public!' One year a storm blew up, and the committee barges were dispersed by the wind. The women and children came ashore at Sheerness, wet, bedraggled, rather patchy where the colour had run from their garments, but unhurt. The men did not reappear until later that night; they had been driven ashore by the wind at Queenborough. It was an anxious afternoon for the ladies, who could only wait.

The saga in the papers continued. Some boys aged thirteen were given twelve lashes for stealing rope to sell. There was a mysterious murder, a man called Elliott was shot and a father and son named Johnson suspected, but nothing could be proved.

There were Sunday school treats, a drum and fife band, and people were drowned in the moat and the fleets. A woman in court for assault and bad language was requested by the judge 'Oh speak louder, as a Sheerness woman ought to do'!

The editor wrote an indignant editorial about the 'slur' in the County Court, Sheerness was not that bad! The ships captains and the pier master were quarrelling, and making life difficult for boat passengers. There was a brisk boat trade until 1878, when the *Bywell Castle* and the *Princess Alice* collided in Woolwich Reach, resulting in the loss of the *Princess Alice* with six hundred drowned, after which the boat traffic slumped.

The advertisements were hilarious, they are time wasters, but a few examples are worth repeating. 'Premature Debility! A popular medical work.' 'The Silent Friend on Marriage. A medical work. To those who have imperilled the power of manhood by youthful indiscretions.' Another says simply 'Try Sasparilla!' And again: 'Do you want Beautiful Hair, Whiskers, etc? Get Dr. Russells Lixivene. Mr. Saffery, Chemist'.

The pathetic lists from the Board of Guardians are published regularly. 'Mrs. Powell to have relief, her husband is on half pay and it is not enough for her and five children. Two shillings increased to two and six, for Mr. Crockford of Eastchurch, he being ninety-two.' Mr. Shrubsole, the grocer, moved from Blue Town to Mile Town, where the shop remained until the 1970's. With a patronising air the paper stated: 'Agricultural matters are not of absorbing interest to readers. The Agricultural Society is not flourishing, and bread and other articles of foodstuff are going up in price.' Perhaps if there had been more interest in agriculture at that time things would have been better all round. Sheerness yard advertised for oakum pickers 'if any of the poor in the neighbourhood were desirous to be employed'. They were paid five shillings a hundredweight for the job.

In 1868 there was a General Election pending, and there was a real anxiety about the future of the yard. A rumour was about that it might be closed, and everyone was ready to fight the closure. It was a false alarm, and the dockyard continued to provide work.

Things improved slowly. The streets were to be watered, and lighted by gas. There were the usual fights over the water, but in the end it was settled. The workhouse doctor ordered a new diet for the children. It was disliked, because it cost more, but the good doctor stuck to his guns, and the children benefited.

Hard labour was ordered for a man who stole a chicken, and for a girl who stole ribbons. There was a fire in Mile Town in 1867, in fact fires were quite common, but after this one the houses were rebuilt facing the High Street.

There were complaints of dangerous riding and driving in the town, and one poor farm labourer was fined three shillings and ninepence or fourteen days' hard labour for falling asleep on the rods of his master's waggon on the Highway in Minster. He earned twelve shillings weekly, worked for a man at Milton, and he was very tired — he pleaded. The little settlement at Westminster was told it could not have any main water laid on, it would cost too much. James Anstey of Mile Town, stationer and greengrocer, was arrested for trying to blow up his shop and murder his wife and family.

It was a compound of parish pump politics, fights, thefts in an out of brothels, entertainments and trotting matches, but somehow Sheerness took shape and grew up. The dockyard church was burnt down in 1882, with the loss of two lives, but it was rebuilt and in use again by 1900.

In 1897 there was a great flood; the island was used to floods, there had been a bad snow storm in 1881 and several very hard winters, but this one was exceptional. Acres of land were flooded, crops ruined, and people and cattle drowned. The sea wall gave way at Westminster, streets in Sheerness were under water, and the pier was washed away. Actually, the pier was already in a bad state of repair before the flood, and there had been many arguments about repairing it. The town mopped up, dried out, sea walls were repaired, and the pier was rebuilt and opened again in 1900. The Conservative Club was built and opened that year, and has stayed open ever since, some might say with very little alteration until recently, when it was redesigned and considerably brightened up.

One of the results of the new railway station was an increase in summer visitors. Usually family parties, or people looking for a quiet and cheap seaside holiday, they provided a new and welcome source of income.

By the end of the century Sheerness had an Urban District Council of its own, water, drains, many thriving businesses and shops, a town crier to ring his bell and warn people to open their windows as the big guns were going to fire, a new class of professional residents, a bandstand, a music hall, a pavilion for entertainments, the yearly regatta, a first-class livery stables in Royal Road, and could be said to be doing quite nicely, thank you. On the debit side, the little wooden houses of Blue Town and Mile Town in their courts and alleys were still there, housing the poorest of the townspeople. There were far too many public houses, and heavy drinking was a problem, as it was in many places in that era. Visitors came to Sheerness, but few of them ventured into the alleys, pubs and brothels of Blue Town. The Forces were a mixed blessing, bringing trade to the town, but also bringing fights and commotions at times. The flood had affected Naval plans adversely, because the new building once considered for the Navy was vetoed, and the new barracks were built at Brompton.

The dockyard was attracting local labour by now, and many boys worked at school with the idea of passing the entrance examination for the dockyard, and perhaps getting an apprenticeship there. The pay was not marvellous, but it was regular, and there was a job for life with a pension at the end. At that time, Sheerness looked like a town with a future.

Queenborough was slowly recovering from its many troubles, and had left behind the lean days of the 1830's, when the beadle's salary was reduced because the parish was so poor. The oyster grounds had never recovered from the mismanagement of earlier years, but fishing had become more lucrative, and there were stories of fishermen earning £49 a week from whitebait.

The copperas factory quietly bowed out in the middle of the century, but the glue and chemical works soon replaced it. This was owned and run by Josiah Hall, who was mayor for some years and genuinely concerned about the town's welfare. He would speak proudly of the times when Nelson had visited the borough, and insisted that there were documents with Nelson's signature among the town's records.

Nelson rented a house in Queenborough opposite the church, and Lady Hamilton stayed in the house next to the churchyard, now called Church House. They attended services in Queenborough Church, so the story tells. The Georgian house opposite the church is still known as Nelson's house, and naturally there is reputed to be a tunnel under the road connecting the two houses. This is hardly likely, as Nelson was not the sort of man to bother with subterfuge.

The glue works was liable to fires in its early days, and presumably the inhabitants grew accustomed to the smell, but any employment was better than abject poverty.

Another industry starting was Castle's cement works at Queenborough Creek, which continued in business until 1912. Alf Castle also ran a fleet of barges, and fetched the flint and chalk to build the railway embankment at Queenborough. The railway brought prosperity to Queenborough in various ways. In the 1861 census it was noted that there were two hundred railway labourers billeted there, which meant an increase in local trade, and extra money for those willing to take lodgers.

Another bonus the railway brought was the Flushing boat trade. The ships to and from Flushing put in to Queenborough pier, where the passengers went on board, or came ashore as the case might be, and were conveyed to Queenborough station. It was a popular service, and widely used, with, so it is claimed, royalty amongst the passengers. There was a temporary interruption in the service in 1875, but it was soon running smoothly again. The pier was burnt down in 1882, with the loss of two lives. This put the pier out of action for a time, but it was rebuilt, and apart from a hitch in 1897 the Flushing boat service ran until 1914, when the first world war brought it to an end.

There was a neat row of brick-built cottages by the pier, called Pier Cottages, comfortable little dwellings. In 1857 Queenborough had the horror and excitement of a murder, when a woman named Eliza Coppins was murdered near the Guildhall by a man called Prentis, and this was alleged to be a crime of passion.

In 1883 George Banks was drowned while he was out shooting in the marshes, his punt overturned, but there were some odd stories about that which were repeated for many years. In fact, if local stories are anything to go by, many queer things happened on the marshes — they were a great place for levelling old scores.

So in various ways Queenborough attracted industry, and the town hauled itself above the poverty line. A National school was built, and the children had to attend school whether they wanted to or not.

Queenborough Railway Station was built on ground that had once belonged to the castle, and the castle well was re-opened by the Railway Company to provide water for the engines.

Like all the other island churches the church at Queenborough was not in a state of good repair, and the vicar, the Reverend Palmer, appealed for funds for the work of restoration.

The work that needed doing was described as an absolute necessity, i.e. the repairing of the church, the restoration of the fabric, the rehanging of the bells and re-casting the broken tenor bell.

This started in May 1884, and during the year the vicar was offered another living, and replaced by the Reverend William Bartlett. There was some delay, but in August 1885 the work had commenced, the *Sheppey Church Magazine* announced. The gallery and pews put there by a former M.P. for the borough in 1721, were removed, and the church was repaired, replastered, and new pews built.

Parts of a carved wooden screen were found beneath the old floor, and there were traces of former 'illuminations' under the whitewash on the walls. The vicar was busily employed collecting more money in order to restore the tower, and the church was closed. Services were held in the large room of the town hall.

Queenborough had lost the right to send two M.P.s to Parliament in 1832, when the Great Reform Bill was passed, which had added to the town's troubles at the time. However, when the west gallery in the church which one of this departed race of M.P.s had dreamed up, was removed, it was found that both sides of the nave had once been painted in sepia tints, to represent a series of semicircular arches resting on fluted pillars. This was presumed to have been done in Elizabeth I's time. In the chancel the coloured 'illuminations' could not be preserved.

The most curious story was that of the eggs. When some loose stones were removed from the south wall of the nave four hens' eggs were found in a cavity in the wall, twelve feet above ground and surrounded by masonry. The explanation for this, and it was pure conjecture, was that when the tower subsided and tipped sideways in 1630 a fissure appeared in the south wall of the nave where it joined the spiral stairway of the tower. Two strong buttresses were set against the western face of the tower to secure it, and the crack was filled with masonry. This work took some time, and while the fissure was still open a hen must have started a nest among the loose stones, and the workmen did not notice the eggs and so built the wall with the eggs inside. Two of the eggs were broken, the contents had shrunk and solidified, but they had retained their 'bad eggs' smell. One of the remaining eggs was kept by the mayor, the other by the vicar. The shells were rough, and had become 'smoky coloured' during two centuries in the wall. It was found that further repairs were necessary to the tower, and although the church was in use by Christmas 1885, the formal reopening did not take place until the following spring.

Queenborough Church is a delightful little church, it looks very old, the tower is well buttressed and the body of the church looks very low, but it does not appear very low ceilinged inside. The coat of arms is Queen Anne's and the stone font is engraved with a picture of Queenborough Castle. There is a great deal of history hidden in Queenborough, and until the town chooses to reveal it no-one can really do the subject justice.

The borough was granted a new charter in 1885, as the old charter granted by Charles I and renewed by Charles II expired in that year. It retained the right to elect a mayor and councillors, and entered the twentieth century in a happier state than the town had known for many years.

There was a strange story told to a District nurse in 1950. Apparently at some time earlier in this century there were things described as 'arrows' sticking out of the wall of the church tower. The vicar was very proud of them, saying that they had been shot from a bow, and embedded in the wall many years ago. The townspeople listened politely, if a trifle unbelievingly.

One evening, two young lads full of mischief scrambled up somehow and pulled these 'arrows' out, taking them home in triumph. Their mothers were appalled, and, frightened of the vicar's wrath, they confiscated the 'arrows' and threw them down the outside privy, which apparently was of the deep pit variety. They cuffed their sons and swore them to secrecy, and when the vicar went round looking for his missing 'arrows', no-one knew anything about them. 'It was the only way' the now elderly mother explained. It would be interesting to know just what was at the bottom of this weird tale.

Sheerness was settling down as a dockyard town and Queenborough was starting a new phase as an industrial town; only Minster seemed to be lagging behind in this forward movement, for farming was at a low ebb, and the village had lost its place of importance on the island.

CHAPTER XXIII

The old order changeth

Not only Minster, but all the Sheppey farms were feeling the effect of the farming depression, and it was no exaggeration to say that the workhouse did loom large, rather like a bogey-man, in the lives of the farm workers. The weekly reports in the papers were not very reassuring to people who knew they might end there, nothing was omitted and some of the reports of meetings must have sounded ominous.

At the Guardians meeting in 1875 there were requests for more and larger schools on the island, which was a good sign. From that point the discussion became trivial. It was suggested that the Union girls should wear hats instead of bonnets, the bonnets were horrible. The committee all agreed, and hats were decided upon. Then someone recollected that bonnets had been ordered this time, and Matron had bonnets in store that must be used up, so the hats were dismissed; back to bonnets! This was followed by a heated argument about the width of the workhouse stairs, because someone had complained that they were not wide enough for coffins. An even grimmer note was struck with the memo. 'No Coffins!' Not reassuring, to very poor villagers.

The Union was continually 'falling down' and being rebuilt, and having extra buildings added. After one such addition, it was reported that 'the old men with bald heads' were complaining of the draughts from the new ventilation. Eventually these ventilators had to be blocked with paper.

A more serious meeting was the one about the school-mistress, who had been found out sending the boys for her beer and spirits, and beating the girls and shutting them up for a day or more in solitary confinement in the punishment cells. The Guardians were furious, and the schoolmarm was sent packing. The Master of the Union was severely reprimanded for not being aware of the situation, for beating the girls was not allowed; it was strictly against the rules. This may come as a surprise, for most people imagine cruel treatment was the norm, whereas in fact it was discouraged and prevented. Infections were common, and frequently it was announced that the girls were all in the infectious ward with 'the itch'. There were serious diseases, too, and in 1893 Helena Winter died. Her tombstone is inscribed 'Late Nurse of Sheppey Workhouse Infirmary'. The story has been handed down that she died from an infection caught while nursing a seriously ill patient. It has also been suggested that she is the 'Grey Lady' who is sometimes seen on the wards at night. Not surprisingly, for it is very old, the hospital has its full quota of ghosts.

There were more lighthearted moments. The granddaughter of one of the Guardians told this story, and swore it was true. Her grandfather was a farmer, a butcher, and on the Board of Guardians. He was driving his pony and trap up Minster Hill one day when he noticed two old ladies from the Union up the hill ahead of him. There was a strong north-east wind blowing, it blew their long skirts up over their heads and he was embarrassed to see that they had nothing on underneath. At the next meeting, 'and he had to put it very delicately, mind, because there was ladies there', he said that he had noticed, due to the strong wind, that some of the inmates were not very warmly clothed. He thought the old women ought to have some...er... underthings, it was too cold for them out in these bitter winds. The result was told triumphantly. 'After that every old woman was allowed two yards of calico (unbleached) to make two pairs of drawers with!' Not the height of comfort, but a definite improvement, and it could well be true.

In 1894 the farmers of Eastchurch, Leysdown, Warden and Harty called a meeting and voted to start a branch of the National Agricultural Union, to try to find a solution to the depression. Officers were elected, and a large number of farm-workers joined. The records are sparse, but all the names are recorded, and the chief industry of the area is given as farming and corn growing. A branch was started at Minster at the same time, and again the chief industry was given as farming and corn growing. Mr. Alfred Coultrip of Norwood Farm was secretary to both branches. In May a discussion on 'State aid Pensions' was held by the Eastchurch branch, and the secretary read a petition, which was 'carried unanimously'.

The petition, composed and written by Mr. Coultrip, was a plea to the Government for Old Age pensions for farm labourers, and it was years ahead of its time. The following extracts are included here to illustrate the plight of the farm-workers at the time, and the concern of the farmers, who were not wealthy themselves. The petition starts with the hope that the N.A.U. will survive and flourish, and the writer continued by saying that if he did not support some reasonable scheme like this (the pension) he should say with the greatest of sorrow, that he deserved to die. The largest part of the organisation consisted of farm-workers, and 'I believe there is no-one in the other classes from this great Association, who does not feel very great sorrow for the large number of worthy, honest, hardworking agricultural labourers of England, who, under the present circumstances, are unfortunately almost doomed to end their days in the Workhouse'.

He describes the degradation and the misery which darkens their old age, and the plight of old farm-workers, 'Labourers getting older and older, day by day, and many of us have watched their stepps gett more shorter and their backs gett more bowed and they are able to do less and less work'. He admitted that farmers 'made work' for the old workers when they could, to keep them from the workhouse. He did not add that financially no-one could keep this up indefinitely. It appeared that some Friendly Societies had been known to let men down, and leave them with no alternative but the workhouse. He expanded the theme of a State pension, certain that England would honour such a contract, and that the men would not be afraid to save their money if the agreement was made with the State. The petition continued with criticism of the Poor Law, which many people thought was 'unsound' and finished, by giving reasons for a State pension and reasons why the N.A.U. should support the petition. Of course, the N.A.U. supported the petition, but nothing came of it, and the N.A.U. did not survive for very long. It was a great effort by a very far-seeing man, and it is unfortunately the case that when the island lists past heroes and notables the men of Alfred Coultrip's honest and unassuming worth are usually forgotten. For all his efforts and compassion, the workhouse remained the farm labourer's bogey-man for many years.

There are farm accounts and wage sheets, showing the average wage of the time, less than three shillings a day. There were 'boys watching sheep on the grattens', the old Kentish word for stubbles after harvest. Nowadays the stubble is burnt, no-one watches sheep there. In the in-between times the waggoner and his mate fetched shingle from the beach, probably for the roads, and did 'barge work' — a queer thing for the waggoner to do, but it referred to the barges that came up Windmill Creek loaded with dung from the livery stables and the zoo in London. This was unloaded at one of the farm quays, to be used on the fields, and the barges went back to London loaded with hay.

Windmill Creek was no longer an important inland water way for the transport of goods, the trains had altered that, but the barge traffic continued well into this century.

There was a list of farms entitled the 'Isle of Sheppey from 1875 to 1902', and there is hardly any difference from the list given by the parish clerk in 1745. Stone Pit was spelt Stone Petts, as it was pronounced, and it had been called Stane Pett in 1300. Church Farm at Leysdown was given an alternative name, Paradise Farm, by which it is known now. There is a fleet called Paradise Fleet nearby. Little Groves was also known as Pump Farm; it was lucky, there was a pump there. Now it is a holiday camp. Garretts Farm, still there on the hill just past the 'Plough' inn, was also known as Louse Hall, and no-one has ever come up with a reason for this off-putting name. Foxenden Farm is still there, up at Warden, but has since gone to sea, as have Spiders Castle and Cliff Farm. They would not know, these worried farmers, that many of the farms they were fighting for would soon be gone, and the sea would not be the only robber, all that would be left would be names and memories.

The Parish Council took over from the Vestry in 1894, with a Rural District Council to refer to. The Parish Council produced little to start with, apart from refusing to adopt the street lighting bill, because it was too expensive, but in 1898 a company formed to promote a railway for the island, and that really gave them something to argue about.

Most people welcomed the idea of a train service, as the residents 'up the Island' had no means of getting to any other part except by walking, unless they owned a pony. There were carriers' carts to Sheerness from Eastchurch and Minster, but the journey was a slow one. Transport would be welcome. The bone of contention in council was the proposed route. No-one wanted it to cross their land, or to give up any ground. Compensation, fencing, route, all were fiercely debated, but permission for the line was officially given, and so affairs had to be settled. The line was built, and the Sheppey Light Railway was opened in August 1901.

The Sheppey Light linked with the main line trains at Queenborough station. At Queenborough passengers from the Sheppey Light could catch the London train, and here they left the London train on their return journey. The bay the little train used can still be seen at Queenborough station. Queenborough was a busy station then, for until 1914 the trains from Queenborough pier started and ended their journey there. From Queenborough the island train went across the marshes to Sheerness East, where the power station is now, on to East Minster, which was beside the present Centra Market shop in Minster Road, then to Minster Station which is completely gone but the station was down Scocles Road, almost opposite the turning into Harps estate; thence to Eastchurch, and the line ended at Leysdown very near the beach. A well was sunk there for water for the engines. Two halts were added later, one at Brambledown and one at Harty Road. The station at Minster caused much heart-searching. A road had to be made down Jointer's Hill, good farm land, to reach it. It was called Station Road, and is

Scocles Road today. It was continued past Minster Station to meet Stickfast Lane and the road that ran to the Lower Road.

Brambledown was little more than a farm or two, and some cottages. Other cottages appeared later in the century, odd places built of corrugated iron, or asbestos sheeting. Many were built in Poore's Lane, which leads to Poore's Farm, and a bridle-way out to the creek. It is now renamed Elmley Road. Locally it once had a far more descriptive name, which it would be unfair to the residents of today to repeat.

The train consisted of two, sometimes three, carriages drawn by a small engine called 'Little Tich'. In the early days a steam rail motor-car was used, but later the engine and carriages took over. Later 'Little Tich' was replaced by a tank engine and two coaches. There was also a goods train daily, which was used for transporting cattle and horses, as well as parcels and other merchandise. The line was built with minimum disturbance to the ground; there were no bridges and no cuttings.

There were many level-crossing gates, and on less frequented roads cattle guards were put down, and speed had to be reduced to ten miles an hour for three hundred yards approaching such crossings. As the maximum speed allowed was twenty-five miles an hour, it was a leisurely journey.

The train was staffed by a driver and guard. The guard issued the tickets on the train, and apart from the gates at stations, he had to work the level-crossing gates. The driver stopped the train before reaching a crossing, the guard would get down and shut the gates, and the train would chug slowly across, and stop again. The guard then reopened the gates, climbed back on the train, and away they would go again.

The first stations were built of railway sleepers, which was considered to be very economical. Later they were replaced by corrugated iron buildings, with a waiting-room which contained a stove for use in cold weather. The duty man at the station had an office, and, it was stated proudly, lavatory accommodation. The telephone was in the office, for the line was run by telephone communication. Once the 'line clear' signal was phoned through the station-master would lower the signal and close the crossing gates. It all worked very well, and the train ride was an enjoyable one.

There are many tales about the old Sheppey Light. Old ladies would arrive at Minster Station as the train was leaving, and storm across the field, umbrellas waving and shopping bags jolting. The driver would stop and the guard would get down and hoist the late-comers up, and one especially was no mean size, saying cheerfully 'Up you go, Ma!' Accidents were infrequent. A man was killed, walking in front of the train on a crossing with no gates. The District nurse drove cheerfully across, her mind far away as usual, and the engine caught the back end of her car. Everyone was speechless, except the nurse, who climbed out of the car and said 'Thanks be, no great harm done and it could have been worse!' Her passenger was shivering in a state of shock. Nothing ruffled the District nurse. She arrived in 1933, the first proper nurse Minster had ever had, she had more qualifications than most nurses dream about, but she chose to be a District nurse and she set the village to rights. Her transport was a sit-up-and-beg bike — the car came much later — and she cycled miles, at all hours of the day and night. She told someone once: 'When I first came to the village, their idea of getting ready for a confinement was a roll of cotton wool and a bottle of lysol — we have better methods now'. She worked right through the war, unselfishly and unfailingly, until illness stopped her in 1946. After that she only lived a few more years. The village loved her, the doctors respected and admired her, and she had a close liaison with the local maternity ward. She is another example of an unsung hero, but it was her sort that the village depended on.

With the advent of the train the villages were opened up. It became possible to go visiting in the next village, or shopping in Sheerness. It made a great difference to everyone's life, and the little train was soon regarded with affection.

The railroad from London had brought something else to the island, the land companies. In 1896 the despoliation started, when Abbey Farm was bought by a company from London, and then offered as building land. The Abbey Gate House, with three acres of land, was put up for sale for £2300, but no-one wanted it. An attempt was made to sell it to the vicar for use as a parsonage, but he was not playing. Later it was sold without the three acres for £1000 and continued to be used as a dwelling-house until 1922. The vicar later bought some of the ground and had the present vicarage built; it was completed in 1924.

Whybournes Farm and Upper and Lower Wards Farms followed the Abbey Farm. In each case the procedure was the same; the house plus two or three acres was sold, and the land offered for building. There is a local story about the Wards Farms. The two farms were divided by a fence that went through the middle of the pond, allowing half the pond to each farm. The tale was that once it was one farm, but two brothers had quarrelled violently over a girl, and then split the farm in half, building another farmhouse and buildings. Of course, no-one knew who they were!

In 1760 it was known simply as Wards, and probably had no more than one or two cottages. By 1840 the Nettlefold family in London had acquired it, with other land in Minster. In the tithe records one farm belonged to William Nettlefold and the other to Edward Nettlefold, so probably the farm was divided for reasons of inheritance.

In the church register, there is a baptism entry for Robinson of New Wards, but which farm was New Wards there is no way of knowing.

Upper Wards was a pleasant red-brick house, and inside it seemed a maze of small rooms. After the second war it was sold to developers, and there is now a housing estate where barns, paddocks and orchards were. Even part of the pond is filled in and built on.

Lower Wards has seen better days, but is still there, just. It is a tall Georgian house that was renovated in 1937. Before that it had no plumbing or sanitation, one water tap in the kitchen, stone-flagged kitchen floors and unplastered brick walls, and a bread oven over the broken-down range in one of the kitchens. There is some evidence of previous alterations, and it is thought to have started life as a small cottage. There is a big cellar beneath the kitchen, and next to the cellar is an underground water tank, a big place a man can stand up in and walk around, as large as the cellar. The surface water drained into this tank, and was pumped up as wanted. There was once a pump outside the back door, and a wash house, complete with sink and copper, opposite. Drinking water had to be fetched from the Union well, as some of the older local people can remember from their mothers' stories. The farm has been used as a riding school for many years.

When the land was scheduled for building, elaborate maps were made showing the layout of the streets on the cliffs and on Breackneck, now called the Glen. Curb stones were laid as guide-lines for roads and pavements, and children tripped over them for years, for the land did not sell, and acres of farm land lay empty and unused.

Land sales were held, notices were published in London offering a free train ticket and champagne lunch, and train loads of Londoners came for a free day out. Some bought land, at £5 a plot, and then forgot all about it when the champagne had worn off. Others registered it before they forgot it, but not many built on it. It was a terrible thing, really, but there was no money in farming at the time, and the landowners were not island people, and did not care about the land.

In 1903 and 1904, the Garrison had two murders to its credit. In each case a corporal was shot by a soldier, who afterwards committed suicide. Doubtless the Army officers had many questions to ask at the time.

Also in 1903, the first electric trams ran from the pier at Sheerness to Cheyney Rock and Sheerness East. They were not able to extend the line, as they could not cross the railway lines at Sheerness East. They were primarily for the dockyard men, but never achieved a great deal of success, and closed down in 1917.

Knocking-off time in the yards is something never to be forgotten. Whistles and hooters blew, the big gates flew open and crowds of men literally shot out, some on bikes, some walking, and later, some to catch one of the fleet of buses waiting. At mid-day everyone kept out of their road, they had to move fast for they only had an hour for dinner.

Nineteen hundred and nine saw the start of flying on the island, and Mr. J. T. C. Moore-Brabazon, later Lord Brabazon, made the first circular mile flight in Great Britain at Leysdown, in a British plane, winning £1000 for his daring.

There was a flying ground at Leysdown, and Mussel Manor was used as a club for the airmen. Later Stone Pit Farm at Eastchurch was taken by the fliers, the Short brothers had a factory there for making aeroplanes, and later the aerodrome developed. One of the first casualties recorded was of a 'blue jacket' who was killed by a propeller in 1912. During the First World War planes were worked on here, and young men came to learn to fly; Winston Churchill was one of them. At that time the Royal Air Force was part of the Navy, the Royal Naval Air Service. Later it became the Royal Flying Corps.

The church magazines of those war years record the deaths of young airmen 'due to their machines falling', and one pioneer, the Honourable Charles Rolls, is commemorated by a stained glass window in Eastchurch Church. There is also a large stone memorial to the airmen opposite the church, at the top of the road which once led down to the aerodrome.

Shortly before the first war the coastguard cottages at Shellness were empty, unused and becoming derelict. There was a land company at work in Leysdown, the cottages were offered for sale, and bought by one of the sons of the swimming family, who had had so much to do with Sheerness Regatta. He was married and had a son himself by now, and thought he might make some sort of holiday home there.

The war in 1914 turned everything upside down. Sheppey became security-conscious, and also developed spy mania. There are stories of German shopkeepers having their windows broken by stones, and their lives made unbearable. Anyone who owned a boat, or lived near the sea front and showed a light at night, was instantly suspect. A pass was necessary to cross the Ferry Bridge, and another was necessary to enter Sheerness. The canal outside Sheerness, locally known as 'Klondyke bridge', was the entrance point from Minster.

The swimmers ran into trouble when Father innocently lent his pass to a friend of the son's. The friend's wife had been ill, and the idea was to get her to Shellness for a change of air. Sheerness took the incident seriously despite knowing the family well, and Father was fined heavily for his misdemeanour. He was not pleased, and said he would never go to Sheerness again, and he meant it.

The island was very vulnerable. It had a dockyard, a garrison, and an aerodrome. Soldiers were billeted everywhere, at Minster, at Shurland Hall, at Leysdown and Shellness. It is noticeable in the old parish magazines how often the officers officiated at prize givings and sports days, and often provided a band for 'Treats'.

This had started in the last years of the previous century,

when Army and Naval officers frequently attended events at Minster. Formerly they had only been prominent in Sheerness. One of the Army officers mentioned as coming to Minster School was Colonel Le Mesurier. Many older people are convinced that he was an ancestor or relative of John Le Mesurier, the actor so popular in the television series, 'Dad's Army', and that is a story that cannot be either confirmed or denied.

All the empty land was taken into cultivation, for farming was suddenly vitally important again, the farmers, and everyone else, were being exhorted to grow more food. Many young men left the island never to return, and despite the high-flown rhetoric of the condolences to the bereaved families, now it all seems rather hypocritical and a shocking waste of young life.

In 1917 Sheerness suffered a daylight raid by German aircraft, and seventeen people were killed. The island was shocked and frightened. The people had not had an easy time during the war. In 1914, in November, H.M.S. *Bulwark* had blown up in Sheerness harbour, with a loss of six hundred lives. In May 1915 H.M.S. *Irene* had blown up, with the loss of all her crew except one man, and seventy-six dockyard employees. This tragedy was remembered for many years.

There was a second air raid, in 1917, this time by moonlight, and four people were killed in Invicta Road. After this there was some reluctance to run trains at night, in case German aircraft were about and used the trains as direction finders. People were also advised to show as little light as possible.

The end of the war brought a sense of relief, the island started the clean up, and to remove the barbed wire from the beaches. A young lady from a local concert party, 'Topsy' Raymond, wrote a small book entitled 'Barbed Wire Island', about Sheppey during the first war, but it is doubtful if any copies remain.

During the war, in 1916, the vicar was ordered to remove the ivy that was growing all over Minster Abbey. He was not very happy about this, since he was fond of it, and thought it must be 'of four or five hundred years growth'. When the ivy was stripped from the chancel buttress, it was so deeply rooted that the stone had to be removed, this stone was found to be carved on the inner side, and 'the stone is carved in two portions, the upper forms a complete square and in it is a beautifully carved wreath and looped on it so that the other portion is spread out to fill the corners. In the centre is a slightly carved boy's head. The larger portion of the stone is oblong, and has on it a damsel draped in a long flowing garment with full sleeves and one hand raised holding in it the three nails that would be used at the Crucifixion. Her face is most mournful. . . .' Another stone was found to be carved, and on it was a man's head that had been cut way to make this stone fit into the buttress. At the foot of that they found a figure 'broken in two, showing only the upper portion of a boy holding seemingly on his head a brazier with much flame proceeding from it'. Whatever they found, it was never followed up, and leaves one wondering just how many stones are carved, and what with. On the outside of the north wall of the abbey there are several gargoyles and a carved angel to be seen, also the remains of Saxon arches.

In 1904 a new lifting span bridge replaced the old Ferry bridge, it was the newest model available, and thought to be a great improvement. Just before the war started, in 1913, the first bus arrived in Sheerness, and the town was startled by the first double decker. It was a solid tyred 'boneshaker', and it needed an army of mechanics, carpenters and upholsterers to keep it in condition. Arthur Standen from Sittingbourne was the proprietor of the new venture, and before the year was out he had six buses on the road. If it could be called a road. It was made of hard-packed earth, it was sprinkled with water in the summer to lay the dust, and became a mud track in the winter.

Till then the train and the trams, backed up by horse-drawn cabs, had had things all their own way, and a feud between the tram company and the buses was inevitable. The trams, belonging to the Electric Traction Company, were joined by two Daimler buses, and the fight was on. Every trick was tried to attract passengers, and the heckling and arguments in Sheerness High Street led to more than one booking for obstruction. It was not unknown for starting handles to be stolen, but once under way the bus would bounce over the unmade roads with passengers hanging on for dear life. There were no official stops, and people would flag the bus driver who would stop and cram his bus as full as he dared, for a penny a trip. People living up the island found the bus service cheaper, and they ran more frequently than the Sheppey Light Railway. Driving at night was hazardous, the streets were unlit and the bus lamps were oil or carbide lamps, and not very bright. The feud stopped when the rival firms started operating on a fifty-fifty basis; other firms tried to cut in but as the various companies kept undercutting each other the services could not pay their way, and the newcomers gave up. The Traction Company and Arthur Standen's company finally merged, and Sheppey Motor Transport Company was established. Mr. Standen ordered the removal of the tramlines and the work was done by German prisoners of war in 1917.

Buses for Minster would drive up the hill past the 'Prince of Waterloo', then reverse down and swing round to face downhill for the return journey. Buses for Eastchurch would creep up Minster Hill and sway round Back Lane and up into Chapel Street. When the first diesel buses, double deckers with open tops, arrived on the island, many people were afraid to go up Minster Hill in them.

In 1923 another rival company appeared, the Enterprise, owned and controlled by Bob Grimer. Another and better feud started at once, to the delight of the passengers who were rejoicing in cheap fares and a choice of buses. In 1926 Arthur Standen sold out to the Maidstone & District Bus Company, and left them to cope with the Enterprise. For Arthur, the heckling, the attracting passengers, the getting from point A to point B in the least time at the least possible cost was over. In 1931 the Maidstone & District took over the Enterprise, and all the fighting stopped. Fares were cheaper then, threepence from Minster to Sheerness, and the buses ran very frequently. There was a 'last bus' at midnight on Saturdays and Sundays, as there were always plenty of passengers from the R.A.F. at Eastchurch.

After the war, the island returned to work. The dockyard was now recognised as the chief industry. The Technical School for Boys had been built in 1910, and boys from primary schools all over the island had the chance of attending there if they could pass the entrance examination, instead of leaving school at fourteen. There were also scholarships to the grammar schools at Sittingbourne for boys and girls.

The 'Tech' had high standards and produced some notable scholars, among them Sir William Penney of atom bomb fame. The regatta never regained its pre-war eminence, but 'The Pictures' were becoming popular and the Hippodrome became a picture house.

Before the war, the Conservative Club and the Victoria Club had been noted for their children's parties. The children were given a wonderful afternoon out, usually on Pye Marshes, a stupendous tea, and then marched home in the dusk carrying lanterns on sticks, often with a band to accompany them. The town would turn out to watch the procession. These parties recommenced after the war, and many people can remember them.

Queenborough was still attracting industry, and was soon to boast an iron foundry, the bottle works, and Pilkington's glass factory, as well as the 'Glue Works'. The glass factory was started by a Belgian firm, and twenty-four houses were built near the glass works for the workers. When the factory changed hands, the houses continued to be used, and a community on its own developed there.

The cement factory had finished in 1912, and the remainder of its stock had been used by the Army to build the roads on the island, for the earth and shingle roads had proved quite unsuitable for Army vehicles.

The war had seen the end of the old Court Tree. This originally stood on a green in front of Kingsborough Farm, and the road from Chequers ended there. A rough track ran across Norwood Farm to the Lower Road. When the councils came into being, and the highways were in process of being sorted out, the road from Chequers to the Lower Road was taken from Norwood Farm and run through the green in front of Kingborough, leaving the Court Tree in the hedge on the Norwood side of the road. Here it stood for some time, old and hollow, and children would play in it. One boy was told that it was the Court Tree, and could not understand why it had this name. He thought for a long time that it was where people used to go courting. In 1915 it fell down, it was thought as a result of the vibration from the Army lorries. A young tree has been carefully grown at Kingsborough in memory of it.

The swimming family returned, this time to Shellness. There was nothing at Shellness but the coastguard cottages, two Army huts, and a large cart lodge where the cart horses that pulled the shell carts were stabled. It was a wonderful place, sea, sky, and beaches of sand and little shells. Water was fetched from the pump behind the cottages, and everyone camped in the huts. Grandma had a cottage, she was fetched from Leysdown Station in a shell cart, sitting in state on a kitchen chair. It was a mile walk to Leysdown for shopping, along the Mile Road. The long sandy beach between Shellness and Leysdown was called Shotton, it is now Shellness beach, complete with chalets and a place for 'Naturists'.

At that time there was an R.A.F. firing range at Shotton, and the beach was out of bounds when the red flag was flying. In the early 1930s two girls went out in a small boat when the flag was up, and were mistaken for the firing target. It caused a sensation locally, and made the daily papers.

In the early 1920s there was nothing at Leysdown but one or two farms, the pub — the 'Rose and Crown', a post office, a general store and very few bungalows. The land company up there had not sold much ground, either. There was some indecision about the development of Shellness, and part of the large family moved away to Minster. The owner developed Shellness as a quiet holiday place for relatives and friends, with a limited number of bungalows. The pump and the oil lamps were retained, it was not meant to become a popular seaside resort, simply a place for a complete change and rest by the sea. It was a wonderful place for children, and the tone of the hamlet was geared to families and children. Naturally there were clubs, a magazine, a yearly dinner and the usual suburban trimmings, but for children it was paradise. The magazine gave a vivid account of the storms and floods of 1928, with the sea frozen, and the flooded marshes all over the island. It was claimed to be as bad as the snow storms of 1881, and the time in 1895 when the Swale froze over, but it was not as devastating as the 1897 flood.

At Shellness the sea wall was almost destroyed, but no-one went crying to the council — the owner repaired it. He really cared for 'The Ness', and considered that it was his responsibility. No-one lived there in the winter, except the caretaker, it was not built for that, or suitable for it. It still is not. The locals regarded it with curiosity, struggling to obtain water and light themselves, they could not imagine

116

why anyone would pay to do without it. Stories spread that it was a nudist colony, or that there were 'carryings on' up there, but there was no truth in any of them. It was wholesome, clean, and fun, rather precious at times, but basically sound. It has changed hands since the war and looks rather pathetic now. There are still some of the original settlers there, but the place seems to need a coat of paint, it has lost its former joyousness. Water is still pumped from the well at the back of the coastguard cottages and there is no electricity, but that is not a real problem, and can be easily overcome. In days past Shelless had much less of a water problem than other places on the Island.

In 1903 a small portion of the Abbey Farm estate was sold for a water works site. One of the old abbey wells was used for a start, and Minster had water laid on. Eastchurch, Leysdown and Brambledown remained dependent on rainwater and the itinerant water cart for many years to come, until 1930 approximately. None of the farms had water laid on, many had wells or springs, and others had underground water tanks for the collection of surface water. Norwood Farm had, and still has, Choules spring. There were springs at Tadwell Farm, and in the 1920s one Brambledown boy used to earn a few pennies by driving to Tadwell in a donkey cart, to fetch drinking water.

The council discussed main water for 'up the island' many times, but could not seem to find a way to supply it. They were also worried by the land company in 1912–14 who were very keen for Minster to become an Urban District. The council would not give way to this, declaring that they were rural, and wanted to remain so. The war ended this argument.

In 1922 a ship struck the Ferry Bridge, and Sheppey was cut off for several weeks. People who had to travel were reduced to ferrying across the Swale, or going by train to Port Victoria on the Isle of Grain and then crossing to Sheerness by steamer. These accidents were not uncommon, and the same thing happened in 1936, when the island was isolated for a week. The island managed, it had doctors, nurses and the workhouse, and enough food for a short while, there was more produced locally than there is now.

An Act of Parliament in 1929 altered the method of workhouse administration, and Sheppey Union was gradually run down. The chapel that had been in the workhouse in 1892 had long since ceased to be used, and more recently the schools for the boys and girls had stopped. The Union children attended the village school, not always to the great joy of the village children. By 1938 the Union had been altered and re-opened as a hospital, Sheppey General Hospital. It was a training school for State registered nurses, with medical and surgical wards, and later, a small maternity ward, for local mothers who could not arrange to have their babies at home.

The island was delighted with this, journeys to the mainland for hospital treatment were difficult and expensive.

The Great Depression of the late 1920s and early 1930s hit Sheppey as much, or more, than the rest of Britain. The dockyard had work, but there was not much other work about. Sheerness had a dispirited air, the streets of residential houses looked shabby, and there had been very little improvement in living conditions. True, most of the houses now had gaslight, a water tap and a flush lavatory, but there were few with hot-water systems or bathrooms, and the 'houses of office' were still 'out the back'. There was not much

anyone could do with the little wooden huts, but the brick-built houses could have been improved, only no-one could afford it. Dockyard wages were not high.

The acres of land at Minster remained empty, and the local people continued to use it. Flocks of sheep and herds of cows wandered unchecked over the cliffs and around the village houses. Queens Road, one of the new roads that led from Union Road to the fields at the back of Windmill Hill, was frequently invaded by animals. The road was unmade, a muddy track with deep ruts where children used to paddle after rainstorms. Horses were grazed there, too. Not many people owned a car, several of the new doctors went round on bicycles when they first came to the island, but with all that free grazing and hay it was possible to keep a pony, and horse transport was still common on the island long after it had ceased in other areas. The land company disapproved, and occasionally there were notices in the local paper stating the penalties for allowing animals to stray, but no-one took any notice.

In 1926 Borstal Hall and the Abbey Gate House were put up for sale, together with the Beach Hotel and sundry pieces of land. The sale was held at Queens Hall, an old Army hut that stood where the Co-op shops and the new houses are in Queens Road now. Queens Hall was used as a small shop, and as a village hall for whist drives and parties. There were five bungalows and a house in Queens Road then, and nothing else.

Union Road had been built in, there were five houses opposite the new burial ground, a piece of ground that had once been part of Abbey Farm, and was only acquired by the vicar with some difficulty. The five houses are still there, and the burial ground is sadly overgrown, suggesting that the return of the sheep might be an advantage.

Borstal Hall was offered with twenty acres of ground. The last tenant had used the large, elegant dining-room as a kitchen, but the hall did have water laid on and 'a bathroom with bath'. Tenants had not been kind to Borstal Hall. Mr. Swift had rebuilt it, but the hall had been sold when he died, and the new owner let it as a farm. The tenant promptly cut down the large grove of trees, leaving the place denuded, with empty meadows. Very little of the ground offered was sold. The Beach Hotel, allegedly the scene of doubtful parties, was later burnt down, to be rebuilt and run as a hotel, later a holiday camp. It is still in use. Borstal Hall was either bought or retained by a gentleman involved in the land company, he moved into it and lived there until it was burnt down.

The Abbey Gate House was not sold. The last tenants had left in 1922, and then the owner had stripped the interior of lathe, plaster, and false partitions to reveal the original walls, ceilings and Tudor fireplaces. There were five rooms, and, at that time, a small walled garden.

The owner, who seemed to be stuck with it, made a gift of it to Dr. Randall Davidson, the Archbishop of Canterbury, who accepted it on the condition that he could transfer the gift to the people of Minster. Once that was settled the Parish Church Council of Minster made an appeal for £1000 for restoration. In this they were supported by the Kent Archaeological Society, who recorded that in 1929 the society had supported the appeal for funds for the repair of the Abbey Gate House and the president had sent a letter to the *Times*. It was a lovely idea, and the gate house was in dire need of rescue, but it seemed a forlorn hope at that time of depression.

CHAPTER XXIV

And gives way to the new

There was no work at Minster, farm work had gone with the farms, and agriculture was in the throes of a depression that continued to get worse with the years. Local men without regular work could, and did, turn their hands to all sorts of things. They fished, they poached, they did odd jobs when they could find them, and some of them went logging in the winter, going round Sheerness with logs in a horse and cart. This needed a certain amount of cheek and back-chat, and several childish little rhymes still endure from that time.

> Cheerio, shan't see you termorrer
> Donkey's dead, broke its head,
> Jumped right dro the collar!

Stupid, but it helped sell logs!

Holiday people came in the summer, not in droves, but a fair number. The island was a cheap holiday, many of them brought tents and camped out on the cliffs, and the island could be reached by bicycle, so saving fares. People discovered the sandy beach at Leysdown and picnicked there. A small fair sometimes visited there in the summer. Enterprising local lads would drive up there with a cart filled with fruit, and trade was brisk. There were, as they said, all sorts of dodges.

The island still had a language of its own then. The accent was not so heavy as in the south-west of England, but there was a distinct burr. The islanders habit of greeting each other with the one word 'Alright!' usually nonplussed strangers. The reply to this greeting was, quite simply, 'Alright'. It is still in use. They say a child from Sheppey can be picked out by the way he, or she, says 'whaaat?' when spoken to. People 'chogged' everything, to prop it up, stop it rattling, or wedge it. 'Put a chog in it' was a usual solution. Bad ground was 'stoggy', a cow 'pooked' when annoyed, and if it would not go on when driven it was 'progged'. If a thing was done well it was 'a tidy job'. Famous expressions, and there were many more. They are not often heard now.

The gate house presented a problem. A committee was formed, and the usual sales, fêtes and raffles were held, but this time things were more enterprising than usual, and for two years Minster held its own carnival, and the money rolled in for the gate house.

Under the supervision of an architect who understood old buildings, the big arch that led under the gate house was unbricked and the smaller one beside it. Other restoration work was carried out, and the vicar was able to write to *Archaeologia Cantiana* and tell them that the Abbey Gate House was officially opened by the Archbishop of Canterbury on November 4th, 1933, after its recent restoration. Over £1,000 had been raised over five years, and another £200 was wanted. There are still a few people left in Minster who can remember all that happening.

After the restoration, the gate house was used for meetings, bazaars, and other parish activities. People were shown round if they evinced an interest. During the war the fire watchers took the place over, and after the war orange juice and cod liver oil were dispensed from a downstairs room—once a porters room. A youth club was run there, but after a while the gate house was regarded as unsafe, and closed. In 1967 it was handed over to the local council, and remained closed.

In the 1970s the local history society started to raise money for its restoration and grants were obtained from official sources. This year, 1981, the Abbey Gate House was reopened to visitors, after much hard work by several local young men. The gate house is of very great age, and full of interest. In the large upstairs room where pilgrims once lodged the pilgrim 'marks' can be seen, carved on window sills, and the great stone fireplace. Unfortunately, present-day fire regulations have made it necessary to install another staircase, the old stone stairway being considered inadequate in case of fire, and this, with other modern alterations, rather spoils the overall effect. It is a really great job that the history society have done, for all that, and many people have visited the gate house and enjoyed seeing what it was really like in years gone by.

In 1929 an attempt was made privately to stop the continual fall of the cliffs. Acres were still going yearly, and the cliff path leading to the 'Royal Oak' had gone to sea taking a great slice of East End Farm's land with it. At that time it was still possible to walk to Warden along the cliffs, passing farm land and fields of corn along the way. That walk is now impossible, due to cliff falls and holiday camps.

The council had built groins at Scrapsgate, but there were no cliffs there, although the groins improved the beach. Scrapsgate was a favourite place for visitors, as it is easy to reach the beach there. Although it is frequently referred to over the centuries, the origin of the name Scrapsgate is obscure. The earliest references to this area describe it as Scrape Hope Marsh, so it evidently derives from that.

A man who was deeply concerned about the cliff falls studied the subject closely, and then bought land on the cliff edge at the end of Imperial Avenue, Minster. He hired a mechanical digger, and had the cliffs terraced, then groined the beach, and put a cement terrace at the foot of the cliffs, so that people could walk there. The village was curious and somewhat sceptical, but the scheme brought both work and diversion, so they went along with it. Flights of steps were erected to get down the cliffs, and a teashop built at the bottom. It was a successful idea, visitors flocked there. It was hard work, too, for everything, including water and means to heat it had to be carried down the cliffs at the beginning of the business.

The shop paid a little toward the initial outlay, and would have done better if it had had a reliable manager, but as it was the business deteriorated through bad management.

The cliffs stopped slipping and the experiment had proved this could be done, but no one in authority locally was interested, so the whole enterprise was allowed to go to waste, and the war finished all hope of further work. Last year work started to halt the fall of the cliffs; several houses were getting too near the edge for comfort or safety. Once again the cliffs are being terraced, and groins built, backed up by a large and ugly cement wall at the foot of the cliffs. Now the work will cost millions, and acres of land have been lost in the meantime. Perhaps it would have been cheaper to adopt and continue the original scheme in 1930.

The Kent County Council paid the Railway £50,000 as compensation for lifting the bridge toll in 1929. Anyone could now drive, walk or ride over the Ferry Bridge for free, and opinions were very divided about it. Some welcomed it, others felt that it was a bad move, as it would let undesirables onto the island. Certainly there were more visitors after the removal of the toll, and there was also a local saying that if the police were looking for a criminal they would find him hiding in Sheppey, as all the rogues congregated there. In actual fact, this view was rather exaggerated, and Sheppey was no worse for not having to pay to enter.

Whether the removal of the toll had any bearing on the next business to start in Sheppey is hard to say, but in early 1930s the first riding school started on the island. In spite of the local Jonah's gloomy forecasts that horses were finished, the school was a success, for there are always those who like a horse, in any century. The horses then were a mixed bag, for show ponies and hunters belonged to the well-to-do, and other people took what they could get. There was no such thing as 'an ordinary child's pony' as it is understood now, and many children bumped round Minster on a pony that had come out of a butcher's cart, or a United Dairy's reject or even an antique high-stepping hackney, that had seen better days. These children were as happy as kings, and would not have changed places with anyone. They liked their riding master, and they had all the space they wanted for riding. The riding school continued, with various changes of base, until the war. After the war it reopened, and is still going strong, which is quite a record, and bears out the boast the owner made as a young man 'when all the others are gone, I'll still be there!' and he is.

Towards the end of the 1930s the depression was easing, and things were improving generally. There were more visitors coming, and the islanders developed the summer trade. There was a fair at Sheerness, and a carnival during the summer season. Visitors came to Leysdown, and a few new bungalows were built there. Eastchurch benefited from the visitors who came from Leysdown and Shellness to shop, and also from the R.A.F. station, which had grown with the years and now had a sizeable barracks. Minster attracted more visitors, too, but not many of them wished to buy land, or build houses. The vast tracts of land stayed empty, and were used by the local people for grazing, riding and playing on.

The clock had been placed at the bottom of Edward Street, Sheerness (now renamed The Broadway) to mark King Edward VII's coronation. Now accepted as a fixture, it became the centre of many pictures of the town, with sailors, and soldiers, much in evidence. Sheerness was still a typical Victorian small naval and garrison town. The bandstand, and the pavilion with its summer concert parties, were still there, and there were picture houses and weekly dances. Many girls now went down to Sheerness and there was always entertainment and an escort to be had; and equally, many girls were not allowed down there, especially at night. They had to be content with village dances in the parish hall.

In the early 1930s the man who had terraced the cliffs became interested in the housing situation. The Sheerness houses were by now well behind the times, and he decided that it was high time the men in the dockyard had the chance of a decent house.

To this end he bought the thirty-five acres, a field that had once grown excellent corn but after the land carve-up had lain empty for years. This land was adjacent to the Scrapsgate Road, with Minster Broadway, new and not yet made up, on the other boundary. Here he built new houses costing £250 or £350, whichever type was preferred. Roads were laid first, unlike more recent developments, and the houses, with bathrooms, a hot-water system, and indoor sanitary arrangements, soon found buyers. The business did not earn any money, nor was it expected to. All it was asked to do was pay its way. It provided work, too, a large army of tradesmen and workmen moved in, and all had to be catered for. As the war drew nearer, business concerns were upset, and the building stopped. After the war, the remainder of the ground was bought by the council, and developed as a council estate, which it is now.

Work was still short on the island. The farmers were the worst off, and many farmhouses were sadly in need of repair, with buildings in the same condition. It was difficult to make a living by farming. One farmhouse had a bathroom installed, a bold move, as the occupants had no idea when they would be able to provide the bath with water. The grand plans for the development of Minster at the beginning of the century, which included a seven hundred foot long pier, had come to nothing. The village had hardly changed since the 1700s. It consisted of little wooden houses on each side of the narrow High Street. The pavements were cobbled. One or two of the houses had been converted into shops, and several had been demolished, following complaints about their bad condition. Two more had caught fire, and burnt down. The 'Highlander' and the 'Kings Arms', formerly built of wood and thatched, had been rebuilt in brick at the end of the nineteenth century. There was an old house on the corner of Back Lane that doubled as a sweet shop (it has been pulled down now, and the road widened) the slaughter house still stood on the waste opposite the corner of the churchyard, the forge was working as it always had, and the little houses in Chapel Street, some wood, some built of brick, huddled together closely.

New houses had been built at the end of Queens Road and the road had been extended to meet a new road that ran at right angles to it and went through the fields to join Chapel Street, and that, in time, made an easier and safer route for the buses. Queens Road was made up in the early 1930s, and Minster Broadway not long afterwards. No-one could see why, the Scrapsgate Road had always been good enough, so why waste money on the Broadway. Then someone had the bright idea that the council had made up the Broadway because they owned the White House, a restaurant on the sea front at the end of Scrapsgate Road, and they wanted a straight road through to it. There was once a small brickfield at that end of Scrapsgate Road, but it had gone by the end of the nineteenth century.

All the coastguard houses were put up for auction, unless, like the ones at Barrows Brook and Warden Point, they had gone to sea. The coastguard houses at East End were taken down, they were getting too near the cliff edge. At East End the officers school kept a pack of beagles kennelled, and the pups were a great attraction in the spring. So was the pussy willow that grew up there on the cliffs, and up Oak Lane to East End was a pleasant country walk, with tea at the 'Royal Oak' at the end of it. Now the 'Royal Oak' and the cliffs have all gone to sea, and Oak Lane is built up for the whole of its length.

The world seemed changeless to Sheppey, then the war came. After the first false alarm came an equally false quiet. Blackout went up, lights went out, everyone worked, farming came into its own again and all land was soon well in use. As usual, the island was a key position and troops moved in, bringing ack-ack batteries and barrage balloons. A boom was built round the harbour, and the menfolk disappeared into the services. The first winter was a cold and snowy one: Eastchurch and Harty were cut off and the troops stationed at Harty could get no supplies. Local men come to the rescue with horses and carts, digging the path through the snowdrifts so that the horses could get through. Strangely, the island was a reception area for evacuees at the beginning, then someone thought again and they were all moved, and many local children with them.

The Army requisitioned houses and families moved out, and often away, for the duration, especially if there was no man at home. In the latter part of the war Sheppey was in the front line, and was bombed, shelled, doodle-bugged (attacked by flying bombs) and generally shattered. There were many civilian deaths; it was no joy to stay home on the island — they certainly were not out of the war. After one of these bombing raids, Mr. Coultrip of Norwood found the wall round the fireplace was loose — he pulled it gently and the whole wall came away, revealing a rather beautiful Tudor fireplace. Two of these were uncovered after raids; they had been plastered over in an earlier century and small fireplaces put in.

After the war it was clearing-up time again, and then the changes came so fast that it was impossible to keep up with them. There was a disgusting winter in 1946–7, when everywhere was snowed up and frozen up for months, and at times Eastchurch, Harty and the top part of the island were completely cut off.

The first shock came in 1950, when the Sheppey Light Railway was closed. No amount of objections had been able to stop this closure, and on the last run there was a great crowd of passengers. A draped coffin was carried by men dressed as undertakers, but it was not funny — it was sad. It was thought that the closure was premature, for during the next ten years the caravan and chalet sites developed, and soon the island from Minster to Leysdown seemed a mass of caravans and chalets in the fields and on the cliffs. Often farmland was used, but the farmers were afraid of being caught in a recession again, as they had been after the first war. Of course there were many tales about the war, fortunes made from growing canary seed, smuggling, illicit slaughtering, and such like black market activities; there was a grain of truth in some of them, but nothing really widespread or sinister.

Then the houses came. Land was cheap in Sheppey, and young couples found it easier to buy a house there than nearer London. The developers and speculators had a wonderful time. Many of the houses slipped, or cracked, or did other odd things for the Sheppey ground is notoriously difficult to build on, and things thrown up in a hurry do not last here.

Suddenly everywhere was housing estates, for the council had been building too, and then it seemed there were almost no open spaces left. The local people were dismayed, they had been used to having the run of the cliffs and the Glen for so long that they could not imagine it would ever alter. No one had expected the building would ever come, but now it had. There had been all sorts of difficulties about the plots, too, ownership was hard to prove at times, and it was not unusual for two owners to claim the same ground. The council bought what was left of the Glen, and made it a public open space, filling in the stream that ran along the bottom and restricting horse riding. The roads were phased out, but the strange thing is that the roads were not part of the Glen land, they were, and are, privately owned. Many people have wondered about this.

In Sheerness, at last, the wooden houses, courts and alleys were demolished, and the occupants rehoused. The courts were a nightmare by now; still with outside privies and a stand pipe for water, they were flea and bug infested, and a sore trial to the District nurse. The houses in Marine Town were, for the main part, still lit by gaslight as late as 1952, and the residents still had no indoor lavatories, or bathrooms. They are sound terraced houses, and have nearly all been bought and modernised now, to make comfortable homes.

Nineteen fifty-three was the year of the flood. Sheppey was cut off from the mainland, and travellers had to come from Rochester by boat to Sheerness. At Sheerness the journey ended, for Minster and the upper part of the island were cut off from Sheerness by a large sheet of water, as the marshes were completely flooded. The marshes at Harty and Eastchurch were flooded too, Windmill Creek came over its banks to cover the farmland around it, and hundreds of sheep, cattle and horses were drowned. Many were saved, too, as foolhardy farmers and stockmen risked drowning to rescue their animals.

The people on the island were surprised and shocked, which seems a little ingenuous on their part when the history of flooding in Sheppey is considered. It took a long time to clean up and dry out, because many of the streets in Sheerness had been flooded, and people had of necessity been moved, or rescued, from water-logged houses. When it was all over there was a great deal of talk about better sea defences, but nothing was done in Sheerness. It was decided to fill in part of Windmill Creek, and dam it so that it was no longer a tidal waterway. To do this a cement dam was built at the creek's mouth, where it entered the Swale near Harty, and the end of the creek, behind Poor's Farm, was filled in by being used as a council rubbish tip, and then grassed over. This ended the creek's life as a waterway for shipping, and is now an inland stretch of water, much narrower than it was in earlier days, and a haven for water fowl.

The hospital had been inspected, and judged to be too small for modern training schemes for State registered nurses, so it was regraded as a training school for State enrolled nurses. Later this ceased, and the hospital was run by trained staff and auxiliaries. A new maternity unit was built to cope with the increasing population, and the midwives, always in short supply, worked all hours. Over the years wards have been closed, and the island has engaged in a running battle to keep the hospital open. On this point the people are completely united, cut off from the mainland too often, they need their hospital.

In 1960 the dockyard closed, and this seemed the end. The R.A.F. station had already gone, to be replaced by a prison, which created a great furore to start with. Now it is accepted with no comment. The Army was moved, and the dockyard and garrison were closed. Although many of the men were given jobs at Chatham Dockyard, school leavers who had been relying on the yard for an apprenticeship or a job found themselves on the dole. For the next few years the work situation was very bad for the young people.

Houses and holiday camps had increased in number, but fares were increasing too, and as many of the new islanders were commuters life began to get difficult for them. Some came to the island and liked it. Others came and hated it, and lived to get away again. The third group were perhaps the worst, the ones who came and wanted to alter it all, and make it just like Gillingham, or London, or Birmingham, or wherever they had come from.

There were many grumbles about unmade roads. Councils made sympathetic noises, but the local people's attitude was 'you knew it was unmade when you moved here, that's why you got it cheap'. The unmade roads had once been green rides, but builders lorries and delivery vans quickly churned them into a morass.

Abbott's laboratories were built at Queenborough, but in 1973 Pilkington's glass works closed, putting more people out of work. The workers who lived in the glass works houses were allowed to remain there, but the estate deteriorated, and the residents became apprehensive about the future. The vicar of Queenborough intervened on their behalf, and now new houses are being built for them in the area, after a great deal of argument and persuasion.

In 1971 British Rail made news when a train did not stop at Sheerness Station, but charged across the platform into the station forecourt, killing one woman and injuring seven other people. After that fiasco, the station was rebuilt and modernised.

A new Ferry Bridge was built in 1960, and opened by the Duchess of Kent. The old Ferry Road was straightened and remade, much to everyone's surprise. During these alterations the 'Lord Nelson', a public house on the mainland side of Swale, had to be demolished to make way for the road. It was an old house, and popular, and the demolition met with much opposition.

The roads on the island are much as they always were, narrow horse and cart roads, at present in bad condition. When the Army left, the firing range at Bartons Point was no longer needed, and the coast road was made up to provide another road from Sheerness to Minster. This made Wards Hill into a major road, and as it was only a narrow lane it was a danger to traffic and pedestrians, so it had to be widened, and lost all the hedges and trees in the process.

In 1968 building for the new comprehensive school was begun, and hoards of coins were dug up at Clark's Farm. In an inverted crock set on a tile, eighteen inches below the original ground level, were four hundred and fifteen coins, among them shillings dated from Edward the Sixth to Charles the First, and half-crowns dated Charles the First. The pot which contained them was of brown glazed china, and made in Kent. It is thought that the money was hidden in the time of the Commonwealth, as so much else was hidden from the Roundheads. In 1631 Clarke's Farm belonged to Sir Edward Hales, and the tenant was Mrs. Bateman, a widow.

In 1970 the three-tier system of schooling began in Sheppey, children no longer left the island for Grammar School, they all had to attend the new Comprehensive School. To everyones horror the Technical School was discarded, it was used for a further year as an 'overflow' school, then shut up, and finally demolished in 1975. People still mourn for it. The latest scheme is to build an old people's home on the site.

In 1972 the steel works came to Blue Town, and was welcomed warmly. It has provided work, good conditions and good wages ever since. It was opened officially by the Duke of Edinburgh in 1972. In 1980 it became famous for its refusal to strike, and the island backed this decision wholeheartedly, and put up with the invading army of pickets cheerfully. To the islanders work seemed too precious to risk throwing it away by striking.

In January 1975 the Olau Line started a ferry service from Sheerness to the Continent, and that brought more jobs. The dockyard had been sold, various light industries had moved in, and by now the docks were in business, and expanding steadily.

On the last day of 1978 a violent storm was followed by floods, and New Year's Day found Sheppey cut off from the mainland by snow, and flooded, the mixture as before. It was bitterly cold and rescue parties went round Sheerness getting people out of flooded houses. The floods had not spread quite so extensively as in 1953, but they were bad enough to frighten everyone. Flood warnings were organised, the old air raid sirens were used, and instructions issued on what to do in the event of a further flood. The island was snowed up for four or five days before the roads were cleared for traffic. After this, it was decided that the sea walls must be strengthened, and work was started at once. Now Sheerness is surrounded by high sea walls, ugly but very necessary, and the work is continuing round the sea wall at Queenborough. In Sheerness many of the houses still have water beneath the floor boards as a legacy from these floods.

The road leading onto the island and the docks was by now a problem. Queenborough and Sheerness were shaken and deafened by heavy lorries, and a bypass was considered from Cowstead Corner to the docks. The railway bridge at Queenborough had been weakened by the heavy traffic, and single line traffic was enforced while repairs were undertaken.

The little village of West Minster was sacrificed to the new road and the inhabitants left the rows of old houses, the shop, and the pub unwillingly. They were a little community on their own, and had their own ways and traditions.

Over the years the councils had been forced to amalgamate, despite their many refusals to do so. Minster, Sheerness and Queenborough and the rest of the rural area were all united unwillingly, to become Queenborough in Sheppey District Council. The grumbling from all areas had hardly died down before the island had to amalgamate with towns and villages on the mainland to become Swale District Council. This does not suit Sheppey at all, and the majority of the people are convinced that it was the wrong thing to do, for Sheppey is different, they say, and her problems are her own.

Now Minster is a built-up area, and Eastchurch and Leysdown are full of holiday camps. Nothing is left of the famous Shurland Hall but the ruined gate house. In the latter part of the eighteenth century one of the battlements was blown down, the remainder were then taken down as they were considered unsafe. At the end of the nineteenth century the farmer living there replaced the battlements and made a rather imposing farmhouse of the gate house, but the place changed hands several times and deteriorated after the First World War. It has not been lived in since early in this century. Several attempts have been made to rescue what remains of the hall, but no-one has been successful so far, and soon it will be too late, and Sheppey will have lost another one of her more notable buildings.

Leysdown had developed into a noisy sea-side town, with bingo, candy floss, amusement arcades, discos, hotels and many fights in the summer season, often with broken bottles as weapons. There is no trace now of the once quiet road to the beach, or the little spinney on the green at the side of it.

If anyone questions any of these happenings, they are told unctuously that one cannot resist progress, but progress is not necessarily improvement. Much of the summer trade is catered for by people who have come to the island especially for that purpose, and many islanders who cannot cross the road, get on to the beach, or on to a bus in the summer, sometimes wonder if the profit from the summer trade is really so great. To the average ratepayer it is not.

All the churches are well cared for and kept in good repair, but at Minster and Eastchurch they have suffered from vandals, and have to be kept locked. During the summer a rota of watchers enables Minster Abbey to stay open, so that visitors may come in. It is reminiscent of the old 'Watch and Ward' days.

The royal coat of arms in the abbey is the coat of arms of George I, 1716, and not many people know that on the reverse side is the coat of arms of Queen Anne. The board was made to be suspended, so that both faces could be seen.

On one of the central pillars there are several marks and crosses carved, and something that looks remarkably like a scratch dial, but this has not been verified by anyone knowledgeable in these matters. Holy Trinity Church in Sheerness has been restored this year (1981). It was 'built on uncertain ground' and the footings slipped, causing the pews on both sides of the centre aisle to slope at a distinct angle to the centre. Walking up the centre aisle was rather like walking with one foot on the pavement and one in the gutter. Now all this has been straightened out, and there is only a slight list to centre. The church has a quality all its own, it gives an impression of space and sunlight, even in dull weather.

Things are not brilliant on the island at the present time. There are many empty shops, many houses with 'for sale' notices up, and a very high rate of unemployment.

People can no longer afford to pay the high fares to commute, and if they could the bus and train services have been so reduced that to get to work on time would be difficult. The cost of petrol rules out too much car travel, and many families are moving away, for there is no work to spare on the island. The prospects for school leavers are very poor, although the council is running work schemes to help them.

It is impossible to guess what the future holds for Sheppey. Many business people are confident that when the general recession ends, the docks will bring more trade, and so more work, to the island. The steel works are surviving well, although they have had a slight set-back of late. The farmers are very much at the mercy of Common Market policies, and the latest farm machinery plus the current trend of ploughing everything up for corn growing, reduces the number of farm jobs. Harty, once famous for its grazing, has been drained, at great expense, and is now down to corn. The ditches have to be pumped out continually, the equipment is very sophisticated and the cost of the operation must be enormous; it will take a whole lot of corn to pay for it.

Sheppey lost most of its trees with Dutch Elm disease, and may lose what few remain to make way for the big machines now in use on the fields.

If the docks are as successful as is hoped, presumably the 'for sale' notices will come down, houses will be bought and trade improve generally, but this year even the holiday camps have suffered from lack of visitors. The island has survived many hard times during its history, so there is no reason to suppose it will not survive this one, and return to prosperity through one scheme or another.

Sheppey has changed more rapidly in the last twenty years that at any time previously, and it is too soon to judge whether this is for better or worse; only time can provide an answer.

Here is Sheppey for anyone who is interested. It would be foolhardy to claim that this is a complete history. The writer is sure to have omitted something that another person would like to have seen included.

Fresh evidence from the past is continually being uncovered, and documents may be found that show past events and people in a different light altogether. Last, but not least, this is a period of rapid changes, and today's happenings are tomorrow's history, which makes it impossible to keep up with the times. When writing a book like this, one can only try to do the best work possible in the circumstances.

CETERA DESUNT

Acknowledgements

I owe many thanks to many people for their help in the collection of material for this book.

Firstly, without the financial assistance of the South East Arts Association in the form of a generous travel grant, the book would probably never have been started.

I must also thank the staff of the Public Records Office, the British Museum Library, the National Register of Archives, and the library at Canterbury Cathedral for their unfailing and very patient help, as I was often uncertain as to what I was looking for.

Also the staff of the Maidstone Archives at County Hall, whom I bedevilled with queries, questions, and almost impossible demands for old manuscripts, none of which was ever refused. Their help has been beyond price.

I would like to thank the staff of Minster and Sheerness libraries, who have produced old books and papers so willingly, and always showed interest in any work going forward.

Finally, and this has been much appreciated, thanks are gratefully given to all those people who have answered innumerable questions, supplied stories, and kindly lent old deeds and papers for study. Among these are William Mills, esq. of Ripney Hill Farm, Charles Love, esq. of Kingsborough Farm, Mrs. Coultrip formerly of Norwood Manor, and the late Harold Ingleton, whose memory for dates and local incidents was so accurate that it made checking and research a formality. There are many more who must be left un-named, but their help was of great value, and thanks are due to them.

I hope this covers all those who have assisted me in many ways, for if they are not mentioned they are certainly not forgotten.